Ultimate C# for High-Performance Applications

Master Multithreading, Parallelism, and Async Techniques to Engineer High-Performance, Enterprise-Grade Software with C# 13 and .NET 9

Jeff McNamara

www.orangeava.com

First Published: November 2025

Published By: Orange Education Pvt Ltd, AVA®

Address: 9, Daryaganj, Delhi, 110002, India

275 New North Road Islington Suite 1314 London,
N1 7AA, United Kingdom

ISBN (PBK): 978-93-49888-26-5

ISBN (E-BOOK): 978-93-49888-43-2

Scan the QR code to explore our entire catalogue

www.orangeava.com

Dedicated To

My Beloved Wife, Julie

And

Suzanne, Sean, Samantha, Karen, Paul, and Paige.

You are the most important people in my life!

About the Author

Jeff McNamara has been passionate about technology for as long as he can remember. What began as a childhood curiosity—experimenting with early programming languages and tinkering with computers—grew into a lifelong pursuit of creating high-performance software. By the time he was in college, Jeff had already turned that passion into a business, building technological solutions for clients, and gaining firsthand experience in entrepreneurship and software development.

After college, Jeff took this talent of his into the corporate world, where he worked on technological projects across diverse industries, including banking, insurance, and healthcare. This wide-ranging experience exposed him to the unique challenges of building reliable, scalable, and secure systems in highly regulated and fast-moving environments. Over the years, Jeff has developed a reputation for combining deep technical expertise with a practical, result-oriented approach to solving complex business problems.

Today, Jeff works as a consultant specializing in cloud architecture and API design. His focus is on helping organizations modernize their applications, optimize performance, and deliver value faster. Drawing on decades of hands-on experience, he guides companies through the process of building systems that are not only robust and secure, but also flexible enough to support innovation.

Jeff's expertise is grounded in both theory and practice. He has spent years refining his understanding of performance optimization, multithreaded programming, and cloud-native development—knowledge he now shares through his writing. His work is aimed at helping both new and experienced developers gain the insights they need to build applications that can stand up to the real-world demands of today's digital landscape.

Beyond technology, Jeff is an avid outdoor man, who enjoys hiking, biking, and camping in the beautiful landscapes of Utah, where he lives. When he is not exploring trails or spending time in nature, he can often be found gaming—another lifelong passion that continues to fuel his interest in interactive technology and immersive experiences.

With a career that bridges entrepreneurship, corporate consulting, and advanced technical problem-solving, Jeff brings a unique perspective to his writing. His mission is to make high-performance programming concepts approachable, practical, and relevant for developers, who want to push the limits of what their applications can achieve, and make it really big in their lives!!

About the Technical Reviewer

Samiksha is a Senior Software Developer with over 6 years of experience in C# and the .NET ecosystem. Her expertise includes building scalable, high-performance applications using ASP.NET Core, multithreading, and modern database technologies. Samiksha contributed her practical knowledge and technical depth as a technical reviewer for the book, *Ultimate C# for High-Performance Application*, ensuring its accuracy and quality.

Acknowledgments

Writing this book has been both a professional challenge and a personal journey, and it would not have been possible without the support, inspiration, and generosity of many people.

First, I want to thank the countless authors, bloggers, and community contributors whose posts, articles, and shared code samples have taught me more than I could ever measure. Much of what I know about building high-performance applications has been sharpened by learning from the experiences of others. Their willingness to share your knowledge has had a lasting impact on me, and on developers everywhere.

I am also grateful to the great teams at Microsoft, whose innovation and guidance in building high-performance and distributed systems laid the foundation for much of my own work. The lessons I have learned from Microsoft's engineers and community resources have been invaluable.

A heartfelt 'thank you' goes to the editorial team at Orange Education Pvt. Ltd. Their patience, thoughtful feedback, and steady encouragement helped transform these pages into a finished work that I am proud to share.

Finally, I thank my wife, family, and friends for their unwavering support throughout this process. From the late nights of writing to the weekends spent revising, their encouragement, support and belief in me kept this project moving forward. This book is as much theirs as it is mine.

Preface

Every developer has faced it: The application that works fine in testing but slows to a crawl in production, the code that seems correct but bottlenecks under load, or the system that cannot keep up with the demands of modern users. Performance issues are not just frustrating–they can mean the difference between success and failure for an application.

That is why this book exists. ***Ultimate C# for High-Performance Applications*** gives you the knowledge and tools to design software that is fast, scalable, and resilient. By combining the latest features of .NET 9 and C# 13 with proven patterns and best practices, this book equips you to write applications that do not just work–they excel!

You will learn how to think about performance from the start, how to leverage multithreading and asynchronous programming effectively, how to debug and profile with confidence, and how to apply everything in real-world scenarios. Thus, whether you are building enterprise software, cloud services, or data-heavy systems, this book will help you write codes that stand up to modern performance demands.

By the end, you will not just understand what makes applications fast–you will also know how to make your applications fast.

Chapter Overview

Chapter 1: Introduction to High-Performance Computing in .NET – Understand why performance matters, and how .NET 9 and C# 13 empower you to build applications that scale.

Chapter 2: Understanding Parallelism in C# – Build a foundation in threads, and async programming so that you can fully unlock parallel execution in your code.

Chapter 3: Creating and Running Tasks in C# – Learn how to create, cancel, and manage tasks to keep your applications responsive and reliable.

Chapter 4: Data Sharing and Synchronization – Gain confidence in managing shared data safely, avoiding race conditions, and writing thread-safe code.

Chapter 5: Threading and Synchronization Primitives – Take control of complex concurrency scenarios with semaphores, mutexes, and reader-writer locks.

Chapter 6: Understanding Concurrent Collections – Discover how concurrent collections let you share data across threads, without sacrificing performance.

Chapter 7: Parallel Loops in .NET – Learn to speed up large-scale processing with Parallel.For and Parallel.ForEach, and apply profiling to optimize results.

Chapter 8: Language-Integrated Query (LINQ) for Parallelism – Use PLINQ to supercharge your queries, and handle large data sets with ease.

Chapter 9: Advanced Task Management – Explore advanced techniques like task continuations, custom schedulers, and complex task hierarchies for maximum flexibility.

Chapter 10: Asynchronous Programming with `Async/Await` – Master async/await to write modern, non-blocking applications that remain responsive under heavy workloads.

Chapter 11: Threading and the Thread Pool – Learn how the .NET thread pool operates, and how to optimize it for different workloads.

Chapter 12: Debugging Parallel Applications Using Visual Studio – Gain the ability to diagnose and fix multithreaded issues using Visual Studio's powerful debugging tools.

Chapter 13: Practical Performance Challenges and Solutions – See how to solve real-world performance bottlenecks, from CPU-bound loops to I/O-heavy systems.

Chapter 14: Building a Chat Application – Apply everything you have learned by building a responsive, real-world chat application from scratch.

Chapter 15: Conclusion – Reflect on the best practices, revisit lessons learned, and get guidance for continuing your journey into high-performance development.

Get a Free eBook

We hope you are enjoying your recently purchased book! Your feedback is incredibly valuable to us, and to all other readers looking for great books.

If you found this book helpful or enjoyable, we would truly appreciate it, if you could take a moment to leave a short review with a 5 star rating on Amazon. It helps us grow, and lets other readers discover our books.

As a thank you, we would love to send you a free digital copy of this book, and a **30%** discount code on your next cart value on our official websites:

www.orangeava.com

www.orangeava.in (For Indian Subcontinent)

☑ **Here's how:**

Leave a review for the book on Amazon.

Take a screenshot of your review, and send an email to **info@orangeava.com** (it can be just the confirmation screen).

Once, we receive your screenshot, we will send you the digital file, within 24 hours.

Thank you so much for your support – it means a lot to us!

Downloading the code bundles and colored images

Please follow the links or scan the QR codes to download the
Code Bundles and Images of the book:

https://github.com/ava-orange-education/Ultimate-C-for-High-Performance-Applications

The code bundles and images of the book are also hosted on
https://rebrand.ly/1219a5

In case there's an update to the code, it will be updated on the existing GitHub repository.

Errata

We take immense pride in our work at **Orange Education Pvt Ltd,** and follow best practices to ensure the accuracy of our content to provide an indulging reading experience to our subscribers. Our readers are our mirrors, and we use their inputs to reflect and improve upon human errors, if any, that may have occurred during the publishing processes involved. To let us maintain the quality and help us reach out to any readers who might be having difficulties due to any unforeseen errors, please write to us at :

errata@orangeava.com

Your support, suggestions, and feedback are highly appreciated.

DID YOU KNOW

Did you know that Orange Education Pvt Ltd offers eBook versions of every book published, with PDF and ePub files available? You can upgrade to the eBook version at **www.orangeava.com** and as a print book customer, you are entitled to a discount on the eBook copy. Get in touch with us at: **info@orangeava.com** for more details.

At **www.orangeava.com**, you can also read a collection of free technical articles, sign up for a range of free newsletters, and receive exclusive discounts and offers on Print Books and eBooks.

PIRACY

If you come across any illegal copies of our works in any form on the internet, we would be grateful if you would provide us with the location address or website name. Please contact us at **info@orangeava.com** with a link to the material.

ARE YOU INTERESTED IN AUTHORING WITH US?

If there is a topic that you have expertise in, and you are interested in either writing or contributing to a book, please write to us at **business@orangeava.com**. We are on a journey to help developers and tech professionals to gain insights on the present technological advancements and innovations happening across the globe and build a community that believes Knowledge is best acquired by sharing and learning with others. Please reach out to us to learn what our audience demands and how you can be part of this educational reform. We also welcome ideas from tech experts and help them build learning and development content for their domains.

REVIEWS

Please leave a review. Once you have read and used this book, why not leave a review on the site that you purchased it from? Potential readers can then see and use your unbiased opinion to make purchase decisions. We at Orange Education would love to know what you think about our products, and our authors can learn from your feedback. Thank you!

For more information about Orange Education, please visit **www.orangeava.com**.

Table of Contents

CHAPTER 1
Introduction to High-Performance Computing in .NET

Introduction

In our modern, fast-paced, and competitive world, the demands placed on the software sector are extremely high. Companies count on their websites to respond within milliseconds and scale to millions of users. Financial systems require millions of transactions to be processed in seconds. Scientific research requires processing of enormous data sets in minutes, and video games must provide fluid, real-time experiences. The need for high-performance software is critical in every industry, and it is foreseeable that the future demands will only be higher.

For professionals and organizations to remain competitive and meet these ever-increasing performance benchmarks, deep expertise in high-efficiency development platforms is essential. In this book, we will explore how C# and .NET provide the tools you need to meet all these challenges while granting you the knowledge and strategies you need to create fast, scalable, and highly efficient applications.

To get the most out of this book, you should have a solid understanding of the C# language and be comfortable with the basics of the .NET framework. Familiarity with object-oriented programming principles and foundational data types such as strings, integers, and doubles is vital. A working knowledge of common data structures, algorithms, and design patterns will be helpful later as we dive into advanced topics. It is assumed that you must be comfortable with troubleshooting and debugging C# code. Considering that you might already be well-versed in these foundational principles, this book uses hands-on examples and practical insights to elevate your understanding about the subject.

Structure

In this chapter, we will cover the following topics:

- The High Cost of Poor Performance
- Evolution of Software Performance
- Concept of Concurrency
- Importance of Parallelism
- Multithreading vs. Asynchronous Programming
- Efficient Performance in C# 13 and .NET 9

The High Cost of Poor Performance

Applications that perform poorly can cost companies millions. For instance, imagine that you have written an e-commerce platform for your employer. The site works well and becomes popular. But then the company decides to run a big sale. Thousands of customers suddenly flood the site. Pages take too long to refresh, and frustrated customers start abandoning their carts. Every second of delay costs the company thousands of dollars in lost sales. You might wonder what is the problem with the website. The answer to it is that while you have built the code functionality correctly, you have not created the system to handle this type of load, and as a result, the cost to the company is high.

High-performance implications are not limited to large-scale cloud applications. Consider another example where you have written a desktop application for employees to perform their jobs. The application works correctly, but there are complaints that the screens freeze sometimes, and the users also must wait a long time for some processes to complete. Again, you might have written the functionality properly, but you did not build the application to be highly responsive. With many employees waiting around for your application to respond instead of doing their job, the company is losing money due to untapped productivity.

It may not have been true in the past, but in the modern world, every application requires developers to consider the aspect of performance. Even small inefficiencies can easily escalate and affect user experience, scalability, and revenue. Therefore, an in-depth understanding of the tools available in .NET and how to properly apply them will make all the difference in your programming career.

Evolution of Software Performance

During the early days of computer software, performance was a secondary concern. Computers back then had single-core processors and the amount of data being processed was small. Some of the earliest personal computers commercially available were only able to address 64k of RAM. That limit was quickly raised to 640k in the early 1980s. In that period, most computers could only run one program at a time and the software was very simple compared to today's feature-rich programs.

Still, the power of word processing and spreadsheet software was enough to make desktop computers a standard feature in most offices in just a few years. Keyboards and monitors replaced typewriters as businesses recognized the increased efficiency of digital computers for employees. As different software programs were created, businesses began to see the need for more powerful systems.

Imagine being an assistant in those early days. You might be typing a letter when the boss calls and asks you to schedule a meeting. You would save what you were doing, exit the word processor, pull up the calendar, check the schedule, create a new appointment, and then save and exit the calendar. Then you could revisit the word processor, load your letter document, and pick up where you left off. The more programs you had to work with, the worse the situation became. An innovation was clearly required to increase efficiency.

One such innovation emerged in 1985 in the form of the 80386 processor from Intel corporation, or the 386 as it was popularly referred to. This new processor had a faster clock speed than previous CPUs, was able to address more memory than ever before, and could run more than one program at a time, through a new feature called **multitasking**. Using this new feature, with the right software implementations, employees and businesses enjoyed efficiencies they had not even dreamt of before.

Imagine being that same assistant with the new generation of software, which was closer to what we have today. Now, you might be in the middle of typing the letter, but in the background, the calendar program would also be running. When the boss calls, you just use a hotkey to switch over to the calendar, schedule the meeting, and then switch back. Little savings like that add up over days and weeks and make employees more efficient at their jobs.

Multitasking is the ability of a CPU to run more than one program, or task, at a time. An important part of multitasking is the ability for a single program to be divided into separate tasks that can make progress independently. This concept is called **concurrency**. To implement **concurrency**, programs could use smaller units of execution called **threads**, or they could use cooperative programming techniques. The use of **threads** to implement **concurrency** is called **multithreading**.

The 386 had the ability to handle **multitasking** and **multithreading** but it carried out the functions via a single core. That means that technically, the CPU only ran one instruction at a given point in time, but the clock speeds were so fast compared to the software load that it seemed like multiple things were happening at once. This is a process called **time-slicing**. It is important to note that in time-slicing, multiple tasks are making progress independently, but they are not actually running at the same time. The said capability requires more sophisticated hardware that came later.

Before long, it became impossible to increase the clock speeds of individual CPUs meaningfully – technology hit physical limits. Also, concurrency could not solve every problem. Some applications required capabilities that simply were not possible with cooperative programming techniques or time-slicing provided by concurrency. The solution was multicore processors, that provided the ability to run tasks truly in **parallel**, with separate tasks running on different CPU cores.

From a modern perspective, both **concurrency** and **parallelism** can be implemented using **threads**. However, **concurrency** does not always imply **parallel** execution. The underlying operating system typically handles scheduling details for **threads**, but in some cases, **concurrency** can be achieved using cooperative programming methods. We will explore **threads** in more detail in later chapters.

Concept of Concurrency

Concurrency, as we have discussed, is the ability to break a program down into tasks that can make progress independently, but they do not necessarily need to be executed simultaneously. Such applications can run on single-core systems and still perform well. There are two main ways in which applications can implement **concurrency**.

One way to implement **concurrency** is to use **threads** that are **time-sliced**. In **time-slicing**, the CPU runs a **thread** for a short period of time and then forcibly interrupts the **thread** and quickly switches to running another **thread**. This process is called **context switching**. The following diagram illustrates it:

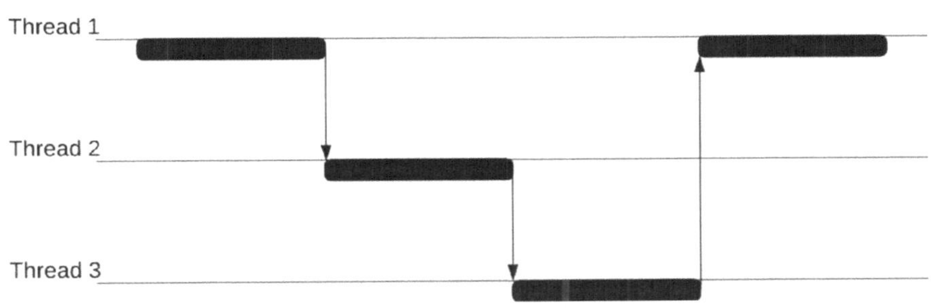

Figure 1.1: *Context-Switching*

In *Figure 1.1*, the arrows follow the flow of execution by the CPU as it runs a **thread** for a short time (usually a few milliseconds) and then forcibly switches to run another **thread**. This process, known as **preemption**, is a key feature in **Preemptive Multithreading**. In this type of system, the **threads** are not aware of being interrupted. It is because the CPU, which is under the control of the operating system's scheduler, manages the switching based on predefined scheduling and prioritization rules. Nearly all modern hardware including servers, desktops, tablets, and phones are designed to support **Preemptive Multithreading**. Likewise, modern operating systems such as Windows, Unix/Linux, macOS, and Android are designed with appropriate schedulers and rules to support preemption.

Another way to implement a type of **concurrency** in software is called **Cooperative Multithreading**. In this system, a **thread** can execute until it yields execution to other **threads**. Unlike **Preemptive Multithreading**, where the CPU forces switch between **threads**, in **Cooperative Multithreading**, the **threads** themselves are responsible for voluntarily yielding execution control. This approach can lead to more efficient execution and use of resources if threads cooperate well, but it runs a greater risk of poorly designed **threads** hogging CPU resources, preventing other **threads** from running and causing unresponsiveness.

Importance of Parallelism

Parallelism can be thought of as a subset of **concurrency**. The specific difference is that in **parallelism**, **threads** are truly running at the same time, on different CPU cores, whereas in **concurrency**, **threads** may be executed at different times or even out of order, but not necessarily at the same time. **Concurrency** can be achieved on single-core systems, but **parallelism** must leverage multiple CPU cores for efficiency. It is important to understand this key difference as some problems benefit more from **parallelism** while others can be solved using **concurrency** and task management.

Figure 1.2 illustrates **parallelism** with three **threads**.

Figure 1.2: *Parallel Execution of Threads*

As you can see, in comparison with *Figure 1.1*, the code in each **thread** runs truly simultaneously with the other **threads**.

Parallelism is the backbone of high-performance software. With it, desktop applications can be highly responsive, even when many applications are running at once. It is the reason video games can provide immersive and fluid experiences, even with many players. Websites and social media serve thousands or even millions of simultaneous users because of **parallelism**. Artificial Intelligence would not be possible without it. Let us look at some real-world examples:

With **parallelism**, it is possible to have background tasks run without interrupting the main program task. This is essential in any UI/UX application as the main program thread can run and focus on updating the screen in response to any user input. When the user issues a command, the command is processed in the background, and then the UI is updated with the result. Using this pattern, slow operations like accessing Internet sites, or loading database records can happen without making the UI appear to freeze. The application is always fluid and responsive, regardless of what it is doing.

Suppose you have a large database with millions of records that all need to be processed. Processing each record sequentially will take a long time. But, with **parallel threads** running, each **thread** could process a separate record, which reduces the time it takes to get the entire job done significantly. Meanwhile, any errors could be tabulated and reported at the end of the job for someone to follow up with later.

Service applications that drive the processing of websites and social media allocate **threads** to respond to user requests. By efficiently using **parallelism**, these sites can scale seamlessly and provide each user with a quick response to each request. Services can use hardware and system resources to economically handle thousands of users simultaneously. Meanwhile, each user feels like they have the system all to themselves.

Some applications must operate within specific time constraints. These applications are called real-time applications. For example, in video streaming, video and audio frame data must delivered in a timely manner to keep up with the display needs. If the data is not delivered quickly enough, the video can become jittery and stutters often. To accomplish this, **parallel threads** are used on the server and client side of a video streaming app. On the server side, **parallel threads** manage client connections, encoding for different formats, transcoding to handle different resolutions, managing asynchronous I/O, and more. On the client side, they manage asynchronous I/O, decoding, buffering and pre-fetching, rendering video and audio, and controlling playback. Handling modern video streaming sites like YouTube would be impossible without **parallelism**.

Another example of real-time applications is a financial system such as a stock trading system. These systems handle millions of transactions per second and each trade is extremely time-sensitive, due to market fluctuations. A stock trading system relies on **parallel threads** to execute trades, tabulate pricing data, manage risk analysis, and update market positions in real-time. Such systems are only possible because of **parallelism** in computing.

Parallelism and **concurrency** are not a guarantee of high performance by themselves. Distributing work across **threads** often requires careful planning and testing. **Threads** introduce new challenges in the form of **deadlocks**, **synchronization**, and resource starvation that need to be avoided. It is possible to reduce performance in a solution by introducing threads due to context switching or synchronization overhead. As we dive deeply into these and other topics in this book, we will explore strategies to avoid these pitfalls and discover and fix problems when they inadvertently arise in your code.

Multithreading versus Asynchronous Programming

Some problems are most efficiently solved via an asynchronous approach. Consider the tasks you might need to do on laundry day as an example. Typically, doing laundry requires sorting, washing, drying, and folding. Because of modern washers and dryers, it is possible to break up these operations into asynchronous tasks. We start by sorting different fabrics and colors and then load the result into a washer. While the washer is doing its job, we can do something else, like reading a book. When the washer is finished, the load is placed into the dryer and another load is loaded in the washer. Both drying and washing continue from that point. When the dryer is finished, folding begins as more loads are washed and dried. This process continues until the entire job is finished.

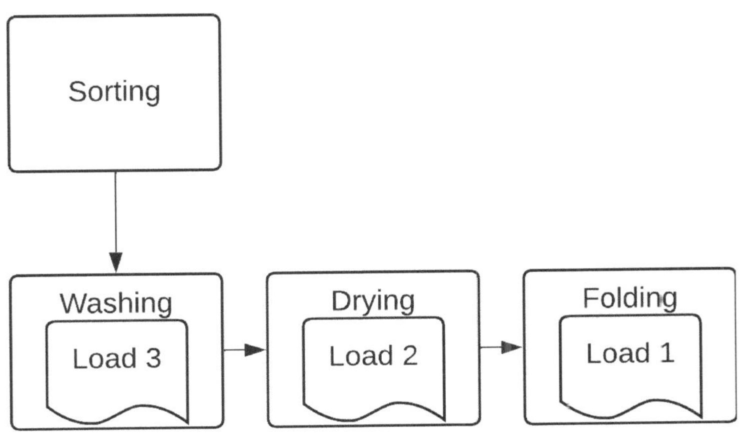

Figure 1.3: *Asynchronous Laundry*

A synchronous approach to this problem would be to wash a load and wait for it to finish, then dry that load and wait for it to finish, fold that load, and then begin afresh with another load. However, one would never do this because in that case, laundry day would take hours longer to finish. Thus, synchronous work is less efficient than an asynchronous approach if we are dealing with multiple loads.

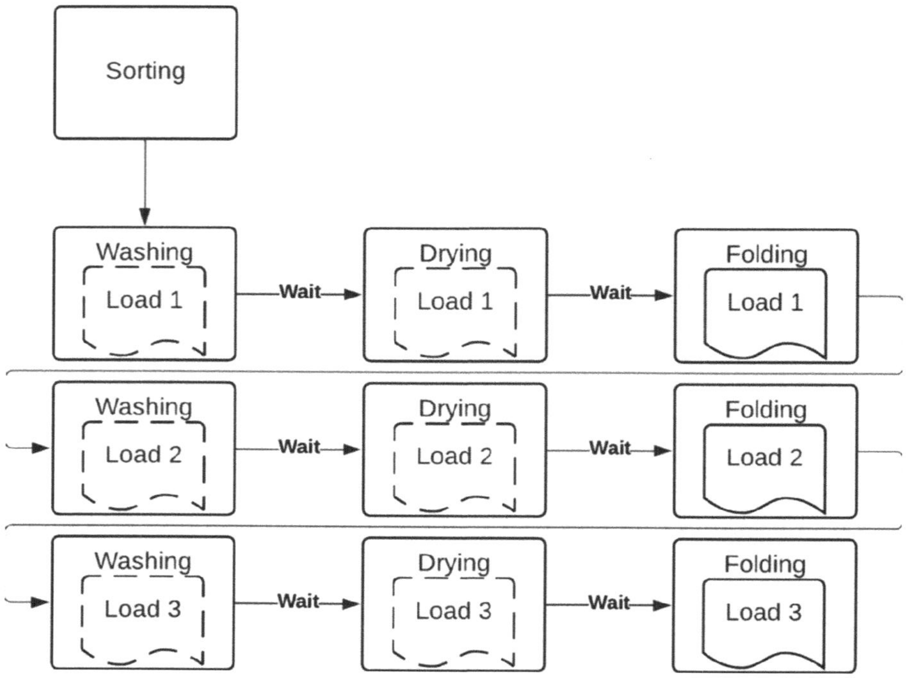

Figure 1.4: *Synchronous Laundry*

Laundry day is a good example of a problem where performance benefits greatly from an asynchronous model. There are many computing problems that fit this model. Modern programming languages like C# provide methods of programming asynchronous solutions. This concept is called **asynchronous programming**.

Asynchronous programming is an example of cooperative programming, where one operation voluntarily yields to another. While planning an asynchronous solution, the problem is broken down into discrete operations that can start, run, and finish independently, like washing, drying, and folding in the laundry example. Operations can start and finish completely independently or they can wait for each other in a chained fashion. Because of this flexibility, **asynchronous programming** is different from multithreading.

To illustrate, let us think about planning an asynchronous solution to the laundry problem. After sorting is completed, loads are created. From that point on, each load is required to go through washing, drying, and folding, in that particular order. However multiple loads can be washed, dried, and folded simultaneously, assuming that proper resources are available. We could structure the solution to chain folding to wait for drying, which in turn waits for washing for a specific load. We could then have sorting create several loads and launch the chain for each load. The facilities of the language used would help us create the chained operations for the loads, launch the process and wait for the result. Under the covers, the compiler would create and use threads where appropriate to handle the various in-flight operations, without blocking threads when waits are encountered. The final solution would use system resources efficiently while still preserving the required ordering. The **asynchronous programming** solution for the laundry problem is illustrated in *Figure 1.5*.

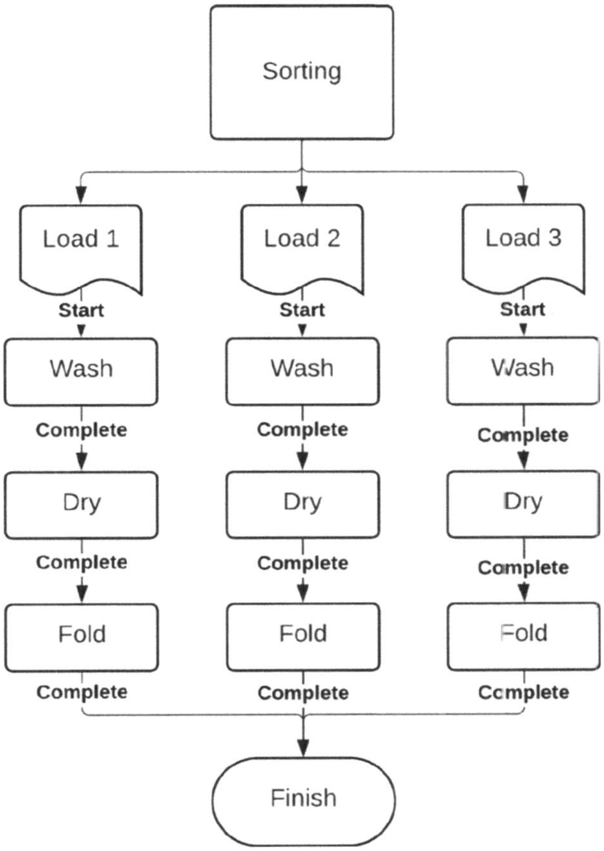

Figure 1.5: *Laundry Solution with Asynchronous Programming*

Notice that *Figure* 1.5 illustrates the conceptual solution as it would be programmed, but not the technical details of thread management. Managing threads at a low level for this solution would complicate the design and hide the meaning and purpose of the code. Therefore, modern programming languages like C# provide facilities to program the solution closer to the conceptual design, while the framework and compiler take care of the more technical details underneath.

Asynchronous Programming is different from **Multithreading** in several ways. Both strategies are important in their respective ways as each of them is used to solve specific problems in programming. The following table summarizes the key differences between **Multithreading** and **Asynchronous Programming** and why each is useful:

	Multithreading	**Asynchronous Programming**
Definition	Operations must run in parallel or make progress independently	Operations that can be started, run, and completed without blocking
Execution Model	Relies on threading or multi-process strategies including blocking synchronization	Allows operations to yield and resume without dedicated threads or low-level synchronization
Parallelism	Executes parallel on capable hardware	Concurrent as a form of cooperative programming
Appropriate Use Case	CPU-bound applications	I/O bound applications

Table 1.1: *Comparison of Multithreading and Asynchronous Programming*

One of the most common uses of **asynchronous programming** is **asynchronous I/O**. Programs often need to access files, databases, or networks. These operations take time as compared to processing in memory. If a synchronous approach is used, thread resources are allocated and blocked while I/O operations are complete. With **asynchronous I/O**, however, the calling thread can do other work while the I/O operation completes, and then the program can resume afterwards. This approach utilizes system resources more efficiently than a traditional synchronous I/O approach.

Figure 1.6 shows the conceptual difference between synchronous and asynchronous I/O

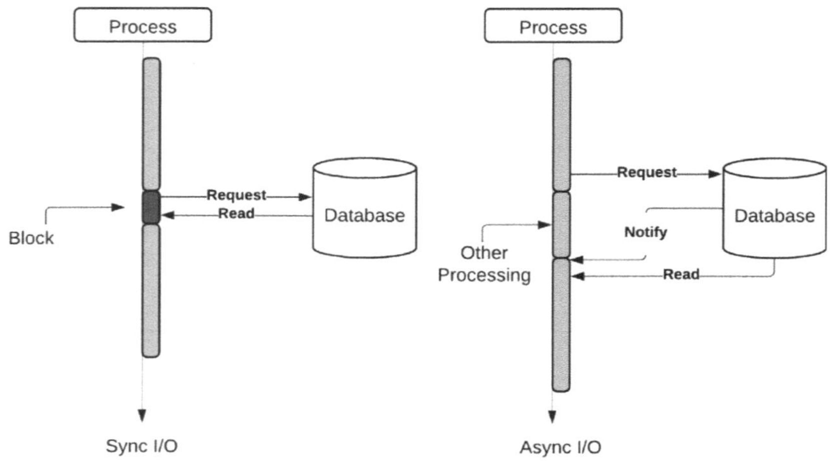

Figure 1.6: *Synchronous vs. Asynchronous I/O*

As shown in *Figure* 1.6, synchronous I/O blocks a thread while the I/O operation completes. This ties up system resources that could be used for other CPU work. **Asynchronous I/O** does not block anything, and frees up the thread to be used for processing. When the I/O operation is complete, processing can resume. This efficient use of system resources makes **asynchronous I/O** a popular choice for most modern software.

Efficient Performance in C# 13 and .NET 9

Throughout this book, we will explore the powerful tools and techniques in C# 13 and .NET 9 that drive high-performance applications. These tools support the critical concepts introduced in this chapter, offering everything you need to tackle complex performance demands. In the following chapters, we will cover the key areas that every developer working on modern applications should master. Here is a glimpse of what lies ahead:

- **Creating and Managing Threads:** Learn to harness the `Thread` class to run multiple tasks simultaneously, a fundamental skill for developing responsive, efficient applications.
- **Using the Thread Pool:** Discover why the `ThreadPool` is a core element in .NET's concurrency model, allowing you to manage and optimize background work in resource-intensive applications.
- **Tasks and the TPL:** Understand how the Task Parallel Library simplifies parallel programming, enabling you to manage dependencies, exceptions, and results across multiple tasks with ease.
- **Data Protection with Monitor and Lock:** Explore tools for safe data sharing, using the `Monitor` class and `lock` keyword to prevent race conditions and ensure data consistency across threads.
- **Thread Synchronization Techniques:** Master advanced synchronization with `Semaphore` and `ResetEvent` classes to coordinate threads and manage access to resources, a must for high-performance and real-time applications.

- **Concurrent Collections:** Learn how concurrent collections provide safe, high-speed data access across threads, essential for handling large volumes of data efficiently.
- **High-performance Data Processing with Parallel Loops:** Gain skills in parallel loops to boost data processing speed, ideal for applications where time is critical, such as real-time analytics or data transformation.
- **Parallel LINQ (PLINQ) for Efficient Data Queries:** Discover how PLINQ unleashes the power of parallelism for data querying, enabling your LINQ queries to run faster by utilizing multiple cores.
- **Asynchronous Programming with `async/await`:** Master **`async/await`** and other asynchronous programming models that improve responsiveness by handling long-running tasks seamlessly in the background.

In each chapter, you will find practical examples and real-world case studies designed to deepen your understanding and prepare you for professional scenarios. From improving user experience in UI applications to optimizing backend processing for large data sets, you will learn not just how each tool works but also when to use it and why. Thus, whether you are working on high-performance web applications, responsive desktop software, or cutting-edge cloud solutions, this book will provide you the insights needed to tackle performance challenges in today's demanding software environments.

Conclusion

The demands on software systems have never been higher and will continue to grow. Modern developers must be equipped with the right knowledge and strategies. In this chapter, we explored essential concepts in high-performance programming - **parallelism**, **concurrency**, and **asynchronous programming**–highlighting their importance and unique roles. We also looked at some of the powerful tools provided by C# and .NET that support these strategies, which we will examine in greater depth in future chapters.

In the next chapter, we will learn the basics of parallelism in C# and .NET. We will learn how to create and control dedicated threads, explore legacy asynchronous programming models with the Asynchronous Programming Model and the Event-based Asynchronous Pattern, and the modern asynchronous pattern called the Task-based Asynchronous Pattern. Finally, we will discover the benefits and drawbacks of these patterns and when they should be used in modern software development.

Points to Remember

- Programs can often be broken down into tasks that can progress independently. These are called threads.
- Concurrency is the ability to break a program down into smaller tasks that can make progress independently, but do not necessarily need to execute simultaneously.
- Parallelism is a subset of concurrency where the tasks benefit from truly simultaneous execution.
- Asynchronous programming is an example of cooperative programming, and may or may not be multithreaded while executing.
- Asynchronous I/O is a good use case of asynchronous programming that helps programs be more efficient in resource usage.

Multiple Choice Questions

1. In computer science, a thread is defined as:
    a. A section of code that accesses the sensitive data.
    b. A sub-program, controlled by a main program.
    c. A smaller unit of execution within a program.
    d. The path of code execution.
2. Which of the following is not a part of Preemptive Multithreading?
    a. Time-slicing
    b. Context-switching
    c. Scheduling
    d. Yielding execution
3. Which of the following is true of Cooperative Multithreading?
    a. The threads themselves are responsible for voluntary yield control.
    b. The CPU and Operating System work together to switch threads without the threads participating.
    c. It requires multiple CPU cores for efficiency.
    d. There is no such concept in programming.
4. Which of the following is true of parallelism?
    a. It requires multiple CPU cores for efficiency.
    b. Threads run truly simultaneously.
    c. It is used in server and desktop applications.
    d. All of the above.
5. What is the definition of asynchronous programming?
    a. Programs that can run on the same computer.
    b. Operations that can be started, run, and completed without blocking.
    c. Operations that are started on one thread and completed on another.
    d. None of the above.
6. Why is asynchronous I/O an important concept?
    a. It helps improve the lifespan of attached devices.
    b. It uses less power than synchronous I/O.
    c. It does not block the calling thread during I/O, making more efficient use of system resources.
    d. It greatly improves I/O operation speeds.

Answers

1. c
2. d
3. a
4. d
5. b
6. c

Questions

1. How can programs be broken down into threads?
2. What are the two main types of concurrency? How do they differ in implementation?
3. How is parallelism different from concurrency?
4. What are some types of applications that benefit most from parallelism?
5. What is the difference between multithreading and asynchronous programming?
6. What types of problems do candidates likely face for asynchronous programming?
7. Is asynchronous programming guaranteed to use multiple threads?
8. How is asynchronous I/O beneficial over a synchronous approach?

Key Terms

- **Thread**: A smaller unit of execution within a program.
- **Multitasking**: The ability to run more than one task at a time by quickly switching between tasks.
- **Concurrency**: The ability to break a program down into smaller tasks that can make progress independently, but do not necessarily need to execute simultaneously.
- **Preemptive Multithreading**: A form of concurrency where the CPU forcibly stops executing a thread and quickly switches to another thread.
- **Time slice**: A predetermined length of time that a thread executes before the CPU forcibly stops it to switch to another thread.
- **Context Switching**: The process of switching to another running thread after forcibly stopping the current thread.
- **Cooperative Multithreading**: A type of concurrency where each thread is responsible for voluntarily yielding execution to other threads.
- **Parallelism:** A subset of concurrency where threads run simultaneously on multiple CPU cores.
- **Asynchronous Programming**: A form of cooperative programming where operations can start, run, and finish without blocking.
- **Asynchronous I/O:** A type of I/O programming that does not block threads while the operation runs.

CHAPTER 2
Understanding Parallelism in C#

Introduction

In the previous chapter, we learned about the concepts of high-performance software in general terms. We explored the concepts of concurrency, parallelism, and asynchronous programming and looked at some examples where each can be applied.

In this chapter, we will learn about how to turn these concepts for practical use in the C# language using .NET foundational classes. We will begin this chapter with the `Thread` class, and will go on to explore how threads are created and controlled. We will then look at some of the legacy models of asynchronous programming available in .NET. Finally, we will learn about when each of these models should be used.

Structure

In this chapter, we will cover the following topics:

- Understanding Threads
  - Review of Threads
  - Introduction to the Thread Class
- Creating and Controlling Threads
  - Basic Thread Creation
  - Controlling Thread Execution
  - Working with Parameters
- Introduction to Asynchronous Programming Models in .NET
  - Asynchronous Programming Model
  - Event-based Asynchronous Pattern
- Benefits and Drawbacks of Legacy Threading Models
  - Benefits of Traditional Threading
  - Drawbacks of Legacy Threading Models
  - Guidance for Using the Legacy Models

Understanding Threads: Review of Threads

In *Chapter 1, Introduction to High-Performance Computing in .NET*, we introduced the concept of a thread in the context of programming. Remember that a thread is a unit of work within the program that can make progress independently. Complex programs can often be broken down into several independent units of work. For example, in a desktop application with a user interface, drawing and updating the user interface components on the screen is a unit of work by itself. Other units of work in such an application might be reading and writing data to a database, sending messages across a network, or performing complex calculations on large sets of data. All these elements can be programmed to execute independently in different threads.

Each application in a system contains at least one thread, known as the **main thread**. The main thread is always a **foreground thread** in .NET. This **main thread** manages the application's execution flow, and when it exits, the entire program stops running, unless there are other **foreground threads** running.

In .NET, threads can be designated as either foreground or background threads, which affect the application's lifecycle.

Foreground threads keep the application running while they are active, meaning the application will not exit until all foreground threads have completed. Unlike them, background threads do not prevent the application from terminating. If all foreground threads are complete, the application will end even if background threads are still running.

Background threads are commonly used for non-critical tasks, such as logging or cleanup operations. Foreground threads, on the other hand, are reserved for essential tasks that should be completed before the program exits, such as critical database operations or data processing workflows.

Introduction to the Thread Class

In .NET threads are represented by the **`Thread`** class. The **`Thread`** class was introduced in the first release of the .NET Framework in 2002, allowing developers to create, start, and control the execution of threads. Threads created using the **`Thread`** class are managed by the .NET runtime and are considered **managed threads**, as opposed to **unmanaged** or **native threads** which are directly handled by the operating system. Each thread created using the **`Thread`** class is considered a **dedicated thread** because it operates independently, with its lifecycle controlled explicitly by the developer's code.

The **`Thread`** class gives developers fine control over individual threads. However, it does not support asynchronous programming or other advanced concepts. Therefore, some of the early uses of the **`Thread`** class ended up becoming very complex solutions with large amounts of code dedicated to thread management. Other libraries were added to address these shortcomings, namely the **Asynchronous Programming Model**, the **Event-based Asynchronous Pattern**, and the **Task-based Asynchronous Pattern**, which we will explore later in this chapter.

Creating and Controlling Threads

The **`Thread`** class is in the **`System.Threading`** namespace. To use a thread, you must define a method on a class that the thread will call when it starts. This method is called a **target method**. You then pass that method into the constructor of a special delegate called the **`ThreadStart`** delegate, then pass the **`ThreadStart`** delegate to the **`Thread`** class constructor.

Creating and Starting Threads

Let us define a simple thread method to illustrate this concept. We will create a class with a public method that displays a simple "**`Hello World!`**" message and create a thread to run it.

```
namespace ThreadClassDemo
{
    internal class Program
    {
        static void Main(string[] args)
        {
```

```
            var workerThread = new Thread(new ThreadStart(Worker.PrintMessage));
        }
    }

    internal class Worker
    {
        public static void PrintMessage()
        {
            Console.WriteLine("Hello world from another thread!");
        }
    }
}
```

In the preceding code snippet, the Main method creates a new thread that will run the **PrintMessage()** method on the **Worker** class when it starts. The instance of the **Thread** class is stored in the **workerThread** variable for later use. If we run the program at this point, nothing appears to happen because the thread does not actually run with the code in this state, it is only created at this point.

Note that it is also possible to create a **Thread** using a Lambda expression, which is shown as follows:

```
namespace ThreadClassDemo
{
    internal class Program
    {
        static void Main(string[] args)
        {
            var workerThread = new Thread(() => Worker.PrintMessage());
        }
    }

    internal class Worker
    {
        public static void PrintMessage()
        {
            Console.WriteLine("Hello world from another thread!");
        }
    }
}
```

Now that we have created a thread, let us add code to start the thread and run it.

To start a thread, call the **Thread.Start()** method. This method immediately starts the thread running and calls the defined delegate.

```
namespace ThreadClassDemo
{
    internal class Program
    {
        static void Main(string[] args)
        {
            var workerThread = new Thread(() => Worker.PrintMessage());
            workerThread.Start();
        }
    }

    internal class Worker
    {
        public static void PrintMessage()
```

```
            {
                Console.WriteLine("Hello world from another thread!");
            }
        }
    }
```

Notice that when we run the program this time, we will see the "**Hello world from another thread!**" message. The **Start()** method starts the thread running and it calls the **PrintMessage()** method on the **Worker** class.

Let us take a deeper look at what is happening from a threading level in this code:

1. The **Main** method is called by the operating system. This method is running on the **main thread**
2. A new instance of the **Thread** class is created, with a lambda that calls the **Worker.PrintMessage()** method. The thread is not started at this point
3. The **main thread** continues to run the **workerThread.Start()** method. This starts the thread represented by the **workerThread** instance. The new thread that starts is a new **foreground thread**
4. The **main thread** has no more work to do, so it completes and exits
5. The worker thread continues and calls the **Worker.PrintMessage()** method, which prints the message
6. The worker thread has nothing more to do and so it completes and exits
7. There are no more active **foreground threads**, so the program exits

The program always prints the message because the **workerThread** instance is defined as a **foreground thread**. This is the default behavior of the **Thread** class.

Now let us see what happens if we change the definition of **workerThread** to be **a background thread**. We can do this by setting the **IsBackground** property to **true**.

```
namespace ThreadClassDemo
{
    internal class Program
    {
        static void Main(string[] args)
        {
            var workerThread = new Thread(() => Worker.PrintMessage());
            workerThread.IsBackground = true;
            workerThread.Start();
        }
    }

    internal class Worker
    {
        public static void PrintMessage()
        {
            Console.WriteLine("Hello world from another thread!");
        }
    }
}
```

When we run the program this time, it usually will not print the message. This is because the **main thread** usually exits before the worker thread has a chance to initialize and run the **Worker.PrintMessage()** method, because it is now defined as a **background thread**.

Passing Parameters to Threads

The **ThreadStart** delegate represents a thread **target method** without any parameters. There is also a **ParameterizedThreadStart** delegate that accepts parameters defined by the **target method**. The easiest and most maintainable way to use this delegate is to use the lambda syntax and pass a parameter in the **target method** in the **Thread** class constructor itself. Let us modify our code to support parameters.

```
namespace ThreadClassDemo
{
    internal class Program
    {
        static void Main(string[] args)
        {
            var workerThread = new Thread(() => Worker.PrintMessage(5));
            workerThread.Start();
        }
    }

    internal class Worker
    {
        public static void PrintMessage(int number)
        {
            Console.WriteLine($"You passed the number: {number}");
        }
    }
}
```

Running the preceding code produces the message "**You passed the number: 5**" before exiting. Note that we passed a constant in this example, but a variable could have been passed as well. Any number of parameters can be passed to thread **target methods** in this way.

Pausing Thread Execution

It often becomes necessary to pause thread execution temporarily, especially while implementing polling loops or rate limiting. The **Thread.Sleep()** method allows you to pause a running thread for a specified period.

To pause the thread, call **Thread.Sleep()** with either an integer (representing milliseconds) or a **TimeSpan**. If an integer is provided, it specifies the number of milliseconds to wait. If a **TimeSpan** is provided, the thread will pause for the duration specified by the **TimeSpan** before resuming.

Let us see the **Thread.Sleep()** method in action.

```
namespace ThreadClassDemo
{
    internal class Program
    {
        static void Main(string[] args)
        {
            var workerThread = new Thread(() => Counter.CountTo(10));
            workerThread.Start();

            Console.WriteLine("Main thread completed.");
        }
    }

    internal class Counter
```

```
        {
            public static void CountTo(int number)
            {

    Stopwatch sw = Stopwatch.StartNew();
    for (int i = 1; i < number + 1; i++)
    {
    Console.WriteLine($"Count: {i} (Elapsed seconds: {sw.Elapsed.Seconds})");
        Thread.Sleep(TimeSpan.FromSeconds(1));
    }
            }
        }
    }
```

In the code above, the **workerThread** is created to call the **Counter.CountTo** method. **CountTo** contains a loop that counts from 1 to the number passed in the number parameter, pausing for 1 second between each loop iteration. The output will look something like this:

```
Main thread completed.
Count: 1 (Elapsed seconds: 0)
Count: 2 (Elapsed seconds: 1)
Count: 3 (Elapsed seconds: 2)
Count: 4 (Elapsed seconds: 3)
Count: 5 (Elapsed seconds: 4)
Count: 6 (Elapsed seconds: 5)
Count: 7 (Elapsed seconds: 6)
Count: 8 (Elapsed seconds: 7)
Count: 9 (Elapsed seconds: 8)
Count: 10 (Elapsed seconds: 9)
```

It is important to remember that the **Thread.Sleep()** method causes the thread to **block**, which means the thread is temporarily halted and does not continue executing until the specified time has passed. **Blocking** a thread means it is in a waiting state and cannot perform any actions, effectively pausing its operations. While the thread is **blocked**, it does not use CPU resources, but other threads or parts of the application may depend on its completion, which can lead to performance issues or inefficiencies if **Thread.Sleep()** is overused. For this reason, it should be used sparingly. Later in this chapter, we will explore alternative methods that allow for more efficient waiting and asynchronous processing.

Waiting for Threads to Complete

It is often necessary for threads to wait for other threads to complete before proceeding. As you saw in the preceding counter code example, the message "**Main thread completed.**" is printed before the count finishes. This is because the **main thread** continues and prints its message before the worker thread concludes.

But what if we need the worker thread to finish before the **main thread** continues? We need a way for the **main thread** to wait for the worker thread to do its work. This is where the **Thread.Join()** method is useful.

The **Thread.Join()** method blocks the calling thread until the thread it is waiting on (the "**called**" thread) completes its execution. This means that the calling thread cannot continue its own operations until the specified thread finishes. **Thread.Join()** is useful when one thread needs to wait for another to complete before proceeding, ensuring that any resources or data created by the other thread are fully available. However, using **Join** can also introduce delays in the calling thread, so it should be used thoughtfully to avoid unnecessary blocking in your application.

Let us modify the counter example to have the **main thread** wait for the counting to complete before proceeding:

```
namespace ThreadClassDemo
{
    internal class Program
    {
        static void Main(string[] args)
        {
            var workerThread = new Thread(() => Counter.CountTo(10));
            workerThread.Start();

            Console.WriteLine("Main thread waiting for counting to complete.");

            workerThread.Join();

            Console.WriteLine("Main thread completed.");
        }
    }

    internal class Counter
    {
        public static void CountTo(int number)
        {
            for (int i = 1; i < number + 1; i++)
            {
                Console.WriteLine($"Count: {i}");
                Thread.Sleep(TimeSpan.FromSeconds(1));
            }
        }
    }
}
```

The output from this new code would look like this:

```
Count: 1
Main thread waiting for counting to complete.
Count: 2
Count: 3
Count: 4
Count: 5
Count: 6
Count: 7
Count: 8
Count: 9
Count: 10
Main thread completed.
```

Note that the message "`Main thread waiting for counting to complete`." may appear before or be interleaved with the counting messages. This behavior is not directly controlled by the program's logic but is instead influenced by factors such as operating system scheduling and resource availability. However, the message "`Main thread completed`." will always appear at the end of the counting sequence. This is because the `workerThread.Join()` method blocks the main thread until the worker thread completes its execution and exits.

Stopping a Thread Gracefully

It is often necessary to control the execution of a thread and tell it to exit gracefully. This is especially useful for threads that run loops. One simple way to stop a thread is to define a flag that the thread can periodically check. If the flag is set, the thread can abort gracefully and exit.

Let us update the counting example to support stopping if a flag is set:

```
namespace ThreadClassDemo
{
    internal class Program
    {
        static void Main(string[] args)
        {
            var counter = new Counter();
            var workerThread = new Thread(() => counter.CountTo(10));
            workerThread.Start();

            Console.WriteLine("Main thread waiting for counting to complete.");
            Thread.Sleep(1000);
            counter.StopRunning = true;

            workerThread.Join();

            Console.WriteLine("Main thread completed.");
        }
    }

    internal class Counter
    {
        public bool StopRunning { get; set; }

        public void CountTo(int number)
        {
            for (int i = 1; i < number + 1; i++)
            {
                if (StopRunning)
                {
                    Console.WriteLine("Counter stopping.");
                    break;
                }
                Console.WriteLine($"Count: {i}");
                Thread.Sleep(TimeSpan.FromSeconds(1));
            }
        }
    }
}
```

In the previous block, a new property is added to the **`Counter`** class called **`StopRunning`**. Each iteration of the counting loop checks to see if this property is set to **`true`**. If it is, a message is printed, and the loop is aborted using the **`break`** keyword. The Main method is also altered to set this flag before the **`workerThread.Join()`** method is called. This aborts the counting thread early. Note that the **`Counter`** class was also changed to eliminate the static method to be closer aligned to best coding practices.

Note: *In some legacy applications you may see code that uses the* **`Thread.Abort`** *method to abort threads. This method does not stop thread execution gracefully and is considered unsafe to use. Older code that relies on* **`Thread.Abort`** *should be upgraded to a safer method of control such as the flag method mentioned earlier.*

Controlling Thread Priority

Threads can be **prioritized** using the **`Thread`** class. Assigning a tread **priority** allows a developer to define an importance or urgency to a thread, relative to other threads in the application. This indication acts as a hint to the operating system scheduler as to the order and amount of CPU time the thread receives relative to the other threads. Threads with a higher **priority** are typically scheduled for execution sooner or more frequently than threads with a lower **priority**.

Let us see how thread **prioritization** affects thread execution with a simple example.

```
namespace ThreadClassDemo
{
    internal class Program
    {
        static bool StopRunning;

        static void Main(string[] args)
        {
            var higherPriorityThread = new Thread(() => Count());
            higherPriorityThread.Priority = ThreadPriority.AboveNormal;
            higherPriorityThread.Name = "higherPriorityThread";

            var normalPriorityThread = new Thread(() => Count());
            normalPriorityThread.Priority = ThreadPriority.Normal;
            normalPriorityThread.Name = "normalPriorityThread";

            var lowerPriorityThread = new Thread(() => Count());
            lowerPriorityThread.Priority = ThreadPriority.BelowNormal;
            lowerPriorityThread.Name = "lowerPriorityThread";

            higherPriorityThread.Start();
            normalPriorityThread.Start();
            lowerPriorityThread.Start();

            Console.WriteLine("Main thread waiting for counting to com-
plete.");
            Thread.Sleep(1000);
            StopRunning = true;

            Console.WriteLine("Main thread completed.");
        }

        static void Count()
        {
            long currentCount = 0;
            while (!StopRunning)
            {
                currentCount++;
            }
            Console.WriteLine($"Thread {Thread.CurrentThread.Name} with
priority {Thread.CurrentThread.Priority} counted to: {currentCount:N0}");
        }
    }
}
```

In the previous example, three threads are created, one with a higher priority, one with a normal priority, and one with a lower priority. Each thread runs a tight loop that counts until the **StopRunning** flag is set. The output from this example will be like the following sequence:

```
Main thread waiting for counting to complete.
Main thread completed.
Thread normalPriorityThread with priority Normal counted to: 1,557,592,684
Thread higherPriorityThread with priority AboveNormal counted to: 1,572,485,382
Thread lowerPriorityThread with priority BelowNormal counted to: 1,449,173,272
```

The higher priority thread counted slightly more than the normal **priority**, and the below normal counted slightly less. This reflects the higher **priority** thread executing more often than the normal **priority** thread and the lower **priority** thread executing less often. The default thread **priority** is normal. Thread **prioritization** is useful for scenarios where higher responsiveness or other precedence is needed in a multithreaded application.

The following thread priorities are supported in .NET:

- Lowest
- Below Normal
- Normal
- Above Normal
- Highest

Note: *Thread priority is a hint to the operating system scheduler, not an absolute guarantee. Many factors affect thread execution including system load, CPU availability, and even operating system policies*

The **Thread** class provides very fine control over individual **dedicated threads** in an application. This is useful in applications where such control is necessary for the overall design of the solution. However, the **Thread** class does not support complex scenarios such as asynchronous programming. For that, we will need to explore other .NET models.

Introduction to Asynchronous Programming Models in .NET

There are three primary models for asynchronous programming in .NET, namely, the **Asynchronous Programming Model (APM)**, the **Event-based Asynchronous Pattern (EAP)**, and the **Task-based Asynchronous Pattern (TAP)**. The **APM**, sometimes called the "Begin/End" pattern, is one of the earliest approaches and is found in some .NET Framework APIs. It requires a **Begin** method and an **End** callback method with state objects to handle results. Later, in .NET 2.0 the **EAP** was introduced. It leverages events to signal the completion of asynchronous tasks. **TAP**, the most recent and widely used model was introduced in .NET 4.0 and uses the **Task** and **Task<Result>** classes to support asynchronous programming. In this section, we will look at the **APM** and **EAP** approaches. We will dive deeply into the **TAP** in the next chapter.

Asynchronous Programming with APM

The **APM** relies on delegates and callbacks to support a begin/end pattern for asynchronous programming. To use this pattern, use the following steps:

1. Define a delegate with a signature that matches a method to be called asynchronously.
2. Define a method that does the work and matches the delegate signature.

3. Define a callback method that will be called when the work is finished.
4. Start the work method with **BeginInvoke**.
5. Wait for the work to complete by calling the **WaitOne** method on the **IAsyncResult** instance returned from **BeginInvoke**.

Let us see this pattern in action by creating a program to calculate a factorial asynchronously:

```
using System;

public class Program
{
    delegate long FactorialDelegate(int n);

    public static void Main()
    {
        int number = 10;
        FactorialDelegate factorialDelegate = new FactorialDelegate(Calculate-
Factorial);
        IAsyncResult asyncResult = factorialDelegate.BeginInvoke(number, End-
FactorialCallback, factorialDelegate);

        Console.WriteLine("Calculating factorial asynchronously...");

        asyncResult.AsyncWaitHandle.WaitOne();
    }

    public static long CalculateFactorial(int n)
    {
        long result = 1;
        for (int i = 1; i <= n; i++)
        {
            result *= i;
        }
        return result;
    }

    public static void EndFactorialCallback(IAsyncResult asyncResult)
    {
        FactorialDelegate factorialDelegate = (FactorialDelegate)asyncResult.
AsyncState;

        long factorial = factorialDelegate.EndInvoke(asyncResult);

        Console.WriteLine("Factorial calculation complete. Result: " +
factorial);
    }
}
```

Note: *The APM is not supported in .NET Core because it is considered less efficient than the Task-based Asynchronous Pattern (TAP) and Microsoft wants to encourage TAP use for newer code. We will cover the TAP in Chapter 3: Creating and Running Tasks in C# and Chapter 9: Advanced Task Management. To run this code, you will need to create a solution for .NET 4.8 or below. Alternatively, you can run the sample code using the online C# compiler at https://dotnetfiddle.net.*

The output from this program should be like the following:

```
Calculating factorial asynchronously...
Factorial calculation complete. Result: 3628800
```

We can see the calculation is run asynchronously and work on the main thread is allowed to continue until the wait operation is called.

Asynchronous Programming with the EAP

The **Event-based Asynchronous Programming (EAP)** model uses events and callbacks to handle asynchronous operations. This model is particularly well-suited for applications that rely heavily on events, such as UI-based applications. **EAP** typically involves the following steps:

1. Create a custom **`EventArgs`** class to encapsulate the data that will be passed when the event is raised. This can include the result of the asynchronous operation, any errors, or progress information
2. Define an event in a class. This event should be based on the custom **`EventArgs`** class created in the first step. The event will be raised once the asynchronous operation completes or reaches a certain state
3. In the method that performs the asynchronous operation, invoke the event when the operation completes or when a significant change occurs (e.g., progress update). The event is typically raised using the **`Invoke`** method or by directly calling the event handler
4. In another class (such as a UI or caller class), create a method that will handle the event. This method should match the event's delegate signature
5. Use the += operator to attach the event handler to the event. This ensures that when the event is triggered, the appropriate method is called

To illustrate this approach, let us create a simple timer that displays a message after a delay has passed.

```
namespace EAPDemo
{

    using System;
    using System.Threading;

    internal class CompletedEventArgs : EventArgs
    {
        public bool IsSuccessful { get; }
        public string Message { get; }

        public CompletedEventArgs(bool isSuccessful, string message)
        {
            IsSuccessful = isSuccessful;
            Message = message;
        }
    }

    internal class MessageTimer
    {
        private TimeSpan _delay;
        private string _message;
        private Timer _timer;
```

```
            public event EventHandler<CompletedEventArgs> Completed;

            public MessageTimer(TimeSpan delay, string message)
            {
                _delay = delay;
                _message = message;
            }

            public void Start()
            {
                _timer = new Timer(OnTimer, null, _delay, TimeSpan.Zero);
            }

            private void OnTimer(object state)
            {
                Completed?.Invoke(state, new CompletedEventArgs(true, _message));
            }
        }

        internal class Program
        {
            static void Main()
            {
                var messageTimer = new MessageTimer(TimeSpan.FromSeconds(2),
    "Timer completed successfully.");
                messageTimer.Completed += MessageTimer_Completed;
                messageTimer.Start();
                Console.WriteLine("Timer started.");
                Console.ReadLine();
            }

            private static void MessageTimer_Completed(object? sender, Completed
    EventArgs e)
            {
                Console.WriteLine(e.Message);
            }
        }

    }
```

The output from the preceding code should be like the following:

```
Timer started
Timer completed successfully
```

Both the **Asynchronous Programming Model (APM)** and the **Event-based Asynchronous Programming (EAP)** are legacy asynchronous programming models that developers may encounter in older programs or libraries. While it is useful to be familiar with these models when working with legacy code, the **Task-based Asynchronous Pattern (TAP)** is the recommended approach for new development. We will explore **TAP** in the next chapter.

Benefits and Drawbacks of Legacy Threading Models

This section explores on the benefits and drawbacks of threading models.

Benefits of Traditional Threading

The `Thread` class provides fine-grained control over individual **dedicated threads**. Through it, developers can start threads and control thread execution, as well as provide thread scheduling hints in the form of **prioritization** that the operating system tries to honor. This type of control is very beneficial in some applications.

For example, IoT applications or other real-time systems may require highly responsive polling loops. This scenario requires precise control over execution timing. Starting dedicated polling and monitoring threads for these applications ensures these critical operations run independently from other parts of the application.

Banking or high-frequency trading applications rely on real-time transactions at high volumes. These types of applications often benefit from **dedicated threads** for trading algorithms or real-time data processing tasks. Using **dedicated threads** in these scenarios avoids task scheduling and queueing to ensure more consistent responsiveness.

Video games and other simulations often require **dedicated threads** to ensure consistent fluidity of visual and audio experiences. These **dedicated threads** handle intensive tasks such as rendering graphics, processing audio, and managing input events in real-time. By isolating these tasks from other computational processes, games can avoid delays or stuttering, providing players with a smooth, responsive experience. This approach also helps to manage latency and ensure that user actions, visual updates, and sound cues synchronize effectively, enhancing immersion and performance.

Background tasks that run continuously such as logging, database replication, file system monitoring, or telemetry processing in an application can be created as **background threads** and set to appropriate priorities to not interfere with main application tasks. **Dedicated threads** provide predictable execution in these types of scenarios.

In general, tasks that require non-standard thread scheduling, tight control, or specific thread management benefit from the use of the `Thread` class. The `Thread` class is often chosen for scenarios where developers need to set priorities, manage thread states explicitly, or apply custom scheduling that isn't well-suited to the managed threading provided by higher-level abstractions.

From an asynchronous programming perspective, the legacy models—namely the **Asynchronous Programming Model (APM)** and the **Event-based Asynchronous Pattern (EAP)** offer no significant benefits over modern techniques. They are covered in this chapter because professional developers may still encounter these older patterns in existing codebases. However, for new developments, the **Task-based Asynchronous Pattern (TAP)** should be used, as it provides a simpler, more flexible, and more powerful framework for handling asynchronous operations. We will explore the **TAP** in the next chapter.

Drawbacks of Legacy Threading Models

While dedicated threads have advantages in specific situations, they also come with significant drawbacks that limit their usefulness in general. Here are the main drawbacks:

- Thread lifecycle management and synchronization are complex topics that require significant thought and planning
- Multithreaded code can be difficult to debug. Race conditions and deadlocks can be hard to detect and correct
- Dedicated threads consume more resources than higher-level abstractions, leading to overhead from context switching and memory use. They are hard to scale effectively, and too many threads can degrade performance by causing CPU contention and resource exhaustion

Thread lifecycle management and synchronization can quickly become complex in larger-scale applications, as the demands on resources grow and the intricacies of coordinating multiple threads multiply. Ensuring each thread completes its task without conflicts, managing shared resources, avoiding deadlocks, and optimizing for performance under heavy loads all add layers of complexity. This requires careful planning and potentially implementing mechanisms like thread pools, synchronization constructs, and monitoring to track thread states. Additionally, failing to properly manage threads can lead to resource leaks, application instability, and even system crashes, all of which can be difficult to debug.

Dedicated threads often need to wait for other threads to complete tasks before they can proceed. If two or more threads enter a state where each is waiting for the other(s) to release resources or finish operations, none of the threads can continue, resulting in a **deadlock**. **Deadlocks** are often intermittent and challenging to resolve, especially when they occur under conditions that are difficult to reproduce in debugging sessions.

Threads that update and access shared data present a different type of complexity. Without careful synchronization, updates can happen out of order, or a thread with stale data may overwrite more recent updates. This situation called a **race condition**, can occur intermittently and is often difficult to detect and debug due to its dependence on timing and thread execution order. We will cover the details of handling shared data in a later chapter.

Compared to abstractions such as thread pools and asynchronous models, **dedicated threads** consume more system resources. As the number of **dedicated threads** increases, overhead from context switching, memory consumption, and CPU contention can lead to significant performance issues. This makes **dedicated threads** more challenging to scale effectively in high-concurrency scenarios compared to other options.

Conclusion

The Thread class provides a powerful tool for creating, starting, controlling, and **prioritizing dedicated threads** in applications that require precise thread management for optimal performance. While **dedicated threads** are generally not recommended for routine tasks due to their resource costs, they are essential in specific use cases, such as real-time systems, complex simulations, or dedicated background tasks requiring strict control.

Understanding legacy asynchronous programming models in .NET, such as the **Asynchronous Programming Model (APM)** and **Event-based Asynchronous Pattern (EAP)**, is valuable for maintaining and integrating with legacy .NET Framework libraries. However, these models offer no substantial advantages over modern approaches like the **Task-based Asynchronous Pattern (TAP)** and **`async/await`**, and they are generally unsuitable for new development.

In the next chapter, we will cover the **Task-based Asynchronous Pattern (TAP)**. **TAP** evolved from **APM** and **EAP**, consolidating and simplifying asynchronous programming and multithreading in .NET. It provides a more efficient, scalable, and developer-friendly approach to managing asynchronous tasks.

Points to Remember

- The **`Thread`** class provides a way to create, control, and prioritize dedicated threads in an application.
- Dedicated threads are useful in specific scenarios, but higher-level abstractions are better for more general use.
- Thread prioritization settings provide hints to the operating system scheduler about relative thread priority, but do not provide execution guarantees.

- The legacy asynchronous programming models in .NET like the Asynchronous Programming Model and the Event-based Asynchronous Pattern, are useful to understand from a maintenance perspective but should not be used in new development.

Multiple Choice Questions

1. Which of the following is not true of the **`Thread`** class?
   a. **`Thread.Abort()`** should be called to stop threads after they have been started.
   b. The **`IsBackground`** property is used to mark a thread as a background thread.
   c. The **`Join()`** method is used to wait for a thread to complete before continuing.
   d. All of the above.
2. Which of the following best defines thread priority?
   a. The order in which threads are created and destroyed in an application.
   b. A determination of which threads to delay and which to run.
   c. An operating system hint that suggests the order and amount of CPU time a thread receives in relation to other threads.
   d. The timing of thread execution, used for debugging purposes.
3. What is a foreground thread in an application?
   a. A type of thread used only in UI applications.
   b. A thread that is scheduled before other threads in the application.
   c. A thread that uses more memory and CPU for higher levels of performance.
   d. A thread that prevents the application from exiting while it is active.
4. Which of the following is a type of application in which dedicated threads are useful?
   a. An e-commerce application where scalability is critical to handle fluctuations in user demand.
   b. An IoT application that requires consistent, precision polling loops.
   c. A UI application that does not require dedicated background processing.
   d. None of the above.
5. In which of the following scenarios is the Asynchronous Programming Model useful?
   a. In maintaining a legacy application that uses it.
   b. In new applications where scalability is a key requirement.
   c. Only for .NET 9 applications, since it is a new feature in this release.
   d. In all applications that require dedicated background processing.

Answers

1. a
2. c
3. d
4. b
5. a

Questions

1. What types of applications benefit from the use of dedicated threads?
2. In what scenarios would dedicated threads become unwieldy or difficult to debug?
3. In what ways does programming dedicated threads differ from asynchronous programming?
4. In what ways is asynchronous programming the same as programming dedicated threads?
5. How can thread prioritization be used to fine tune performance?
6. What are good uses of background threads?

Key Terms

- **Main Thread:** a thread started by the operating system that runs the application
- **Foreground Thread:** a thread that prevents the application from exiting if it is active
- **Background Thread:** a thread that does not prevent the application from exiting if it is active
- **Managed Thread:** a thread controlled by the .NET runtime
- **Unmanaged or Native Thread:** a thread controlled directly by the operating system
- **Dedicated Thread:** a thread created by the `Thread` class that operates independently and whose lifecycle is controlled entirely by developer code
- **Asynchronous Programming Model (APM):** a legacy .NET model for asynchronous programming that relies on delegates, and state objects to function. Also called the "`Begin/End`" model
- **Event-based Asynchronous Pattern (EAP)**: a legacy asynchronous programming model in .NET that relies on events to function
- **Task-based Asynchronous Pattern (TAP)**: the modern asynchronous programming model in .NET that relies on the `Task` and `Task<Result>` classes to function
- **Target Method**: The method a thread will call when it starts
- **Block, Blocking, Blocked**: a thread in a waiting state, unable to perform any actions
- **Priority, Prioritization, Prioritized:** a hint to the operating system scheduler that suggests the order and amount of CPU time a thread receives in relation to other threads in the application

CHAPTER 3
Creating and Running Tasks in C#

Introduction

In the previous chapter, we explored low-level thread programming and management in .NET, along with legacy asynchronous programming models. In this chapter, we will dive into a higher-level abstraction that simplifies parallel programming by eliminating the need to manage threads directly, which is known as the .NET **`Task`** class.

Structure

In this chapter, we will cover the following topics:

- Introduction to the **`Task`** Class
    - Understanding the **`Task`** Class
    - Core Properties and Methods of the **`Task`** Class
    - How to Create and Run Tasks
    - Running Tasks Directly and Using Factory Methods
    - Task Continuations and Chaining
    - Completing Tasks Synchronously
- Task Cancellation
    - Using Cancellation Tokens
    - Checking for Task Cancellation
    - Best Practices for Task Cancellation
- Proper Error Handling in Tasks
    - Understanding Exceptions in Tasks
    - Using Wait Methods with Exception Handling
    - Error Handling in Continuations
    - Best Practices for Error Handling in Asynchronous Code
- Task-based Asynchronous Pattern (TAP)
    - Overview of the TAP
    - How the TAP Builds on the Task Class
    - Guidelines and Best Practices for TAP Methods

Introduction to the `Task` Class

The **`Task`** class is the backbone of modern parallel and asynchronous programming in .NET. Unlike the **`Thread`** class, which represents a dedicated thread in an application, the **`Task`** class represents the higher-level concept of a logical unit of work that can run asynchronously. Internally, the **`Task`** class utilizes threads and thread pools, managing their allocation and scheduling, which allows for efficient resource use and minimizes the overhead associated with manually managing threads. This abstraction makes parallel programming much more accessible and efficient, allowing developers to focus on application logic rather than low-level threading details.

The **`Task`** class is at the core of the **Task Parallel Library (TPL)** in .NET. **TPL** provides built-in support for parallelism through constructs such as parallel loops and parallel queries, allowing developers to harness multi-core processing power more efficiently. Additionally, the **`Task`** class is fundamental to asynchronous programming in .NET, serving as the backbone of the **Task-based Asynchronous Pattern (TAP)**. Through **TAP**, developers can create asynchronous methods, which simplify the structure and readability of asynchronous code. We will discuss the **TAP** later in this chapter and discover parallel loops and queries in later chapters.

With the **`Task`** class, developers can write asynchronous delays and waits that do not block threads. This is achieved using asynchronous programming patterns which allow the thread to continue executing other tasks while waiting for the delay or operation to complete. This approach helps improve scalability and performance, particularly in I/O-bound or high-concurrency applications, as it frees up resources and prevents thread starvation, which can occur when threads are unnecessarily blocked.

Understanding the `Task` Class

The **`Task`** class is found in the **`System.Threading.Tasks`** namespace. It is meant to represent a logical unit of work in an application, which is a method accessed using a delegate or lambda, very similar to the way the **`Thread`** class works. Though they have some similarities, the **`Task`** class differs from the **`Thread`** class in important ways.

Level of Abstraction

The **`Task`** class represents a logical unit of work rather than a physical thread. It is designed for efficient workload management, leaving the details of how tasks run to the .NET runtime. Tasks may run asynchronously or synchronously as determined by the .NET runtime.

The **`Thread`** class is a lower-level abstraction of a physical operating system thread. It is designed focused on fine-grained thread management. Threads always run asynchronously as controlled by the developer code.

Thread Scheduling and Management

Tasks are scheduled on the **Thread Pool**, which allows the .NET runtime to reuse and manage threads automatically, optimizing system resources and reducing overhead. We will discuss the **Thread Pool** in detail in later chapters.

Threads are directly created and managed by the developer, with no connection to the **Thread Pool**. Each thread consumes system resources and must be carefully managed by the developer.

Performance and Scalability

Tasks are more efficient for short-lived or high-frequency operations because they use pooled threads. This allows the .NET runtime to allocate and reuse threads efficiently. This reuse also allows for greater scalability.

Threads are more efficient for long running and dedicated operations. Each thread requires significant memory resources to manage its stack and consumes system resources to create and destroy the thread. Creating many threads can lead to performance bottlenecks or resource exhaustion.

Asynchronous Programming Support

Tasks are well suited for asynchronous programming support. They are integrated with the **Task-based Asynchronous Pattern (TAP)** and support the **`async/await`** keywords and continuations, making developing asynchronous code easier to work with.

Threads do not support asynchronous programming directly and are not integrated with **`async/await`** or continuations. Asynchronous programming can be achieved using threads, but requires significant manual coding, often involving callbacks and state management.

Error Handling

Tasks have built-in support for exception processing, capturing and rethrowing exceptions gracefully. This simplifies exception handling and makes exceptions easier to work with in multi-task scenarios.

Exceptions thrown in a thread can terminate the thread unless they are caught and handled in the thread's execution context. This requires more careful thought and planning in concurrent scenarios.

Cancellation Support

Tasks have integrated support for cancellation using the **`CancellationToken`** and **`CancellationTokenSource`** classes. These classes facilitate simple cooperative cancellation.

Threads have no built-in cancellation support. Developers must manually design and build methods to signal cancellation and stop running threads. This often involves careful use of shared variables or other synchronization mechanisms.

The following table summarizes the key differences between the **`Thread`** and **`Task`** classes:

Feature	**`Task` Class**	**`Thread` Class**
Abstraction Level	High (Logical Unit of Work)	Low (Physical Thread)
Managed by Runtime	Yes, via the Thread Pool	No, manually managed
Performance	High for short-lived tasks	More thread overhead
Asynchronous Support	Supports async/await and Continuations	No built-in support
Error Handling	Aggregates exceptions and rethrows later	Unhandled exception can terminate thread
Cancellation Support	Built-in	Manual
Use Cases	Short-lived parallel tasks	Long-lived or specific needs

***Table 3.1**: Comparison of Task and Thread Classes*

Core Properties and Methods of the Task Class

The **`Task`** class implements the **`IAsyncResult`** interface that was originally introduced in the

Asynchronous Programming Model (APM). While the **IAsyncResult** interface is less commonly used in modern development due to the shift towards the Task-based Asynchronous Pattern (TAP), it is included in the Task class to provide seamless compatibility between the older APM model and newer programming paradigms.

By implementing **IAsyncResult**, the **Task** class serves as a bridge between APM and TAP, enabling developers to leverage the benefits of modern asynchronous programming while maintaining compatibility with older frameworks and APIs.

The Task class has the following properties:

Property	**Description**
`AsyncState`	Returns the state object passed to the `Task` constructor. This is part of the `IAsyncResult` interface and is used mainly for backwards compatibility with the APM
`CompletedTask`	A pre-completed static `Task` instance. This is useful for returning a completed task in a TAP method that completes synchronously, avoiding the overhead of creating a new `Task`
`CurrentId`	A static property that returns the ID of the currently executing `Task`
`Exception`	Returns the `AggregateException` instance for a failed `Task`
`Factory`	A static property that exposes factory methods used for creating `Task` instances
`Id`	Returns the ID of a specific `Task` instance
`IsCanceled`	Returns a value indicating whether a `Task` instance completed due to being canceled
`IsCompleted`	Returns a value indicating whether a `Task` instance is completed processing
`IsCompletedSuccessfully`	Returns a value indicating whether a `Task` instance completed without failing
`IsFaulted`	Returns a value indicating whether a `Task` instance failed due to an unhandled exception
`Status`	Returns a value indicating the current status of a `Task`

***Table 3.2**: Properties of the Task Class*

Creating and Running Tasks

The **Task** class in .NET provides several mechanisms to create and start tasks, catering to a variety of development needs:

- **Constructors**: The **Task** class includes constructors that allow developers to create individual tasks with specialized options. These constructors can be used to define tasks with specific behaviors, such as specifying a cancellation token, a task scheduler, or custom continuation options.
- **Factory Methods**: The **Task.Factory** property provides factory methods, such as **StartNew**, which combine task creation and execution in a single step. These methods are particularly useful when tasks need to start immediately after being defined.
- **Static Methods**: The Task class includes static methods to:

  a. Create and run tasks in a simplified manner, such as using **Task.Run**.

  b. Create specialized tasks, such as **Task.CompletedTask** for a pre-completed task or methods like **FromResult**, **FromException**, and **FromCanceled** for explicitly initialized task states.

Like the **Thread** class, the **Task** class requires a delegate that specifies the code to execute when the **Task** starts. However, **Task** uses the pre-defined **Action** and **Func<T>** delegates, rather than allowing custom delegates like **Thread** does.

An **Action** in .NET is a pre-defined delegate that has no return value and accepts up to 16 parameters. The Task class uses **Action** for methods that perform operations without returning results. This simplifies the design of the **Task** class, making it easier to distinguish between tasks that return values and those that do not.

The **Func<T>** delegate is another pre-defined delegate in .NET. Like **Action**, it can accept up to 16 parameters. Unlike **Action**, **Func<T>** returns a value of the type specified by the generic parameter **T**. The **Task<T>** class, which is a generic subclass of **Task**, uses **Func<T>** to encapsulate methods that return results.

Creating Tasks Using a Constructor

To create a Task using the constructor, define a method to be run and call one of the constructors as shown in the following code:

```
var task = new Task(PrintMessage);

void PrintMessage()
{
    Console.WriteLine("Hello world from Task!");
}
```

The constructor does not start the task, so if we run the previous code example, it does not print the message. To start a task that's waiting to run, we need to call the **Start()** method.

```
var task = new Task(PrintMessage);
task.Start();

void PrintMessage()
{
    Console.WriteLine("Hello world from Task!");
}
```

If we run the previous example, we will not be able to see the message. The reason is that even though we started the task, the main thread of the application continued and completed, exiting the program before the task had a chance to be scheduled and run. Given that tasks are a higher level of abstraction than threads, they cannot prevent a program from exiting. Therefore, to see the message, we need the main thread to wait until the task is scheduled and completed. One way to do this is to use the **Wait()** method. Let us add the wait method to the example:

```
var task = new Task(PrintMessage);
task.Start();
task.Wait();

void PrintMessage()
{
    Console.WriteLine("Hello world from Task!");
}
```

After adding the **Wait()** method, the message is printed. Let us walk through what is happening in this sample in detail:

1. The **Main()** method is called by the operating system and a new **Task** is created using an **Action** that points to the **PrintMessage()** method as a target.

2. The **Start()** method on the task instance is called. This schedules the task to be run.
3. The **Wait()** method is called on the task instance. This blocks the main thread, allowing the task to be scheduled and run.
4. When the task completes its work, the main thread completes and exits the program.

The **Task** class also supports lambdas, which the compiler converts to **Action** or **Func<T>** depending on whether they return values or not. Let us convert the "**Hello world**" example to use a lambda:

```
var task = new Task(() => Console.WriteLine("Hello world from Tasks!"));
task.Start();
task.Wait();
```

The use of the lambda simplifies the code and makes the sample a bit easier to read, although it behaves the same way as the original "**Hello world**" example.

Tasks that return values are created and used similarly. Let us create a sample that calculates Fibonacci sequences:

```
var task = new Task<long>(() => CalculateFibonacci(10));
task.Start();

Console.WriteLine("Calculating fibonacci...");
var result = task.Result;
Console.WriteLine("The 10th fibonacci number is " + result);

long CalculateFibonacci(int n)
{
    if (n <= 1)
    {
        return n;
    }

    return CalculateFibonacci(n - 1) + CalculateFibonacci(n - 2);
}
```

The output of the previous example is as follows:

```
Calculating fibonacci...
The 10th fibonacci number is 55
```

The Fibonacci example uses **Task<T>** to calculate the value and return it. This is different in a few ways from the previous **Task** examples. Instead of creating a **Task** instance, we create a **Task<long>** instance, matching the method signature of the **CalculateFibonacci()** method. Also, we use the **Result** property instead of the **Wait()** method. The **Result** property also blocks the calling thread, but it returns the result of the method, where **Wait()** does not.

Waiting for Multiple Tasks

The **Wait()** method waits for a single task to complete, as we have seen in previous examples. Often, it is necessary to wait for multiple tasks to complete at once. For example, you might be making parallel calculations or waiting for multiple API requests, and you need to be sure all the results are available before proceeding. In such cases, the **Task.WaitAll()** method is used to block the thread and wait for a set of tasks to complete. The following example demonstrates waiting for multiple tasks.

```
var task1 = Task.Run(() => Counter(10));
var task2 = Task.Run(() => Counter(5));

Task.WaitAll(task1, task2);
Console.WriteLine("Finished all tasks.");
```

```
void Counter(int limit)
{
    for (int i = 0; i < limit; i++)
        Thread.Sleep(100);
    Console.WriteLine("Counted to " + limit);
}
```

In the prior example, two tasks are created with different completion times. **`Task.WaitAll()`** is called to block and wait for both tasks to complete before continuing. The output is as follows:

```
Counted to 5
Counted to 10
Finished all tasks.
```

In some specific scenarios, it is useful to wait for the quickest task in the list to complete before continuing. For example, in a highly available application, you may send a request to multiple APIs and use results from the first one to respond. In this scenario, **`Task.WaitAny()`** is used to block and wait for the quickest task to finish before proceeding. Let us see how the prior example behaves using **`Task.WaitAny()`**:

```
var taskList = new List<Task>();
taskList.Add(Task.Run(() => Counter(10)));
taskList.Add(Task.Run(() => Counter(5)));

int completedIndex = Task.WaitAny(taskList.ToArray());
Console.WriteLine($"Finished quickest task {taskList[completedIndex].Id}.");

void Counter(int limit)
{
    for (int i = 0; i < limit; i++)
        Thread.Sleep(100);
    Console.WriteLine("Counted to " + limit);
}
```

The output from the prior example is as follows:

```
Counted to 5
Finished quickest task 1.
```

The difference here is that **`Task.WaitAny()`** returns when the first task to finish is completed. **`Task.WaitAny()`** returns an integer that is the index of the completed task in the array of tasks passed. This can be used to access the completed task for further processing.

Using Task Constructors

Creating tasks using constructors is useful in the following specific scenarios.

1. When task execution needs to be delayed after creation until specific criteria is met or additional initialization occurs, creating using a constructor allows creation to be separated from the start.
2. In advanced scenarios where specific task options need to be set, task options provide fine control over task chaining behavior and setting preferences for long running tasks.
3. The **`Task`** constructor can accept a custom task scheduler. This is useful in advanced scenarios where the default scheduling behavior is not sufficient.
4. In debugging and testing scenarios, it is often useful to create a task before executing it to examine or manipulate states and other properties before starting the task.

5. Creating a **Task** with the constructor provides backwards compatibility with APM. This may be useful for upgrading legacy code or integrating with some frameworks.

Using **Task** constructors has some disadvantages as well. These limitations are as follows:

1. Tasks must be manually started after they are created. While this is an advantage in some scenarios, it can easily be overlooked. As we have seen in our examples so far, if the task is not started, it will not run. This can lead to defects that may be difficult to debug.
2. Using the constructor bypasses some of the runtime optimizations that can be leveraged using other methods such as the **Run()** method or **StartNew()**. These optimizations enable better resource allocation and scheduling.
3. Constructors do not allow for creating completed, faulted, or canceled tasks, requiring additional work if used in these scenarios.
4. In most scenarios, using the constructor leads to code that is harder to read and less maintainable.

Note: *The Task constructor supports providing a custom scheduler. While threads are scheduled by the operating system, tasks in .NET are managed by software schedulers provided by the Task Parallel Library (TPL). The default scheduler,* **TaskScheduler.Default**, *is highly optimized for general scenarios and typically meets most application needs. However, in specialized cases, such as when using a specific synchronization context, providing custom task prioritization rules, or simulating constrained environments for testing, creating a custom task scheduler may be beneficial. Details on creating a custom task scheduler are covered later in this book.*

Running Tasks Directly and Using Factory Methods

In most cases, it is preferable to create a task and start it immediately, rather than using the constructors. The **Task** class provides two methods for creating and starting tasks.

The first method is to use the **Task.Factory.StartNew()** method. This method has the advantage of exposing many of the options available in the constructors while immediately starting the task after creation. The **StartNew()** method can be used to start either a **Task** or **Task<T>** instance. Let us see the **StartNew()** method in action:

```
int number = 7;
var task = Task.Factory.StartNew(() => IsPrime(number));
Console.WriteLine("Checking prime asynchronously...");
bool result = task.Result;
Console.WriteLine($"The number {number} {(result ? "is" : "is not")} prime.");

bool IsPrime(int number)
{
    if (number <= 1)
    {
        return false;
    }

    for (int i = 2; i <= Math.Sqrt(number); i++)
    {
        if (number % i == 0)
        {
            return false;
        }
    }
```

```
        return true;
    }
```

The previous example outputs the following:

```
Checking prime asynchronously...
The number 7 is prime.
```

Tasks can also be run directly using the **Run()** method. This is the most common method for starting tasks. The **Run()** method also supports starting **Task** or **Task<T>** instances. Let us refactor the prime number example to use the **Run()** method:

```
int number = 7;
var task = Task.Run(() => IsPrime(number));
Console.WriteLine("Checking prime asynchronously...");
bool result = task.Result;
Console.WriteLine($"The number {number} {(result ? "is" : "is not")} prime.");

bool IsPrime(int number)
{
    if (number <= 1)
    {
        return false;
    }

    for (int i = 2; i <= Math.Sqrt(number); i++)
    {
        if (number % i == 0)
        {
            return false;
        }
    }

    return true;
}
```

The **Run()** method in the **Task** class does not provide the advanced configuration options that the **StartNew()** method supports, such as specifying a custom task scheduler, cancellation tokens, or options like **TaskCreationOptions**. However, it is less verbose and simpler to use, making it well-suited for most common scenarios where fine-grained control is not required.

Task Continuations and Chaining

Logical work in applications often requires different units of work to be completed in a specific order. The **Task** class supports this concept by allowing tasks to be scheduled sequentially or chained together. When structured this way, tasks later in the chain are executed only after the preceding tasks have been completed. This is particularly useful when the output of one task serves as the input for another.

Chaining tasks in .NET is commonly accomplished using the **ContinueWith()** method. This method schedules a **continuation** task that will be executed once the preceding task is completed. The **ContinueWith()** method requires a delegate (such as an **Action<Task>** or **Func<Task, TResult>**) as a parameter. The delegate receives the preceding task as its input, allowing the continuation task to examine the state of the prior task.

Because of the chaining nature of **ContinueWith()**, it is often most readable to use method chaining syntax to construct **continuations**. Let us look at a simple example:

```
Task.Run(() => Console.WriteLine("Executing the first task."))
    .ContinueWith(task => Console.WriteLine("Executing continuation task."))
    .Wait();
```

The output from the prior example is as follows:

```
Executing the first task.
Executing continuation task.
```

Let us break down the prior example step by step.

1. The **Task.Run()** method creates and starts a new Task with a delegate that prints the first message
2. The **ContinueWith()** method creates and schedules another **Task** that prints the second method. This task receives a **Task** instance as a parameter. This **Task** instance is the completed task originally created with **Task.Run()**
3. The main thread calls **Wait()** on the second task, which blocks until both tasks in the chain are complete

Examining the state of the prior task in the chain allows **continuation** tasks to use the output from that task. For example, the **Result** property can be read and used in **continuation** processing.

```
int number = 7;
Task.Run(() => IsPrime(number))
    .ContinueWith(task => Console.WriteLine($"The number {(task.Result ? "is"
: "is not")} prime."))
    .Wait();

bool IsPrime(int number)
{
    if (number <= 1)
    {
        return false;
    }

    for (int i = 2; i <= Math.Sqrt(number); i++)
    {
        if (number % i == 0)
        {
            return false;
        }
    }

    return true;
}
```

In the prior example, the first task calculates whether the number passed is prime and returns the result. The **continuation** task then uses the **Result** property to print whether the result is or is not prime. Examining the prior task's properties allows the **continuation** task to control its behavior depending on the outcome of the prior task. This allows the **continuation** task to handle error conditions as well as use result values.

Handling Errors in Continuations

A **continuation** task can directly check the prior tasks success status and determine whether to handle the error or continue normally. A **continuation** task should always do this to avoid propagating exceptions. The following code demonstrates proper error handling in a **continuation**.

```
RunContinuation(10).Wait();
RunContinuation(0).Wait();

Task RunContinuation(int number)
{
    return Task.Run(() => ProcessData(number))
        .ContinueWith(task =>
        {
            if (task.IsCompletedSuccessfully)
                Console.WriteLine($"The result is: {task.Result}");
            else
                Console.WriteLine($"Task failed with message: {task.
Exception?.Flatten().Message}");
        });
}

decimal ProcessData(int number)
{
    if (number == 0)
    {
        throw new ArgumentException("Invalid argument.");
    }

    return 100.0M / number;
}
```

In the prior example, the first task calls **`ProcessData()`** which will fail if the number zero is passed. The **continuation** task checks to see if the first task was successful by examining the **`IsCompletedSuccessfully`** property. If the task is successful, it prints the result, if not, it prints the task exception message. The output is as follows:

```
The result is: 10.0
Task failed with message: One or more errors occurred. (Invalid argument.)
```

Limitations of Continuations

Continuations using **`ContinueWith()`** allow task workflows to be created and executed, enabling developers to define subsequent operations to run once a task is completed. However, **`ContinueWith()`** has the following limitations that developers should consider:

- By default, the **continuation** is not guaranteed to run on the same thread as the preceding task. To control this behavior, developers can specify the desired execution context using the **`TaskContinuationOptions`** parameter in the **`ContinueWith()`** call. Failing to account for this can lead to synchronization issues, especially if shared data is accessed or modified across tasks. Strategies for handling shared data and ensuring proper synchronization will be explored in future chapters.
- Managing complex chains of tasks using **`ContinueWith()`** can lead to verbose and difficult-to-read code. Such chains often become harder to maintain and debug as the task workflow grows in complexity. This is especially true when dealing with multiple dependent continuations or error-handling scenarios.

Because of these limitations, modern code often favors **`async/await`** instead of **continuations** for task chaining. The **`async/await`** model provides more readable and maintainable code while achieving similar outcomes. We will fully explore **`async/await`** in future chapters.

Completing Tasks Synchronously

While tasks are primarily designed for asynchronous execution, there are scenarios where a task must be completed synchronously, such as when returning a result immediately from a method that expects a Task or when handling error conditions without awaiting an actual operation. The Task class provides several optimized members for these cases:

- **`Task.CompletedTask`** returns a cached, already-completed task, useful when no result is needed
- **`Task.FromResult(T result)`** creates a successfully completed **`Task<T>`** with a specified result
- **`Task.FromException`** and **`Task.FromCanceled`** create faulted or canceled tasks, respectively, allowing you to represent error or cancellation states without running asynchronous code

These members are especially useful for quickly returning task-based results in synchronous code paths and are covered in more detail in *Chapter 10, Asynchronous Programming with Async/Await.*

Task Cancellation

Suppose you have written a web service application. To fulfill requests, the application accesses a database and performs computations on the returned data. These operations can be time-consuming and resource intensive.

Now, consider what happens if, during this processing, the user disconnects or cancels their request. Without a proper mechanism, the application will continue executing the task even though the result cannot be returned to the user. This leads to wasted resources, reduced system performance, and potentially increased costs.

To address this issue, the **Task Parallel Library (TPL)** provides a standard way to cancel tasks. Using cancellation tokens, tasks can be monitored and safely terminated when a cancellation request is issued. This approach ensures that resources are freed up promptly and the application remains responsive and efficient under varying conditions.

The **TPL** contains two classes that provide a standard way to signal and respond to cancellation of tasks. These are the **`CancellationTokenSource`** class and **`CancellationToken`** struct. These classes provide a uniform, cooperative approach to task cancellation.

Using Cancellation Tokens

The **`CancellationTokenSource`** class acts as a controller and is used to signal a **`CancellationToken`** that cancellation has been requested. This signal can be controlled manually by calling the **`Cancel`** method. Cancellation can also be scheduled by calling the **`CancelAfter`** method or by assigning a timeout in the **`CancellationTokenSource`** constructor. The **`CancellationTokenSource`** class has a **`Token`** property that exposes the **`CancellationToken`** that will be signaled when cancellation is requested.

Cancellation in the **TPL** is designed to promote a cooperative model rather than a forced interruption. This design ensures a cancelled task can respond in a controlled way, avoiding issues such as a corrupted state or other inconsistent results that could arise from an abrupt termination. According to this model, the task code must detect that cancellation was requested and take appropriate action to respond by quickly cleaning up resources and returning to a consistent state. The **CancellationToken** class is the mechanism tasks use to monitor for cancellation.

The simplest way to check if cancellation has been requested is to check the **CancellationToken.IsCancellationRequested** property. This property is designed to be checked periodically by a task, such as in a loop. The **IsCancellationRequested** property returns **false** if cancellation has not been requested, and **true** if it has. The following example shows how to cancel tasks and check for cancellation:

```
using System.Threading;
using System.Threading.Tasks;

var cts = new CancellationTokenSource();
var token = cts.Token;

var task = Task.Run(() =>
{
    while (!token.IsCancellationRequested)
    {
        Console.WriteLine("Task working...");
        Thread.Sleep(1000);
    }

    Console.WriteLine("Task cancelled.");

 }, token);

Thread.Sleep(4500);
cts.Cancel();
task.Wait();
cts.Dispose();
Console.Read();
```

In the prior example, the main thread starts a task that loops forever until canceled, simulating some ongoing work. The task starts and the main thread waits for 4.5 seconds before cancelling the task and waiting for it to complete. The output looks like the following:

```
Task working...
Task working...
Task working...
Task working...
Task working...
Task cancelled.
```

In this case, the task simply stops when it detects the cancellation, but the developer has the flexibility to write any type of code necessary to ensure a stable state or resource cleanup before exiting.

The previous example also passes the **CancellationToken** as a parameter to the **Run()** method. This approach allows the **Run()** method to check for cancellation before starting the task, avoiding unnecessary work if cancellation has already been requested. This behavior facilitates proper handling of cancellation scenarios in asynchronous programming workflows.

Cancellation can also be monitored using the **ThrowIfCancellationRequested()** method available in the **CancellationToken** struct. This method throws a **OperationCanceledException** if cancellation has been requested for the associated **CancellationToken**. This is useful in scenarios where long-running or potentially blocking operations need to be aborted promptly when a cancellation request is issued. If a task throws an **OperationCanceledException** in this way and does not catch it, the task **Status** property will be set to **Canceled** and the **IsCanceled** property will be set to true.

This approach is commonly used in asynchronous programming, especially in conjunction with **async** and **await**. Many of the asynchronous I/O methods in the .NET framework (such as those in the **System.IO** or **System.Net.Http** namespaces) support cancellation by taking a **CancellationToken** as a parameter. These methods internally use **ThrowIfCancellationRequested()** or similar logic to observe the cancellation token and abort operations when necessary.

Let us modify our example to use **ThrowIfCancellationRequested()**:

```
var cts = new CancellationTokenSource();
var token = cts.Token;

var task = Task.Run(() =>
{
    try
    {
        while (true)
        {
            token.ThrowIfCancellationRequested();
            Console.WriteLine("Task working...");
            Thread.Sleep(1000);
        }
    }
    catch (OperationCanceledException)
    {
        Console.WriteLine("Task cancelled.");
        throw;
    }

}, token);

Thread.Sleep(4500);
cts.Cancel();
try { task.Wait(); } catch (AggregateException) { }
Console.WriteLine("The task status is: " + task.Status);
cts.Dispose();
```

The output from the prior example is as follows:

```
Task working...
Task working...
Task working...
Task working...
Task working...
Task cancelled.
The task status is: Cancelled
```

Note: *The CancellationTokenSource class supports the IDisposable interface and should be disposed after use, for proper resource management.*

Advanced Cancellation

The **CancellationTokenSource** class supports linking to another **CancellationTokenSource** through its static **CreateLinkedTokenSource()** method. This method creates a new instance of **CancellationTokenSource** that will enter the canceled state when any of the tokens provided as arguments to the method are canceled. This allows you to create hierarchies or chains of cancellation sources, enabling centralized or parent-child-style cancellation management. This is especially helpful in complex scenarios where multiple tasks need coordinated cancellation.

```
var ctsParent = new CancellationTokenSource();
var ctsChild = CancellationTokenSource.CreateLinkedTokenSource(ctsParent.Token);

var task1 = Task.Run(() => DoWork(ctsParent.Token, "one"), ctsParent.Token);
var task2 = Task.Run(() => DoWork(ctsChild.Token, "two"), ctsChild.Token);

Thread.Sleep(3000);
ctsParent.Cancel();
task1.Wait();
task2.Wait();
ctsParent.Dispose();
ctsChild.Dispose();

void DoWork(CancellationToken token, string taskName)
{
    int count = 0;
    while (!token.IsCancellationRequested)
    {
        count++;
        Thread.Sleep(1000);
    }

    Console.WriteLine($"Task {taskName} canceled after count of {count}");
}
```

The prior example cancels just the parent source, but because the child source is linked, it is also canceled. The output is as follows:

```
Task one canceled after count of 3
Task two canceled after count of 3
```

The `CancellationToken` struct supports an advanced feature called **delegate registration**, which allows you to associate a delegate with a token. When cancellation is requested for that token, the registered delegate is invoked. This mechanism can be particularly useful for scenarios such as advanced resource cleanup, logging, or coordination tasks that are independent of the code being directly canceled.

To register a delegate, use the `Register` method, as shown in the following example:

```
var cts = new CancellationTokenSource();
var token = cts.Token;

token.Register(() =>
{
    Console.WriteLine("Cancellation has been requested. Performing cleanup...");
});

cts.Cancel();
```

Running the prior example produces the following message in the delegate:

```
Cancellation has been requested. Performing cleanup...
```

Best Practices for Task Cancellation

Although it is part of the **Task Parallel Library (TPL)**, task cancellation can be used with threads or anywhere else that cancellation support is needed. Using **TPL** cancellation provides a standard, easy to read, predictable way to enable cancellation in .NET. The following are best practices for cancellation using **TPL** cancellation support:

1. Use a shared `CancellationTokenSource` instance when possible. When multiple `Task` instances need to be cancelled together, it is better to use a single shared source and pass its `Token` to each `Task`.
2. Always pass `CancellationToken` to methods that support it. This may require methods that do not need cancellation to accept the token to pass it to methods that do need cancellation support. Always expose cancellation token parameters in asynchronous API methods.
3. Check for cancellation regularly. As we have seen in the prior loop examples in this section, it is critical to check for cancellation in long running or loop-based tasks, to respond to cancellation and stop processing quickly.
4. Avoid hard exits such as `Thread.Abort()`. Using `CancellationToken` instead of abrupt stops avoids invalid state or resource cleanup issues.
5. Always dispose `CancellationTokenSource` when finished, to release managed and unmanaged resources. This avoids resource leaks.
6. Avoid passing `CancellationToken` after cancellation. Passing a canceled token to an operation can cause unexpected behavior. Consider creating a new `CancellationTokenSource` instead.
7. Use linked tokens for composite cancellation. In some scenarios, cancellation can occur for multiple reasons. For example, an operation could be cancelled by a user or by a timeout. In these scenarios, combine sources using the `CancellationTokenSource.CreateLinkedTokenSource()` method.
8. Handle `OperationCanceledException` gracefully. This exception should not be treated as an error. It signals cancellation. Catch it where cancellation is expected, but do not overuse try-catch. Do not unintentionally catch this exception, for example in a try-catch that catches the `Exception` class.
9. Avoid over cancellation. Cancellations should be intentional and should not cause downstream tasks to fail unnecessarily.
10. Avoid relying on cancellation tokens for cleanup in critical scenarios. The `using` keyword or try-finally blocks may be more reliable for guaranteed cleanup.

By following these best practices, you can create robust, responsive, and well-structured applications that handle cancellation gracefully.

Proper Error Handling in Tasks

Error handling in tasks is primarily done using exceptions, consistent with standard practices in .NET applications. However, tasks introduce unique considerations for exception processing, such as how exceptions are encapsulated, propagated, and observed. Understanding these nuances is essential for developers to handle errors effectively and ensure the stability of asynchronous code.

Understanding Exceptions in Tasks

Exceptions that occur in tasks can typically be caught and handled within the task code. However, if an unhandled exception occurs in a task, it is wrapped in an `AggregateException` object. This wrapped exception is stored in the `Exception` property of the task to facilitate scenarios where multiple exceptions might arise.

This behavior is particularly important in the following contexts:

1. When tasks are linked using continuation methods like **`ContinueWith()`**, multiple exceptions might propagate from different tasks in the chain.
2. When using methods like **`Task.WaitAll()`**, exceptions from all the awaited tasks are aggregated into a single **`AggregateException`**.

To correctly handle exceptions from tasks, exception handlers must be aware of this wrapping mechanism and handle the **`AggregateException`** appropriately. This typically involves inspecting the **`InnerExceptions`** collection to analyze or rethrow individual exceptions.

Unobserved Exceptions

If a task exception occurs, but no code accesses the task's **`Exception`** property or handles it via the **`await`** keyword, the exception remains unhandled. This is called an **Unobserved Exception**. **Unobserved Exceptions** can lead to code unstable code, resource leaks, or inconsistent states. In older versions of .NET, **Unobserved Exceptions** would cause the application to terminate. Current .NET versions do not behave this way by default. However, they can be configured to terminate if the **`ThrowUnobservedTaskExceptions`** runtime is explicitly set.

Unobserved Exceptions can be difficult to debug because they may not immediately surface in the code path where they originated. The **`TaskScheduler`** contains an event called **`UnobservedTaskException`** that can be used to log **Unobserved Exceptions** and diagnose missed cases. Adding a handler for this event can provide a safety net in complex applications. The following code simulates an **Unobserved Exception** caught by this handler:

```
TaskScheduler.UnobservedTaskException += TaskScheduler_UnobservedTask
Exception;

RunTask();

Thread.Sleep(20);

GC.Collect();
GC.WaitForPendingFinalizers();
GC.Collect();

Console.ReadLine();

static void TaskScheduler_UnobservedTaskException(object sender, Unobserved-
TaskExceptionEventArgs e)
{
    Console.WriteLine("Unobserved exception: " + e.Exception.ToString());
    e.SetObserved();
}

static void RunTask()
{
    Task.Run(() =>
    {
        Thread.Sleep(10);
        throw new InvalidOperationException("This will not be observed.");
    });
}
```

Calling the **SetObserved()** method on the **UnobservedTaskExceptionEventArgs** instance ensures that the application will not exit in .NET 4.0 or if the application is configured to exit in higher .NET versions.

Note: *The* **UnobservedTaskException** *event is only called when tasks are garbage collected, as shown in the prior example. This makes* **UnobservedTaskException** *unsuitable for normal error handling. Use this event only as a safety net to ensure unobserved exceptions can be logged for further analysis and debugging.*

Using Wait Methods with Exception Handling

Synchronous blocking methods like **Wait()**, **WaitAll()**, and the **Result** property throw an **AggregateException** if an exception occurs in the task or tasks being awaited. The **WaitAny()** method does not throw **AggregateException**, leaving the developer with the responsibility to manually examine tasks for faulted states when using **WaitAny()**.

Handling AggregateException

The **AggregateException** class is a subclass of **Exception** and is used to provide a single **Exception** instance that aggregates one or more exceptions that occurred during task processing. To access the individual exceptions for analysis or logging, **AggregateException** provides the **InnerExceptions** property, which is a collection of all the exceptions that occurred during task processing. The following code illustrates a common use case for handling **AggregateException**:

```
var task = Task.Run(() => ProcessData(0));

try
{
    task.Wait();
}
catch (AggregateException ex)
{
    foreach (var exception in ex.Flatten().InnerExceptions)
        Console.WriteLine(exception.Message);
}

decimal ProcessData(int number)
{
    if (number == 0)
    {
        throw new ArgumentException("Invalid argument.");
    }

    return 100.0M / number;
}
```

Exceptions contained within **AggregateException** may still contain inner exception hierarchies themselves. **AggregateException** does not change those hierarchies. **AggregateException** exposes the **InnerException** (singular) property inherited from **Exception**. In the case of **AggregateException**, the **InnerException** property contains the first exception in the **InnerExceptions** collection. This acts as a convenience in situations where only one exception would be present, such as when waiting on a single task using **Wait()**. In these cases, a developer could treat **AggregateException** like any other exception and access inner exceptions using the **InnerException** property.

In some chained task hierarchies, it is possible to encounter multiple nested **AggregateException** instances. Writing loops to process exceptions in these scenarios can become complex and error prone. To simplify exception handling under such circumstances, the **AggregateException** class provides the **Flatten()** method.

Calling **Flatten()** creates a single **AggregateException** instance that contains a flat collection of all inner exceptions, including those extracted from any nested **AggregateException** instances. This ensures that all exceptions, regardless of their original nesting level, are accessible in a single-level **InnerExceptions** collection.

Error Handling in Continuations

Continuations create tasks that are executed after a preceding task (called the **antecedent**) has completed. When defining **continuations** using **ContinueWith()**, you can specify options that control how the **continuation** behaves. Two commonly used options, **NotOnFaulted** and **OnlyOnFaulted**, determine whether the **continuation** is executed based on the success or fault state of the **antecedent** task.

- **NotOnFaulted**: This option schedules the **continuation** only if the **antecedent** task completes successfully (that is, without throwing an unhandled exception). This simplifies continuation code by eliminating the need to check for faults explicitly.
- **OnlyOnFaulted**: This option schedules the continuation only if the **antecedent** task throws an unhandled exception. It allows the continuation code to focus exclusively on error handling.

The **Task Parallel Library (TPL)** supports defining multiple **continuations** for the same **antecedent** task. This enables chaining conditionally executed **continuations**. If a **continuation's** conditions are not met, the **continuation** transitions to the **Canceled** status without running.

Let us rewrite the **continuation** exception sample from earlier in this chapter to use conditional **continuations**:

```
RunContinuation(10);
RunContinuation(0);

void RunContinuation(int number)
{
    var task = Task.Run(() => ProcessData(number));
    task.ContinueWith(antecedent => Console.WriteLine($"The result is:
{antecedent.Result}"), TaskContinuationOptions.NotOnFaulted);
    var continuation = task.ContinueWith(antecedent => Console.Write-
Line($"Task failed with message: {antecedent.Exception?.Flatten().Message}"),
TaskContinuationOptions.OnlyOnFaulted);
    try { continuation.Wait(); } catch (AggregateException) { }
}

decimal ProcessData(int number)
{
    if (number == 0)
    {
        throw new ArgumentException("Invalid argument.");
    }

    return 100.0M / number;
}
```

In the prior example:

1. Two **continuations** are added to a task that runs the **ProcessData()** method

2. The first **continuation** prints the result and is scheduled only if the **antecedent** task completes successfully (`NotOnFaulted`)
3. The second **continuation** handles errors and is scheduled only when the **antecedent** task faults (`OnlyOnFaulted`)
4. The second **continuation** is awaited. If the **antecedent** succeeds, the second **continuation** is canceled, and an `OperationCanceledException` is raised. This is caught in the `try-catch` block

Best Practices for Error Handling in Asynchronous Code

The following best practices should be followed when writing error handling for tasks:

- Consider using `async/await` instead of directly writing task code when possible, to ensure more natural exception handling
- Ensure blocking calls such as `Wait()`, `Result`, or `WaitAll()` are wrapped in `try-catch` blocks and that exceptions are properly logged
- Consider using the `TaskScheduler.UnobservedTaskException` event to create a global handler to log exceptions that may have been missed in complex task chains
- Avoid mixing blocking and fully asynchronous code (`async/await`) to avoid deadlocks and missed exceptions
- For unrecoverable issues, allow the application to terminate gracefully in a controlled manner

By adhering to these guidelines, developers can write robust asynchronous code that handles errors predictably and efficiently.

Task-based Asynchronous Pattern (TAP)

The **Task-based Asynchronous Pattern (TAP)** is a modern programming model introduced in .NET to simplify and standardize asynchronous programming. **TAP** leverages the `Task` and `Task<T>` classes to represent asynchronous operations, enabling developers to build responsive and scalable applications with minimal complexity. This section explores **TAP**'s role, its connection to the `Task` class, its relationship with `async/await`, and best practices for implementing **TAP**-compliant methods.

Overview of the TAP

The **TAP** was introduced in .NET 4.5 to address challenges with earlier asynchronous programming models, the Event-based Asynchronous Pattern (EAP) and the Asynchronous Programming Model (APM). These earlier models rely heavily on callbacks and events, which often results in verbose, difficult to maintain code. Additionally, the earlier models took differing approaches to I/O bound and CPU-bound tasks, causing unnecessary confusion and complexity.

In **TAP**, asynchronous operations are standardized as methods that return either `Task` or `Task<T>` instances. This approach has significant benefits over the older models which are mentioned as follows:

- The **TAP** streamlines asynchronous code by eliminating the need for callbacks, making the code more intuitive.
- When integrated with `async/await`, it improves readability by making asynchronous code appear synchronous, improving code clarity.

- It unifies CPU-bound and I/O-bound tasks under the same programming model, reducing complexity and enhancing consistency.

TAP is the standard for asynchronous programming in .NET, enabling developers to build complex high-performance applications that are responsive and scalable.

The TAP Builds on the Task Class

The foundation of the **TAP** is the **`Task`** class, which represents an asynchronous operation. **TAP** methods are implemented by returning a **`Task`** or **`Task<T>`** from asynchronous methods, allowing the calling code to interact with them in a consistent manner. Tasks provide the following key features that enable the **TAP**:

- A **`Task`** represents an operation that may not yet be complete. This allows the operation to finish on a separate thread, independent from the calling thread.
- Any exceptions thrown during **`Task`** execution are captured and can be handled by the calling code.
- Using **`ContinueWith()`** or **`await`**, tasks can be designed with follow up operations that run after the task completes.
- Tasks support cancellation natively by integrating with **`CancellationToken`**.

Building on **`Task`** allows the **TAP** to provide a uniform and predictable way to implement and consume asynchronous operations across the .NET ecosystem.

TAP is implemented by creating methods that return **`Task`** or **`Task<T>`** instances. Let us rewrite the Fibonacci example from earlier in the chapter to follow the **TAP** standard:

```
try
{
    Console.WriteLine("The 5th Fibonacci number is: " + FibonacciAsync(5).
Result);
    Console.WriteLine("The 11th Fibonacci number is: " + FibonacciAsync(11).
Result);
}
catch (AggregateException ex)
{
    foreach (var exception in ex.Flatten().InnerExceptions)
        Console.WriteLine(exception.Message);
}

Task<long> FibonacciAsync(int n)
{
    return Task.Run(() => CalculateFibonacci(n));
}

long CalculateFibonacci(int n)
{
    if (n <= 1)
    {
        return n;
    }

    return CalculateFibonacci(n - 1) + CalculateFibonacci(n - 2);
}
```

This example leverages the **TAP** by providing a `Fibonacci` method that returns a `Task<long>` which asynchronously calculates the required number in the Fibonacci sequence. Using this pattern, the CPU intensive code is handled asynchronously, but using patterns that appear to be synchronous. This approach simplifies error handling and maintainability.

Guidelines and Best Practices for TAP Methods

When implementing **TAP** methods, the following best practices should be followed to ensure consistency, maintainability, and optimal performance:

- Return a `Task` for void methods and `Task<T>` for methods with a result.
- Follow the naming convention of appending "`Async`" to the method name. This is a Microsoft standard and helps avoid errors by clearly identifying the method as an asynchronous method that should be awaited to calling a code.
- Ensure exceptions are properly propagated to the returned `Task`. This allows for proper exception handling at higher levels.
- Implement cancellation support by providing `CancellationToken` parameters and checking for cancellation regularly at appropriate points in the code.
- Avoid mixing blocking code such as `Wait()` or `Result` with `async/await` code. Mixing these models can lead to intermittent deadlocks which can be very difficult to detect and fix.
- Avoid using **TAP** without `async/await` unless there is a specific need to do so. Some high-performance applications require explicit control over continuations or task management and require using **TAP** directly as we have done in this chapter. But most general applications are more scalable and performant using `async/await`. We will cover `async/await` in later chapters.

By following these guidelines, you can create asynchronous applications that are highly performant, scalable, reliable, and easy to maintain.

Conclusion

The `Task` and `Task<T>` classes represent logical units of work in an application and are at a higher level of abstraction than the Thread class, which represents an operating system thread. Tasks are part of the **Task Parallel Library (TPL)**, a robust framework for asynchronous and parallel programming. The TPL also includes support for standard patterns such as cancellation tokens, to enable graceful termination of operations.

Tasks are the foundation of asynchronous programming in .NET and support the **Task-based Asynchronous Pattern (TAP)**. **TAP** unifies and simplifies the handling of asynchronous programming and asynchronous I/O, making asynchronous programming more accessible and consistent.

Mastering task programming is essential for achieving high-performance programming in C#, as it allows developers to take full advantage of modern multi-core processors and efficient resource utilization.

In the next chapter, we will delve into the challenges of shared data in parallel programming and explore techniques for properly managing shared variables to avoid common pitfalls like race conditions and deadlocks.

Points to Remember

- A `Task` represents a logical unit of work in an application which may progress independently.
- Tasks are higher level abstractions than threads and may complete synchronously or asynchronously.

- Tasks are better for short lived operations, where threads are often better for long-running operations.
- The **Task Parallel Library (TPL)** includes a standard pattern for cancelling tasks using **`CancellationTokenSoure`** and **`CancellationToken`**. These are integrated with tasks but can be used in any situation requiring a cooperative cancellation model.
- The **Task-based Asynchronous Pattern (TAP)** is an asynchronous programming model that unifies asynchronous I/O and asynchronous programming in a common model. It is realized by writing methods that return tasks.

Multiple Choice Questions

1. Which of the following is true of the **`Task`** class?
    a. It always runs asynchronously.
    b. It represents a logical unit of work.
    c. It is best for long-running operations.
    d. It is used to return values from calculations.
2. What is the **`Task<T>`** class used for?
    a. Isolating shared data for safe processing.
    b. Handling exceptions in parallel processing.
    c. Representing an independent logical unit of work that returns a value.
    d. None of the above.
3. What is an exception that happens in a task that is not handled or accessed called?
    a. An unhandled exception.
    b. An aggregated exception.
    c. A cancellation exception.
    d. An Unobserved Exception.
4. Which of the following is true of the **TAP**?
    a. It is a standard and unified asynchronous programming model in .NET.
    b. It is the foundation for modern asynchronous programming in .NET.
    c. Both a and b.
    d. None of the above.

Answers

1. b
2. c
3. d
4. c

Questions

1. How does using tasks simplify parallel and asynchronous programming compared to using threads?
2. How does the **TAP** simplify asynchronous programming compared to the APM or EAP?
3. In what ways could parallel programming with tasks be complicated or hard to debug?
4. How could **continuations** be used to create efficient workflows?
5. In what ways does **`AggregateException`** simplify exception handling for tasks?

Key Terms

- **Task**: A class that represents a logical unit of work that can progress independently and may complete synchronously or asynchronously
- **Task Parallel Library (TPL)**: A .NET library that contains support for tasks, task cancellation, and parallel and asynchronous programming
- **Task-based Asynchronous Pattern (TAP)**: An asynchronous programming model in .NET that unifies asynchronous programming and asynchronous I/O in a single, simplified, and cohesive model
- **Thread Pool**: A way for .NET to reuse and manage threads automatically
- **`CancellationTokenSource`**: A class that requests cancellation via an associated cancellation toke
- **`CancellationToken`**: A struct that allows notification of a cancellation request for cooperative cancellation support
- **Continuation**: An operation that is designed to execute after the completion of a prior task
- **`AggregateException`**: An exception designed to consolidate and encapsulate exceptions that occur in task processing
- **Unobserved Exception**: An exception that occurs in a task but is not caught using try-catch or accessing the **`Exception`** property
- **Antecedent**: The prior task in a continuation chain that must complete before the continuation is scheduled to run

CHAPTER 4
Data Sharing and Synchronization

Introduction

In prior chapters, we covered the fundamentals of parallelism and asynchronous programming. By now, you should have a solid understanding of how to start and stop threads, as well as manage tasks using their respective classes and tools. In this chapter, we will delve into one of the most common and challenging aspects of multithreaded programming: managing **shared data**. Proper handling of shared resources is critical to ensuring thread safety, maintaining data integrity, and avoiding issues such as race conditions and deadlocks.

Structure

In this chapter, we will cover the following topics:

- Introduction to **Shared Data** in Multithreaded Applications
  - Defining **Shared Data** in Multithreaded Contexts
  - **Race Conditions**, Data Corruption, and Unpredictable Behavior
- **Atomic Operations** with the **`Interlocked`** Class
  - Understanding **Atomicity**
  - Introduction to the **`Interlocked`** Class
  - Common Methods of the **`Interlocked`** Class
  - Practical Example: Safely Updating a Shared Counter
- Ordered Memory Operations
- Managing **Critical Sections** with the **`Monitor`** Class
  - Understanding **Critical Sections**
  - Overview of the **`Monitor`** Class
  - Common Methods of the **`Monitor`** Class
  - Practical Example: Protecting Shared Resources
- Comparing the **`Monitor`** and **`Lock`** Classes
  - Introduction to the **`Lock`** Class
  - Key Features of the **`Lock`** Class
  - Using the **`Lock`** Class for **Thread Safety**
  - Functional Overlap of **`Monitor`** and **`Lock`** Classes
  - Differences Between **`Monitor`** and **`Lock`** Classes
  - Performance Considerations

- Choosing Between `Monitor` and `Lock` Classes
- Simplifying **Synchronization** with the `Lock` Keyword
  - Introduction to the `Lock` Keyword
  - Internal Mechanics of `Lock` Keyword
  - Code Example: Using `Lock` for **Thread Safety**
- Identifying and Avoiding Common Pitfalls
  - The Problem of **Deadlocks**
  - Avoiding **Over-Synchronization**

Introduction to Shared Data in Multithreaded Applications

In the examples we have covered so far in this book, the data being used has been local, which is either passed as parameters or scoped within methods. This type of data is inherently **thread-safe** because it resides on the call stack and each thread maintains its own call stack. However, there are scenarios where threads need to access and modify the same data. This **shared data** introduces challenges related to concurrency and **synchronization**, which will be the focus of this section.

Defining Shared Data in Multithreaded Contexts

In the context of multithreaded applications, **shared data** refers to any data or resources in a program that multiple threads can access simultaneously. This data may reside in the heap, static memory, or global variables, and its accessibility must be carefully managed to ensure consistency and prevent **race conditions**. **Shared data** often requires **synchronization** mechanisms, such as **locks**, semaphores, or **atomic operations**, to maintain **thread-safety** and to coordinate access between threads effectively.

Proper management of **shared data** requires developers to identify all instances of **shared data** in any multithreaded application. This includes identifying implicit data sharing through libraries and frameworks and implementing appropriate **synchronization** techniques to ensure data integrity and application performance.

The term **"thread-safe"** refers to a property of code, methods, or objects that ensures correct behavior and predictable outcomes when accessed or executed by multiple threads simultaneously. **Thread-safe** code allows the user to effectively manages access to shared data or resources, to prevent race conditions, data corruption, or unexpected behaviors in a multithreaded environment. Therefore, while using third-party libraries or .NET framework components in a multithreaded application, it is crucial to understand whether the code is **thread-safe**. A **Thread-safe** code can be safely used across multiple threads. Conversely, a non-thread-safe code requires developers to implement proper **synchronization** mechanisms to ensure safe usage in shared environments.

Note: *In prior code samples we have used the* `Console` *class to print results to the console screen. For example, see Chapter 3, Creating and Running Tasks in C# under Creating Tasks Using a Constructor. The static methods we have used are documented as* ***thread-safe*** *and can therefore be used freely between threads.*

Race Conditions, Data Corruption, and Unpredictable Behavior

Let us look at a simple example of two threads updating the same variable at the same time without any precautions. The following example simply increments a shared variable 500,000 times for each thread and prints the results:

```
namespace DataSyncDemo
{
    internal class Program
    {
        static int loopCount;

        static void Main(string[] args)
        {
            var thread1 = new Thread(() => PlayLoop());
            var thread2 = new Thread(() => PlayLoop());

            thread1.Start();
            thread2.Start();

            thread1.Join();
            thread2.Join();

            Console.WriteLine($"Final loop count is: {loopCount:N0}");
        }

        static void PlayLoop()
        {
            for (int i = 0; i < 500000; i++)
            {
                loopCount++;
            }
        }
    }
}
```

Since there are two threads in the prior example, we would expect the **loopCount** variable to be 1,000,000 after both threads exit. However, if we run the example, the actual result printed is some number less than 1,000,000. In this case it is the following:

```
Final loop count is: 658,194
```

In the prior example, the loop executes exactly 500,000 iterations in each thread. The problem is that the threads will interfere with each other as they update the **shared data** in the **loopCount** variable, with one thread overwriting the results of the other and losing data. This situation is called a **race condition**. The following diagram illustrates the **race condition** in the previous example:

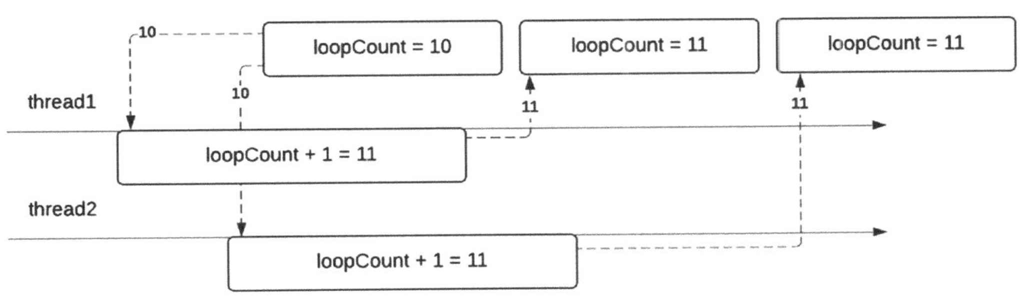

***Figure 4.1**: Race Condition*

In *Figure* 4.1, **`thread1`** reads data from **`loopCount`** to increment it. Before it can save the result back to the **`loopCount`** storage in RAM, **`thread2`** reads the value of **`loopCount`** to increment it. Both threads increment the value of 10 to 11 and store the result. The expected result of 12 was not achieved because of the timing of the independent thread operations. However, if **`thread2`** had read **`loopCount`** after **`thread1`** had successfully updated its results, the correct outcome could have been achieved. As you can see after executing the example, the correct outcome surfaces often, but not always.

In fact, if we execute the prior example multiple times, we are likely to get different results every time. This is because the operating system schedules threads independently and the timing of their execution is unpredictable.

The root cause of the inconsistency is that both threads are attempting to update the shared **`loopCount`** variable simultaneously without any **synchronization** mechanism. Each thread reads the current value of **`loopCount`**, increments it, and writes it back. However, since these steps are not atomic, a thread can overwrite the value written by the other thread, leading to lost updates.

This situation creates a "*race*" between the threads to update the counter variable. The specific outcome is influenced by factors such as thread priorities, CPU load, and the operating system's scheduling algorithm, which collectively contribute to the unpredictable results. This phenomenon is called a **race condition,** because the threads are effectively racing to access and modify the shared resource.

Race conditions can lead to unpredictable behavior, data loss, or even data corruption. Their intermittent and unpredictable nature makes them particularly challenging to diagnose and resolve. To prevent race conditions, shared data and resources in multithreaded applications require meticulous planning and the use of appropriate **synchronization** mechanisms. By applying the tools and strategies outlined in this chapter, you can ensure your code is robust and **thread-safe**.

Atomic Operations with the Interlocked Class

The .NET framework provides a solution to the simple case of a race condition causing unpredictable behavior in the case of updating shared variables, which is called the **`Interlocked`** class. It is designed to provide low-level atomicity to shared variable updates, making it the perfect solution to the problem demonstrated in the previous example.

Understanding Atomicity

Let us revisit the race condition illustrated in *Figure* 4.1. A race condition occurs because the operations of reading a variable, modifying its value, and storing the result back are performed as separate steps. During this process, another thread can intervene, leading to unexpected behavior or incorrect results.

However, if these steps were combined into a single, indivisible operation, called an **atomic operation,** no other thread could observe or modify the state during its execution. **Atomic operations** ensure consistency and eliminate the possibility of a race condition by preventing concurrent access to shared resources during critical operations. This concept is the cornerstone of multithreaded programming and critical for maintaining data integrity.

Figure 4.2 illustrates the fix to the race condition using atomic operations.

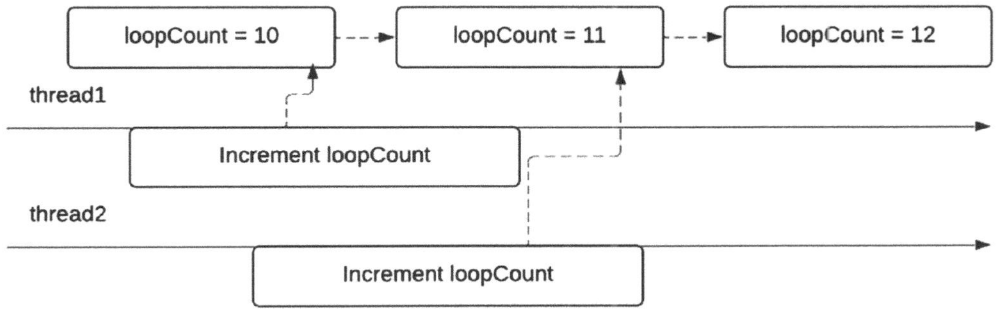

Figure 4.2: *Atomic Variable Updates*

Introduction to the Interlocked Class

The **Interlocked** class in .NET provides atomic operations for updates to shared variables. Using methods on the **Interlocked** class instead of normal operators ensures that the operations are **atomic** and can't be observed or interfered with by another thread while they are in-progress.

The methods on the **Interlocked** class are **thread-safe** and can be used by multiple threads simultaneously without requiring any additional **synchronization** mechanisms. The **Interlocked** class methods are also high-performing because they leverage low-level processor instructions to implement **atomicity**, avoiding the overhead of higher-level locking mechanisms.

The **Interlocked** class contains methods for simple arithmetic and bitwise operations for specific .NET primitive data types. There are some primitives that are not supported and cannot be used with **Interlocked**. For those types, other **synchronization** mechanisms are required. The types supported by **Interlocked** are as follows.

- **Int32**, **int**
- **Int64**, **long**
- **UInt32**, **uint**
- **UInt64**, **ulong**
- **Double**, **double**
- For exchange operations only:
    - **IntPtr**
    - **UIntPtr**
    - **Object**, **object**
    - **Single**, **float**

Common Methods of the Interlocked Class

The **Interlocked** class contains the following methods for the supported data types. Each provides an atomic operation for the given operation. The most common methods are summarized as follows:

Property	Description
Add()	Adds two numbers and replaces the first number with the sum. Using a negative number as the second parameter effectively performs a subtraction operation

And()	Performs a bitwise "**and**" operation on two numbers and replaces the first number with the result
CompareExchange()	Compares two numbers given in the first two parameters and if they are equal, replaces the first with the value in the third parameter. This method supports generics and can be used to replace object references
Decrement()	Decrements the variable and stores the result
Exchange()	Sets the variable to the given value and returns the original value. This method supports generics and can be used to replace object references
Increment()	Increments the variable and stores the result
Or()	Performs a bitwise "**or**" operation on the given numbers and replaces the first number with the result
Read()	Reads a `long` or `ulong` value **atomically** on 32 bit systems

Table 4.1: *Common Methods of Interlocked Class*

The **Read()** method provides a way to read 64-bit values **atomically** on 32-bit systems. This is necessary because 32-bit CPUs can't read 64-bit values in a single operation. On 64-bit systems, the **Read()** method is not strictly necessary because the CPU has the ability to read these values in a single operation. Applications that may run on either 32-bit or 64-bit systems should use **Read()**.

The Interlocked class includes two additional methods: **MemoryBarrier()** and **MemoryBarrierProcessWide()**. These methods enforce specific ordering of memory operations at the assembly level. They are primarily used in advanced scenarios, such as implementing low-level custom **synchronization** primitives or safely publishing singleton instances in multi-threaded environments. For most applications, there are higher-level, easier-to-maintain abstractions available to achieve these goals. As a result, detailed usage of these methods is beyond the scope of this book.

Practical Example: Safely Updating a Shared Counter

Let us update the race condition example to solve the race condition using the **Interlocked** class. The race condition occurs during the increment operation on the **loopCount** variable, so we will replace the increment operator with the **Interlocked.Increment()** method.

```
namespace DataSyncDemo
{
    internal class Program
    {
        static int loopCount;

        static void Main(string[] args)
        {
            var thread1 = new Thread(() => PlayLoop());
            var thread2 = new Thread(() => PlayLoop());

            thread1.Start();
            thread2.Start();

            thread1.Join();
            thread2.Join();

            Console.WriteLine($"Final loop count is: {loopCount:N0}");
        }

        static void PlayLoop()
        {
```

```
                for (int i = 0; i < 500000; i++)
                {
                    Interlocked.Increment(ref loopCount);
                }
            }
        }
    }
```

When the above example is executed, we will always get the following message:

```
Final loop count is: 1,000,000
```

The **Interlocked** class provides **atomicity** in a highly performant manner for scenarios where race conditions involve simple updates to individual shared variables. However, it is limited to certain supported data types and specific operations, such as addition, subtraction, or exchange of values. In more complex scenarios, such as updating unsupported data types, performing non-atomic compound operations, or coordinating multiple updates that must occur together, the **Interlocked** class alone is insufficient. In such cases, it is necessary to explore other **synchronization** mechanisms to ensure **thread-safety**.

Ordered Memory Operations

In some cases, **atomicity** can be achieved simply by avoiding certain compiler optimizations, such as ensuring that the data is stored and accessed from memory instead of via a CPU register. In these cases, C# provides the **volatile** keyword. Using the **volatile** keyword ensures that every read and write for the variable goes directly to memory, bypassing optimizations such as CPU registers. The volatile keyword also guarantees that reads operations for variables follow write operations, resulting in **atomicity**.

Let us see an example of using volatile with a flag to stop a process loop:

```
namespace DataSyncDemo
{
    internal class Program
    {
        static volatile bool stopRequested;

        static void Main(string[] args)
        {
            var thread1 = new Thread(() => PlayLoop());
            var thread2 = new Thread(() => PlayLoop());
            thread1.Name = "Thread A";
            thread2.Name = "Thread B";

            thread1.Start();
            thread2.Start();

            Thread.Sleep(2000);
            stopRequested = true;

            thread1.Join();
            thread2.Join();

            Console.WriteLine("Thread work complete.");
        }

        static void PlayLoop()
        {
```

```
                int count = 0;
                while (!stopRequested)
                {
                    Thread.Sleep(500);
                    count++;
                    Console.WriteLine($"{Thread.CurrentThread.Name} = {count}");
                }
            }
        }
    }
```

Due to the **volatile** keyword, assigning the value true to the **stopRequested** flag guarantees that the reads in the threads running the loop happen after the write and that the data is in memory where it is visible to all threads. Without **volatile**, the behavior is unpredictable.

Reads and writes to variables protected with volatile are atomic, but other operations such as increment, addition, and others are not. Use volatile in situations where shared variables are updated but not used in calculations, such as in the **stopRequested** flag example.

The **volatile** keyword can only be applied to simple data types. Here is a list of the data types that support its use:

- Reference types
- Pointer types in an unsafe context
- Simple primitives such as **sbyte**, **byte**, **short**, **ushort**, **int**, **uint**, **char**, **float**, and **bool**
- Enums based on one of the supported simple primitives
- Generic types that are known to be reference types
- **IntPtr** and **UIntPtr**

The .NET framework provides a **Volatile** class that provides the same functionality as the **volatile** keyword but supports additional types such as **double** and **long**. To use the Volatile class, all reads to a variable should be done using the **Volatile.Read()** method and all writes should be done using **Volatile.Write()**.

Managing Critical Sections with the Monitor Class

We have seen how **atomic** operations can resolve **race conditions** in scenarios where updating single variables is required. However, it is often necessary to synchronize more complex logic. The **Monitor** class in .NET is designed to support these more complex compound operations in a multithreaded environment.

Understanding Critical Sections

A **critical section** is any segment of code in a multithreaded application that interacts with shared resources (such as variables, data structures, or hardware devices) and must not be accessed by more than one thread at a time. If threads are allowed to access **critical sections** without **synchronization** mechanisms, **race conditions** can occur, leading to unpredictable behavior. **Critical sections** can be simple operations or complex, multi-statement blocks of code.

Overview of the Monitor Class

The **Monitor** class in .NET provides thread **synchronization** for **critical sections** involving multiple statements. It does this by managing a **lock** on a specific object, referred to as the **lock object**, through methods such as **`Enter()`**, **`TryEnter()`**, and **`Exit()`**. Acquiring a **lock** on the **lock object** associates the locked object with the calling thread, which prevents other threads from accessing the **critical section** protected by that **lock object** until the **lock** is released by the thread that owns it.

The **`Monitor`** class ensures that access to the **critical section** is restricted based on the **lock object**. For this mechanism to work correctly, *all threads accessing the **critical section** must use the same **lock object** instance*. If a different **lock object** instance is used by a thread, the Monitor will treat it as a separate **lock**, allowing unintended access to the **critical section**.

This behavior highlights the importance of designing code to ensure that a single, consistent **lock object** instance is used by all threads for synchronizing access to a shared resource. Failure to do so can result in race conditions, data corruption, or other concurrency issues.

The **`Monitor`** methods are designed to work with reference types, but they will accept value types as parameters. When a value type is passed to **`Enter()`** or **`TryEnter()`**, it is boxed into a new object instance before being used. Since each call boxes the value type into a distinct object instance, the **lock** mechanism will fail to work as intended:

1. **Locking Behavior:** Each boxing operation creates a new object instance, so calls to **`Enter()`** or **`TryEnter()`** will always succeed, even if another thread is already inside the **critical section**. This means that the critical section is effectively unsynchronized, as the **lock objects** used by different threads are not the same.
2. **Exit Behavior:** When calling **`Exit()`** on a boxed value type, the lock object passed to **`Exit()`** will not match the lock object used in **`Enter()`** or **`TryEnter()`** due to separate boxing instances. This mismatch will result in a **`SynchronizationLockException`** being thrown because **`Monitor.Exit()`** can only release locks held by the calling thread on the exact same object instance.

For these reasons, *value types should never be used as **lock objects** in **`Monitor`** methods*. Always use reference types like instances of object for lock objects to ensure correct **synchronization** behavior.

The Lock Object

The **`Monitor`** class in .NET maintains the following references for each **lock object**:

1. A reference to the thread that currently owns the **lock**. This thread holds exclusive access to the **critical section** protected by the **lock**.
2. A reference to a **waiting queue**: This queue contains threads that are waiting for the lock to become available. These threads are blocked until they are either signaled or the lock is released.
3. A reference to a **ready queue**: This queue holds threads that are ready to acquire the **lock**. When the **lock** becomes available, one of the threads from this queue will be selected to acquire it.

The methods on the **`Monitor`** class affect threads in these queues to support different patterns of behavior. The **waiting queue** works with methods that manage thread **synchronization**, particularly in scenarios where conditional waits or signals between threads are required. The **ready queue** works with methods that control acquisition of the lock itself.

Common Methods of the Monitor Class

The **Monitor** class exposes the following methods:

Methods	Functions
`Enter()`	Acquires a **lock** on a **lock object** and afterwards enters a **critical section**
`TryEnter()`	Acquires a **lock** on a **lock object** and afterwards enters a **critical section**. Accepts a timeout parameter for failing the attempt to acquire the **lock** after the specified period, if the **lock** was not acquired
`Wait()`	Releases a **lock** on a **lock object** and blocks the current thread until the thread re-acquires the **lock**
`Pulse()`	Notifies a thread in the waiting queue that a change has occurred in the **lock object**'s state. The first thread in the **waiting queue** will receive this notification and be moved to the **ready queue**
`PulseAll()`	Notifies all threads in the waiting queue that a change has occurred in the **lock object**'s state. All the threads in the **waiting queue** will be moved to the **ready queue**
`Exit()`	Releases the **lock object** and exits the **critical section**

Table 4.2: *Monitor Class Methods*

The **Enter()**, **TryEnter()**, and **Exit()** methods work together to control access to the **lock object** and the protected **critical section**. These methods work with threads in the **ready queue**.

The **Wait()**, **Pulse()**, and **PulseAll()** methods must be called from within the **critical section** code and are used for thread signalling. These methods work with threads in the **waiting queue**.

Practical Example: Protecting Shared Resources

The **Monitor** class supports many simple and complex use cases. Let us have a look at a simple example of protecting a **critical section** that updates two shared variables:

```
namespace DataSyncDemo;

internal class Program
{
    static object lockObject = new object();
    static int totalCount;
    static int evenCount;

    static void Main(string[] args)
    {
        var thread1 = new Thread(() => PlayLoop());
        var thread2 = new Thread(() => PlayLoop());

        thread1.Start();
        thread2.Start();

        thread1.Join();
        thread2.Join();

        Console.WriteLine($"Total count: {totalCount:N0}");
        Console.WriteLine($"Even count: {evenCount:N0}");
    }

    static void PlayLoop()
```

```
        {
            for (int i = 0; i < 500000; i++)
            {
                Monitor.Enter(lockObject);
                try
                {
                    totalCount++;
                    if (i % 2 == 0)
                    {
                        evenCount++;
                    }
                }
                finally
                {
                    Monitor.Exit(lockObject);
                }
            }
        }
    }
```

In the prior example, two shared variables are updated, one to contain the total loop count (**totalCount**) and one to hold the number of times the loop count was an even number (**evenCount**). Because the critical section contains multiple statements, the **Montior** class is used along with a dedicated **lock object** instance contained in **lockObject**. The output is as follows.

```
Total count: 1,000,000
Even count: 500,000
```

The **critical section** in the prior example is the code that increments **totalCount** and conditionally increments **evenCount**. Hence, this code is surrounded by calls to the **Enter()** and **Exit()** methods of the **Monitor** class. Both of these methods require the same instance of a lock object to be passed, which is the **lockObject** instance in this case.

Once the **Enter()** method is called, it is imperative that the **Exit()** method also be called, even if an exception occurs. Failure to follow this pattern can result in **deadlocks**, where threads are waiting for the lock to be released when it never will be. Therefore, the **critical section** is surrounded by a **try-finally** block with the call to **Exit()** in the finally section. This is the recommended pattern because it ensures **Exit()** will always be called if the section completes successfully or if an exception occurs.

Note: *The prior example uses the normal increment operations instead of the atomic methods because the critical section is already protected by* **Monitor** *methods, which makes using* **Interlocked** *redundant and unnecessary.*

Using TryEnter

Using **Enter()** will force the calling thread to wait indefinitely to acquire the **lock**. This behavior may not be desirable in all cases. In some cases, you may prefer to avoid indefinite waiting. To handle this, **TryEnter()** provides a way to attempt acquiring the **lock**, but it allows you to specify a time limit by specifying a timeout. If the **lock** is not acquired within the specified time, **TryEnter()** will return **false**, allowing you to implement retry logic or alternative methods instead of waiting indefinitely.

Let us see the **TryEnter()** method in action:

```
namespace MonitorTryEnter;

internal class Program
{
    static object lockObject = new object();
```

```
        static object secondaryObject = new object();
        static int totalCount;
        static int primaryCount;
        static int secondaryCount;

        static void Main(string[] args)
        {
            var thread1 = new Thread(() => PlayLoop());
            var thread2 = new Thread(() => PlayLoop());

            thread1.Start();
            thread2.Start();

            thread1.Join();
            thread2.Join();

            Console.WriteLine($"Total count: {totalCount:N0}");
            Console.WriteLine($"Primary count: {primaryCount:N0}");
            Console.WriteLine($"Secondary count: {secondaryCount:N0}");
        }

        static void PlayLoop()
        {
            var random = new Random();
            for (int i = 0; i < 100; i++)
            {
                Interlocked.Increment(ref totalCount);
                if (Monitor.TryEnter(lockObject, 50))
                {
                    try
                    {
                        primaryCount++;
                        var waitPeriod = random.Next(75);
                        Thread.Sleep(waitPeriod);
                    }
                    finally
                    {
                        Monitor.Exit(lockObject);
                    }
                }
                else
                {
                    Monitor.Enter(secondaryObject);
                    try
                    {
                        secondaryCount++;
                    }
                    finally
                    {
                        Monitor.Exit(secondaryObject);
                    }
                }
            }
        }
    }
```

In the prior example, a simulated **critical section** that may be long running is protected by **TryEnter()**. An alternative method is protected by **Enter()** using a secondary **lock object**. If the **TryEnter()** fails to acquire the **lock object** within the given timeout period of 50 milliseconds, the alternative method is used. The output is something like the following:

```
Total count: 200
Primary count: 120
Secondary count: 80
```

Note: *`Monitor.Enter()` and `Monitor.TryEnter()` can be called multiple times by the same thread without deadlocking, as would be the case with a recursive method. If this is done, care must be taken to ensure the thread calls `Monitor.Exit()` exactly the same number of times as the `Enter()` or `TryEnter()` methods were called.*

Thread Synchronization with Wait and Pulse

Let us say you work for a game company and are assigned to write a process to correctly build the game's textures, sound assets, and scripts in the correct order. Such a process must account for textures being built before shaders that depend on them. Sound assets must be converted before scripts referencing them can execute. The build system must enforce these dependencies.

Multithreading is a natural choice to optimize the build process and maximize CPU resources. However, managing dependencies between tasks introduces unique challenges. To handle this effectively, you need a mechanism for communication and **synchronization** between threads that also preserves the order of building dependencies first.

The **Monitor.Wait()** and **Monitor.Pulse()** methods are instrumental in this scenario. **Wait()** waits for a signal from **Pulse()** while both execute within **critical sections**. Calling **Wait()** blocks the thread and puts the calling thread in the **waiting queue**. Calling **Pulse()** moves the first thread in the waiting queue into the **ready queue** where it will wait to obtain the **lock**. The following code illustrates how **Wait()** and **Pulse()** work together to solve the build system problem.

Note: *The following code is for .NET 9 and will not work with .NET Framework.*

```
class BuildSystem
{
    private readonly Dictionary<string, TaskNode> _tasks = new();

    public BuildSystem()
    {
        // Define tasks and their dependencies
        _tasks["A"] = new TaskNode("A", new[] { "B", "C" });
        _tasks["B"] = new TaskNode("B", new[] { "D" });
        _tasks["C"] = new TaskNode("C", Array.Empty<string>());
        _tasks["D"] = new TaskNode("D", Array.Empty<string>());
    }

    public void StartBuild()
    {
        foreach (var task in _tasks.Values)
        {
            new Thread(() => RunTask(task)).Start();
        }
    }

    private void RunTask(TaskNode task)
    {
```

```
        task.WaitForDependencies();

        Console.WriteLine($"Task {task.Name} is starting.");
        Thread.Sleep(1000); // Simulate work
        Console.WriteLine($"Task {task.Name} is completed.");

        foreach (var dependentTask in _tasks.Values)
        {
            if (dependentTask.Dependents.Contains(task.Name))
                dependentTask.DependencyCompleted();
        }
    }

    class TaskNode
    {
        private readonly object _lockObject = new();
        private int _remainingDependencies;

        public string Name { get; }
        public List<string> Dependents { get; } = new();

        public TaskNode(string name, IEnumerable<string> dependencies)
        {
            Name = name;

            Dependents.AddRange(dependencies);
            _remainingDependencies = Dependents.Count;
        }

        public void WaitForDependencies()
        {
            Monitor.Enter(_lockObject);
            try
            {
                while (_remainingDependencies > 0)
                {
                    Monitor.Wait(_lockObject); // Wait for all dependencies
                }
            }
            finally { Monitor.Exit(_lockObject); }
        }

        public void DependencyCompleted()
        {
            Monitor.Enter(_lockObject);
            try
            {
                _remainingDependencies--;
                if (_remainingDependencies == 0)
                {
                    Monitor.Pulse(_lockObject); // Wake waiting threads
                }
            }
            finally { Monitor.Exit(_lockObject); }
        }
    }
```

```
    }

    class Program
    {
        static void Main()
        {
            BuildSystem buildSystem = new();
            buildSystem.StartBuild();
        }
    }
```

Let us break down the work in the prior code example:

1. The work of the build system is defined in the **BuildSystem** class.
2. The **BuildSystem** class maintains a list of **TaskNode** classes which represent each build action along with any other tasks on which the task depends. In this case, task A depends on B and C, B depends on D, and C and D have no dependencies.
3. The operating system calls the **Main()** method in the **Program** class. This method creates a new instance of the **BuildSystem** class, which sets up the tasks and dependencies described in point 2, and calls **buildSystem.StartBuild()**.
4. **StartBuild()** runs every task in the task list on a separate thread.
5. When each task runs, it first waits for any dependencies to finish by calling **WaitForDependencies()**. This method enters a critical section which enters a loop that checks to see if the remaining dependency count is above 0. If it is, the critical section calls **Monitor.Wait()** to block and release the lock.
6. Once **WaitForDependencies()** exits, the task does its work. This is simulated by printing some messages and sleeping for 1 second.
7. Once the work is done, each task searches the task list in the build system for any tasks that are dependent on the current finished task. If found, the task calls **DependencyCompleted()** on the dependent task.
8. **DependencyCompleted()** enters a critical section and decrements **_remainingDependencies**. When it is zero, **Monitor.Pulse()** is called. Remember that this call is made from the thread running the dependency, not from the thread waiting for dependencies to complete. That thread will be blocked and in the waiting queue.
9. The **Pulse()** call signals the thread that something has changed and it needs to check again. On the dependant thread, this cycles through the **WaitForDependencies()** loop and checks the remaining dependencies count again. If it is zero, the loop exits, and the thread can do its own work.
10. Finally, all threads complete their work. The proper order has been preserved.

The relationship between **Wait()** and **Pulse()** in the prior example is illustrated in *Figure* 4.3.

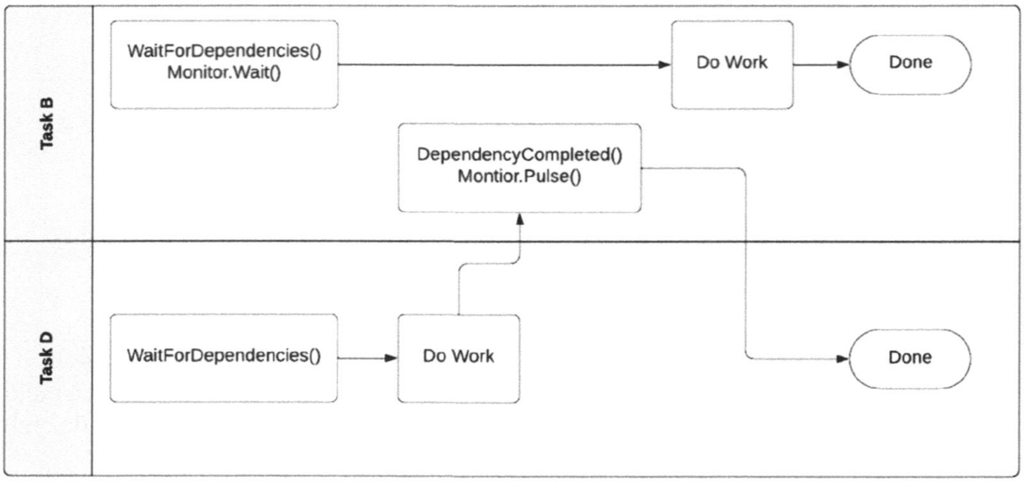

***Figure* 4.3:** *Wait-Pulse Logical Flow*

As shown in *Figure* 4.3, Task D and Task B run on different threads. The thread running Task B checks for dependencies, which it has, and then blocks using **`Monitor.Wait()`**. Meanwhile Task D runs on its own thread, checks for dependencies which it does not find and does its work. Then Task D's thread calls **`DependencyCompleted()`** on Task B, which decrements the dependency count and calls **`Monitor.Pulse()`**. This signals Task B's thread that something has changed. Task B's thread then receives the lock and checks for dependencies again. This time it does not find any and is able to do its work. This is how order is preserved between threads in the build system sample.

The **`Monitor.Wait()`** and **`Monitor.Pulse()`** methods are for more advanced scenarios that require signalling between threads. These methods of the **`Monitor`** class are flexible enough to provide support for a variety of complex scenarios where threads must wait for each other to complete the overall workload.

Comparing the `Monitor` and `Lock` Classes

The **`Monitor`** class was introduced in .NET 1.0 and has been foundational for multithreaded programming throughout .NET history. In .NET 9, a new class was introduced with improved performance and functionality as an alternative to some of the functionality **`Monitor`** provides, and is called the **`Lock`** class.

Introduction to the `Lock` Class

Introduced in .NET 9 and C# 13, the **`Lock`** class is intended as a replacement for the **`Enter()`**, **`TryEnter()`** and **`Exit()`** methods in the **`Monitor`** class. It is designed to address performance issues with **`Monitor`** while also providing new safety features in the form of compiler warnings and additional syntax that **`Monitor`** does not support. The **`Lock`** class does not provide signalling with **`Wait()`** and **`Pulse()`**, and so, it is not an absolute replacement for **`Monitor`**.

Key Features of the `Lock` Class

The **`Lock`** class provides **`Enter()`**, **`TryEnter()`**, and **`Exit()`** methods, mirroring their counterparts in **`Monitor`**. These methods follow the same rules and precautions as **`Monitor`**, ensuring compatibility and easing code upgrades from **`Monitor`** to **`Lock`**. Unlike **`Monitor`**, these methods are instance-based and require an instance of **Lock** rather than a separate lock object, encapsulating **synchronization** concerns.

The **Lock** class introduces a new method, **EnterScope()**, specifically designed for use with the **using** keyword. This method returns a **Lock.Scope** object, which implements **IDisposable**. Upon disposal, the **Lock.Scope** exits the critical section and releases the lock. This pattern simplifies syntax and ensures proper lock management even in the presence of exceptions.

Finally, the **Lock** class introduces a new property called **IsHeldByCurrentThread** that returns **true** if the current thread owns the lock. This property can be used to avoid calling **Exit()** if the current thread does not own the lock, producing safer and more predictable **synchronization** code.

Using the Lock Class for Thread Safety

When writing new code using **Lock**, it is recommended to use the **EnterScope()** method in a **using** statement or to use the lock keyword, which we will explore later in this chapter. The following example shows proper usage of the **Lock** class:

```
namespace DataSyncDemo;

internal class Program
{
    static Lock lockObject = new();
    static int totalCount;
    static int evenCount;

    static void Main(string[] args)
    {
        var thread1 = new Thread(() => PlayLoop());
        var thread2 = new Thread(() => PlayLoop());

        thread1.Start();
        thread2.Start();

        thread1.Join();
        thread2.Join();

        Console.WriteLine($"Total count: {totalCount:N0}");
        Console.WriteLine($"Even count: {evenCount:N0}");
    }

    static void PlayLoop()
    {
        for (int i = 0; i < 500000; i++)
        {
            using (lockObject.EnterScope())
            {
                totalCount++;
                if (i % 2 == 0)
                {
                    evenCount++;
                }
            }
        }
    }
}
```

The prior example shows proper use of the **Lock** class for new code using **EnterScope()** in a using statement instead of using **Monitor** with a separate lock object. The code is functionally equivalent to using **Monitor,** but is slightly more performant.

Functional Overlap of Monitor and Lock Classes

The **Monitor** and **Lock** classes provide overlapping functionality for thread **synchronization** through their methods for acquiring and releasing locks. Both classes are designed to implement **thread safety** by protecting critical sections from simultaneous access by different threads, by ensuring that only one thread can access the critical section at any given time. Both provide similar methods as demonstrated in the following table:

Monitor	Lock	Purpose
Enter	**Enter**	Acquires the lock, potentially blocking until the lock is available.
TryEnter	**TryEnter**	Attempts to acquire the lock with optional timeouts.
Exit	**Exit**	Releases the lock.

Table 4.3: *Monitor and Lock Overlap*

Both classes base the locking functionality on the same low-level primitives provided by the CLR.

Differences between Monitor and Lock Classes

Although they are similar, there are some important differences between **Monitor** and **Lock**.

- **Monitor** is a static class with static methods that are designed to be used with an associated **lock object**, while **Lock** is an instance-based class which encapsulates the locking logic within its instance. This simplifies code structure by reducing the need for additional **lock objects**, improving readability and maintainability.
- **Lock** introduces the new **EnterScope()** method, which simplifies syntax and improves readability and maintainability when used with the **using** keyword. This syntax is less verbose than the **try-finally** syntax required by **Monitor**. The **Lock** class also natively integrates with the **lock** keyword.
- **Monitor** provides simple thread signalling via the **Wait()** and **Pulse()/PulseAll()** methods, which **Lock** does not provide. These methods can be used within a critical section protected by the **Lock** class by using the **Lock** class instance as the required **lock object**.
- **Lock** provides the **IsHeldByCurrentThread** that Monitor does not provide. This property simplifies detecting that the lock is held by the current thread. It is also highly performant, using thread local operations to streamline thread-specific lock logic in complex systems.
- Finally, the compiler will issue code warnings if a **Lock** object is cast to another type and locked. This ensures correct usage and helps prevent potentially hard to detect **synchronization** errors or **deadlocks**.

Performance Considerations

- The **Lock** class is performance-optimized as a part of the overall performance theme of .NET 9. While both **Monitor** and **Lock** offer similar performance, **Lock** contains some optimizations that may enhance performance in high-contention scenarios.
- Because the **Lock** class is instance based, it saves a small amount of overhead that **Monitor** has due to the need to resolve the **synchronization** object in each method call. **Lock** does not need to resolve a **synchronization** object because it encapsulates the lock logic in its instance.

- For scenarios where detecting whether the current thread owns the lock is required, **IsHeldByCurrentThread** might avoid some small overhead introduced by manual detection mechanisms a developer might use with **Monitor**. This property is highly optimized and simple to use.
- Ultimately the performance optimizations in **Lock** are negligible in common low-complexity scenarios. Most applications will not see a noticeable performance difference between **Montior** and **Lock**. These applications will benefit more from the simplified syntax and enhanced compiler safety features of **Lock** than from its performance enhancements.

Choosing between Monitor and Lock Classes

The **Lock** class contains important enhancements over the **Monitor** class when used to protect **critical sections**. Use the following as best practices when choosing between **Monitor** and **Lock**.

- When writing new multithreaded code, you must prefer the **Lock** class for protecting **critical sections**. Its clearer semantics, optimized performance, and compiler warnings help prevent common threading issues.
- When maintaining or extending existing multithreaded codebases, use **Monitor** to ensure consistency and compatibility, adhering to best practices like using dedicated **lock objects** and minimizing lock durations.
- For signaling within critical sections, use **Monitor.Wait()** and **Monitor.Pulse()** with the same **lock object**, regardless of whether it is an object or **Lock** instance.

These guidelines offer a balanced approach for leveraging the best of both **Monitor** and **Lock** in multithreaded programming.

Simplifying Synchronization with the Lock Keyword

The C# **lock** keyword provides a concise and effective way to protect critical sections of code. It abstracts the complexity of acquiring and releasing locks, ensuring that the thread executing the code gains exclusive access to the specified object and automatically releases the lock when the critical section completes, even if an exception is thrown.

Introduction to the Lock Keyword

The **lock** keyword was introduced in .NET 1.0 as a standard way of enforcing mutual exclusion for **critical sections**. Prior to C# 13, **lock** integrated with the **Monitor** class to enforce **thread safety**. In C# 13, **lock** integrates with the **Lock** class.

The **lock** statement has the following syntax:

```
lock(lockObj)
{
    //critical section
}
```

Using the **lock** keyword is preferable to using methods of the **Lock** or **Monitor** classes directly in general-purpose multithreaded programming. It handles the mechanics of entering and exiting the critical section automatically, ensuring proper use even in the case of exceptions. The simplified and standard syntax makes the code easier to read and less error-prone.

Internal Mechanics of Lock Keyword

In the prior example, if **lockObj** is an instance of the **Lock** class, it is exactly equivalent to the following.

```
using(lockObj.EnterScope())
{
    //critical section
}
```

For backwards compatibility, **lock** can be used with a dedicated **lock object**. When used in this way, it is exactly equivalent to the following.

```
object lockObj = new();
bool lockWasTaken = false;
try
{
    System.Threading.Monitor.Enter(lockObj, ref lockWasTaken);
    // critical section
}
finally
{
    if (lockWasTaken) System.Threading.Monitor.Exit(lockObj);
}
```

In both cases, the lock is released properly even if an exception occurs. Using **lock** with an instance of the **Lock** class is the preferred usage for new code.

As we might expect given the above explanation of how the **lock** keyword behaves internally, **Monitor.Wait()** and **Monitor.Pulse()/Monitor.PulseAll()** can safely be used within the **lock** statement block.

Code Example: Using Lock for Thread Safety

Let us use the lock keyword in a simple example. The following code uses two threads to add items to a list, then prints the results:

```
namespace DataSyncDemo;

internal class Program
{
    static List<string> sharedList = new();
    static Lock lockObject = new();

    static void Main(string[] args)
    {
        var thread1 = new Thread(() => AddItems());
        var thread2 = new Thread(() => AddItems());
        thread1.Name = "Thread One";
        thread2.Name = "Thread Two";

        thread1.Start();
        thread2.Start();

        thread1.Join();
        thread2.Join();

        foreach (var message in sharedList)
            Console.WriteLine(message);
```

```
        }

        static void AddItems()
        {
            for (int i = 0; i < 10; i++)
            {
                lock (lockObject)
                {
                    if (i % 2 == 0)
                        sharedList.Add($"{Thread.CurrentThread.Name} - {i}");
                }
            }
        }
    }
```

The output from the prior example is something like the following:

```
Thread One - 0
Thread One - 2
Thread Two - 0
Thread One - 4
Thread One - 6
Thread One - 8
Thread Two - 2
Thread Two - 4
Thread Two - 6
Thread Two - 8
```

Using the `lock` keyword makes the code simple and easy to read. Using `lock` makes it clear that the block of code within the `lock` statement block is a **critical section** and the entry and exit logic is handled correctly by the compiler.

Identifying and Avoiding Common Pitfalls

Code that blocks threads, including `Monitor` and `Lock`, can cause problems if not used carefully and thoughtfully. Developers should be aware of these pitfalls and take proactive steps to avoid them.

The Problem of Deadlocks

The locking patterns discussed in this chapter cause threads to block in various ways. As with all blocking operations, there is a risk of the thread being blocked in such a way that it cannot be unblocked. This can result in a **deadlock**, where two or more threads are waiting on each other indefinitely, and none can proceed.

A thread **deadlock** is a situation in a multithreaded application where two or more threads are blocked indefinitely, each waiting for resources held by the other. This creates a cycle of dependency that prevents any of the threads involved from progressing. In essence, a **deadlock** occurs when each thread in the cycle is holding a resource and waiting for a resource that another thread in the cycle is already holding. **Deadlocks** typically arise when multiple threads acquire locks in an inconsistent or circular manner.

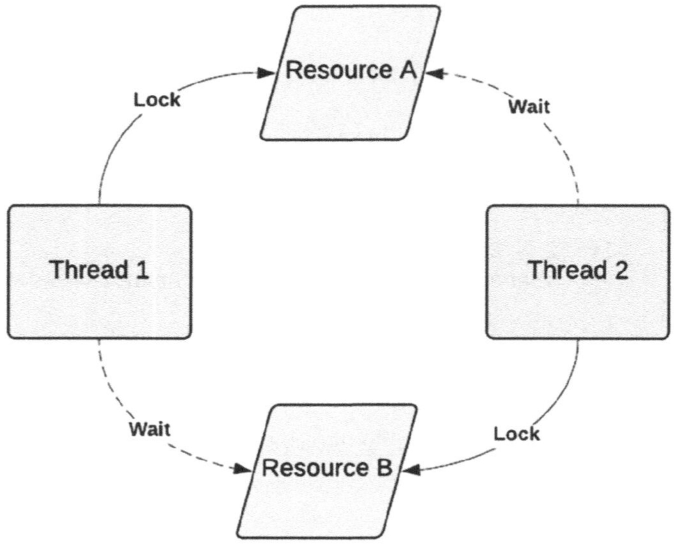

Figure 4.4: *Example Deadlock*

Figure 4.4 shows a type of circular deadlock, where Thread 1 locks Resource A which Thread 2 is waiting for, meanwhile Thread 2 locks Resource B, which Thread 1 is waiting for. Both threads are waiting for resources that can never be unlocked. In this situation, both threads wait forever, and the application seems like it is hanging.

Avoiding Deadlocks

Given the potential for **deadlocks** in blocking code, it's important to adopt strategies that prevent circular dependencies and ensure threads can acquire resources safely. The following are some best practices for avoiding **deadlocks**:

- **Always acquire locks in a consistent order**. If all threads acquire locks in the same order, it avoids circular wait conditions, which is the hallmark of **deadlocks**.
- **When appropriate, consider using a timeout for lock acquisition**. Using a timeout with `TryEnter()` allows a thread to unblock if it cannot obtain the lock within the timeout period. This allows the thread to release any locks it may be holding and try again.
- **Avoid holding multiple locks simultaneously**. Where possible, avoid holding multiple locks at once. Use fine-grained locks in small sections of code instead of larger sections.
- **Keep critical sections as small as possible**. This is important for overall performance as well as avoiding deadlocks. The fewer instructions in a critical section, the less risk of a deadlock occurring and the higher the overall performance of each thread will be.
- **Use lock-free data structures or atomic operations where feasible**. These tools avoid the possibility of deadlocks by avoiding locking altogether.
- **Use higher level concurrency mechanisms**. If applicable, higher-level mechanisms like semaphores, mutexes, and concurrent collections can provide solutions that avoid locking. All these will be discussed in future chapters.
- **Minimize or avoid nested locking and lock hierarchies**. Avoid scenarios where threads need to lock resources in a nested or hierarchical manner, if possible. Often, more design work can be employed to simplify the code and avoid the complexity of nesting and hierarchies.
- **Use proven safe design patterns**. Apply patterns such as reader-writer lock or producer-consumer to handle concurrency in a more controlled manner, reducing the risk of **deadlocks**. These patterns will be discussed in future chapters.

Avoiding Over-Synchronization

The use of mutually exclusive **synchronization** techniques, such as those provided by Monitor and Lock, is a critical part of dealing with shared resources in multithreaded code. It is possible to overuse **synchronization**, which can lead to performance degradation and potential errors such as **deadlocks**.

To avoid **over-synchronization**, consider the following in addition to the guidance for avoiding `deadlocks`:

- **Prefer atomic operations using `Interlocked` or `volatile` when possible**. These operations avoid **synchronization** locks and are performance optimized.
- **Use immutable objects or collections where possible.** Updates to immutable objects result in new instances, avoiding concurrent updates.
- **Avoid unnecessary locking.** Carefully evaluate whether locking is necessary at all. Sometimes local variables can be used instead of shared resources, thread local storage, or lock free solutions such as concurrent collections. These will be discussed in future chapters.
- **Leverage asynchronous programming when possible.** Use tasks and `async/await` to avoid locking while waiting for task completion. `Async/await` will be covered in later chapters.

Conclusion

Shared resources and data pose unique challenges in multithreaded code, often leading to issues such as data corruption and unpredictable behavior. Addressing these challenges requires careful planning and design, as well as a thorough understanding of the tools available in the programming language to ensure **atomicity** and **synchronization**. The tools presented in this chapter will help you ensure predictability and accuracy in multithreaded code.

In the next chapter, we will delve into **synchronization** best practices and discover specific **synchronization** primitives.

Points to Remember

- **Shared data** and resources can cause data corruption and unpredictable behavior in multithreaded applications.
- Solutions to **shared resource** problems include **atomic operations** and **synchronization** strategies such as **locks**.
- **Critical sections** should be kept as small as possible to avoid performance issues and **deadlocks**.
- Using the `Lock` class for synchronization is safer and more performant than using the `Monitor` class.

Multiple Choice Questions

1. The `volatile` keyword indicates what about a shared variable?

   a. That the variable is not safe for use outside the class that defines it.

   b. That the variable is random and could change at any time.

   c. That access to the variable is protected from some compiler optimizations and reads and writes are ordered.

   d. There is no `volatile` keyword in C#.

2. The Interlocked class in .NET provides what benefit to multithreaded applications?
    a. **Thread-safe**, optimized **atomic operations**.
    b. Interleaving of data in a shared collection.
    c. Detection and resolution of deadlocks.
    d. **Thread-safe** synchronization for **critical sections**.
3. What does the `lock` keyword do in C#?
    a. Locks a memory location, isolating it from unauthorized access.
    b. Locks the computer screen, requiring a user to log in again to unlock.
    c. Pauses the scrolling of text, allowing a user to read before continuing.
    d. Provides consistent, safe mutual exclusion for **critical sections**.
4. How does the `Monitor` class protect critical sections in .NET applications?
    a. Provides **lock** management using a dedicated **lock object**.
    b. Provides cooperative ordering of access to **critical sections**.
    c. Both a and b.
    d. All of the above.

Answers

1. c
2. a
3. d
4. c

Questions

1. What types of shared data access would benefit from the use of the `volatile` keyword or `Volatile` class?
2. In what situations is the `Interlocked` class the best choice for shared data management?
3. When should the `Monitor` class be used instead of the `Lock` class?
4. Why is the `lock` keyword useful if there is a `Lock` class that accomplishes similar goals?

Key Terms

- **Shared Data/Shared Resources:** Data or resources that must be accessed simultaneously by two or more threads in a multithreaded application
- **Race Condition:** Unpredictable behavior and incorrect results related to reading, updating, and writing data and resources by multiple threads in a multithreaded application
- **Thread-safety:** A property of a program, function, or code segment that ensures correct behavior and predictable outcomes when accessed by multiple threads in a multithreaded application

- **Atomic/Atomicity/Atomic Operations:** The property of an operation or a sequence of operations that guarantees it occurs as a single, indivisible step, ensuring thread-safety
- **Critical Section: Any segment of co**de in a multithreaded application that interacts with shared resources (such as variables, data structures, or hardware devices) and must **not be accessed by** more than one thread at a time
- **Locks:** A synchronization mechanism that ensures only one thread can access a critical section at any given time, blocking other threads until the lock is released
- **Lock Object:** An reference type instance used exclusively to control lock synchronization in a multithreaded application
- **Waiting queue:** The queue of threads waiting for a lock object protected by Monitor to be signalled
- **Ready queue:** The queue of threads waiting for a lock object protected by Monitor to be released
- **Deadlock:** A condition in multithreaded code where two or more threads are waiting for each other indefinitely and none can proceed
- **Over-synchronization:** The unnecessary over usage of synchronization mechanisms in multithreaded code
- **Synchronization:** The coordination and control of access to shared resources in a multithreaded application

CHAPTER 5
Threading and Synchronization Primitives

Introduction

Having explored the challenges of shared data and resource contention, along with basic techniques to manage them, we now turn our focus to mastering **thread synchronization**. This chapter will introduce best practices and the key primitives provided by .NET for efficient and safe thread coordination, focusing on specialized classes such as `Mutex`, `Semaphore`, `AutoResetEvent`, and `ReaderWriterLockSlim`. Understanding these tools is crucial for writing high-performance applications where synchronization between threads is required.

Structure

In this chapter, we will cover the following topics:

- Inter-Process Synchronization
  - Key Distinctions between Mutex and Other Primitives
  - Using Mutex to Coordinate between Processes
  - Handling Mutex Exceptions and Timeouts
- Controlling Resource Pools
  - Differences between `Semaphore` and `SemaphoreSlim`
  - Use Cases for Pool Management
  - Best Practices
- Pausing Threads and Resuming Threads
  - Differences in Reset Event Classes
  - Use Cases for Signaling Between Threads
  - Avoiding Common Pitfalls
- Implementing Single-Write Multi-Read
  - Defining the Reader-Writer Problem
  - Reader-Writer Use Cases
  - Performance Benefits

Inter-Process Synchronization

In the previous chapter, we explored how the `Lock` and `Monitor` classes provide **thread synchronization**. These classes are primarily designed to **synchronize** threads within the same process. While this limits the scope of these classes to **synchronization** within a single process, certain scenarios require **synchronization** across processes. For such cases, the `Mutex` class offers a robust solution.

Key Distinctions between Mutex and Other Primitives

Unlike `Lock` and `Monitor`, the `Mutex` class can **synchronize** threads not only within the same process but also across multiple processes, making it ideal for scenarios such as inter-process communication or managing shared resources between independent applications.

The `Mutex` class achieves this by leveraging low-level operating system resources, specifically kernel objects, designed for inter-process signaling and **synchronization**. This capability allows it to function across process boundaries, a feature not available in managed **synchronization primitives**. However, this reliance on OS-level resources makes the Mutex a heavyweight solution. Each operation involves a transition between user mode and kernel mode, introducing additional overhead compared to managed implementations like `Lock` and `Monitor`.

Despite its relative cost, the `Mutex` class is indispensable in scenarios where inter-process **synchronization** is critical, such as ensuring only one instance of an application accesses a shared file or resource at a time.

Mutexes can be created as either **local** or **named**. A **local Mutex** is restricted to a single process and is primarily used to synchronize threads within that process, offering functionality similar to the **Lock** class but with additional overhead due to its reliance on operating system resources. While `Lock` is purely managed, a **local Mutex** uses OS kernel objects, making it less efficient for purely intra-process **synchronization** tasks.

A **named Mutex**, on the other hand, allows **synchronization** across multiple processes. When a **named Mutex** is created, it is registered in the operating system's global namespace, enabling other processes to access the same Mutex instance by specifying its name. This allows processes to share the same kernel **synchronization** object and coordinate access to shared resources. **Named Mutex** objects are particularly useful for scenarios like ensuring that only one instance of an application writes to a shared log file or accesses a critical resource.

Using Mutex to Coordinate between Processes

One common use of the `Mutex` class is to ensure that only a single instance of an application is running at any given time. This approach is particularly common in desktop applications where running multiple instances could confuse users, lead to resource contention, or result in improper use of shared resources, such as configuration files or databases.

To implement this functionality, the application typically creates a **named Mutex** during startup. If the **named Mutex** already exists it indicates that another instance of the application is already running, and the new instance can exit gracefully or notify the user.

This technique is often used in applications like media players, backup utilities, or tools that access hardware devices, where multiple simultaneous instances could cause performance issues or data corruption.

Let us create a simple application that uses this approach to ensure only a single instance can run at a time:

```
bool createdNew = false;
Mutex singleInstanceMutex = new Mutex(true, "MutexDemo", out createdNew);
try
{
    if (createdNew)
    {
        Console.WriteLine("The application is running. Press any key to
exit.");
        Console.ReadKey();
    }
    else
        Console.WriteLine("Another instance is running. Exiting now.");
}
finally
{
    singleInstanceMutex.Dispose();
}
```

In the prior example, a **Mutex** is created with the name "**MutexDemo**" and a flag indicating the process should own the **Mutex** initially. The **createdNew** flag is passed to the constructor to check if the running process created the kernel object or if it existed already. This flag will be **false** if the kernel Mutex already existed before the constructor ran. If **createdNew** is true, the application runs normally. If it is **false**, the application knows another instance is already running and exits gracefully.

Because the **Mutex** class relies on system resources to function, it is critical that each **Mutex** instance be disposed after use, even if exceptions occur. The prior example accomplishes this by using a **try-finally** block to ensure **Dispose()** is always called.

Controlling Access to Shared Resources

Threads can take ownership of the **Mutex** and release ownership by using **WaitOne()** to take ownership and **ReleaseMutex()** to release it. This is like locking and unlocking a **Lock** instance using **Enter()/TryEnter()** and **Exit()**. Ownership can be initially set in the constructor, as it is in the prior example, or the **Mutex** can be created without ownership set.

Calling **WaitOne()** while another thread owns the **Mutex** causes the thread to block until ownership is released or the timeout period expires, just as calling **Enter()** or **TryEnter()** on **Lock** causes the thread to block. This mechanism is useful for controlling access to a shared system resource, such as a common log file.

The following code demonstrates the use of **WaitOne()** and **ReleaseMutex()** to control access to a shared log file:

```
var logFileName = Path.Combine(
    Environment.GetFolderPath(Environment.SpecialFolder.MyDocuments),
    "MutexLogFile.txt");
using (var logFileMutex = new Mutex(false, "LogFileMutex"))
{
    Console.WriteLine("Writing to log file.");
    for (int i = 0; i < 60; i++)
    {
        logFileMutex.WaitOne();
        try
        {
            File.AppendAllText(logFileName,
```

```
                    $"{Environment.ProcessId} - Logging instance {i}\n");
            }
            finally
            {
                logFileMutex.ReleaseMutex();
            }
            Console.Write(".");
            Thread.Sleep(500);
        }
        Console.WriteLine("\r\nWork finished.");
    }
```

In the prior example, the **Mutex** instance is created in a using statement, which ensures later disposal. As the loop progresses, **WaitOne()** is called to attempt to gain ownership of the **Mutex**. Calling **WaitOne()** without parameters indicates that the thread will be blocked indefinitely waiting for the signal that ownership was obtained. The loop appends data to the log file in a critical section and then releases the **Mutex** by calling **ReleaseMutex()**. Note that the critical section is surrounded by a **try-finally** block to ensure **ReleaseMutex()** is called in all cases.

The log file will be written to your Documents folder. The file will contain interleaved log entries from each instance of the application that was running, like the following.

```
36824 - Logging instance 8
39428 - Logging instance 2
36824 - Logging instance 9
39428 - Logging instance 3
36824 - Logging instance 10
39428 - Logging instance 4
36824 - Logging instance 11
```

The process **id** is the first number, which is different depending on the process writing to the log at that point in time.

The **WaitOne()** method also supports specifying a timeout period. When used in this way, the effect is like **Lock.TryEnter()** where **true** is returned if ownership of the **Mutex** was signaled, and **false** is returned if the timeout expired. This allows the thread to do other work and retry for access to the shared resource later.

Handling Exceptions and Timeouts

When working with Mutex for synchronization in C#, handling timeouts and exceptions is crucial to ensure robust and deadlock-free applications. A thread attempting to acquire a Mutex may be blocked indefinitely if another thread fails to release it, leading to potential performance bottlenecks or application hangs. To mitigate this, the **WaitOne()** method provides an overload that accepts a timeout value, allowing a thread to attempt acquiring the Mutex for a specified duration before proceeding with an alternative execution path. Additionally, exception handling is essential to deal with scenarios such as **AbandonedMutexException**, which occurs when a thread holding a Mutex terminates unexpectedly without releasing it. Properly managing these cases ensures that Mutex-based synchronization remains reliable and does not lead to unpredictable behavior or resource contention in multithreaded applications.

Handling Mutex Timeouts

When a timeout occurs, **WaitOne()** returns **false**, indicating that the critical section cannot be entered because the `Mutex` could not be acquired within the specified time. This allows the thread to gracefully handle the contention by:

- Implementing retry logic to attempt to acquire the `Mutex` again
- Performing other work that is unrelated to the critical section, ensuring the thread remains productive
- Notifying the user or logging the event for monitoring and diagnostics

Timeouts are a normal part of contention management and should be handled to maintain application responsiveness and avoid deadlocks.

Handling Mutex Exceptions

If a thread exits while owning the `Mutex` without calling `ReleaseMutex()`, the `Mutex` is considered **abandoned**. When another thread tries to acquire the **abandoned** `Mutex` by calling `WaitOne()`, an `AbandonedMutexException` is thrown. This behavior is designed to signal a potential critical issue with the software, as it may indicate incomplete or inconsistent operations in the protected resource.

Handling this exception provides an opportunity to:

- Log the event or notify the user for diagnostics and debugging
- Verify the integrity of the protected resource
- Retry the `WaitOne()` call **only if the resource can be confirmed to be in a consistent state**

Catching and handling `AbandonedMutexException` carefully is a best practice to prevent cascading failures and ensure system stability.

Controlling Resource Pools

The **synchronization** strategies we have explored so far focus on controlling access to critical sections, ensuring that only one thread can execute a given section of code at a time. These primitives are essential for preventing race conditions and ensuring thread safety in situations where shared resources might be accessed concurrently.

However, not all **synchronization** problems involve exclusive access to a critical section. Sometimes, we need to manage a limited number of resources shared among multiple threads. For example, a fixed number of database connections or file handles might need to be shared efficiently. In computer science, such a limited set of resources is often referred to as a **resource pool**.

To manage **resource pools** in .NET, the framework provides the `Semaphore` and `SemaphoreSlim` classes. These synchronization primitives are designed to limit the number of threads that can access a **resource pool** concurrently, enabling effective control over shared resources in multithreaded environments.

Both `Semaphore` and `SemaphoreSlim` are designed to allow up to a specified number of threads to concurrently access a shared **resource pool**. This maximum limit is defined in the constructor when an instance is created and cannot be increased later. However, the current count, which represents the number of available slots in the **resource pool**, can be dynamically adjusted using the `Release()` method or decremented with one of the `Wait()` methods.

Threads desiring access to the **resource pool** call one of the `Wait()` methods. If the current count has not reached the maximum limit, the thread is granted access, and the count is decremented. If the limit has been reached, the thread is blocked and will wait until another thread releases a resource back to the **pool** using the `Release()` method.

Note: *The* **Semaphore** *and* **SemaphoreSlim** *classes offer no guaranteed order such as FIFO or LIFO to access the pooled resources.*

The following code simulates a **resource pool** using a queue and controls access using a semaphore:

```
var pool = new Queue<string>(["One", "Two", "Three"]);
var lockObject = new Lock();
var semaphore = new SemaphoreSlim(3, 3);
try
{
    var threadList = new List<Thread>();
    for (int i = 0; i < 10; i++)
    {
        threadList.Add(new Thread(UseResource));
        threadList[i].Start();
    }

    foreach (var thread in threadList)
        thread.Join();

    Console.WriteLine("Work completed.");
}
finally
{
    semaphore.Dispose();
}

void UseResource()
{
    semaphore.Wait();
    try
    {
        var resource = Dequeue();
        Console.WriteLine($"Using resource {resource}");
        Thread.Sleep(1000);
        Enqueue(resource);
    }
    finally
    {
        semaphore.Release();
    }
}

string Dequeue()
{
    lock (lockObject)
    {
        return pool.Dequeue();
    }
}

void Enqueue(string resource)
{
    lock (lockObject)
    {
        pool.Enqueue(resource);
    }
}
```

In the prior example, ten threads are started that all share use of the three simulated resources a **resource pool** implemented using the **Queue** class. The **Semaphore** controls access to the queue resources. The **Queue** class itself is not thread safe, so access to the shared queue is controlled using a **Lock** instance. The output will be something like the following:

```
Using resource One
Using resource Three
Using resource Two
Using resource Three
Using resource Two
Using resource One
Using resource One
Using resource Three
Using resource Two
Using resource Two
Work completed.
```

Differences between Semaphore and SemaphoreSlim

Like the **Mutex** class, the **Semaphore** class relies on underlying kernel resources for its implementation. This means it incurs some overhead compared to purely managed **synchronization primitives** like **SemaphoreSlim**, which operates entirely in user space.

A **Semaphore** can be created as a local instance or as a named system-wide object. When a **named semaphore** is created, it can be shared between processes, making it suitable for inter-process **synchronization** scenarios. This capability is analogous to named mutexes, which also allow **synchronization** across process boundaries. **Named semaphores** can be useful for coordinating access to shared resources, such as files or shared memory, among multiple applications.

It is important to note that when using a **named semaphore**, all processes sharing it must reference the semaphore by the same name. Care must also be taken to handle potential naming conflicts or ensure that the semaphore is properly released to prevent resource leaks.

The **SemaphoreSlim** class is a lightweight alternative to the **Semaphore** class, as indicated by the "Slim" in its name. Unlike **Semaphore**, **SemaphoreSlim** does not rely on underlying kernel resources and operates entirely in managed code. As a result, it is more efficient and incurs less overhead, making it ideal for scenarios where inter-process **synchronization** is not required.

Since **SemaphoreSlim** is purely managed, it can only be used for local semaphore instances within an application. This limitation is acceptable for most intra-process **synchronization** tasks and is why **SemaphoreSlim** is the recommended choice for managing concurrent access to shared resources within a single application.

Its efficiency and reduced overhead are particularly beneficial in high-performance or highly concurrent applications, where minimizing system calls and kernel transitions can have a significant impact on overall performance.

In addition to supporting timeouts in its **Wait()** methods, which the **Semaphore** class also supports, **SemaphoreSlim** uniquely supports cancellation through the use of cancellation tokens. This feature allows a waiting thread to cancel its request for a semaphore slot in response to user input, application state changes, or other conditions, providing more flexibility and responsiveness in multithreaded scenarios.

Another key distinction is that **SemaphoreSlim** supports non-blocking, asynchronous versions of the **Wait()** method, such as **WaitAsync()**. This makes **SemaphoreSlim** the only semaphore class suitable for use in asynchronous programming. By enabling threads to release control during asynchronous waits, **SemaphoreSlim** helps improve resource utilization and responsiveness in applications that rely heavily on asynchronous code.

These additional features make **SemaphoreSlim** not only more lightweight but also more versatile for modern .NET applications, especially those using asynchronous programming patterns.

Use Cases for Pool Management

There are many uses for resource pool management techniques using semaphores, some of which are shown in the following table:

Use Case	Description
Database Connection Pool	An application can limit the number of concurrent database connections using a semaphore to control the maximum number of concurrent connections
API Rate Limiting	APIs sometimes limit the number of calls allowed per second. A semaphore can be used to limit the number of threads allowed to call the API at any given time, enforcing the rate limit
Hardware Resource Limit	Devices like printers, GPUs, or IoT devices may have a limit to the number of threads that can access them at any given time. Semaphores can be used to limit access, ensuring that only the allowed number of threads access the hardware at any given time
Managing Concurrent Licenses	A software product may have a limited number of licenses for concurrent use. A semaphore might be used to track and enforce the license count
Limiting Resource Intensive Tasks	An application may need to run multiple CPU-intensive or memory-intensive tasks at the same time. A semaphore could be used to limit the number of tasks that can execute concurrently, balancing performance and resource usage

Table 5.1: *Semaphore Use Cases*

Any scenario where a limited number of resources need to be accessed by a larger number of threads is a candidate for using a semaphore. This ensures that resource usage stays within safe and manageable limits, prevents contention, and promotes efficient concurrency by allowing only a specified number of threads to access the **resource pool** at any given time.

Best Practices

The following best practices should be observed when using **Semaphore** or **SemaphoreSlim** to control access to **pooled resources**:

- Only use **Semaphore** when inter-process **synchronization** is required. Prefer **SemaphoreSlim** in cases where the **synchronization** will be within a single process.
- Always call **Release()** after any **Wait()**, **WaitOne()**, or **WaitAsync()** method call to avoid deadlocks. Use **try-finally** blocks to ensure that **Release()** is called in all cases.
- Avoid nesting calls to **Wait()** methods, such as calling **Wait()** in recursive methods. It is better to design code to only require a single call to **Wait()** if possible, and ensure that call is paired to a **Release()** call. Use structured patterns like hierarchies to manage multiple semaphores.
- Ensure that **Release()** is called no more than once for each **Wait()** call. Calling **Release()** more times than **Wait()** is called can lead to runtime exceptions.
- Keep critical section code as brief as possible and optimize it to minimize the time each thread holds a semaphore slot.
- Use the asynchronous **SemaphoreSlim.WaitAsync()** method in asynchronous code. Never use blocking operations in asynchronous code.

- Use timeouts or cancellation tokens to avoid waiting indefinitely. Respond to timeouts gracefully by doing other work or retrying the wait.
- Log calls to **Wait()** and **Release()** to identify over or under usage at runtime.
- Semaphores do not implement fairness (FIFO or LIFO for example) to waiting threads. If fairness is critical, consider other **synchronization primitives** or custom implementations.
- Test with high concurrency to ensure your semaphore logic scales and handles edge cases correctly. Ensure that timeouts are handled gracefully and situations like thread pool starvation are avoided. Thread pool starvation will be discussed in detail in Chapter 11, *Threading and the Thread Pool.*

By adhering to these best practices, you can build robust, efficient applications that avoid common pitfalls like thread pool starvation or over-releasing, ensuring smooth resource management and system performance.

Pausing Threads and Resuming Threads

In multithreaded applications, threads often need to wait for other threads to complete specific tasks or reach certain milestones before proceeding. These tasks, milestones, or special occurrences are commonly referred to as **events**.

In .NET, the **AutoResetEvent** and **ManualResetEvent** classes provide mechanisms for signaling and managing such **events** between threads. These classes enable one thread to notify one or more others that a task has been completed, a milestone has been reached, or a special occurrence has happened, allowing the waiting threads to proceed accordingly.

Differences in Reset Event Classes

Both the **AutoResetEvent** and **ManualResetEvent** classes maintain a **signaled** or **non-signaled** state. When the state is **signaled**, threads waiting for the **event** are allowed to proceed. When the state is **non-signaled**, waiting threads are blocked until the event is set to **signaled**. Resetting these **event** classes refers to changing the state to **non-signaled**, whereas setting refers to changing the state to **signaled**.

The main difference between **AutoResetEvent** and **ManualResetEvent** is the way in which each is reset. **AutoResetEvent** resets automatically as soon as a single thread is released by calling the **Set()** method, allowing only one thread to release per call to **Set()**. **ManualResetEvent** only resets when the **Reset()** method is called, allowing many threads to respond to the **event**. This difference makes **AutoResetEvent** more suitable for fine-grained control of threads, and **ManualResetEvent** more suitable for broader synchronization scenarios.

The following example shows one use of **AutoResetEvent**:

```
ConsoleKeyInfo keyInfo = new ConsoleKeyInfo();
var threadList = new List<Thread>();
var autoResetEvent = new AutoResetEvent(false);
try
{
    for (int i = 0; i < 2; i++)
    {
        threadList.Add(new Thread(PlayLoop));
        threadList[i].Name = "Thread " + i;
        threadList[i].Start();
    }

    do
```

```
    {
        Console.WriteLine("Press a key to do work. Press 'q' to quit.");
        keyInfo = Console.ReadKey();
        autoResetEvent.Set();
    } while (keyInfo.KeyChar != 'q');
    foreach (var thread in threadList)
    {
        autoResetEvent.Set();
        thread.Join();
    }
}
finally
{
    autoResetEvent.Dispose();
}

void PlayLoop()
{
    while (true)
    {
        autoResetEvent.WaitOne();
        if (keyInfo.KeyChar != 'q')
        {
            Console.WriteLine($"{Thread.CurrentThread.Name} working...");
            Thread.Sleep(500);
        }
        else
            break;
    };
}
```

In the prior example, two threads are created and both run the **`PlayLoop()`** method. This loop waits for the **`autoResetEvent`** to be **signalled**. The main thread signals **`autoResetEvent`** every time a key other than 'q' is pressed. Each time the event is signalled, one thread is allowed to do its work at a time. Pressing a key alternates between threads doing work. The output looks like the following:

```
Press a key to do work. Press 'q' to quit.
Thread 0 working...
 Press a key to do work. Press 'q' to quit.
Thread 1 working...
 Press a key to do work. Press 'q' to quit.
Thread 0 working...
 Press a key to do work. Press 'q' to quit.
Thread 1 working...
```

Contrast the prior example with the following example which demonstrates **`ManualResetEvent`**:

```
ConsoleKeyInfo keyInfo = new ConsoleKeyInfo();
var threadList = new List<Thread>();
bool paused = false;
var manualResetEvent = new ManualResetEvent(true);
try
{
    Console.WriteLine("Press space to pause.");
    for (int i = 0; i < 3; i++)
    {
        threadList.Add(new Thread(PlayLoop));
        threadList[i].Name = "Thread " + i;
        threadList[i].Start();
```

```
        }

        while (true)
        {
            if (paused)
                Console.WriteLine("Press space to resume. Press 'q' to quit.");
            keyInfo = Console.ReadKey();
            if (keyInfo.KeyChar == ' ')
            {
                paused = !paused;
                if (paused)
                    manualResetEvent.Reset();
                else
                    manualResetEvent.Set();
            }
            else if (keyInfo.KeyChar == 'q')
            {
                manualResetEvent.Set();
                break;
            }
        };
        foreach (var thread in threadList)
            thread.Join();
    }
    finally
    {
        manualResetEvent.Dispose();
    }

    void PlayLoop()
    {
        while (true)
        {
            manualResetEvent.WaitOne();
            if (keyInfo.KeyChar != 'q')
            {
                Console.WriteLine($"{Thread.CurrentThread.Name} working...");
                Thread.Sleep(500);
            }
            else
                break;
        };
    }
```

In the prior example, three threads are created and each runs the **PlayLoop()** method. A **ManualResetEvent** is created with an initial state of **signalled**, indicating that waiting threads are allowed to proceed. The threads do their work until the space key is pressed, which pauses all the threads by calling **Reset()**, blocking them when they call **WaitOne()**. If the space key is pressed while the threads are blocked, **Set()** is called, which releases the threads and they are allowed to work again. The output will be something like the following:

```
Press space to pause.
Thread 0 working...
Thread 2 working...
Thread 1 working...
Thread 0 working...
Thread 2 working...
Thread 1 working...
```

```
Press space to resume. Press 'q' to quit.
Thread 1 working...
Thread 0 working...
Thread 2 working...
```

The prior two examples show the stark contrast between **`AutoResetEvent`**, which allows a single thread to be released each time it is **signaled** by calling **`Set()`**, and **`ManualResetEvent`**, which allows many threads to be released when **signaled**. This difference in behavior allows each class to be used for very different use cases.

Note: *Both Reset Event classes use kernel resources and should be disposed when no longer in use by calling **`Dispose()`** to avoid resource leaks.*

Use Cases for Signalling between Threads

The **`AutoResetEvent`** class is useful for fine-grained signaling between threads. Some of its common use cases are shown in the following table:

Use Case	Description
Thread Coordination	A thread sets up a resource for another thread to use. The second thread must wait for the resource to be available before proceeding
Producer-Consumer Pattern	A producer thread generates data that is processed by a consumer thread. The producer signals each time a unit of data is available to be processed
Event-Driven Execution	A controller thread waits for user input or a time-critical event and signals another thread to process the input or event
Throttling Access	Multiple threads need to use a resource but only one can use it at any given time
Background Job Completion Notification	A background thread completes a calculation or download and signals the main thread that the work is complete
Simplifying Polling Scenarios	Replace polling with `AutoResetEvent` to make code efficient and event driven

Table 5.2: *AutoResetEvent Use Cases*

Use the **`AutoResetEvent`** for one-to-one signaling between threads and for scenarios where releasing a single thread at a time is required.

The **`ManualResetEvent`** class can be used for cases where signaling must be manually controlled. Some common use cases for **`ManualResetEvent`** are listed in the following table:

Use Case	Description
Pausing and Resuming Threads	A controller thread pauses worker threads in response to user input or another event, then resumes processing in response to a different event
Multiple Thread Coordination	A controller sets up resources for many threads to use. They must all wait for the resources to become available before use
Barrier for Thread Execution	Ensuring that a group of threads do not proceed until all are ready or a specific condition is met
Signalling Between Multiple Tasks	Worker threads wait for a loader thread to complete preparing resources before a multithreaded batch process can proceed

Table 5.3: *ManualResetEvent Use Cases*

ManualResetEvent is ideal for one-to-many signalling between threads, and for cases where the signalling should not be immediately reset.

Using Reset Events between Processes

Both **AutoResetEvent** and **ManualResetEvent** are child classes of the **EventWaitHandle** class. **EventWaitHandle** can be used to construct instances of either class. The main reason to do this is to provide a named instance of the event to signal between processes, like the functionality of **Mutex**.

When used in this way, one process will normally be a signaler, and another process will be a waiter. The signaler process will create the **Reset Event** and define the name. The waiter process will open the existing **Reset Event** by name. The waiter will call **WaitOne()** to wait for the signal and the signaler will call **Set()** to signal and **Reset()** to reset as needed.

The following examples show simple code to signal between processes with Reset Events:

```
using (var autoResetEvent = new EventWaitHandle(false, EventResetMode.AutoRe-
set, "EventWaitDemo"))
{
    Console.WriteLine("Press any key to signal waiter process.");
    Console.ReadKey();
    autoResetEvent.Set();
    Console.WriteLine("Event set.");
}
```

The prior example shows a signaller process creating an **AutoResetEvent** using the **EventWaitHandle** class constructor to name the event. The event is initially not signalled but is switched to signaled after the user presses a key.

```
using (var autoResetEvent = new EventWaitHandle(false, EventResetMode.Auto
Reset, "EventWaitDemo"))
{
    Console.WriteLine("Waiting for signal.");
    autoResetEvent.WaitOne();
    Console.WriteLine("Event set.");
}
```

This example shows the waiter process opening the same named event using the same parameters in the **EventWaitHandle** constructor. This process waits for the signal using a call to **WaitOne()**. When the signaller process calls **Set()** the waiter process will continue and print the "Event set." message.

Using **EventResetMode.AutoReset** in the **EventWaitHandle** constructor creates an **AutoResetEvent** instance. Using **EventResetMode.ManualReset** creates a **ManualResetEvent** instance.

Avoiding Common Pitfalls

The **Reset Events** are powerful tools for signaling between threads. While using them can be critical for some applications, care must be taken to avoid inadvertently causing problems at runtime. The following are common pitfalls and suggestions to avoid them:

- The **Reset Events** use kernel resources and are therefore higher overhead than **SemaphoreSlim** or **Monitor**, which are fully managed synchronization primitives. Consider the use of **Monitor.Pulse()/PulseAll()** or **SemaphoreSlim** in situations where signalling happens at high volume or in performance critical situations.
- If the signaling thread never calls **Set()** due to incorrect logic, waiting threads may block indefinitely. Carefully test to ensure the signaling thread always calls **Set()** when expected.

Consider using timeouts in `WaitOne()` calls to gracefully exit waiting threads to avoid deadlocks.

- The **Reset Events** are best used in simple scenarios. Using them for complex coordination can lead to brittle, difficult to maintain code. Consider using higher level abstractions such as `Task`, `Monitor`, or `SemaphoreSlim` for more complex scenarios.
- It is possible for race conditions to exist between `Set()` and `WaitOne()` calls. For example, if multiple threads wait for an `AutoResetEvent` signal, a thread might call `WaitOne()` waiting for a signal that has already happened, leading to a deadlock or unexpected behavior. Consider different **synchronization** mechanisms or use `Task` based programming to avoid complex timing issues.
- Unhandled exceptions in signaling or waiting threads can cause signals to be missed, resulting in deadlocks, unexpected behavior, or even process crashes. Always ensure proper exception handling is in place to handle these situations gracefully.

By being mindful of these pitfalls, you can ensure that your use of `AutoResetEvent` and `ManualResetEvent` in .NET is both efficient and reliable.

Implementing Single-Write Multi-Read

There are often scenarios where threads can be divided into **reader** threads and **writer** threads. In other words, threads that only read data and threads that modify or write data. In such cases, the number of reader threads is usually greater than the number of writer threads. This distinction introduces unique challenges in synchronization, as multiple **readers** can safely access the shared resource simultaneously, but **writers** require exclusive access to prevent data corruption. Effectively balancing these competing requirements, while avoiding issues like deadlock or starvation, is at the heart of the **reader-writer problem**.

Defining the Reader-Writer Problem

Multiple **readers** can access shared data or resources simultaneously, but **writers** usually require exclusive access to safely update the shared resource. Efficiently and safely balancing readers and writers is the main problem in **reader-writer** scenarios.

The key challenges in **reader-writer** scenarios are as follows:

- **Readers** and **writers** cannot access the same resource at the same time.
- Many **readers** can access the resource concurrently without conflict.
- Only a single **writer** can access the resource at any given time.
- Threads should not be blocked indefinitely to avoid deadlocks due to improper **synchronization.**
- **Readers** and **writers** must not be perpetually delayed due to priority imbalances, such as allowing **readers** to always proceed leaving **writers** perpetually waiting.

Solving Reader-Writer with `ReaderWriterLockSlim`

The `ReaderWriterLockSlim` class in .NET is specifically designed to address the single-write, multi-read concurrency problem. It provides separate methods for acquiring **reader** and **writer** locks, allowing multiple threads to read concurrently while ensuring that only one thread can write at a time. This class also supports upgrading a reader lock to a writer lock through its upgradeable read-lock mechanism, minimizing the risk of deadlocks when a thread needs to transition from reading to writing. Additionally, `ReaderWriterLockSlim` offers fine-grained control over locking behavior and is optimized for scenarios where **readers** outnumber **writers**.

Using **ReaderWriterLockSlim** follows the familiar pattern found in other synchronization primitives. **Readers**, **upgradeable readers**, and **writers** all have enter and matching exit methods designed to surround critical sections that access the protected shared resources. Exit methods should be called from within **finally** blocks to ensure they are always called, even if exceptions occur.

Let us see how **ReaderWriterLockSlim** can be used to solve a real-world scenario. Suppose we are writing a weather app that analyzes temperature data from a temperature sensor. The application maintains a list of the last 10 readings and calculates the average temperature and detects significant temperature changes, all in separate threads. **Writer** threads are responsible for adding sensor readings to the list and removing old entries. **Reader** threads are used to calculate the average temperature and find significant changes. **ReaderWriterLockSlim** will be used to manage these different threads efficiently.

Since the following example is too long to include in this book. it can be found at the following URL:

https://github.com/ava-orange-education/Ultimate-C-for-High-Performance-Applications/blob/main/Chapter%2005/ReaderWriterLock/Program.cs

In the prior example, a list of temperatures is protected by **ReaderWriterLockSlim**. Any access to the list is considered a critical section because it is shared by many threads. The **reader** threads use **EnterReadLock()** and **ExitReadLock()** to ensure reads can happen without writes interfering. **Writer** threads use **EnterWriteLock()** and **ExitWriteLock()** to ensure no **readers** or other **writers** are accessing the list while updates occur.

The scenario requires two **writers**, one to read and add the sensor data to the list and one to remove old temperatures from the list. The sensor access is simulated by a random number generator. There are also two **readers**, one that calculates the average temperature and one that detects significant changes in temperature. Finally, there is a thread that updates the display. The main thread simply waits for a key to be pressed before shutting everything down and exiting. The output looks something like the following:

```
Average temperature: 18.6 - Significant temperature change detected.
Average temperature: 18.1 - Temperature changes normal.
Average temperature: 19 - Temperature changes normal.
Average temperature: 19.3 - Significant temperature change detected.
Average temperature: 19.5 - Temperature changes normal.
Average temperature: 18.6 - Temperature changes normal.
```

Upgrading Readers to Writers

Sometimes a **reader** thread may require logic that conditionally updates the shared resource. Coordinating this type of update between a **reader** thread and a separate **writer** thread would be complex and error prone. To simplify this scenario, **ReaderWriterLockSlim** provides **EnterUpgradeableReadLock()** and **ExitUpgradeableReadLock()** methods. These methods are useful when the **reader** normally enters the critical section in read mode but may decide to enter write mode if a certain condition is met.

For example, let us say you need to create a thread safe way to add a number to a shared list, but only if the number is not already in the list. Using **ReaderWriterLockSlim**, the add method would be implemented like the following example:

```
var numberList = new List<int>();
var readerWriterLock = new ReaderWriterLockSlim();

void AddIfNotExist(int number)
{
    readerWriterLock.EnterUpgradeableReadLock();
    try
```

```
        {
            if (!numberList.Contains(number))
            {
                readerWriterLock.EnterWriteLock();
                try
                {
                    numberList.Add(number);
                }
                finally
                {
                    readerWriterLock.ExitWriteLock();
                }
            }
        }
        finally
        {
            readerWriterLock.ExitUpgradeableReadLock();
        }
    }
```

The **AddIfNotExists()** method in the prior example enters an upgradeable read lock by calling **EnterUpgradeableReadLock()** then checks to see if the number exists in the list. If it does, the method calls **ExitUpgradeableReadLock()** and exits. If the number does not exist, the method upgrades to a write lock by calling **EnterWriteLock()** and then adds the number to the list. In this case, **ExitWriteLock()** is called to exit the write lock. After that, **ExitUpgradeableReadLock()** is called to exit the read lock.

Note: *.NET provides both the* **ReaderWriterLock** *and* **ReaderWriterLockSlim** *classes. However,* **ReaderWriterLock** *has lower performance compared to* **ReaderWriterLockSlim** *and lacks some of the more modern features found in* **ReaderWriterLockSlim**. *As a result,* **ReaderWriterLock** *is only recommended for maintaining legacy codebases, while* **ReaderWriterLockSlim** *should be used for new code to take advantage of its improved performance and enhanced features.*

Reader-Writer Use Cases

ReaderWriterLockSlim is ideal for cases where **readers** are more frequent than **writers**, because **readers** do not block each other, but **writers** block **readers** and other **writers**. It is beneficial in most cases where **readers** and **writers** can be clearly separated. The following table contains some of the more common use cases for **ReaderWriterLockSlim**:

Use Case	Description
Shared Caching	Multiple **readers** can access the cache simultaneously. A single thread updates the cache, locking out **readers** in the process
Configuration Management	Many **readers** can access configuration objects simultaneously. One thread can be dedicated to updating configuration objects when necessary
Shared Collections	Shared Dictionaries, Lists, or HashSets can be accessed by many **readers**. Additions, deletions, and updates are handled by **writers** as needed
File or Resource Management	Many **readers** can read shared files or memory resources. **Writers** restrict access while making updates
Analytics and Metrics	Multiple threads read metrics for reporting and alerts. A single thread updates counters or statistics

Real-time Data Monitoring	A single thread updates data from a sensor or IoT device. Multiple **readers** process the data for analysis or display
Gaming or Simulation	Data that is accessed frequently by the user but is updated occasionally by the engine

Table 5.4: ReaderWriterLockSlim Use Cases

Performance Benefits

`ReaderWriterLockSlim` has several performance benefits over other **synchronization primitives** in situations where **readers** and **writers** can be clearly separated, especially in cases where **readers** are more frequent than **writers**. The following list is a summary of the key performance benefits:

- **Optimized for Read-heavy Workloads:** Read requests do not block each other and are handled efficiently by the lock. Write requests are queued and processed after active reader's finish. This reduces contention compared to other locks such as `Mutex` or `Montior` which block all threads regardless of the operation.
- **Reduced Context Switching: Readers** are allowed access to the lock without forcing frequent context switches, which are costly in terms of CPU cycles.
- **Fine-grained Control:** Support for upgradeable locks allows a read lock to be acquired initially and later upgrade to a write lock if needed. This reduces the need to release and reacquire locks, which can save time and resources.
- **Thread Priority Handling**: **Writer** threads are given a fair chance to acquire the lock even under heavy read load, avoiding "*starvation*" scenarios where **writers** are delayed for long periods waiting for **readers.**

By balancing the needs of concurrent **readers** with exclusive **writers**, `ReaderWriterLockSlim` can significantly enhance the performance of multithreaded applications, especially when read operations dominate.

Conclusion

The **synchronization primitives** covered in this chapter are designed for specialized scenarios that go beyond basic shared resource protection. Whether you need to handle inter-process synchronization, efficiently manage resource pools, respond to asynchronous events, or implement single-write, multi-read patterns, these tools offer tailored and highly optimized solutions. Mastering these classes will empower you to address complex synchronization challenges while maximizing the performance and reliability of your applications.

In the next chapter, we will examine the `System.Collections.Concurrent` namespace, introducing thread-safe, lock-free collections that simplify concurrent programming. We will explore their key features, practical use cases, and the patterns and best practices that enable you to leverage these powerful tools for building efficient and scalable applications.

Points to Remember

- **Synchronization primitives** that use kernel resources, such as `Mutex` and `Semaphore` are higher overhead than .NET native alternatives. Use these only in cases where inter-process synchronization is required
- Keep critical sections as small and optimized as possible to avoid performance degradation
- Avoid nested or reentrant calls to Enter/Exit methods to avoid unnecessary complexity
- Use methods with timeouts, when possible, to avoid deadlocks and increase maintainability

Multiple Choice Questions

1. What is the Mutex class used for?
   a. Throttling calls to an API.
   b. Preventing multiple instances of an application from starting.
   c. Synchronizing between multiple processes.
   d. Both b and c.
2. Implementing a shared cache is a good fit for which synchronization primitive?
   a. `SemaphoreSlim`
   b. `AutoResetEvent`
   c. `ReaderWriterLockSlim`
   d. `Mutex`
3. What are the **`ManualResetEvent`** and **`AutoResetEvent`** classes useful for?
   a. Pausing and resuming threads.
   b. Background job completion notification.
   c. Both a and b.
   d. Managing shared collections.
4. Pooled resources can be shared by using which synchronization primitive?
   a. `Mutex`
   b. `SemaphoreSlim`
   c. `ReaderWriterLockSlim`
   d. `ManualResetEvent`

Answers

1. d
2. c
3. c
4. b

Questions

1. Aside from pooled resources, what other types of applications can benefit from using **`SemaphoreSlim`**?
2. In what circumstances would **`Monitor`** be a better way to implement events than the **Reset Events**?
3. Why is **`ReaderWriterLockSlim`** higher performance for single-write multi-read scenarios than the **`Lock`** class?

Key Terms

- **Thread Synchronization:** Coordination between threads to manage access to shared resources, prevent contention, and avoid data corruption
- **Synchronization Primitives:** Tools that help coordinate access to shared resources in multithreaded or concurrent programming, ensuring correct and predictable behavior
- **Local Mutex: A `Mutex` that i**s accessible only within a single process
- **Named Mutex:** A `Mutex` that is accessible by name between many processes
- **Events:** Synchronization me**chanisms that** coordinate threads by signaling when specific tasks, processes, or conditions are complete, allowing other threads to proceed
- **Reset Events:** The synchronization primitives that maintain a signaled or non-signaled state, such as `AutoResetEvent` and `ManualResetEvent`.
- **Signaled:** The state of a reset event that allows waiting threads to proceed
- **Non-signaled:** The state of a reset event that prevents waiting threads from proceeding
- **Reader:** A thread that exclusively reads from a shared resource
- **Upgradeable Reader:** A thread that normally reads from a shared resource but may write under certain conditions
- **Writer:** A thread that exclusively writes to a shared resource
- **Reader-writer Problem:** Effectively balancing readers and writers to ensure multiple readers can access a shared resource but only a single writer can access at any given time

CHAPTER 6
Understanding Concurrent Collections

Introduction

In some of the examples from the previous chapter, we explored the usefulness of shared collections in multithreaded applications using standard collections. While these collections enable data sharing among threads, they also introduce challenges related to thread safety, data consistency, and performance overhead. In this chapter, we will delve into the thread-safe collections provided by .NET, such as **`ConcurrentBag<T>`**, **`ConcurrentDictionary<TKey, TValue>`**, **`ConcurrentQueue<T>`**, and **`ConcurrentStack<T>`**. Additionally, we will examine how these collections address common concurrency challenges and explore patterns, including the Producer-Consumer pattern with **`BlockingCollection<T>`**. By the end of this chapter, you will gain a deeper understanding of when and how to use these collections effectively in your high-performance applications.

Structure

In this chapter, we will cover the following topics:

- Introduction to Concurrent Collections
    - The Importance of Thread-Safe Collections
    - The Challenges of Standard Collections
    - Solving Challenges with Concurrent Collections
- Using `ConcurrentBag`
    - Features and Design
    - Use Cases
    - Performance Considerations
- Using `ConcurrentDictionary`
    - Features and Design
    - Use Cases
    - Best Practices
- Specialized Collections: `ConcurrentQueue`
    - Characteristics
    - Use Cases
- Specialized Collections: `ConcurrentStack`
    - Characteristics
    - Use Cases

- The Producer-Consumer Pattern
  - Introduction to The Producer-Consumer Problem
  - Simplifying The Producer-Consumer Pattern
  - Cancellation Support
  - Ordering Elements
  - Handling Bounded and Unbounded Collections
  - Array Operations
  - Use Cases

Introduction to Concurrent Collections

Collections are a fundamental component of most applications, including those with multithreading. The .NET framework offers generic collections within the **`System.Collections.Generic`** namespace, which provide flexible and type-safe collection behavior. However, these collections are not inherently thread-safe, which means that they can encounter data corruption or race conditions when accessed simultaneously by multiple threads without external synchronization.

To address these challenges, the .NET framework introduces thread-safe generic collections in the **`System.Collections.Concurrent`** namespace. These collections are designed to handle concurrent operations efficiently and eliminate the need for explicit synchronization mechanisms like locks in many scenarios. They maintain type-safety while optimizing performance, enabling developers to build robust and high-performing multithreaded applications with minimal complexity.

The Importance of Thread-Safe Collections

The thread-safe collections in **`System.Collections.Concurrent`** provide the ability to share collections between threads in multithreaded applications, which provides high-performance behavior with limited complexity compared to using standard collections.

The Challenges of Standard Collections

The collections in the **`System.Collections`** and **`System.Collections.Generic`** namespaces are not designed for concurrent access, meaning they can only be safely used within a single thread. When multiple threads attempt to access or modify these collections simultaneously without proper synchronization, issues such as race conditions, data corruption, and unpredictable behavior can occur.

In the previous chapter, we explored examples of using synchronization primitives like locks to handle collections in thread-safe ways. While effective, these solutions introduce additional complexity into the codebase. Implementing them correctly requires careful attention to detail to avoid issues such as deadlocks, excessive contention, or degraded performance.

Solving Challenges with Concurrent Collections

To address these challenges using standard collections otherwise present in multithreaded scenarios, .NET provides concurrent collections in the **`System.Collections.Concurrent`** namespace. These collections are specifically designed for multithreaded scenarios, offering built-in thread safety and optimized performance. They eliminate the need for manual synchronization, making it easier to build robust and scalable multithreaded applications.

The collections in **System.Collections.Concurrent** are as follows:

- ConcurrentBag<T>
- ConcurrentDictionary<TKey, TValue>
- ConcurrentQueue<T>
- ConcurrentStack<T>
- BlockingCollection<T>

We will discuss each of these in detail in this chapter.

Note: *The other classes in* **System.Collections.Concurrent** *are partitioners. These classes are specifically for use in the Parallel LINQ capability of the TPL. We will discuss these in more detail in Chapter 8: Language-Integrated Query (LINQ) for Parallelism.*

Using ConcurrentBag

A **bag** is a collection data structure used when the order of elements is not important. Unlike a set, a **bag** allows for duplicates, meaning it can contain multiple instances of the same item. It differs from a list in that it does not guarantee any specific order for its elements. **Bags** are particularly useful in scenarios where the frequency of items matters, rather than their arrangement or uniqueness.

The **ConcurrentBag<T>** class is a thread-safe **bag** implementation in .NET. Items can be added, removed, updated, and accessed freely by multiple threads simultaneously. Because it is a **bag** implementation, duplicates are allowed in the collection and there is no guaranteed order of the collection elements.

Features and Design

In addition to being thread-safe, the methods on **ConcurrentBag<T>** are non-blocking for optimal performance in multithreaded scenarios. It is designed to keep operations that occur on the same thread isolated whenever possible, to minimize contention and improve scalability. It also supports dynamic resizing to automatically accommodate new elements. These features make **ConcurrentBag<T>** suitable for scenarios where elements are accessed individually, particularly when threads can interact with their own items in the **bag**.

ConcurrentBag<T> can implement the following interfaces:

- **IEnumerable<T>**
- **IReadOnlyCollection<T>**
- **ICollection**
- **IEnumerable**
- **IProducerConsumerCollection<T>**

Support for **IEnumerable** means that the contents of **ConcurrentBag<T>** can be accessed using a **foreach** loop. However, while the methods of **ConcurrentBag<T>** are thread-safe for additions and removals, the methods implemented to support enumeration are not guaranteed to be thread-safe if the collection is modified concurrently during enumeration. The **foreach** loop and LINQ extension methods create a snapshot of the collection at the moment the enumeration begins, and any modifications made afterward will not be reflected in the enumeration. To ensure consistent behavior during enumeration in a multithreaded environment, external synchronization like a lock statement or other synchronization primitives, might be necessary.

Methods implemented to support the other interfaces are also not guaranteed to be thread-safe. For example, operations like **CopyTo()** or **Count()** may return inconsistent results if the collection is modified concurrently during their execution. To use these methods safely in a multithreaded environment, external synchronization mechanisms such as a lock statement should be applied around the collection operations. It is also important to note that these methods often rely on a snapshot of the collection's state, which may not reflect changes made after the operation starts. Developers should carefully evaluate whether additional synchronization is needed based on the specific requirements of their application.

The **IProducerConsumerCollection<T>** interface supports the Producer-Consumer pattern and is particularly useful when used with the **BlockingCollection<T>** class. We will explore **BlockingCollection<T>** in more detail later in this chapter.

The following example shows how **ConcurrentBag<T>** can be used to implement a dynamic shared resource pool:

```
using System.Collections.Concurrent;

ConcurrentBag<string> pool = new ConcurrentBag<string>()
{
    "Resource 1",
    "Resource 2"
};
var threadList = new List<Thread>();
for (int i = 0; i < 4; i++)
{
    var thread = new Thread(UseResource);
    thread.Start();
    threadList.Add(thread);
}

foreach (var thread in threadList)
    thread.Join();

void UseResource()
{
    string resource;
    if (!pool.TryTake(out resource))
        resource = $"Resource created by thread: {Thread.CurrentThread.
ManagedThreadId}";
    Thread.Sleep(500);
    pool.Add(resource);
    Console.WriteLine($"Thread {Thread.CurrentThread.ManagedThreadId} used
resource: {resource}");
}
```

In the above example, a resource pool is created using **ConcurrentBag<string>** with two resources initially in the pool. The threads try to take resources from the pool for use using the **TryTake()** method. In this case, the pool is dynamic, so if a resource does not exist in the pool, a thread can create it. Once a thread finishes using the resource, it is added back to the pool. The output will be as follows:

```
Thread 9 used resource: Resource created by thread: 9
Thread 7 used resource: Resource created by thread: 7
Thread 8 used resource: Resource 1
Thread 6 used resource: Resource 2
```

Use of **ConcurrentBag<T>** greatly simplifies the code required to manage a resource pool like the one in this example where blocking is not required. In scenarios where blocking is required, consider using **BlockingCollection<T>** or other synchronization primitives.

Use Cases

The **ConcurrentBag<T>** class is designed for situations where multiple threads need to add or retrieve items from a collection without the need for strict ordering. It is high-speed and scalable. The following table highlights some common use cases:

Use Case	Description
Dynamic Resource Pool	Manage resources that can be reused and dynamically created, like threads, database connections, or file handles
Intermediate Results	Parallel algorithms can store intermediate results in ConcurrentBag<T> for later aggregation
Workload Distribution	Tasks or work items can be stored in ConcurrentBag<T>. Threads can retrieve the items for processing without regard for ordering
Logging and Monitoring	Metrics or log data can be collected in ConcurrentBag<T> while processing and a separate thread can write the data to files or databases for persistent storage
Event Aggregation	Collect events or notifications from multiple sources in ConcurrentBag<T> and process them together
Inventory Management in Games	In a multiplayer game, items dropped by players or NPCs can be stored in ConcurrentBag<T> to be picked up later by other players

Table 6.1: *ConcurrentBag<T> Common Use Cases*

Due to the unordered nature of elements in **ConcurrentBag<T>**, it is not suitable for scenarios where ordering is required. If order matters in your application, consider using **ConcurrentQueue<T>** or **ConcurrentStack<T>** instead. These specialized collections will be covered later in this chapter.

Performance Considerations

The **ConcurrentBag<T>** class is highly optimized for scenarios where threads frequently add and remove items. It performs exceptionally well when threads primarily access the items they have added, thus minimizing synchronization overhead. However, there are important performance considerations to be aware of and address in specific use cases, which are mentioned as follows:

- It is optimized for scenarios where multiple threads frequently add and remove items. It is not optimized for bulk add operations. Consider a **List<T>** with external synchronization primitives for bulk operations.
- The **bag** leverages thread-local storage to minimize synchronization overhead when the same thread accesses items it added. In scenarios when items are accessed across threads, this mechanism can add memory and synchronization overhead. Consider **ConcurrentQueue<T>**, **ConcurrentStack<T>**, **BlockingCollection<T>**, or **Channel<T>** if usage is primarily cross-thread.
- Enumerating **ConcurrentBag<T>** is an expensive operation because the entire collection is copied to a snapshot before the enumeration takes place. This can lead to significant performance issues if enumeration is frequent or the data set is large. Avoid frequent enumeration of large data sets.
- In extremely high concurrency scenarios where many threads are adding and removing items, the synchronization cost can become a performance bottleneck. Consider specialized collections such as **BlockingCollection<T>** for highly contentious scenarios.
- **ConcurrentBag<T>** is best when managing medium to large data sets. For smaller amounts of data, the synchronization overhead may outweigh the benefits. Consider **ConcurrentDictionary<TKey, TValue>** or a **List<T>** with an external synchronization primitive for small amounts of data.

- Items can stay in thread-local storage until garbage collection occurs. This can lead to memory pressure as stale items build up. Consider regularly clearing or re-assigning the **bag** to clean up stale items.

ConcurrentBag<T> excels in specific scenarios where thread-local storage minimizes contention and frequent add/take operations are required. However, its performance can degrade in cross-thread scenarios, high-concurrency environments, or when memory efficiency is critical. Always profile your application to validate the suitability of **ConcurrentBag<T>** for your use case.

Using ConcurrentDictionary

The **Dictionary<TKey, TValue>** class is a foundational collection type in .NET, widely used for its efficiency and flexibility in managing key-value pairs with type safety. However, the **Dictionary<TKey, TValue>** is not thread-safe and can lead to unpredictable behavior when accessed by multiple threads simultaneously.

To address this limitation, .NET provides the **ConcurrentDictionary<TKey, TValue>** class, a thread-safe collection designed specifically for concurrent access scenarios. It ensures safe access and modification of key-value pairs in multi-threaded environments, leveraging optimized locking and partitioning mechanisms to maintain high performance.

Features and Design

The **ConcurrentDictionary<TKey, TValue>** class is a robust, thread-safe solution for managing key-value collections in multithreaded environments. It does implement **IDictionary<TKey, TValue>** but the methods used to implement that interface are not guaranteed to be thread-safe. To maintain thread-safety, **ConcurrentDictionary<TKey, TValue>** introduces some new methods to add and remove items from the collection. The following table outlines these methods and their use:

Method	Usage
AddOrUpdate(TKey, Func<TKey,TValue>, Func<TKey,TValue,TValue>)	If TKey does not exist in the dictionary, the add delegate is called and the result is added to the dictionary. Otherwise, the update delegate is called and the value in TKey is updated with the result
AddOrUpdate(TKey, TValue, Func<TKey,TValue,TValue>)	If TKey does not exist in the dictionary, the add value is added to the dictionary. Otherwise, the update delegate is called and the value in TKey is updated with the result
GetOrAdd(TKey, TValue)	If TKey is in the dictionary, its value is returned. Otherwise, the value in TValue is added for TKey and then returned
GetOrAdd(TKey, Func<TKey,TValue>)	If TKey is in the dictionary, its value is returned. Otherwise, the value delegate is called and the result is added for TKey and then returned
dictionary[key] = value	Stores a key/value pair by adding it if the key does not exist or updating the value if the key does exist
TryAdd(TKey, TValue)	Adds the key value pair if the key does not already exist. Returns true if the value was added and false if not
TryUpdate(TKey, TValue, TValue)	Checks to see if the value of key matches the third parameter. If it does, it updates the value to the second parameter. Returns true if the value was updated and false if not
TryRemove(TKey, out TValue)	Attempts to remove the value of TKey and return it in the TValue parameter. Returns true if successful and false if not
TryRemove(KeyValuePair<TKey, TValue)	Attempts to remove the provided key value pair. Returns true if successful and false if not

Table 6.2: *ConcurrentDictionary Add and Update Methods*

The methods in *Table 6.2, ConcurrentDictionary Add and Update Methods* are all thread-safe and atomic, meaning they do not require additional synchronization for use between threads. However, developers should note an important caveat: the **AddOrUpdate()** and **GetOrAdd()** methods accept delegates that are executed outside the internal locking mechanisms. This design avoids performance issues associated with locking while running user-defined code. Consequently, these delegates may be invoked multiple times under high concurrency, and their execution order is not guaranteed. To ensure predictable behavior, developers should ensure that delegate logic is idempotent and thread-safe.

The following code uses the **AddOrUpdate()** method to add an element and then update the element:

```
using System.Collections.Concurrent;

var dictionary = new ConcurrentDictionary<string, int>();

//Add new entry
int addedValue = dictionary.AddOrUpdate("apple", 1,
    (key, oldvalue) => oldvalue + 1);
Console.WriteLine($"apple: {addedValue}");

//Update existing entry
int updatedValue = dictionary.AddOrUpdate("apple", 1,
    (key, oldvalue) => oldvalue + 1);
Console.WriteLine($"apple: {updatedValue}");
```

In this code, a **ConcurrentDictionary<string, int>** is used to demonstrate the behavior of the **AddOrUpdate()** method. In the first call, the key "apple" does not exist in the dictionary so the **addValue** parameter (**1**) is used to insert the key with an initial value of **1**. In the second call, the key "apple" already exists with a value of **1**, so the **updateValueFactory** delegate is invoked. This delegate takes the existing value (**1**), adds **1**, and updates the entry with the result (**2**).

ConcurrentDictionary<TKey, TValue> supports the following features:

- The methods for adding, updating, and removing key-value pairs are thread-safe and atomic so they do not require external synchronization mechanisms.
- Internally, the dictionary uses a lock-striping technique, where different sections are locked independently. This improves performance by reducing lock contention between threads.
- Reading values does not lock the dictionary, making reads extremely fast.
- Like **ConcurrentBag<T>**, enumeration is thread-safe but is done using a snapshot of the collection. The dictionary can still be modified by other threads while being enumerated.
- The dictionary supports a custom equality comparer that implements **IEqualityComparer<TKey>**.

Internally, the dictionary is divided into several segments, each with its own lock. This ensures that multiple threads can update the dictionary with reduced contention. The segmentation is implemented in such a way that operations like enumeration and resizing are always accurate and consistent. This design optimizes the dictionary for high concurrency scenarios and ensures that the dictionary performs well even under heavy load.

The dictionary can resize itself automatically when necessary. The resizing operation is thread-safe and does not block readers or writers unnecessarily.

The following example shows how **ConcurrentDictionary<TKey, TValue>** can be used to implement a shared cache:

```
using System.Collections.Concurrent;

Random rand = new Random();
```

```
ConcurrentDictionary<string, int> cache = new ConcurrentDictionary<string,
int>();
var threadList = new List<Thread>();
for (int i = 0; i < 10; i++)
{
    var keyName = i % 4;
    var thread = new Thread(() => FetchItemData("item" + keyName));
    thread.Start();
    threadList.Add(thread);
}

foreach (var thread in threadList)
    thread.Join();

Console.WriteLine("Cache contents:");
foreach (var kv in cache)
    Console.WriteLine(kv);

void FetchItemData(string key)
{
    var data = cache.GetOrAdd(key, k =>
    {
        Thread.Sleep(500);
        return rand.Next(1, 100);
    });
    Console.WriteLine($"Retrieved data for key {key}: {data}");
}
```

In the prior example, a cache is defined using a **ConcurrentDictionary<string, int>** instance. Ten threads are started that all fetch data from the cache or a simulated external data source, with a given key. A random number generator is used to simulate the data source. Using the **GetOrAdd()** method, the data associated to the key is retrieved from the cache. If the key is not present in the dictionary, it is retrieved from the data source using a delegate. The output looks like the following:

```
Retrieved data for key item3: 36
Retrieved data for key item0: 56
Retrieved data for key item2: 5
Retrieved data for key item1: 98
Retrieved data for key item0: 56
Retrieved data for key item2: 5
Retrieved data for key item3: 36
Retrieved data for key item1: 98
Retrieved data for key item1: 98
Retrieved data for key item0: 56
Cache contents:
[item3, 36]
[item0, 56]
[item2, 5]
[item1, 98]
```

The following interfaces are implemented by **ConcurrentDictionary<TKey, TValue>**:

- IDictionary<TKey, TValue>
- IReadOnlyDictionary<TKey, TValue>
- ICollection<KeyValuePair<TKey, TValue>>
- IReadOnlyCollection<KeyValuePair<TKey, TValue>>
- IEnumerable<KeyValuePair<TKey, TValue>>

- ICollection
- IDictionary
- IEnumerable

Like **ConcurrentBag<T>**, the methods that implement these interfaces in **ConcurrentDictionary<TKey, TValue>** are thread-safe for individual operations, but composite operations (such as checking if a key exists and then adding or modifying it) may not be. Extension methods associated with **ConcurrentDictionary<TKey, TValue>** are not guaranteed to be thread-safe.

Use Cases

The **ConcurrentDictionary<TKey, TValue>** class is very versatile and is suitable for any scenario where managing key-value pairs in a multithreaded environment is necessary. The following table mentions some of the more popular use cases:

Use Case	**Description**
Caching Data	Storing frequently accessed data that may be added, updated, or removed by multiple threads
Dependency Tracking in Dependency Injection	Managing a registry of services or instances in a Dependency Injection Container
Event Subscription Management	Tracking event subscribers in a system where multiple threads may add subscribers
Job Coordination	Keeping track of job statuses in a background processing system
Data Deduplication	A mechanism to detect and reject duplicates in real time
In-Memory Databases	Maintain key-value databases in a multithreaded application

***Table 6.3:** ConcurrentDictionary Use Cases*

Best Practices

The following best practices should be observed when designing solutions using **ConcurrentDictionary<TKey, TValue>:**

- Use **ConcurrentDictionary<TKey, TValue>** for scenarios where frequently accessed data is used between threads. Avoid using it for complex, multi-key transactions. Other synchronization mechanisms or collections may be more appropriate in these situations
- Avoid unnecessary external locking. **ConcurrentDictionary<TKey, TValue>** is designed to handle its own internal synchronization. Adding external synchronization mechanisms can degrade performance when they are not required
- Avoid checking for a key's existence before calling **TryAdd()**, **TryRemove()**, or **TryUpdate()**. This is unnecessary and can lead to race conditions
- Be careful with delegates in **AddOrUpdate()** or **GetOrAdd()** methods. The delegates are not called during locking and so race conditions are possible. They may also be called more than once, so ensure they are idempotent
- If the dictionary manages mutable items such as complex objects, lists, or dictionaries, updates to those values are not thread safe. Prefer immutable objects or provide external synchronization to ensure thread-safety
- Use **TryAdd()**, **TryRemove()**, or **TryGetValue()** to avoid exceptions like **KeyNotFoundException**
- Design your application to avoid frequent updates to the same key if possible

- If you know the approximate size of the dictionary, use the constructor overload to specify the initial capacity
- Regularly clean up unused or stale entries to optimize memory usage
- Profile the dictionary under expected concurrency levels and increase the concurrency level parameter in the constructor if contention becomes a bottleneck

By adhering to these guidelines, you can fully leverage the capabilities of ConcurrentDictionary<TKey,TValue> to handle concurrent operations effectively, without sacrificing thread safety or performance. Whether you are building a caching mechanism, managing shared state, or implementing complex data structures in multi-threaded environments, these best practices will help you design solutions that are both efficient and maintainable. Properly optimizing your use of ConcurrentDictionary<TKey, TValue> ensures that your application can scale seamlessly to meet the demands of modern, high-concurrency workloads.

Specialized Collections: ConcurrentQueue

The collections we have explored so far in System.Collections.Concurrent do not maintain the order of their elements. However, in certain scenarios, preserving the order of items is crucial to the solution. One of the two collections in System.Collections.Concurrent that guarantees the order of elements is ConcurrentQueue<T>.

Characteristics

ConcurrentQueue<T> is a queue implementation that enforces **first-in, first-out** (**FIFO**) order of its elements, meaning items are dequeued in the same order they were enqueued. It is thread-safe and suitable for use in multithreaded scenarios. The following are key characteristics of ConcurrentQueue<T>:

- **Thread-safe:** All operations on the queue are designed to be safe to use by multiple threads without requiring external locks
- **First-in, first-out:** The queue maintains the order of items, guaranteeing that elements are dequeued in the order they were enqueued
- **Lock-free:** ConcurrentQueue<T> employs lock-free techniques for thread-safety, ensuring high performance even under contention
- **Multiple Producers and Consumers:** It supports scenarios where multiple threads add items, and multiple threads remove items simultaneously
- **Atomic Operations:** The queue supports try-based atomic operations for dequeue and peek. These operations return true if successful and provide the object at the beginning of the queue in a single operation
- **Snapshot Capabilities:** The ToArray() method allows creating a snapshot of the queue contents, although it might not represent a fully consistent state if other threads are concurrently modifying the queue
- **Highly Scalable:** Due to its lock-free implementation, the queue performs well under high contention, making it suitable for high-performance scenarios
- **No fixed size:** The queue dynamically expands as items are added
- **Integrated into the TPL:** ConcurrentQueue<T> is integrated into the TPL and is often used with Parallel.ForEach as a partitioning mechanism
- **No Bulk Operations:** The queue is optimized for single add and remove operations and does not support bulk operations. There is a constructor for initializing the queue from an array or other enumeration

- **No Blocking Operations:** The queue is designed to not block producers or consumers. For scenarios that require producers to wait for consumers (or vice versa), use **BlockingCollection<T>**

The following example shows the use of **ConcurrentQueue<T>** in a simulated background job queue:

```
using System.Collections.Concurrent;

var cts = new CancellationTokenSource();
var queue = new ConcurrentQueue<string>();
var tasks = new List<Task>();

tasks.Add(Task.Run(() => QueueJobs(cts)));
tasks.Add(Task.Run(() => RunJobs(cts.Token)));
tasks.Add(Task.Run(() => RunJobs(cts.Token)));

Task.WaitAll(tasks);

Console.WriteLine("Jobs completed.");

void QueueJobs(CancellationTokenSource tokenSource)
{
    for (int i = 1; i < 11; i++)
    {
        queue.Enqueue($"Job {i}");
        Thread.Sleep(100);
    }
    tokenSource.Cancel();
}

void RunJobs(CancellationToken token)
{
    while (!token.IsCancellationRequested || !queue.IsEmpty)
    {
        if (queue.TryDequeue(out string jobName))
        {
            Console.WriteLine($"Running job: {jobName}");
            Thread.Sleep(500);
        }
    }
}
```

In the prior example, one task is started to create and enqueue jobs. Two more tasks are started to dequeue and process the jobs. The jobs are enqueued faster than they are run. A **CancellationTokenSource** is used to signal that job queueing is completed. The **ConcurrentQueue<string>** instance keeps track of jobs and ensures they are run in the order they were enqueued. The output is as follows:

```
Running job: Job 1
Running job: Job 2
Running job: Job 3
Running job: Job 4
Running job: Job 5
Running job: Job 6
Running job: Job 7
Running job: Job 8
Running job: Job 9
Running job: Job 10
Jobs completed.
```

Use Cases

The **ConcurrentQueue<T>** class is ideal for multithreaded applications where **first-in, first-out** processing is required between threads. It is thread-safe and highly scalable, making it suitable for use even when thread contention is expected to be high. The following table contains common use cases:

Use Case	Description
Non-blocking Producer Consumer	One or more threads generate data and enqueue work and one or more threads dequeue work and process the data
Task Scheduling	Managing background jobs in a **first-in, first-out** order
Data Stream Buffering	Storing data temporarily in a buffer to ensure smooth transitions between producers and consumers
Event Handling	Storing asynchronous events for processing in the order they were received
Background Processing	Storing data from multiple sources and processing it in the background
Pipeline Processing	Storing intermediate results between stages in a processing pipeline
Logging	Storing log entries from different threads without locking
Communicating Between Threads	Storing data safely between threads without requiring extra locking mechanisms

Table 6.4: *ConcurrentQueue<T> Use Cases*

The **ConcurrentQueue<T>** class is a thread-safe, lightweight, and efficient solution for implementing **FIFO (first-in, first-out)** operations in multithreaded environments. Its simplicity and performance make it a practical choice for inter-thread communication.

Specialized Collections: ConcurrentStack

Another collection that guarantees order in **System.Collections.Concurrent** is **ConcurrentStack<T>**. It manages items in a **last-in, first-out** order (**LIFO**). This makes **ConcurrentStack<T>** particularly useful in scenarios where the most recently added items need to be processed first, such as undo operations in text editors or managing tasks with a stack-based approach. Its thread-safe design ensures that multiple threads can push and pop items without the need for explicit synchronization, providing a robust solution for concurrent programming challenges.

Characteristics

ConcurrentStack<T> is similar in many ways to **ConcurrentQueue<T>** with the key difference being in the order elements are kept and accessed in the collection. Like **ConcurrentQueue<T>**, **ConcurrentStack<T>** is thread-safe and is implemented without locks. The following list outlines the key characteristics of **ConcurrentStack<T>**:

- **Thread-safe:** All operations are designed to be safe to use from multiple threads without the need for external synchronization.
- **Lock free:** All methods operate without locks for high performance even in highly contentious scenarios.
- **Last in, first out:** The order of elements is **last-in, first-out**, meaning that the last element added to the stack is the first to be removed.

- **Atomic operations:** **ConcurrentStack<T>** Supports atomic operations for stack pop and peek. Methods like **TryPeek()** and **TryPop()** return **true** and provide the last object pushed if they succeed.
- **Batch operations:** In addition to atomic operations for single items, **ConcurrentStack<T>** offers atomic batch operations. **PushRange()** and **TryPopRange()** process multiple elements in a single atomic operation.
- **Snapshot enumeration:** Enumeration and LINQ methods force a snapshot of the collection to be created and then enumerate the snapshot. As with other concurrent collections, the snapshot may not be up to date if the collection is being updated during enumeration.
- **Simple API:** The API is simple and powerful, focusing on thread-safe **LIFO** operations.

The following example demonstrates a job queue that prioritizes processing more recent entries first, implemented using **ConcurrentStack<T>**:

```
using System.Collections.Concurrent;

var jobs = new ConcurrentStack<string>();
var cts = new CancellationTokenSource();
var tasks = new List<Task>();

tasks.Add(Task.Run(() => QueueJobs(cts)));
tasks.Add(Task.Run(() => RunJobs(cts.Token)));
tasks.Add(Task.Run(() => RunJobs(cts.Token)));

Task.WaitAll(tasks);

Console.WriteLine("Jobs complete.");

void QueueJobs(CancellationTokenSource source)
{
    for (int i = 1; i < 11; i++)
    {
        jobs.Push($"Job {i}");
        Thread.Sleep(100);
    }
    source.Cancel();
}

void RunJobs(CancellationToken token)
{
    while (!token.IsCancellationRequested || !jobs.IsEmpty)
    {
        if (jobs.TryPop(out string jobName))
        {
            Console.WriteLine($"Running job: {jobName}");
            Thread.Sleep(500);
        }
    }
}
```

In the prior example, one task is created to push jobs to the job stack. Two tasks are run the process the jobs from the stack. Using **ConcurrentStack<T>** ensures that the most recently added job is processed first, while older jobs wait. The output will look like something like this:

```
Running job: Job 1
Running job: Job 2
Running job: Job 5
```

```
Running job: Job 6
Running job: Job 10
Running job: Job 9
Running job: Job 8
Running job: Job 7
Running job: Job 4
Running job: Job 3
Jobs complete.
```

Thread scheduling plays a role in the order jobs are processed in this case, so the output will vary somewhat. The queue enforces that the last job pushed is the first job taken when the **`TryPop()`** method is called for.

Use Cases

The **`ConcurrentStack<T>`** class is ideal for any scenario that requires **last-in, first-out** processing between threads. Its lock-free thread-safe design makes it highly scalable and performant even in cases where thread contention is high. The following table highlights common use cases:

Use Case	Description
Undo/Redo Functionality	In applications where users can undo and redo actions, `ConcurrentStack<T>` can store prior actions in a thread-safe manner
Graph Search Implementation	Advanced graph search algorithms such as Depth First Search can use `ConcurrentStack<T>` to store nodes or states of the search process. The stack ensures that each thread runs on its own set of nodes, ensuring that multiple searches can run in parallel
Task Scheduling with LIFO Prioritization	Tasks or jobs can be scheduled and processed in most recently added first order
Backtracking Algorithms	Games that require path finding or maze solving can store the state of the search as the algorithm progresses. If dead ends are reached, those states can be pulled off the stack while multiple threads explore different paths
Token Pool Management	Pools of tokens or identifiers can be efficiently pushed and popped to ensure thread-safe access by multiple worker threads
Parallel Parsing	Multiple parser threads can parse large documents or datasets in parallel, pushing results onto the stack. The results can later be safely removed from the stack to ensure no data is lost or overwritten

Table 6.5: *ConcurrentStack<T> Use Cases*

The **`ConcurrentStack<T>`** class is an efficient and thread-safe way to enforce **last-in, first-out** behavior in a multithreaded application. It is easy to use and high-performing, making it a natural choice even for the most demanding multithreaded environments.

The Producer-Consumer Pattern

A common way to organize work in high performance applications is to separate processes that retrieve, create, or organize data from processes that work with the data. The processes that organize or generate the data are called producers, while the processes that consume, process, or otherwise use the data are called consumers. A solution structured using producers and consumers is called the **Producer-Consumer Pattern**.

Introduction to the Producer-Consumer Problem

The **Producer-Consumer Pattern** is typically implemented using a shared-buffer or queue that acts as an intermediary between producers and consumers. Producers add data to the buffer and consumers retrieve data from it. This decoupling allows producers and consumers to operate independently, which can improve application scalability, maintainability, and performance.

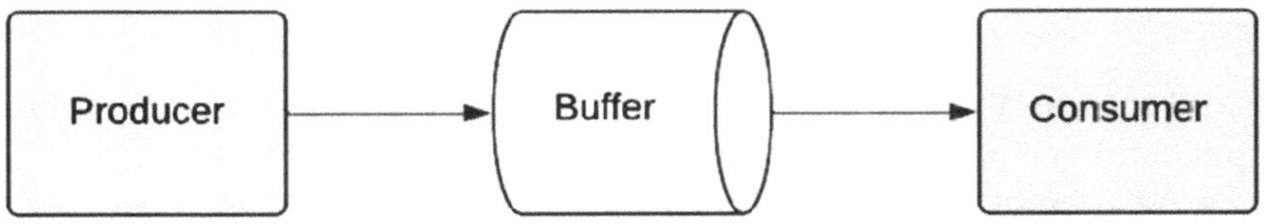

Figure 6.1: *Producer-Consumer Pattern*

Figure 6.1 illustrates the basic Producer-Consumer pattern. A process that produces some data to be processed is called a producer and it adds data to the intermediate buffer. Another process that will act on the produced data is called the consumer and it takes data from the intermediate buffer.

The Producer-Consumer pattern increases efficiency and scalability of an application by allowing producers and consumers to scale independently as shown in *Figure* 6.2.

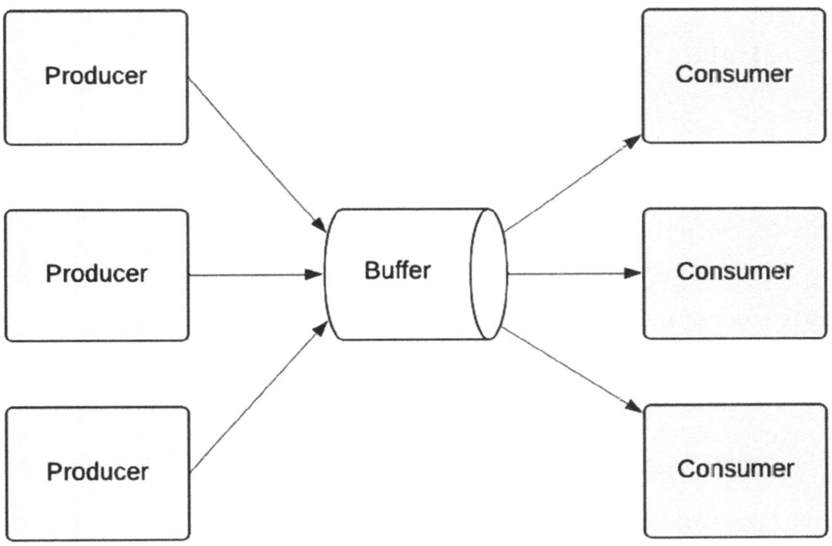

Figure 6.2: *Scaled Producer-Consumer*

The independent nature of producers and consumers presents several challenges to successful implementation. The shared buffer, like all shared data, must be protected to prevent data corruption and race conditions. Producers must be controlled to ensure they do not attempt to add data when the buffer is full. Similarly, consumers must not attempt to retrieve data when the buffer is empty. Additionally, a signaling mechanism is required to inform consumers when producers are finished, indicating no more data will be added.

Many of the synchronization primitives we have studied so far, such as locks and semaphores, can be effectively used to implement the Producer-Consumer pattern. However, manually implementing the pattern using low-level primitives is both time-consuming and error-prone. A higher-level abstraction would help simplify implementation and allow developers to focus on the larger intent of the software.

Simplifying Producer-Consumer

The .NET framework provides a complete implementation of the Producer-Consumer pattern in the **`BlockingCollection<T>`** class. **`BlockingColleciton<T>`** is a thread-safe collection that supports simultaneous adding and taking of items by multiple threads. It implements methods to block producers when the collection is full and block consumers when the collection is empty. It also has "**try**" methods that do not block or that block only for a specified time span. It also supports cancellation using **CancellationToken**. It can act as a fully functioning buffer for most all Producer-Consumer scenarios.

Using **BlockingCollection<T>** greatly simplifies implementing the Producer-Consumer pattern in multithreaded applications. Producers simply call **Add()** or **TryAdd()** to add items and consumers call **Take()** or **TryTake()** to remove items. The collection handles blocking as needed.

Let us see how **BlockingCollection<T>** can help us implement a simple order processing system:

```
using System.Collections.Concurrent;

var queue = new BlockingCollection<string>();
try
{
    var producer = Task.Run(PlaceOrders);
    var consumer = Task.Run(FulfillOrders);

    Task.WaitAll(producer, consumer);

    Console.WriteLine("All orders processed.");
}
finally
{
    queue.Dispose();
}

void PlaceOrders()
{
    for (int i = 1; i < 11; i++)
    {
        queue.Add($"Order {i}");
        Thread.Sleep(100);
    }
    queue.CompleteAdding();
}

void FulfillOrders()
{
    while (!queue.IsCompleted)
    {
        var order = queue.Take();
        Thread.Sleep(200);
        Console.WriteLine("Fulfilled " + order);
    }
}
```

The prior example implements a simple order processing system. A task is created to place orders (the producer) and another task is created to fulfill orders (the consumer), with a **BlockingCollection<T>** acting as the buffer. The producer adds orders to the queue by calling the **Add()** method. The consumer removes orders from the queue by calling the **Take()** method.

After the producer is finished adding items, it calls **CompleteAdding()** to signal to consumers that no more items will be added. The consumer checks the **IsCompleted** property to determine if data is still available. This property will be true if the collection is empty and **CompleteAdding()** has been called, indicating that no more work will be added.

BlockingCollection<T> allocates resources that should be released when no longer needed. Therefore, always ensure the collection is disposed by calling **Dispose()**.

The output is as follows:

```
Fulfilled Order 1
Fulfilled Order 2
Fulfilled Order 3
Fulfilled Order 4
Fulfilled Order 5
Fulfilled Order 6
Fulfilled Order 7
Fulfilled Order 8
Fulfilled Order 9
Fulfilled Order 10
All orders processed.
```

The consumer loop can be simplified further by using the **GetConsumingEnumerable()** method of **BlockingCollection<T>**. This method returns an **IEnumerable<T>** instance that can be used directly in a foreach loop. The **GetConsumingEnumerable()** method provides blocking behavior, which means that it waits until an item becomes available in the collection.

When an item is added to the **BlockingCollection**, it is retrieved by the loop and automatically removed from the collection. The loop continues until **CompleteAdding()** is called, signaling that no more items will be added, and the collection is empty. This approach allows for a clean and straightforward implementation of the consumer side without requiring explicit blocking logic.

The following is a revision of the order fulfillment system using **GetConsumingEnumerable()**:

```
using System.Collections.Concurrent;

var taskList = new List<Task>();
var queue = new BlockingCollection<string>();
try
{
    taskList.Add(Task.Run(PlaceOrders));
    taskList.Add(Task.Run(FulfillOrders));
    taskList.Add(Task.Run(FulfillOrders));

    Task.WaitAll(taskList);

    Console.WriteLine("All orders processed.");
}
finally
{
    queue.Dispose();
}

void PlaceOrders()
{
    for (int i = 1; i < 11; i++)
    {
        queue.Add($"Order {i}");
        Thread.Sleep(100);
    }
    queue.CompleteAdding();
}
```

```
void FulfillOrders()
{
    foreach (var order in queue.GetConsumingEnumerable())
    {
        Thread.Sleep(200);
        Console.WriteLine("Fulfilled " + order);
    }
}
```

In the prior example, the **`FulfillOrders()`** method is updated to use a simple **`foreach`** loop with **`GetConsumingEnumerable()`**. The number of consumers is also increased to demonstrate scalability. Producers and consumers can be scaled independently in the Producer-Consumer pattern. The output is the same as the original example.

Cancellation Support

`BlockingCollection<T>` provides built-in support for cancellation through **`CancellationTokenSource`** and **`CancellationToken`**, enabling producers and consumers to terminate their operations gracefully when a cancellation request is issued.

The **`TryAdd()`** method blocks when the collection is full and waits for a slot to become available so the item can be added. However, it accepts a **`CancellationToken`** parameter, allowing the operation to be cancelled. When cancelled, the method unblocks, and the thread continues execution even though the add operation failed.

Similarly, the **`TryTake()`** method blocks when the collection is empty, waiting for an item to become available. It also accepts a **`CancellationToken`**, enabling the operation to be cancelled. Upon cancellation, the method unblocks, allowing the thread to continue execution even if no item was retrieved.

The **`GetConsumingEnumerable()`** method also supports cancellation through a **`CancellationToken`**. If a cancellation request is issued, the enumeration stops immediately regardless of whether the collection still contains items or **`CompleteAdding()`** has been called. This ensures that consumers can exit cleanly without processing additional items.

Let us see an example of cancelling producers and consumers:

```
using System.Collections.Concurrent;

var cts = new CancellationTokenSource();
var buffer = new BlockingCollection<string>();
try
{
    var producer = Task.Run(() => BufferWork(cts.Token));
    var consumer = Task.Run(() => ProcessWork(cts.Token));

    Thread.Sleep(5000);
    cts.Cancel();
    Task.WaitAll(producer, consumer);

    Console.WriteLine("Items remaining in the buffer: " + buffer.Count);
}
finally
{
    buffer.Dispose();
}

void BufferWork(CancellationToken token)
```

```
    {
        int count = 1;
        while (!token.IsCancellationRequested)
        {
            if (buffer.TryAdd($"WorkItem {count++}", Timeout.Infinite, token))
                Thread.Sleep(100);
        }
    }

    void ProcessWork(CancellationToken token)
    {
        try
        {
            foreach (var workItem in buffer.GetConsumingEnumerable(token))
            {
                Console.WriteLine("Processing work item " + workItem);
                Thread.Sleep(200);
            }
        }
        catch (OperationCanceledException) { }
    }
```

The prior example demonstrates a continuous work stream where tasks are produced and consumed until a cancellation request is issued. The producer uses **`TryAdd()`** to enqueue work items, while the consumer processes them using **`GetConsumingEnumerable()`**.

When a call to **`TryAdd()`** is cancelled, the method returns **`false`** without throwing an exception. This allows the thread to continue working, potentially retrying later. In the example, the thread does not attempt to retry and instead continues processing until cancellation is requested. Similarly, **`TryTake()`** also returns **`false`** if cancelled, enabling the thread to continue without interruption. Both methods will also return **`false`** if the specified timeout expires. If the timeout parameter is set to **`Timeout.Infinite`** or -1, the method waits indefinitely, and cancelling it is the only way to unblock the operation.

When **`GetConsumingEnumerable()`** is cancelled, it throws an **`OperationCanceledException`**, which terminates the enumeration and exits the foreach loop. Threads must handle this exception to continue operating gracefully. In the example, the exception is caught but not explicitly processed, leading to the thread exiting as part of the cancellation process.

Ordering Elements

`BlockingCollection<T>` is not implemented as an independent collection that manages its own elements. Instead, it serves as a thread-safe wrapper around an instance of a type implementing the **`IProducerConsumerCollection<T>`** interface. This interface provides the underlying storage mechanism for the elements in the **`BlockingCollection<T>`**.

As we have seen, other collections in the **`System.Collections.Concurrent`** namespace (such as **`ConcurrentBag<T>`**, **`ConcurrentQueue<T>`**, and **`ConcurrentStack<T>`**) implement **`IProducerConsumerCollection<T>`**. This design allows **`BlockingCollection<T>`** to delegate the actual storage and ordering of elements to any of these collections.

By accepting an **`IProducerConsumerCollection<T>`** implementation as a constructor argument, **`BlockingCollection<T>`** offers flexibility in determining the ordering semantics of its elements. For example, using **`ConcurrentBag<T>`** would not enforce ordering and **`ConcurrentStack<T>`** would enforce LIFO ordering. If no collection is provided during construction, **`BlockingCollection<T>`** defaults to FIFO ordering by using a **`ConcurrentQueue<T>`**.

Handling Bounded and Unbounded Collections

The examples we have seen so far have not specified a limit for the buffer size in **BlockingCollection<T>**. By default, unless a limit is explicitly provided, **BlockingCollection<T>** operates in an unbounded configuration, allowing it to grow to accommodate new items. In this setup, Add operations will never block because the collection size will expand as needed. This behavior may be acceptable in scenarios where producers and consumers are expected to remain in sync, avoiding memory issues.

However, unbounded collections can pose significant risks, such as excessive memory usage or even application crashes due to out-of-memory exceptions, especially in scenarios with a high production rate and slower consumption. To mitigate these risks, it is often better to specify a maximum buffer size.

When a buffer size limit is defined, **BlockingCollection<T>** operates as a bounded collection. In this configuration, if the collection reaches its limit, Add operations will block until the consumer removes an item and frees up space. This mechanism enforces backpressure, ensuring that producers cannot overwhelm the system.

The following example demonstrates the effects of bounded and unbounded collections:

```
using System.Collections.Concurrent;

var bounded = new BlockingCollection<string>(2);
var unbounded = new BlockingCollection<string>();

Console.WriteLine("Unbounded work...");
var producer = Task.Run(() => Produce(unbounded));
var consumer = Task.Run(() => Consume(unbounded));
Task.WaitAll(producer, consumer);

Console.WriteLine("Bounded work...");
producer = Task.Run(() => Produce(bounded));
consumer = Task.Run(() => Consume(bounded));
Task.WaitAll(producer, consumer);

Console.WriteLine("Completed.");

void Produce(BlockingCollection<string> collection)
{
    for (int i = 1; i < 6; i++)
    {
        var item = $"WorkItem {i}";
        Console.WriteLine("Producing: " + item);
        collection.Add(item);
    }
    collection.CompleteAdding();
}

void Consume(BlockingCollection<string> collection)
{
    foreach (var item in collection.GetConsumingEnumerable())
    {
        Console.WriteLine("Consumed: " + item);
        Thread.Sleep(200);
    }
}
```

In the prior example, work is processed using both an unbounded instance of **BlockingCollection<T>** and a bounded instance with a specified capacity. The unbounded collection allows producers to add items without restriction, even when consumers are slow. As a result, producers can significantly outpace consumers, potentially leading to unchecked memory usage and system instability. In contrast, the bounded collection enforces a limit on the buffer size. When this limit is achieved, producers are forced to wait until consumers have processed items, which ensures controlled resource utilization and prevents runaway memory growth. The following output demonstrates that the bounded collection results in a more interleaved sequence of operations, where production and consumption alternate more closely. This interleaving reflects the synchronization enforced by the bounded buffer, promoting balanced processing and reducing the risk of resource exhaustion.

```
Unbounded work...
Producing: WorkItem 1
Producing: WorkItem 2
Consumed: WorkItem 1
Producing: WorkItem 3
Producing: WorkItem 4
Producing: WorkItem 5
Consumed: WorkItem 2
Consumed: WorkItem 3
Consumed: WorkItem 4
Consumed: WorkItem 5
Bounded work...
Producing: WorkItem 1
Consumed: WorkItem 1
Producing: WorkItem 2
Producing: WorkItem 3
Producing: WorkItem 4
Consumed: WorkItem 2
Producing: WorkItem 5
Consumed: WorkItem 3
Consumed: WorkItem 4
Consumed: WorkItem 5
Completed.
```

Array Operations

There are four static methods in the **BlockingCollection<T>** class that operate on arrays of collections, namely **AddToAny()**, **TryAddToAny()**, **TakeFromAny()**, and **TryTakeFromAny()**. These methods enable efficient and thread-safe operations for scenarios requiring inter-thread communication, data partitioning, or coordination, where groups of producers or consumers are involved.

AddToAny() and **TryAddToAny()** allow a producer to add an item to the first available collection in an array of **BlockingCollection<T>** instances. **TakeFromAny()** and **TryTakeFromAny()** allow a consumer to remove an item from the first collection in an array that contains an item.

These methods are especially useful in complex scenarios involving multiple producers and consumers operating on shared resources. Most use cases for these array-based methods involve pairing a single producer method, which can efficiently distribute data to multiple collections, with individual **TakeFromAny()** or **TryTakeFromAny()** calls in consumer groups or vice versa, where multiple producers feed data into an array of collections that a single consumer can process.

A common scenario is when a system needs to balance workload across multiple threads or coordinate data between multiple components. For instance:

- **Load balancing**: Producers can distribute items among several collections, and consumers can process items from these collections based on availability.
- **Fault tolerance**: In distributed or redundant systems, multiple collections may represent separate data queues, and these methods can help ensure no single queue becomes a bottleneck.

Using these methods provides flexibility and scalability, making them a powerful feature in concurrent programming with the `BlockingCollection<T>` class.

Use Cases

The Producer-Consumer pattern is a foundational concept in multithreaded applications, enabling efficient communication and coordination between threads. It is widely applicable in scenarios where one or more threads produce data while others consume it, ensuring optimal resource utilization and seamless task processing.

The following are common use cases for the Producer-Consumer pattern using `BlockingCollection<T>`:

Use Case	Description
Batch Processing of Data	Processes data in groups, allowing producers to add items continuously and consumers to process batches based on size or time thresholds
Task Scheduling	Acts as a task queue for worker threads to pick up and execute jobs, suitable for background operations or distributed workloads
Streaming Data Processing	Handles real-time data streams by enabling concurrent processing of incoming updates without missing or delaying events
Rate-Limiting or Throttling	Controls the rate of data or task processing to prevent system overload, such as limiting API calls or managing resource usage
Event Processing Pipelines	Facilitates sequential stages of processing by passing events through multiple `BlockingCollection<T>` instances, each representing a pipeline stage
Asynchronous Logging	Collects log messages in real-time without blocking the main application thread, with a background thread handling storage or output
File Processing Pipelines	Enables concurrent reading, processing, and writing of files, improving throughput in file conversion or parsing tasks
Task Coordination Between Subsystems	Bridges modular components, allowing one subsystem to produce tasks while another consumes them for processing
Multithreaded Image or Video Processing	Processes frames or image data concurrently, enabling real-time transformations like filtering or compression

Table 6.6: *Producer-Consumer Use Cases*

Conclusion

Concurrent collections provide thread-safe, scalable, and optimized solutions for managing shared data between threads. By leveraging these collections, developers can focus on building robust, high-performance applications without worrying about the complexities of manual synchronization. Whether you are implementing Producer-Consumer patterns, managing task queues, or working with shared resources in a multithreaded environment, concurrent collections offer the tools to ensure that your code is efficient, maintainable, and free of common threading pitfalls.

The next chapter will focus on parallel loops for multithreaded applications, covering topics such as the **Parallel** class, its methods (**Parallel.For**, **Parallel.ForEach**), best practices for maximizing performance, common pitfalls, and scenarios where parallel loops can significantly improve processing efficiency. Examples will include practical use cases like batch processing, data transformation, and computationally intensive tasks.

Points to Remember

- The methods directly implemented by the collections in this chapter are guaranteed to be thread-safe. But methods implemented for interfaces or extension methods are not guaranteed to be thread-safe.
- Enumerating collection elements is possible for each of these collections, but a snapshot is created at the moment of enumeration. The snapshot may not contain all elements if there are threads actively adding to the collection when the enumeration is created.
- **BlockingCollection<T>** uses one of the other collections (**ConcurrentBag<T>**, **ConcurrentQueue<T>**, or **ConcurrentStack<T>**) to manage its elements internally. If no collection is specified in the constructor, **ConcurrentQueue<T>** is used by default. This allows fine control over element ordering.

Multiple Choice Questions

1. Which of the following is not a characteristic of concurrent collections in .NET?
   a. Thread-safe operations.
   b. Improved performance in multithreaded scenarios.
   c. Avoidence of all locks internally.
   d. Designed for concurrent access by multiple threads.
2. Which collection is best suited for storing and accessing objects without regard for insertion order?
   a. ConcurrentQueue<T>
   b. ConcurrentStack<T>
   c. BlockingCollection<T>
   d. ConcurrentBag<T>
3. Which method of ConcurrentDictionary<TKey, TValue> helps in updating values automatically?
   a. The TryAdd() method.
   b. The AddOrUpdate() method.
   c. The GetOrAdd() method.
   d. The ContainsKey() method.

4. How does `BlockingCollection<T>` handle capacity limits when adding items?
    a. Throws an exception when capacity is exceeded.
    b. Discards items when capacity is full.
    c. Blocks the adding thread until space becomes available.
    d. `BlockingCollection<T>` has no ability to limit capacity.

Answers

1. a
2. d
3. b
4. c

Questions

1. Are there scenarios where using concurrent collections might introduce overhead compared to non-thread-safe collections?
2. Imagine a file-processing pipeline where files are read, processed, and then written to a different location. Which collections would you use in each stage?
3. How could you combine collections to produce a complex data structure like a thread-safe priority queue?

Key Terms

- **Bag:** A collection data structure where the order of elements is not important
- **FIFO, First-In, First-Out:** An ordering of elements in a collection guaranteeing that the first element added to a collection is the first element removed from the collection
- **LIFO, Last-In, First-Out:** An ordering of elements in a collection guaranteeing that the last element added to a collection is the first element removed from the collection
- **Producer:** A process that retrieves, creates, or organizes data that will be used later
- **Consumer:** A process that consumes, processes, or otherwise uses data produced by producers
- **Producer-Consumer Pattern:** A solution structured using producers and consumers

CHAPTER 7
Parallel Loops in .NET

Introduction

One of the great benefits of multicore processors is their ability to support true parallel processing, where multiple computations can occur simultaneously. Modern CPUs can run many threads or tasks concurrently, leveraging the power of multiple cores to improve performance. We have seen examples of how threads or tasks can be assigned unique responsibilities in an application, performing these responsibilities simultaneously and cooperatively. However, many scenarios require breaking down, or partitioning, large computational tasks into smaller, independent subtasks that can be executed in parallel. This approach, known as **parallel computing**, is a key technique for optimizing the performance of applications, particularly those with computation-intensive workloads.

This chapter will introduce the **`Parallel`** class in .NET, which supports running arrays of delegates in parallel and supports **parallel loops**.

Structure

In this chapter, we will cover the following topics:

- Introduction to **Parallel Loops**
  - Comparison of Sequential and **Parallel Loops**
  - Benefits of Parallelizing Loops
- **Parallel Loops** behind the Scenes
  - Thread-level implementation
  - Load Balancing
  - Integration with the TPL
- Using `Parallel.For`
  - Syntax and Usage
  - Scenarios for Using `Parallel.For`
  - Simple Computation Example
- Using `Parallel.ForEach`
  - Syntax and Usage
  - Key Differences from Parallel.For
  - Data Stream Example
  - Scenarios for Using Parallel.ForEach
- Handling Loop State
  - Managing State Between Iterations
  - Breaking, Stopping, and Skipping
  - Conditionally Exiting Example

- Error Handling
  - Handling Exceptions
  - Best Practices
  - Logging and Retrying Example
- Performance Considerations
  - Balancing Parallelism with Overhead Costs
  - Understanding Partitioning
  - Reducing Contention
- Real-World Example
  - Data Transformation Problem
  - Step-by-Step Implementation
- Testing and Profiling
  - Testing Correctness
  - Profiling Performance
  - Debugging Common Issues
- Invoking Delegates

Introduction to Parallel Loops

Parallel loops are a programming construct that enable iterative operations to be executed concurrently across multiple threads. This approach leverages modern multicore processors to achieve higher efficiency and reduced execution time, especially for data-intensive or computationally heavy tasks. By distributing the iterations of a loop among available threads, **parallel loops** handle thread coordination, **load balancing**, and thread pooling internally, simplifying multithreaded programming for developers.

In .NET, **parallel loops** are supported by the `Parallel` class in the `System.Threading.Tasks` namespace, which provides methods such as `Parallel.For()` and `Parallel.ForEach()` to execute loops in parallel. These methods take care of dividing the workload, managing threads, and ensuring scalability by dynamically adjusting to the system's available resources.

Comparison of Sequential and Parallel Loops

Sequential loops, implemented using the `for` and `foreach` keywords in C#, are fundamental constructs in programming. They enable developers to iterate through collections or ranges, processing each item individually in the order they appear.

For workloads involving small to medium-sized collections or lightweight operations, `for` and `foreach` loops are highly efficient. This efficiency stems from their straightforward design, avoiding the overhead of managing threads or context switching. However, as the number of elements grows, or the operations become more computationally demanding, these loops may encounter scalability challenges, making parallelization techniques a valuable alternative.

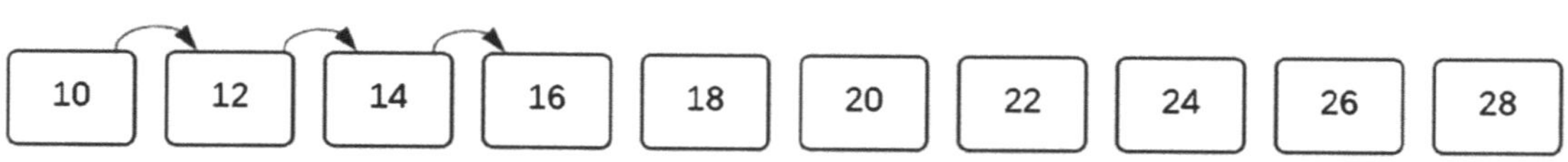

Figure 7.1: *Sequential Loop Collection Processing*

In contrast to **sequential loops**, **parallel loops** can process multiple iterations simultaneously. By **partitioning** collections into smaller chunks, parallel loops enable concurrent processing of these chunks, significantly enhancing performance and throughput. This approach is particularly beneficial for compute-intensive or data-intensive tasks that can be broken down into independent iterations.

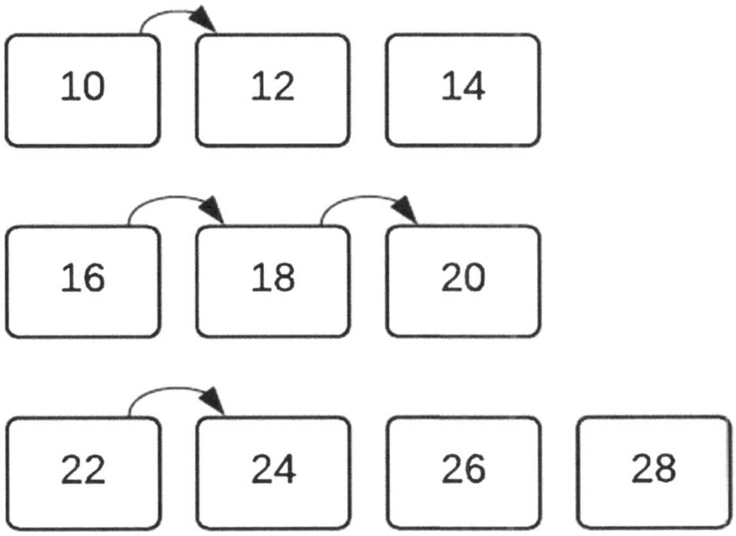

Figure 7.2: *Parallel Loop Collection Processing*

Figures 7.1 and 7.2 illustrate the contrast between **sequential loop** processing and parallel loop processing when handling collections of data. **Parallel loops** can divide large datasets into smaller chunks that are processed concurrently, which provides a significant performance advantage, especially for computationally intensive or large-scale data sets.

Benefits of Parallelizing Loops

Parallel loops introduce more overhead than sequential loops, so they are not applicable to all scenarios. But for situations where each loop iteration will be computationally intense or where the data set is very large, the extra overhead is more than offset by the benefits of parallelism.

Parallel loops have the following general benefits in applicable scenarios:

- **Parallel loops** can significantly improve performance by breaking down the overall workload into smaller chunks and by processing each chunk concurrently.
- Each chunk of work is processed in parallel by different threads, maximizing CPU usage on multicore systems.
- The internal implementation abstracts low-level threading concerns, simplifying the implementation of parallelism.

When deciding whether to use **parallel loops**, it is essential to evaluate the computational intensity and size of the data set. While **parallel loops** can greatly improve performance in suitable scenarios, they introduce overhead that can outweigh their benefits for lightweight or small workloads. By leveraging their ability to maximize CPU usage and abstract low-level threading concerns, **parallel loops** are a powerful tool for optimizing performance in applications where scalability and efficiency are critical.

Parallel Loops Behind the Scenes

Parallel loops in .NET are designed to be easy to use, allowing developers to write multithreaded code with minimal effort. However, behind the scenes, these loops rely on the Task Parallel Library (TPL) to manage the complex orchestration of tasks, thread scheduling, and load balancing. By dynamically splitting work into smaller chunks and assigning them to threads from the thread pool, **parallel loops** adapt to system resources and workload, ensuring efficient execution. Understanding these inner workings provides invaluable insights into optimizing performance, identifying potential bottlenecks, and troubleshooting unexpected behavior in your multithreaded applications.

Thread-Level Implementation

The `Parallel` class in .NET uses the `ThreadPool` to execute its tasks. The `ThreadPool` is a .NET class that manages a pool of worker threads, allowing tasks to execute efficiently by reusing threads and minimizing the overhead of creating and destroying individual threads. By leveraging the `ThreadPool`, the `Parallel` class optimizes task execution, reducing overhead and eliminating the need for developers to manage threads directly.

The `ThreadPool` automatically adjusts the number of threads allocated based on system workload and resource availability, ensuring optimal utilization of system resources without overloading the CPU. When a parallel operation, such as `Parallel.For()` or `Parallel.ForEach()`, is initiated, the `Parallel` class relies on the `ThreadPool` to distribute the work across multiple threads. If the workload is heavy, the `ThreadPool` may allocate more threads to handle the tasks concurrently, while maintaining system performance. Conversely, if the workload is light, the `ThreadPool` can reduce the number of threads, thus conserving resources. This seamless integration of the `ThreadPool` with the `Parallel` class ensures that parallel operations are efficient, scalable, and responsive to system conditions.

We will explore the `ThreadPool` more fully in *Chapter 11: Threading and the Thread Pool.*

Load Balancing

When a **parallel loop** is started, the `Parallel` class uses the `Partitioner` class from `System.Collections.Concurrent` to define a **partitioning** strategy that divides the work into smaller partitions. These partitions are processed concurrently by multiple threads, with the `Partitioner` managing the distribution of work.

To maximize CPU usage, each thread processes chunks of the work from its own queue. It's possible for a thread to finish its work earlier than others. To maintain **load balancing**, the `Parallel` class employs a **work-stealing algorithm**, which works as follows:

1. Threads begin by processing tasks from their own queue.
2. If a thread completes its tasks before others, it "steals" work from another thread's queue to keep busy, usually by taking work from the back of the queue.
3. This process continues until all the work is completed.

This **partitioning** and **work-stealing** mechanism ensures that the workload is distributed as evenly as possible, preventing threads from becoming idle while work remains. By dynamically balancing the load, this approach reduces contention, improves scalability, and helps maximize CPU usage.

Integration with the TPL

The `Parallel` class is part of the Task Parallel Library in .NET. It leverages several other TPL classes and fully supports TPL concepts such as cancellation and error handling. Internally, the **`Parallel`** class depends on the following TPL classes:

- The **`ThreadPool`** is used to manage threads
- The **`TaskScheduler`** is used to schedule tasks
- The **`Partitioner`** performs efficient range **partitioning** for **parallel loops**
- **`ParallelLoopState`** tracks loop state, including whether the loop should exit early

Additionally, methods on the **`Parallel`** class support **`CancellationToken`** to ensure the loop exits safely and efficiently when cancellation is requested. This avoids unnecessary processing when cancellation is requested by the application.

Any errors encountered during processing are aggregated and reported in an **`AggregateException`** instance. This is crucial for understanding and handling any exceptions that arise from **parallel loops** or tasks.

Using `Parallel.For`

The **`Parallel.For()`** method is designed to operate on a range of values from a starting value to an ending value. The range includes the starting value, but does not include the ending value, making it ideal for indexing collections.

The **`Parallel.For()`** method divides the specified range dynamically across multiple threads, which makes it highly efficient for parallelizing tasks that involve iterating over large datasets or performing independent computations for each index. However, because iterations may execute in parallel on different threads, care must be taken to ensure thread safety while accessing shared resources from within the loop delegate.

Syntax and Usage

There are several overloads for **`Parallel.For()`**, the simplest of which takes a starting value, an ending value, and an **`Action`** delegate which will be performed for each iteration. The resulting method call looks like the following:

```
using System;
using System.Threading.Tasks;

Parallel.For(0, 100, i =>
{
    Console.WriteLine("Processing iteration: " + i);
});
```

The example defines a loop that will iterate 100 times and print a message for each iteration. The value of **`i`** will be in the range of 0-99. The method will break the work down into chunks and process each chunk in a different thread. Hence, the output will not be sequential, but exactly one iteration will be processed for each value of **`i`** in the range. The call to **`Parallel.For()`** will block the calling thread until all iterations have completed.

The default chunking behavior is to optimize thread usage dynamically and provide no support for cancellation. This behavior can be customized by using an instance of **`ParallelOptions`** in the method call. This class has three properties that can influence the behavior of the **`Parallel.For()`** loop:

- **`CancellationToken`** can be set to allow the loop to be cancelled.
- **`MaximumDegreeOfParallelism`** can be set to limit the maximum number of concurrent tasks allowed in the loop or -1 if no upper limit is to be applied.

- **`TaskScheduler`** can be set to use a custom task scheduler or left null to use the default scheduler.

Adding cancellation support to the prior example would look something like the following:

```
var cts = new CancellationTokenSource();
var parallelOptions = new ParallelOptions
{
    CancellationToken = cts.Token
};
cts.CancelAfter(50);

try
{
    Parallel.For(0, 100, parallelOptions, i =>
    {
        Console.WriteLine("Processing iteration " + i);
        Thread.Sleep(50);
    });
}
catch (OperationCanceledException) { }
```

The above example adds a **`CancellationTokenSource`** and a **`ParallelOptions`** instance. The **`CancellationTokenSource`** is set to cancel automatically after 50 milliseconds. This causes an **`OperationCanceledException`** to be thrown. However, you must note that the **`OperationCanceledException`** is not wrapped in an **`AggregateException`** instance.

The **`Action`** delegate receives a variable indicating the current iteration as a parameter. In the prior examples, **`i`** is used to represent this value. The delegate can also receive an instance of a **`ParallelLoopState`** class as an optional second parameter. This class allows for gracefully exiting the loop early and detecting whether any unhandled exceptions have been thrown. We will discuss this class in more detail later in this chapter.

Note: *The Action delegate will be called one time for every iteration in the range and the Parallel class takes care of low-level thread synchronization internally, but no synchronization is provided for data accessed by the delegate itself. It is important to provide additional synchronization as necessary for accessing shared objects or data in the Action delegate to avoid race conditions or unexpected behavior.*

Scenarios for Using `Parallel.For`

The **`Parallel.For()`** method is designed for use in processing ranges in large data sets or computationally heavy operations. The following are some common use cases.

Use Case	Description
Data Transformation	Applying one or more transformations to a large set of data
Matrix Operations	Speeding up computationally heavy operations on large matrices, commonly used in machine learning, simulations, or graphic processing
Image Processing	Applying filters, resizing, or modifying images in a batch
Simulation	Running multiple simulations with different parameters in physics engines, game development, or statistical modelling
Data Aggregation and Analysis	Parsing logs, calculating sums or other metrics across large data sets

Rendering 3D Objects	Rendering parts of a 3D scene or animation concurrently
Large-Scale Mathematical Computations	Calculating prime numbers, factorials, or other mathematical sequences

***Table 7.1**: Parallel.For Use Cases*

Simple Computation Example

Let us see how **Parallel.For()** can be used in matrix computations. The following example performs a simple multiplication for each element in a matrix:

```
int[,] matrix = new int[10000, 10000];

var sw = System.Diagnostics.Stopwatch.StartNew();
Parallel.For(0, matrix.GetLength(0), i =>
{
    for (int j = 0; j < matrix.GetLength(1); j++)
    {
        matrix[i, j] = i * j;
    }
});
Console.WriteLine($"Time taken: {sw.ElapsedMilliseconds} ms");

Console.WriteLine("Element at [3, 4]: " + matrix[3, 4]);
Console.WriteLine("Element at [100, 500]: " + matrix[100, 500]);
```

In the above example, a 1000 x 1000 matrix of integers is created. The parallel loop iterates through each row in the matrix in parallel. Each row iteration calls an inner loop that fills each column in the row with the multiplied value of row index * column index. The output is as follows:

Time taken: 51 ms

```
Element at [3, 4]: 12
Element at [100, 500]: 50000
```

There is no additional synchronization applied because every row and column is accessed exactly once by the delegate, so no contention will occur. However, accessing other data sources may require synchronization. Developers should carefully analyze how shared data is accessed by the delegate and plan locking or other synchronization accordingly.

Using Parallel.ForEach

Parallel.For() is designed for efficiently processing ranges of numbers, while **Parallel.ForEach()** is intended for collections that implement **IEnumerable<T>**. The **ForEach()** method takes an **IEnumerable<T>** instance as a parameter and executes an **Action<T>** delegate for each item in the enumeration.

If the enumeration is an array or a list, the framework uses direct indexing to create partitions efficiently. For other types of enumerations, a **Partitioner** instance is used to determine an optimal **partitioning** strategy. This ensures that each item in the collection is processed exactly once, but the processing of items is done in parallel to maximize efficiency and performance.

It is important to note that **Parallel.ForEach()** does not guarantee the order of execution. Additionally, users can pass an **Action<T, ParallelLoopState>** delegate to handle more complex scenarios, such as prematurely breaking or stopping the loop, or to support cancellation. For advanced use cases, custom partitioners can be implemented to fine-tune performance.

Syntax and Usage

The most basic syntax of **Parallel.ForEach()** involves passing an **IEnumerable<T>** instance as the first parameter and passing an **Action<T>** delegate as the second parameter as shown in the following example:

```
var source = new List<string>() { "One", "Two", "Three", "Four", "Five", "Six" };

Parallel.ForEach(source, number =>
{
    Console.WriteLine(number);
});
```

This example creates a list of strings and processes them using **Parallel.ForEach()**. The list is passed as the first parameter and the delegate to process each item is passed as the second parameter. In this example, the variable passed to the delegate is called **number** and the delegate simply prints the contents of this string. Just as **Parallel.For()** does not preserve order, the output from **Parallel.ForEach()** also does not preserve any processing order. The output is something like the following:

```
Four
Two
Six
Five
Three
One
```

The delegate can simply receive the element to process, as the prior example demonstrates, or it can receive more parameters. Like **Parallel.For()**, it can receive a **ParallelLoopState** instance to enable stopping the loop early. Also, it can receive a state parameter, which defaults to the index of the current item in the enumeration but can be customized.

Here are the possible signatures for the **Action** delegate:

- **(T)**: This variable contains the current element being processed
- **(T, ParallelLoopState)**: The element and a **ParallelLoopState** instance, used to safely stop the loop
- **(T, ParallelLoopState, long)**: The element, a **ParallelLoopState**, and the state parameter

A **ParallelOptions** parameter can be passed to provide cancellation support, maximum degree of parallelism control, and a custom task scheduler, the same as with **Parallel.For()**. Let us add cancellation support to the string list example:

```
var source = new List<string>() { "One", "Two", "Three", "Four", "Five", "Six"
};
var cts = new CancellationTokenSource();
var parallelOptions = new ParallelOptions()
{
    CancellationToken = cts.Token
};
cts.CancelAfter(20);

try
{
    Parallel.ForEach(source, parallelOptions, (number, state, index) =>
    {
```

```
            Thread.Sleep(50);
            Console.WriteLine(number + " " + index);
        });
    }
    catch (OperationCanceledException) { }
```

If the source enumeration is not a standard array or list, an instance of the **Partitioner** class is used to partition the data. By default, a system-provided partitioner is used, optimized for most general use cases. For scenarios requiring custom **partitioning** logic, a user-defined **Partitioner** can be created and passed as a parameter to methods like **Parallel.ForEach()**. In such cases, the **Partitioner** is specified in place of the enumeration in the first parameter.

Key Differences from Parallel.For

The parallel loops, **Parallel.For()** and **Parallel.ForEach()** are similar in many respects, but there are some key differences. The following table lists the main differences between them:

Aspect	Parallel.For()	Parallel.ForEach()
Input Type	A numeric range (for example, 0..100)	A collection (for example, **Array**, **List**, **IEnumerable**)
Loop Variable	The numeric index (for example, **int**)	Individual collection item
Use Case	Numeric data processing	Collection or data structure processing

Table 7.2: *Parallel Loop Comparison*

Parallel.For() is designed to iterate over a numeric range, such as a specified "**from**" and "**to**" range of integers. It provides the current index in the range as the loop variable parameter, making it particularly useful for numeric processing tasks. This includes scenarios such as performing operations on arrays or matrices where calculations depend on the index or applying transformations to elements in a computational grid.

In contrast, **Parallel.ForEach()** is designed to process collections such as List, Array, or any enumerable (**IEnumerable**). It provides the current element of the collection as the loop variable parameter, making it ideal for handling non-numeric data or processing large sets of objects. Common use cases include iterating over file paths, applying operations to database query results, or transforming objects in a collection.

Both methods support additional customization using **ParallelOptions**, allowing developers to control the degree of parallelism, enable cancellation, and manage other advanced options for more refined parallel execution.

Data Stream Example

Let us create a simple application that simulates processing a data stream using **Parallel.ForEach()**:

```
using System.Collections.Concurrent;

var source = Enumerable.Range(1, 500);
var squares = new ConcurrentDictionary<int, int>();

Parallel.ForEach(source, number =>
{
    squares[number] = number * number;
});
```

```
Console.WriteLine($"2 squared is {squares[2]:N0}");
Console.WriteLine($"500 squared is {squares[500]:N0}");
```

In the prior example, a simulated data stream is created using the **`Enumerable.Range()`** method. This creates a true **`IEnumerable<int>`** instance. A **`Parallel.ForEach()`** loop is used to calculate the square of each of the numbers in the enumerable and store the result in a **`ConcurrentDictionary<int, int>`** instance. Finally, the sample results are printed. The output is as follows.

```
2 squared is 4
500 squared is 250,000
```

As with **`Parallel.For()`**, **`Parallel.ForEach()`** blocks the calling thread until the loop finishes processing all iterations.

Scenarios for Using `Parallel.ForEach`

`Parallel.ForEach()` is optimized for processing arrays, lists, and other enumerations of any type of data. The following table lists some of the more common use cases:

Use Case	Description
Processing Large Data Sets	Parsing or analyzing data in databases, CSV files, JSON, or other data files
Web Scraping	Scraping data from multiple web sites or APIs simultaneously
Bulk Email	Sending bulk email to a large number of recipients
Data Transformation	Converting or transforming data in a collection
Data Streaming	Real-time processing large or continuous data streams in parallel
Machine Learning and AI	Parallelizing tasks like feature extraction, data augmentation, or batch inference
Bulk Network Operations	Downloading or uploading multiple files in parallel
Bulk File Processing	Processing large directories of files in parallel

Table 7.3: *Parallel.ForEach Use Cases*

Handling Loop State

Parallel loops in C# support two types of state management to handle scenarios where fine-grained control over loop execution or per-thread state is required:

- **ParallelLoopState Parameter**: The **`ParallelLoopState`** parameter can optionally be passed to the body delegate of the loop. This parameter allows for fine control over the loop's execution by enabling features such as:
    - **Stopping the Loop**: Immediately halts execution of the loop iterations that have not yet started but allows already executing iterations to complete.
    - **Breaking the Loop**: Stops iterations from starting beyond a certain point while ensuring that all currently running iterations complete. This is particularly useful for scenarios where an iteration meets a condition and subsequent iterations beyond that point are unnecessary.
- **Local State Parameter**: Parallel loops also support a local state parameter, which allows the custom state to be maintained on a per-thread basis. This state is specific to the thread executing the loop and can be used for tasks such as aggregating data, maintaining counters, or other thread-specific operations. The local state is initialized once for each thread, and its final value can be aggregated after the loop completes.

Managing State Between Iterations

Both parallel loops support a local state parameter in the body delegate. In both loops, this parameter can be defined as needed by implementing an initializer and finalizer delegate. However, in **`Parallel.ForEach()`**, the parameter can be used without an initializer or finalizer. In this case, the local state parameter is of type **`long`** and represents the index of the current element in the enumeration.

To provide a custom state parameter:

1. **Define an initialization function**: This function will return the initial state value for each thread.
2. **Define a main body delegate**: This delegate processes every iteration and returns an updated state. The updated state will be passed to the next iteration that runs on the same thread.
3. **Define a finalization action**: This action receives the final state value for each thread after all iterations assigned to that thread are complete.

When these functions are provided:

- The initializer function is called once per thread before the thread begins processing its iterations.
- The body delegates processes each iteration and manages the thread-local state.
- The finalizer function is invoked after all iterations assigned to a thread have been processed.

This approach is particularly useful for scenarios where **thread-local** computations or resources need to be managed. The following simple example illustrates custom state usage:

```
var source = new List<string>() { "One", "Two", "Three", "Four", "Five", "Six"
};

Parallel.ForEach(source,
    localInit: () =>
    {
        // Initialize thread-local state
        return new List<string>();
    },
    body: (element, state, localState) =>
    {
        // Process the iteration and update thread-local state
        localState.Add(element);
        return localState;
    },
    localFinally: (finalState) =>
    {
        // Handle final thread-local state
        Console.WriteLine($"Thread completed with local state: {string.Join(",
", finalState)}");
    });
```

The output of the previous example looks like this:

```
Thread completed with local state: Two
Thread completed with local state: Five
Thread completed with local state: Four
Thread completed with local state: Three
Thread completed with local state: One
Thread completed with local state: Six
```

Breaking, Stopping, and Skipping

Using the **ParallelLoopState** parameter allows fine control over the loop behavior. With it, you can programmatically break the loop, stop the loop, and determine if individual iterations should continue processing or be skipped.

Calling the **Break()** method indicates that all iterations with an index higher than the current index should be skipped. Iterations with lower indices will still be allowed to process. This is useful in cases where the order of items matters and skipping higher-level indices is sufficient. The **LowestBreakIteration** property can be used to determine the smallest index where **Break()** was called, allowing skipped iterations to check if they should still execute.

The **Stop()** method indicates that all iterations should immediately stop, and any remaining work should be skipped. This is useful in situations where a condition has occurred that requires all processing to halt entirely. Unlike **Break()**, **Stop()** is not index-aware and stops the loop globally.

To determine if the current iteration should continue processing, in the event that **Break()** or **Stop()** has been called, **ParallelLoopState** provides a property called **ShouldExitCurrentIteration**. If this property is true, the current iteration should not process further. A common way to exit the iteration is to use the **return** keyword, but conditional logic can also be used.

Custom logic can also be applied to skip individual iterations. For example, logic can be written to determine if the current index is even and call **return** immediately if true. This would skip every even index in the loop but process all odd indices. Custom logic is independent of **ParallelLoopState** and provides additional flexibility for controlling loop behavior.

Conditionally Exiting Example

The following example uses the **Break()** method to exit a loop conditionally:

```
var source = Enumerable.Range(1, 100);

Parallel.ForEach(source, (number, state, loopState) =>
{
    if (loopState > 9)
    {
        Console.WriteLine("Stopping loop...");
        state.Break();
    }

    if (state.LowestBreakIteration.HasValue && state.LowestBreakIteration.Val-
ue <= loopState)
    {
        Console.WriteLine($"Skipping index {loopState}.");
        return;
    }

    Console.WriteLine($"Processing index {loopState}.");
});
```

In this example, a **Parallel.ForEach()** loop is created to process a stream of numbers. A condition is defined to break the loop if the index of the current number is greater than 9. This condition triggers the **Break()** method of the **ParallelLoopState** object to be called. Another check determines if the **LowestBreakIteration** property has a value and if that value is less than or equal to the index of the current number. If that condition is true, processing is cancelled by using the return keyword. Otherwise, normal processing is allowed to happen.

The output will vary depending on system conditions, but only indices 0 to 9 are processed.

Error Handling

Error handling in parallel loops is critical because the loop iterations are processed on multiple threads. An exception on one of the iterations does not stop processing on any of the other iterations, although it will stop the loop from starting new ones.

Handling Exceptions

Exceptions that are not handled within the loop body stop the loop from starting new iterations and are aggregated into an **`AggregateException`**. When handling this exception, each exception that occurred during loop processing can be accessed through the **`InnerExceptions`** property. Aggregate exceptions are covered in more detail in *Chapter 3, Creating and Running Tasks in C#*.

Alternatively, exceptions can be handled within the loop body itself. This approach allows individual exceptions to be addressed directly and provides an opportunity to take corrective actions, such as retrying the operation or logging the error. It also provides an opportunity to stop further loop processing gracefully in the event of an exception.

Best Practices

The following are general best practices for error handling in parallel loops:

- The parallel loops return a **`ParallelLoopResult`** instance that is used to check if the loop completed successfully. This struct contains two properties. **`IsComplete`** and **`LowestBreakIteration`**. **`IsComplete`** is true if the loop completes successfully and false otherwise. If **`LowestBreakIteration`** has a value, it is the index of the lowest iteration when **`Break()`** was called. This result is useful if the loop may have been stopped prematurely by calling **`Break()`** or **`Stop()`**.
- In many applications, handling exceptions within the loop body provides fine control over exception handling and logging. If transient faults are a possibility, handling exceptions in the loop body provides a way to retry faults. Handling exceptions in this way also allows fine control over stopping the loop in cases where continuing is unnecessary of destabilizing.
- If handling exceptions in the loop body is not beneficial, ensure the **`AggregateException`** is caught in a **`try-catch`** block outside the loop. This enables logging of all inner exceptions that occurred during processing.
- Always log or record all exceptions to avoid "silent failures" which could lead to undiagnosed problems in the application. Silent failures are exceptions that are not handled and logged properly.
- Gracefully exit the loop if exceptions occur, especially when further iterations are unnecessary after an exception. Calling **`Break()`** will stop iterations beyond the current one but allow current and lower iterations to continue. Calling **`Stop()`** will cancel all iterations regardless of index.
- Test your loops under conditions that are likely to cause errors and profile their performance. This ensures that error handling does not introduce bottlenecks or degrade the benefits of parallelism.
- Avoid nested parallel loops. Nesting parallel loops can lead to exponential growth of thread usage and can quickly overwhelm systems.

Logging and Retrying Example

The following example shows how logging and retrying can be implemented in parallel loops:

```
using System.Collections.Concurrent;

var errors = new ConcurrentBag<string>();
var results = new ConcurrentDictionary<int, int>();

Parallel.For(1, 101, data =>
{
    var processed = false;
    while (!processed)
    {
        try
        {
            ProcessData(data);
            processed = true;
        }
        catch (InvalidOperationException ex)
        {
            errors.Add(ex.Message);
        }
    }
});

Console.WriteLine($"Square of 1 is {results[1]}");
Console.WriteLine($"Square of 100 is {results[100]}");
Console.WriteLine($"Errors: {errors.Count}");
Console.WriteLine($"Sample error: {errors.First()}");

void ProcessData(int data)
{
    if (Random.Shared.Next(0, 5) == 0)
        throw new InvalidOperationException($"Simulated failure for item
{data}.");

    results.TryAdd(data, data * data);
}
```

In this example, the **`ProcessData()`** method simulates transient faults using a random number generator. If a fault occurs, an exception is thrown. Otherwise, the loop data is processed. In the loop body delegate, the exception is caught. Logging is simulated by adding the error message to a **`ConcurrentBag<string>`** instance. In the case of an exception, processing is retried until it is successful.

A sample output might look like this:

```
Square of 1 is 1
Square of 100 is 10000
Errors: 27
Sample error: Simulated failure for item 55.
```

Performance Considerations

Parallel loops can be high performance solutions to CPU or I/O bound problems. But they do introduce overhead that is not present in sequential loops. Understanding the overhead and tuning the solution is crucial for achieving optimal performance with parallel loops.

Balancing Parallelism with Overhead Costs

Parallel loops introduce overhead in the form of thread scheduling, thread creation, and synchronization (that is, if shared resources are used). These loops divide the work into chunks and schedule threads or tasks. This incurs some computational overhead. If too many threads are created and scheduled, frequent context switching can reduce performance. And if synchronization occurs locking and managing resources can add to performance overhead.

Therefore, the size of the computational workload needs to be large enough to justify the extra overhead. For smaller size workloads, stick to sequential loops and avoid the extra overhead. Here are a few general rules of thumb that are helpful to know about when working with **parallel loops**:

- Less than 10,000 items, sequential loops are generally faster
- Between 10,000 and 100,000 items, parallel might be faster but should be tested
- At 100,000 or greater items, parallel is usually faster

Since every scenario is different, testing and profiling each one of them is highly recommended.

Too many threads can overwhelm the system, especially in a shared environment like a server or in a resource intensive application. You can compensate for this by adjusting the maximum degree of parallelism. By default, the **parallel loops** use the number of logical cores on the system, which is ideal for CPU bound workloads. I/O bound workloads would benefit from more threads than this to compensate for I/O wait times. To set the maximum degree of parallelism, use the **`ParallelOptions.MaxDegreeOfParallelism`** property.

Understanding Partitioning

By default, the **parallel loops** automatically determine chunk size. However, you can manually adjust this for better performance. Larger chunk sizes reduce thread scheduling overhead but could lead to uneven load distribution. Smaller chunk sizes are better for **load balancing** but increase scheduling overhead. Larger chunks may be better for quicker processing times and smaller chunks more beneficial for longer processing times. Again, testing and profiling will help determine a good balance. To adjust chunk sizes, use the create method on the **`Partitioner`** class. For example, **`Partitioner.Create(0, data.Length, chunkSize: 100)`** will create a ranged partitioner with a custom chunk size of 100.

Note: *It is possible to create a custom partitioner that provides full control of all aspects of **partitioning** by using the Partitioner or **`OrderedPartitioner`** classes as a base. Creating a custom partitioner is beyond the scope of this book.*

Reducing Contention

Sharing data in parallel threads can lead to reduced performance due to locks or other synchronization overhead. Therefore, it is important to consider strategies to avoid synchronization overhead as much as possible.

One way to avoid using shared data is to use the **`ThreadLocal<T>`** class. By using this class, each thread obtains its own instance of the variable and can update it without sharing data. At the end of the loop, the values for each thread instance can be aggregated.

The following code demonstrates the use of **ThreadLocal<T>**:

```
var threadLocalData = new ThreadLocal<int>(true);
try
{
    Parallel.For(1, 1000, number =>
    {
        threadLocalData.Value = number * 5;
    });

    int finalValue = threadLocalData.Values.Sum();
    Console.WriteLine($"The final value is {finalValue:N0}.");
    Console.WriteLine($"Number of threads: {threadLocalData.Values.Count}.");
}
finally
{
    threadLocalData.Dispose();
}
```

The output will show up as:

```
The final value is: 7,175.
Number of threads: 7.
```

In this example, a **thread-local** variable called **threadLocalData** is used to collect data from processing in a **Parallel.For()** loop. The variable is constructed with a flag to indicate that tracking all thread values is enabled. As the loop is processed, the **thread-local** value is updated for the executing thread. Since this value is always local to the currently executing thread, no synchronization or locking is required. After the loop, the final values for each thread are aggregated into one sum and printed. The **ThreadLocal<T>** class implements **IDisposable** so be sure to always call **Dispose()** when finished.

Another way to avoid using shared data is to use local variables initialized in **localInit** delegate and summarized in the **localFinally** delegate. Any type of variable can be initialized and used in this way, even complex classes.

The following example demonstrates the use of **localInit** and **localFinally** delegates to reduce shared data synchronization:

```
int total = 0;

Parallel.For(1, 1000, () => 0, (number, state, localValue) =>
{
    localValue = number * 5;
    return localValue;
}, localValue =>
{
    Interlocked.Add(ref total, localValue);
});

Console.WriteLine($"Total value: {total:N0}");
```

The output shows up as:

```
Total value: 19,575
```

The prior example initializes a local state value to an integer value of 0 in the **localInit** delegate. This is called for each thread processing the loop. The value is passed to the body delegate in the **localValue** parameter. The loop body modifies this value and returns it. The returned value will then be passed to the next iteration processed on the same thread. After each thread finishes processing, the **`localFinally`** delegate is called. This delegate aggregates the thread's final value into a final total, which is printed after the loop finishes.

Other options for reducing contention in parallel loops include the following steps:

- Consider using concurrent collections. These are optimized to minimize synchronization and maximize performance
- Batching work into larger chunks instead of processing each individual item can reduce overall synchronization. Processing batch chunks may include a sequential loop inside the parallel loop body to process individual items
- If locking cannot be avoided, consider using fine grained locks like **`ReaderWriterLockSlim`**. This type of lock is especially useful for scenarios where reads are much more prevalent than writes
- For primitive shared variables, the Interlocked class can avoid synchronization overhead and ensure high performance

It is recommended to avoid shared data as much as possible. If it cannot be avoided, consider the above strategies to optimize performance.

Real-World Example

Developers often need to write software to transform large datasets These transformations can take many forms, such as formatting, aggregation, masking, type conversion, or data cleaning. **Parallel loops** provide an efficient way to process large datasets by applying transformations concurrently, improving performance. In this section, we will build a sample data transformation application that demonstrates many of the parallel processing strategies covered in this chapter.

Data Transformation Problem

Data transformations are often complex with many data elements involved. To keep this example simple, we will be parsing a database of names into their component elements (such as, first name, middle name, and last name) and storing the result in a data store. The names will have a single first name followed by an optional middle name and a last name, all separated by spaces. For example:

- Sarah Connor
- Alan Dwight Maxwell

There will be one million names in the data source and the target data store will be empty. Most often, in a real-world scenario the data source and data store would be files or databases, but to keep the code simple and portable, the data source and data store will be kept entirely in memory.

Step-by-Step Implementation

Most data transformation solutions can be laid out in three steps: obtaining the data from the data source, applying the transformation, and storing the transformed data.

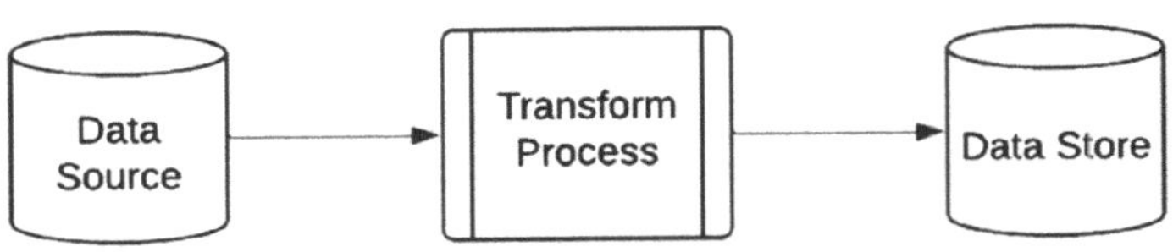

Figure 7.3: *Data Transformation Process*

In our implementation, we will represent the data source and data store in separate classes. The transformation process in this case is not very complex, so we will represent it in a single method.

The first step is to create the data source class. The purpose of this class will be to access the data and present it in an **IEnumerable<string>** instance, which can be consumed by the **Parallel.ForEach()** method. In a production environment, the data would likely be in files or in a database and the data source class would control access to it, but in our case, we will generate the data randomly. The following code uses arrays of names to randomly generate the names:

```
using System.Text;

namespace DataTransformation
{
    class DataSource
    {
        private string[] firstNames = ["John", "Sally", "Deborah",
            "Frank", "Robert", "Giles", "Nancy", "Vincent", "Lisa",
            "Leslie", "Gus", "Mary", "Bruce"];
        private string[] lastNames = ["Brown", "Smith",
            "Corey", "Johnson", "Michaels", "Durant",
            "Mitchel", "Donovan", "O'Riely", "McConnel"];

        public IEnumerable<string> GetData()
        {
            for (int i = 0; i < 1000000; i++)
            {
                var nameBuilder = new StringBuilder();
                nameBuilder.Append(GetRandomElement(firstNames));
                if (Random.Shared.Next(0, 10) < 3)
                    nameBuilder.Append(" " + GetRandomElement(firstNames));
                nameBuilder.Append(" " + GetRandomElement(lastNames));

                yield return nameBuilder.ToString();
            }
        }

        private string GetRandomElement(string[] array)
        {
            return array[Random.Shared.Next(0, array.Length)];
        }
    }
}
```

The prior code defines the **DataSource** class which uses arrays to randomly create names. The code is thread-safe by using **Random.Shared** and static arrays to generate numbers for the enumerable. This code will create one million names when the enumerable is iterated.

The next step is to define the transformation process. The requirement is to take the name string and parse it into individual name components. We will create a class called **StandardData** to hold the transformation results. The transformation logic can be contained in a single method, so we will put that logic into this class as well. If the required transformations were more complex, it might be better to implement them in separate classes. The constructor will call a **parse method** which will transform the incoming data and store the results in the class properties. The following example defines the **StandardData** class:

```
namespace DataTransformation
{
    class StandardData
    {
        public StandardData(string data)
        {
```

```
            ParseData(data);
        }

        public string? FirstName { get; set; }

        public string? LastName { get; set; }

        public string? MiddleName { get; set; }

        private void ParseData(string data)
        {
            var names = data.Split(" ");

            FirstName = names[0];
            if (names.Length == 3)
            {
                MiddleName = names[1];
                LastName = names[2];
            }
            else
                LastName = names[1];
        }
    }
}
```

Next, we will need to define the data store. In a real-world scenario, this class would most likely access files or databases to store the transformation results. In our case we will use a **`ConcurrentBag<StandardData>`** to store the transformed data. The **`DataStore`** class will expose two methods, one to store and one to retrieve data. The following code defines the **`DataStore`** class:

```
using System.Collections.Concurrent;

namespace DataTransformation
{
    class DataStore
    {
        private ConcurrentBag<StandardData> dataStore =
            new ConcurrentBag<StandardData>();

        public void StoreData(StandardData data)
        {
            dataStore.Add(data);
        }

        public IEnumerable<StandardData> GetElements(int count)
        {
            return dataStore.Take(count);
        }
    }
}
```

Now that the details of the solution are implemented, we can now implement the **parallel loop** to finalize the solution. In the main method, we will create an instance of our **`DataSource`** and **`DataStore`** classes. We will need to log any errors encountered during processing. Since we don't have an external logging system for this project, we will simply log any exceptions into a **`ConcurrentBag<string>`**

instance. A **Parallel.ForEach()** loop will be used to process all the data concurrently. The code for the main method is as follows:

```
using System.Collections.Concurrent;

namespace DataTransformation;

internal class Program
{
    static void Main(string[] args)
    {
        var source = new DataSource();
        var dataStore = new DataStore();
        var dataLog = new ConcurrentBag<string>();

        Parallel.ForEach(source.GetData(), data =>
        {
            try
            {
                StandardData standardData = new StandardData(data);
                dataStore.StoreData(standardData);
            }
            catch (Exception ex)
            {
                dataLog.Add(ex.ToString());
            }
        });

        Console.WriteLine("Transformation complete. Sample records:\n");

        foreach (var data in dataStore.GetElements(5))
            Console.WriteLine($"{data.LastName}, {data.FirstName}
{data.MiddleName}");

        Console.WriteLine($"\n{dataLog.Count} errors.");
    }
}
```

The output from the project will be random but will be something like this:

```
Transformation complete. Sample records:

Mitchel, John
Johnson, Vincent Lisa
Mitchel, Bruce
Corey, Sally
Johnson, Vincent Robert

0 errors.
```

As you can see, **parallel loops** can greatly simplify parallel processing problems such as data transformation on large scale datasets. By leveraging the power of parallel computing, we can significantly reduce processing times and improve the efficiency of our algorithms. This not only enhances performance, but also opens new possibilities for tackling complex computational challenges that were previously unmanageable.

Testing and Profiling

When working with **parallel loops**, it is crucial to ensure both speed and correctness. This section covers strategies for testing, profiling, and debugging **parallel loop** code to identify performance bottlenecks and concurrency issues effectively.

Testing Correctness

Parallel loop code must be correct in its basic functionality as well as all edge cases and error paths. The following strategies will help ensure that your code is robust and correct in all cases:

- Unit test using deterministic input. Test both the **parallel loop** and a sequential loop with the same input and ensure the results are identical. If the loop processes random data, ensure that the seed value is fixed for all tests to ensure predictability.
- Test for race conditions using data that might trigger concurrency issues in shared data. This may involve multiple iterations using shared data.
- Perform load testing using a very large data set or under heavy load. This may help reveal issues that may not occur under normal conditions.
- Consider re-running tests in automated loops or performing fuzz testing to uncover sporadic or non-deterministic bugs. Fuzz testing involves testing with massive amounts of randomly generated data.
- Practice defensive programming by inserting assertions and logging into the loop. Ensure that logs are thread-safe and structured.
- If the loop contains locking, be sure to test for deadlock conditions.
- Profile memory usage to ensure that the loop is not leaking resources.
- Ensure that exceptions are properly aggregated and handled. In loops that allow cancellations, ensure that the `OperationCancelledException` is handled correctly.

Profiling Performance

Performance profiling will help to optimize parallel loop code and ensure appropriate use of system resources. Consider the following strategies to achieve this:

- Use Visual Studio Profiler to visualize CPU and thread usage and to help identify hotspots in **parallel loop** code. Consider using Instrumentation or Sampling profiling modes for detailed insights into CPU-bound parallel loops
- Consider a benchmarking tool like `BenchmarkDotNet` to set up benchmarks for **parallel loops**. It provides rigorous statistical measurements and helps you compare the performance of different implementations and options
- Use Visual Studio Concurrency Visualizer to check if the loop is causing too many threads to be created or excessive context switching. We will cover Concurrency Visualizer in *Chapter 12, Debugging Parallel Applications in Visual Studio*
- Monitor CPU and memory usage to ensure that increased performance does not come at the expense of system resources. Use tools such as Task Manager, Performance Monitor (`PerfMon`), or dotnet-counters to track CPU, memory, and garbage collection metrics
- Use ETW-based tools like Windows Performance Analyzer for deeper insights into thread scheduling, context switching, and CPU utilization
- Monitor Thread Pool Usage by checking `ThreadPool.GetAvailableThreads()` to ensure that the loop is not exhausting the thread pool, which could lead to performance bottlenecks

Debugging Common Issues

Debugging parallel loop issues can be challenging, even if best practices are followed. The following guidelines will help detect and fix many common issues:

- If the loop uses shared resources, ensure that proper synchronization is used or use thread-safe collections or methods
- Ensure exceptions are properly caught in the body of the loop or outside the loop. When the **`AggregateException`** is caught, ensure the **`InnerExceptions`** collection is inspected to understand all issues
- Visual Studio Concurrency Viewer can help visualize threads that are waiting on locks or other resources. We will cover Concurrency Visualizer in *Chapter 12, Debugging Parallel Applications in Visual Studio*
- If a bug is hard to reproduce in the parallel loop, try isolating a single iteration or subset of iterations and run them sequentially to better understand the issue
- Leverage the Parallel Stacks and Tasks windows in Visual Studio to visualize what each thread is doing. We will cover these in detail in *Chapter 12, Debugging Parallel Applications in Visual Studio*
- Some types of bugs could be due to resource starvation. Monitor CPU and memory usage to ensure proper system resource usage

Invoking Delegates

Besides providing support for **parallel loops**, the Parallel class also supports running an array of tasks. The **`Parallel.Invoke()`** method accepts an array of Action delegates that will be run in parallel, with an optional **`ParallelOptions`** parameter. The **`Parallel`** class handles the details of task scheduling and thread management.

As with the **parallel loops**, if any exceptions are thrown from any Action delegate in the array, they are wrapped in an **`AggregateException`** instance. Exceptions can also be caught in the body of the Action delegates themselves.

There is no thread synchronization provided for shared data accessed in these delegates, so the same best practices used for shared data in parallel loops also applies to invoked delegates. There is no **partitioning** for data supported by the **`Invoke()`** method.

The **`Parallel.Invoke()`** method provides a simple way to run a set of arbitrary tasks in parallel, without worrying about the details of task or thread management.

Conclusion

Conclusively, **parallel loops** in Visual Studio provide a robust mechanism for managing and optimizing concurrent tasks. By utilizing **parallel loops**, developers can harness the full potential of multi-core processors, enabling efficient execution of code segments. It is essential to implement best practices for thread synchronization and resource management to prevent issues such as race conditions and resource starvation. Understanding and mastering these techniques will not only elevate the performance of your applications but also ensure their reliability and stability in handling parallel computations effectively.

In the next chapter, we will discover how to apply the power of parallelism to LINQ queries. LINQ, or Language Integrated Query, is a powerful feature in .NET that allows developers to write expressive and concise queries for data manipulation. By integrating parallelism with LINQ, we can significantly enhance the performance of these queries, especially when dealing with large datasets.

Points to Remember

- **Parallel loops** improve performance by breaking down work into smaller chunks that are executed concurrently on multiple threads.
- The `Parallel` class provides support for **parallel loops** in .NET. It also provides a way to invoke an array of tasks on multiple threads.
- The `Parallel` class does not provide thread synchronization for shared data accessed in delegates.
- Locking and thread synchronization should be reduced or eliminated to maintain performance in **parallel loops**.
- Proper error handling and logging are crucial to ensure that parallel loop code is robust and maintainable.

Multiple Choice Questions

1. What is the main advantage of using **parallel loops** over traditional sequential loops?
    a. They always execute faster than sequential loops.
    b. They run iterations in parallel, potentially improving performance.
    c. They are easier to debug than sequential loops.
    d. They execute only on a single thread.
2. Which of the following statements about **parallel loops** are true?
    a. They guarantee order of execution.
    b. They always use all available CPU cores.
    c. They automatically partition the workload across multiple threads.
    d. Both a and c
3. How can you stop further iterations in a `Parallel.For()` loop?
    a. By throwing an exception
    b. By using `ParallelLoopState.Break()`
    c. By setting a cancellation token
    d. Both b and c
4. What is the recommended way to handle exceptions in `Parallel.ForEach()`?
    a. Use a `try-catch` block inside the loop
    b. Use a global exception handler
    c. Catch and handle AggregateException
    d. Both a and c

Answers

1. b
2. c
3. d
4. d

Questions

1. Parallel loops can improve performance by utilizing multiple CPU cores. Under what circumstances might they degrade performance instead?
2. What potential race conditions or data corruption issues can arise and how might they be mitigated?
3. How would you decide whether to use parallel loops or `Task.Run()` or `Thread.Start()` in an application?
4. How would you choose between using `Parallel.For()` and `Parallel.ForEach()` in your application?
5. Parallel loops are a powerful way to achieve parallelism. What are some scenarios where other patterns might be more appropriate?

Key Terms

- **Parallel Computing:** breaking down or **partitioning** large computational tasks into smaller, independent subtasks
- **Parallel Loops:** methods that are syntactically like sequential loops but process iterations in parallel
- **Sequential Loops:** built-in loop keywords that run all iterations on a single thread
- **Load Balancing:** ensuring that work is evenly distributed between threads
- **Partitioning:** dividing the work into smaller chunks that can be executed concurrently by multiple threads
- **Work-Stealing:** a process of a thread taking work from another thread when its own work queue is completed
- **Thread-Local:** a variable that is stored separately for each thread. Each thread has its own instance of the variable

CHAPTER 8
Language-Integrated Query (LINQ) for Parallelism

Introduction

Language-Integrated Query or **LINQ** provides a powerful and expressive way to manipulate collections in C#, but it executes sequentially. As datasets expand, sequential execution can become a bottleneck. To address this, .NET introduces **Parallel LINQ** (also known as **PLINQ**), an extension of **LINQ** that leverages multi-core processors to execute queries in parallel. **PLINQ** can significantly improve performance by distributing work across multiple threads, but it also introduces challenges such as partitioning, load balancing, and error handling. This chapter explores how and when to use **PLINQ** effectively, covering syntax, performance considerations, and real-world applications to help you write highly efficient parallel queries.

Structure

In this chapter, we will cover the following concepts:

- Introduction to **LINQ** and **PLINQ**
  - Overview of **LINQ**
  - Evolution of **LINQ** to **PLINQ**
  - Benefits of Using **PLINQ**
- Using PLINQ
  - Understanding Performance Benefits
  - Comparing **LINQ** and **PLINQ**
  - Identifying Workload Bottlenecks
  - Performance Trade-offs
- Basic Syntax and Usage
  - Enabling Parallelism
  - Writing Basic Queries
  - Controlling Degree of Parallelism
  - Parallel Aggregation and Processing
- Partitioning and Load Balancing
  - Partitioning Internals
  - Impact on Performance
  - Load Balancing Strategies

- Controlling **PLINQ**
    - Forcing Parallelization
    - Thread Affinity
    - Combining Control Methods
    - Synchronization Considerations
- Error Handling
    - Exception Handling in **PLINQ**
    - Dealing with Non-Deterministic Failures
    - Strategies for Fault Tolerance
- Real-World Example
    - Processing a Large Dataset Efficiently
    - Implementing Parallel Search
    - Measuring Performance

Introduction to LINQ and PLINQ

Parallel LINQ (abbreviated as PLINQ) is an extension of **LINQ** that enables parallel execution of queries for improved performance. Since **PLINQ** builds upon **LINQ**, a solid understanding of **LINQ** is essential before diving into its parallel counterpart. Therefore, before exploring **PLINQ**, we will first review **LINQ** and its basic usage.

Overview of LINQ

Queries are a foundational aspect of data retrieval and management. They enable developers to filter, join, sort, group, aggregate, and select specific fields from data using a simple, declarative language. Many developers are familiar with these concepts in relational databases through Structured Query Language (SQL), but querying capabilities extend to many other data formats and storage models, including XML, JSON, and NoSQL databases. However, there is no single standard query language for all these models, due to which developers have to learn multiple **query** languages to work with different data sources.

Language-Integrated Query (LINQ) addresses this challenge by making queries a standard part of the C# language and enabling providers to interface with databases and other data formats. **LINQ** supports a declarative syntax that is easy to learn and understand called **query** syntax, as well as a method-based fluent syntax. With **LINQ**, **queries** are written directly in C#, simplifying and standardizing data retrieval across different sources.

LINQ queries work with collections of data, whether in-memory or from external sources such as databases. In-memory data sources must implement **IEnumerable<T>** to support **LINQ** operations, while external sources, such as databases that support deferred execution, must implement **IQueryable<T>**. Although the **query** syntax remains the same for both, **IQueryable<T> queries** are translated into provider-specific commands before execution, whereas **IEnumerable<T> queries** operate directly in memory.

The following example uses **LINQ** to filter a list of numbers from 1 to 100 and only displays those divisible by 10:

```
var source = Enumerable.Range(1, 100);

var tens = from num in source
           where num % 10 == 0
```

```
                select num;

        foreach (var number in tens)
            Console.WriteLine(number);
```

In this example, an enumeration is created called **source** containing the numbers between 1 and 100. Another enumeration is created called **tens** using a **LINQ** query. The **LINQ** statements filter the numbers in **source** to only those divisible by 10 using a **where** clause. Finally, the **tens** enumeration is printed. The output is as follows:

```
10
20
30
40
50
60
70
80
90
100
```

It is important to understand that a **LINQ query** is not executed immediately but uses deferred execution. The **query** is only executed when its results are enumerated, such as in a foreach loop, or when an aggregation method like **Count()** or **Sum()** is called. Additionally, methods like **ToList()** or **ToArray()** force immediate execution by materializing the results into a collection.

This section provides a basic understanding of **LINQ**, which is required to understand **Parallel LINQ**. Providing a more comprehensive tutorial is beyond the scope of this book.

Evolution of LINQ to PLINQ

LINQ revolutionized data processing in .NET by providing a declarative, readable way to manipulate collections. However, traditional **LINQ queries** execute sequentially, which can become a bottleneck when processing large datasets. Since **LINQ** operates on a single thread by default, it fails to take full advantage of modern multicore processors, limiting performance in CPU-intensive scenarios.

To address this limitation, .NET introduced **Parallel LINQ (PLINQ)**, which extends **LINQ** by enabling automatic parallelization of **queries**. **PLINQ** distributes query operations across multiple threads using the Task Parallel Library (TPL), improving efficiency in computationally expensive workloads. It supports **queries** on **IEnumerable<T>** collections of in-memory data while preserving standard **LINQ** syntax.

PLINQ allows developers to leverage parallelism without altering the core structure of a **LINQ** query. However, parallel execution introduces additional overhead, such as thread management and workload distribution, which can sometimes negate performance benefits for smaller datasets or simple operations. As a result, **PLINQ** is most effective for CPU-bound tasks involving large datasets, complex computations, or scenarios where independent operations can be efficiently executed in parallel.

By understanding its strengths and limitations, developers can determine when **PLINQ** is the right tool for optimizing query performance in .NET applications.

Benefits of Using PLINQ

In previous chapter, you may have noticed that **PLINQ** shares similarities with parallel loops. Both work with **IEnumerable<T>** and use parallelism to improve processing time on multicore systems.

The main advantage of **PLINQ** is that it enables **LINQ** queries to execute in parallel, automatically handling data partitioning and workload balancing. In contrast, parallel loops (`Parallel.For()` and `Parallel.ForEach()`) execute a loop body in parallel for each iteration but require more explicit control over thread execution.

PLINQ also optimizes **query** execution by evaluating whether parallelism is beneficial based on factors such as dataset size and **query** complexity. If **PLINQ** determines that parallelism will not benefit performance, the **query** may still run sequentially. By default, **PLINQ** may reorder **query** results for performance reasons, but ordering can be preserved at a potential performance cost using optional method calls.

Using PLINQ

While **PLINQ** offers the benefits of parallelism, it also introduces overhead costs. Understanding both the advantages and trade-offs of **PLINQ** is essential to determining whether it is the right choice for a given workload.

Understanding Performance Benefits

When a **query** is transitioned to **PLINQ**, the following steps occur:

1. The source enumeration is partitioned into chunks using an appropriate partitioning strategy, such as range or hash partitioning based on the query and data structure.
2. The chunks are distributed across multiple threads, which may run on different CPU cores based on system workload and available resources.
3. The results are aggregated after processing, with potential overhead for ordering or synchronization.

By default, **PLINQ** dynamically determines the optimal level of parallelism based on factors such as workload complexity, data size, and available CPU cores. If the overhead of parallelization outweighs the benefits, **PLINQ** may revert to sequential execution. However, this behavior can be overridden using explicit parallel execution modes.

Several factors may cause **PLINQ** to execute a **query** sequentially, including:

- The data set is too small for parallelization to provide meaningful speedup
- The **query** is computationally lightweight (e.g., simple filtering), making parallel execution unnecessary
- The **query** involves stateful computations, such as order-dependent operations (such as `OrderBy`, `GroupBy`, and `Aggregate`)
- The **query** depends on external resources like I/O operations, where parallelism offers limited benefit
- The workload requires frequent synchronization, which can introduce contention and negate parallel gains

For large data sets or compute-intensive **queries**, **PLINQ** can significantly improve performance and scalability. However, careful profiling is recommended to ensure that parallel execution provides tangible benefits over sequential processing.

Comparing LINQ and PLINQ

There are important considerations to account for when designing and implementing **PLINQ queries** that are different than **LINQ** implementations. The following table highlights these differences:

Aspect	LINQ	PLINQ
Execution Mode	Sequential execution on a single thread	Parallel execution using multiple threads
Performance	Suitable for small datasets or light computations	Improves performance for large datasets and heavy computations
Ordering	Preserves original order	Does not guarantee order by default
Exception Handling	Standard exception handling	Requires `AggregateException` handling
Resource Utilization	Uses fewer system resources	Uses more CPU cores and higher memory usage

Table 8.1: *LINQ vs PLINQ Comparison*

Identifying Workload Bottlenecks

Queries that perform complex calculations, transformations, or aggregations can be CPU intensive and may benefit from PLINQ. Distributing these types of calculations across several CPU cores often provides an increase in performance. Complex calculations may include image processing, encryption, matrix operations, or complex custom algorithms.

Likewise, **queries** processing large numbers of elements will also benefit. The following rules can be used as a guideline:

- 10,000 elements or less should be processed by **LINQ**
- 10,000 – 100,000 **PLINQ** may be faster
- More than 100,000 **PLINQ** is likely faster

If a query involves I/O operations, **PLINQ** may not help since these operations do not benefit from partitioning. Asynchronous I/O should be used in these situations.

Visual Studio Profiler can be used to analyze **LINQ queries** and identify CPU bottlenecks that could benefit from **PLINQ**. Using Visual Studio Profiler will be covered in more detail in *Chapter 12: Debugging Parallel Applications Using Visual Studio.*

Check CPU utilization during **LINQ queries**. If a single CPU core is busy while others are idle, **PLINQ** can help distribute the load.

Time queries using Stopwatch before and after applying **PLINQ** to ensure the **query** is benefiting from parallelism. This approach can also be used to fine tune **queries** and apply appropriate options.

Performance Trade-Offs

PLINQ generally excels at optimizing **queries** that perform data transformations (for example, **`Select`**, **`Where`**, and **`GroupBy`**) and aggregations (like Sum, Max, Average). This is especially beneficial for large datasets or when performing complex filtering (in a Where clause) or computationally expensive projections (in a Select clause). By leveraging multiple processor cores, **PLINQ** can significantly speed up CPU-bound operations.

However, **PLINQ** is not always advantageous. It provides little to no benefit and may even degrade performance in the following scenarios:

- **I/O-bound operations**, such as database **queries** or file I/O, where the bottleneck is waiting for external resources rather than CPU computation
- **Queries accessing shared resources** that require synchronization, as locking mechanisms reduce parallel efficiency
- **Scenarios requiring strict ordering**, since **PLINQ** processes data in parallel, often resulting in unordered output. **PLINQ** can be forced to produce ordered output, but this often reduces performance
- **Small datasets**, where the overhead of parallelizing the query outweighs the performance gains of parallel execution

PLINQ is a powerful tool for accelerating CPU-bound queries by parallelizing data transformations and aggregations, particularly on large datasets with complex filtering or computationally expensive operations. However, these benefits diminish while dealing with I/O-bound tasks, shared resource contention, strict ordering requirements, or small datasets where parallelization overhead outweighs performance gains. Understanding these trade-offs is crucial for effectively leveraging **PLINQ** to optimize **query** performance without introducing unnecessary complexity or inefficiencies.

Basic Syntax and Usage

Parallel LINQ is an extension to basic **LINQ** and uses a simple syntax to enable parallelism. **PLINQ** is implemented as a set of extension methods that follow fluent syntax. These methods are applied to the source **`IEnumerable<T>`** instance in a **LINQ query**.

Enabling Parallelism

Enabling **Parallel LINQ (PLINQ)** on a **query** is done by calling the **`AsParallel()`** method on an **`IEnumerable<T>`** instance, allowing **LINQ** queries to execute in parallel using multiple threads. This method is typically applied to **LINQ** queries that operate on in-memory collections (**`IEnumerable<T>`**) rather than deferred-execution data sources like **`IQueryable<T>`**, which are often used with databases.

The following example shows how **PLINQ** can be enabled on a **LINQ query**:

```
var source = Enumerable.Range(1, 10000);

var thousands = from num in source.AsParallel()
           where num % 1000 == 0
           select num;

foreach (var number in thousands)
    Console.WriteLine(number);
```

In the prior example, the **`AsParallel()`** method is applied to the **`IEnumerable<int>`** that is the source for the **LINQ** statement. This ensures that the **LINQ** query can run in parallel. The output is as follows:

```
1000
2000
3000
4000
5000
6000
7000
8000
```

```
9000
10000
```

Note: *PLINQ does not work with* `IQueryable<T>` *sources such as* **LINQ** *to SQL or* **LINQ** *to Entities.* `IQueryable<T>` *is designed to work with external sources such as databases. Parallel* **LINQ** *is designed to work in-memory and will not benefit an external source. It is possible to work with the result of an* `IQueryable<T>` **query** *by converting it to an enumerable using* `AsEnumerable()`*, but this should only be done if parallelism will benefit processing of the resulting enumeration.*

Writing Basic Queries

As noted in the prior example, the `AsParallel()` method is applied to the query source in the query's from clause. This enables **PLINQ** on a **LINQ** query. The **query** is analyzed, and parallelism is applied if the analysis determines a benefit to using it. This analysis is not perfect and should not be relied on exclusively. The `AsParallel()` method is the only required one to enable **PLINQ**.

Because it is based on the TPL, **PLINQ** supports cancellation. Adding a call to `WithCancellation()` adds support for cancellation to a **PLINQ query**. Cancelling a **PLINQ query** causes an `OperationCanceledException` to be thrown.

The following example adds cancellation support to a **PLINQ query**:

```
var source = Enumerable.Range(1, 1000000);
var cts = new CancellationTokenSource();
cts.CancelAfter(50);

var thousands = from num in source.AsParallel().WithCancellation(cts.Token)
                where num % 1000 == 0
                select num;

try
{
    foreach (var number in thousands)
        Console.WriteLine(number);
}
catch (OperationCanceledException)
{
    Console.WriteLine("The operation was canceled.");
}
```

The prior example shows a **PLINQ query** processing a large set of numbers and filtering for every number that is divisible by 1000. A cancellation token source is used to cancel the query before it completes by adding the `WithCancellation()` method call and passing the `CancellationToken`. The output is something like the following:

```
706000
6000
56000
106000
207000
257000
357000
407000
The operation was canceled.
```

PLINQ utilizes fluent syntax to control its behavior, enabling developers to configure various execution aspects by chaining method calls with appropriate parameters. This approach allows for fine-grained control over parallel execution, degree of parallelism, ordering, exception handling, and other features.

Controlling Degree of Parallelism

By default, **PLINQ** determines the degree of parallelism to apply by analyzing several factors, including the structure of the enumeration being processed and the number of available CPU cores. Typically, **PLINQ** will use a number of tasks equal to the logical core count of the system. However, this behavior can be explicitly controlled using the **`WithDegreeOfParallelism()`** method.

The integer passed to **`WithDegreeOfParallelism()`** must be in the range of 1 to 512 and represents the maximum number of concurrent tasks that can be used to process the **query**. **PLINQ** will not exceed this number but may use fewer tasks depending on workload conditions. The following example demonstrates how to control the degree of parallelism in a **PLINQ query**:

```
var source = Enumerable.Range(1, 100000);

var filtered = from num in source.AsParallel().WithDegreeOfParallelism(2)
               where num % 10000 == 0
               select num;

foreach (var number in filtered)
    Console.WriteLine(number);
```

In this example, a list of 100,000 numbers is processed, filtering out numbers that are evenly divisible by 10,000. The **`WithDegreeOfParallelism(2)`** method ensures that a maximum of two tasks are used to process the **query**. Since **PLINQ** executes **queries** in parallel, the output order is not guaranteed. A sample output might look like the following:

```
60000
70000
80000
90000
100000
10000
20000
30000
40000
50000
```

Restricting the degree of parallelism can be useful for optimizing performance in certain environments, such as on a busy server cluster where excessive parallelism might compete for resources. However, limiting parallelism too much may reduce throughput, so careful tuning is essential depending on workload characteristics.

Parallel Aggregation and Processing

PLINQ provides specialized methods for processing **query** results in parallel, including **`Aggregate()`** and **`ForAll()`**, which enable efficient computation and processing by leveraging multiple threads.

The **`Aggregate()`** method in **PLINQ** performs an accumulation operation in parallel. Unlike the standard **LINQ `Aggregate()`**, which processes elements sequentially, **PLINQ**'s version executes the aggregation function across partitions concurrently, improving performance in many scenarios. However, since aggregation operations often require a specific order of execution, care must be taken when designing parallel aggregation logic to ensure correctness.

The following example demonstrates the usage of **PLINQ `Aggregate()`**:

```
var source = Enumerable.Range(1, 100);

var sum = (from number in source.AsParallel()
```

```
                 where number % 2 == 0
                 select number)
                 .Aggregate(0, (subtotal, num) => subtotal + num);

    Console.WriteLine($"The sum of even numbers is: {sum}.");
```

This example uses **PLINQ** to select all even numbers between 1 and 100 and uses the **`Aggregate()`** method to sum the resulting number enumeration. The output is as follows:

The sum of even numbers is: 2550.

The **`ForAll()`** method processes each element of a **PLINQ query** result in parallel using a provided delegate. Unlike **foreach**, which guarantees sequential execution, **`ForAll()`** does not preserve the order of elements and is optimized for performance. It is particularly useful for operations with side effects, such as writing to a database, logging, or updating a UI in a thread-safe manner.

The following example demonstrates the usage of **`ForAll()`**:

```
var source = Enumerable.Range(1, 100);

(from number in source.AsParallel()
 where number % 10 == 0
 select number)
.ForAll(num =>
 Console.WriteLine($"Processing {num} on thread
{Thread.CurrentThread.ManagedThreadId}."));
```

This example runs a process for every number in the source enumeration that is divisible by 10. The output will be something like the following:

```
Processing 70 on thread 14.
Processing 80 on thread 15.
Processing 50 on thread 12.
Processing 40 on thread 11.
Processing 30 on thread 10.
Processing 100 on thread 1.
Processing 20 on thread 4.
Processing 60 on thread 13.
Processing 10 on thread 9.
Processing 90 on thread 16.
```

Since **`ForAll()`** executes operations in parallel, any shared resources must be managed carefully to avoid race conditions. The **`Aggregate()`** function may require a custom combiner function for reducing partial results if the default behavior is not sufficient. Additionally, **PLINQ** does not preserve order by default, which can impact operations that rely on sequential processing.

To ensure that **PLINQ** respects the order of the original enumeration, use the **`AsOrdered()`** method. This method forces **PLINQ** to maintain the original sequence of elements throughout query execution. However, preserving order may introduce additional overhead, potentially reducing parallelization benefits and impacting performance.

Partitioning and Load Balancing

A large part of the work that **PLINQ** does to parallelize queries involves partitioning the source enumeration. To optimize **queries** effectively, it is essential to understand the default partitioning strategies that **PLINQ** provides.

For most general scenarios, the default partitioning works well, distributing work efficiently across available threads. However, in cases where finer control is needed, **PLINQ** supports custom partitioning through the **Partitioner<T>** class, found in the **System.Collections.Concurrent** namespace. This is the same mechanism used for custom partitioning in parallel loops, allowing developers to define how data is split among tasks for better performance in specific workloads.

Partitioning Internals

PLINQ automatically selects a partitioning strategy based on the properties of the **IEnumerable<T>** source and the type of query being processed. It can choose one of three strategies: **Range Partitioning**, **Chunk Partitioning**, or **Hash Partitioning**, which are mentioned as follows:

Range Partitioning

This strategy is used when the source collection has an indexer and a known length, and when the query does not involve grouping or joining. The collection is divided into smaller contiguous ranges, each processed by a different thread. For example, thread A processes the range of indices 0-50, thread B processes 51-100, thread C processes 101-150, and so on.

Examples of collections with indexers and known lengths include arrays, which have a Length property and an indexer; and lists, which have a Count property and an indexer.

Range Partitioning is most effective when the processing time for each element is roughly the same, as it evenly distributes work across threads.

The following example uses **Range Partitioning** to find the square of an array of numbers:

```
var source = Enumerable.Range(1, 1000000).ToArray();

var squares = (from number in source.AsParallel()
               select number * number).ToList();

Console.WriteLine("First 10 squares:");
for (int i = 0; i < 10; i++)
    Console.WriteLine(squares[i]);
```

The output is as follows:

```
First 10 squares:
1
4
9
16
25
36
49
64
81
100
```

This example creates an array of numbers and uses **PLINQ** to find the square of each number, which is then stored in a **List<int>**. The first 10 squared numbers are then printed. **Range Partitioning** is selected automatically because the **query** does not have joins or grouping and the array has a known size and an index.

Chunk Partitioning

Chunk Partitioning is used when the source is an enumerable without an indexer or a known size, and when the **query** does not involve grouping or joining.

With this approach, each thread pulls a chunk of elements from the enumeration, processes them, and then retrieves another chunk. This continues until all elements have been processed.

Chunk Partitioning is especially effective when processing times vary significantly between elements. Threads that complete their work faster can process more chunks, leading to better load balancing.

The following example demonstrates **Chunk Partitioning** in **PLINQ**:

```
var source = Enumerable.Range(1, 1000000);

var roots = (from number in source.AsParallel()
             select Math.Sqrt(number)).ToList();

Console.WriteLine("First 10 roots:");
for (int i = 0; i < 10; i++)
    Console.WriteLine(roots[i]);
```

The prior example calculates the square root of each element in an enumeration of numbers using **PLINQ** and stores the results in a **`List<double>`**. Since the source in this case does not have an index or a known size and there is no grouping or joining, **Chunk Partitioning** is used.

Hash Partitioning

Hash Partitioning is applied when the **query** involves grouping or joining elements. Elements with the same hash key are processed in the same partition, ensuring that related elements are handled together.

The hash key typically corresponds to the key used in **`GroupBy`** or Join operations, making this strategy particularly efficient for such queries.

The following example groups words by first letter using **PLINQ**:

```
var source = new[] {"apple","apricot",
    "avocado","blueberry","strawberry",
    "blackberry","raspberry" };

var groupedWords = from word in source.AsParallel()
                   group word by word[0] into wordGroup
                   select new { Key = wordGroup.Key, Words = wordGroup };

foreach (var group in groupedWords)
    Console.WriteLine(
        $"Words beginning with {group.Key}: {string.Join(", ", group.Words)}.");
```

The output is as follows:

```
Words beginning with b: blueberry, blackberry.
Words beginning with a: apple, apricot, avocado.
Words beginning with s: strawberry.
Words beginning with r: raspberry.
```

The prior example uses an array of words as a source and groups the words by first letter using **PLINQ**. Because the **query** uses grouping, **Hash Partitioning** is used to process the **query**.

Impact on Performance

Each built-in **PLINQ** partitioning strategy affects performance differently and is better suited for specific workloads. Fine-tuning **PLINQ** performance involves structuring the **query** and source enumeration to target a partitioning strategy that minimizes bottlenecks and optimizes thread utilization.

- **Range Partitioning** works well when processing time per element is uniform. **PLINQ** pre-allocates contiguous ranges of elements to each thread, ensuring even work distribution when processing is consistent. However, if processing times vary significantly, some threads may finish their queues early while others remain busy in a phenomenon called **thread starvation**. This results in underutilization of available cores.
- **Chunk Partitioning** is best suited for workloads where processing time varies greatly between elements. Instead of assigning fixed ranges, **PLINQ** dynamically assigns smaller chunks of data to threads as they complete work. This minimizes **thread starvation** by ensuring that no thread remains idle for long periods. However, **Chunk Partitioning** introduces overhead from frequent task scheduling and synchronization, which can slightly reduce efficiency compared to **Range Partitioning** for uniform workloads.
- **Hash Partitioning** is the most effective method for **queries** involving grouping or joining, as it ensures elements with the same key are processed by the same thread. This can reduce contention while processing related elements. However, if the hash function produces an uneven distribution, some partitions may receive more elements than others, causing workload imbalance and reducing overall efficiency.

PLINQ automatically selects an appropriate partitioning strategy, but developers can fine-tune behavior when necessary. Controlling partitioning is a key optimization tool for ensuring even work distribution, reducing contention, and improving throughput in parallel **queries**.

Load Balancing Strategies

Balancing the workload between threads is essential for optimizing **PLINQ queries**. Ideally, each thread should perform an equal amount of work to prevent bottlenecks and minimize task-switching overhead. The first step in achieving this balance is selecting the appropriate partitioning strategy, as different workloads benefit from different approaches.

Range Partitioning works best when each element takes approximately the same amount of time to process. This method minimizes the overhead associated with task switching by dividing the data into evenly sized ranges and assigning them to different threads. On the other hand, **Chunk Partitioning** is more effective when processing times vary significantly. Instead of dividing work upfront, this strategy dynamically assigns chunks to threads as they become available, ensuring that slower threads do not hold back overall execution. While **Chunk Partitioning** introduces some scheduling overhead, it prevents **thread starvation** and improves overall performance in non-uniform workloads.

For queries involving grouping or joins, **Hash Partitioning** ensures that elements with the same key remain together. This can be crucial for operations that require local aggregation before merging results. However, hash collisions can sometimes lead to an uneven distribution of work, so it is most effective when the number of unique keys is large and well-distributed.

When built-in partitioning strategies do not provide optimal performance, custom partitioners can be created using `Partitioner.Create()`. This allows developers to fine-tune how data is distributed across threads to better match the workload's characteristics. The following example demonstrates how to create a partitioner with no buffering, allowing each thread to fetch items from the enumeration one at a time:

```
using System.Collections.Concurrent;

var source = Enumerable.Range(1, 1000000);
var partitioner = Partitioner.Create(source, EnumerablePartitionerOptions.
NoBuffering);
```

```
var squares = (from number in partitioner.AsParallel()
               where number % 1000 == 0
               select (uint)(number * number)).ToList();

Console.WriteLine("First 10 squares:");
for (int i = 0; i < 10; i++)
    Console.WriteLine(squares[i]);
```

The output is as follows:

```
First 10 squares:
196000000
225000000
256000000
289000000
324000000
361000000
441000000
484000000
529000000
576000000
```

This partitioner enforces a fine-grained work distribution strategy, where each thread fetches one item at a time, reducing the risk of an unbalanced workload. However, because no buffering is used, frequent synchronization between threads can increase overhead, especially when operations are short-lived. This trade-off should be carefully considered when tuning performance.

In cases where workloads are highly unbalanced and built-in partitioners do not provide sufficient control, fully custom partitioners can be implemented by inheriting from `OrderablePartitioner<T>`. Custom partitioning allows dynamic adjustments based on processing time, finer control over chunk sizes, and optimizations to reduce thread contention. However, because custom partitioners require additional implementation effort, they should only be used when default strategies fail to distribute work efficiently.

Choosing the right **PLINQ** partitioning strategy is critical to achieving peak performance. **Range Partitioning** is effective when processing times are predictable, while **Chunk Partitioning** adapts to workloads with significant variability. **Hash Partitioning** ensures proper grouping for operations that depend on key locality. When none of these approaches suffice, custom partitioners provide an alternative but require careful tuning. By selecting the right partitioning method, developers can achieve better parallel efficiency, reduce contention, and improve overall throughput.

Controlling PLINQ

PLINQ provides several methods to control parallelism in **queries**, allowing developers to fine-tune execution for performance and resource efficiency. These methods are available for both **query** syntax and fluent syntax; however, they are particularly useful in fluent syntax, which offers greater flexibility for fine control. Therefore, the examples in this section use fluent syntax:

Forcing Parallelization

PLINQ's default behavior is to analyze the **query** structure and source enumeration to determine whether parallelization will provide a performance benefit. If **PLINQ** determines that parallel execution would not be advantageous due to factors like small data size or operations with high overhead, it may automatically fall back to sequential execution. In most cases, this adaptive behavior is beneficial, but there are situations where developers may need to override this decision and force parallel execution.

The **WithExecutionMode()** method allows developers to explicitly control PLINQ's execution strategy. This method accepts a **ParallelExecutionMode** parameter with two possible values:

- **Default**: The default **PLINQ** behavior, where parallel execution is used only if **PLINQ**'s internal analysis determines that it will lead to a performance improvement
- **ForceParallelism**: Forces **PLINQ** to execute the query in parallel, regardless of the default analysis

The following example demonstrates the use of **WithExecutionMode()** to enforce parallel execution:

```
var source = Enumerable.Range(1, 100).ToArray();

var results = source.AsParallel()
              .WithExecutionMode(ParallelExecutionMode.ForceParallelism)
              .Where(number => number % 10 == 0)
              .Select(number => number * number);

foreach (var result in results)
    Console.WriteLine(result);
```

This example has a source with only 100 elements and very simple query operations. This query would normally result in sequential execution, but since **WithExecutionMode()** is specified with **ParallelExecutionMode.ForceParallelism**, the **query** will run in parallel.

Forcing parallel execution should only be used when it is known that parallelism will yield a performance improvement. In some cases, forcing parallel execution can introduce unnecessary overhead, especially when working with small datasets or simple operations. Thorough testing with realistic data is essential to ensure that forcing parallelism results in actual performance gains.

Thread Affinity

Thread affinity refers to a task or operation that must consistently execute on a specific thread or set of threads. This is often required for operations that depend on thread-local storage, UI thread constraints, or native code interactions that require execution on a fixed thread.

PLINQ uses the .NET Thread Pool to automatically assign partitioned work to threads, optimizing for performance through dynamic load balancing and work stealing. This means that **PLINQ** does not guarantee that a particular task will execute on the same thread throughout its lifecycle. As a result, tasks that require **thread affinity** may experience issues when executed within a **PLINQ** query.

Thread affinity is not required in most scenarios, but it is critical in certain cases, such as:

- **Thread-Local Storage (ThreadLocal<T>)**: If a task relies on thread-local data, being scheduled on different threads can lead to lost or inconsistent values
- **GUI Applications (WPF/WinForms)**: UI elements can only be updated from the main UI thread. UI-bound operations should be marshaled back using **Dispatcher.Invoke()** (WPF) or **Control.Invoke()** (WinForms)
- **Interacting with Native Code**: Some unmanaged libraries, such as COM objects or DirectX, require execution on a specific thread due to threading model constraints

PLINQ does not provide a built-in mechanism to enforce **thread affinity** while executing **queries**. Therefore, care must be taken to avoid using **PLINQ** for tasks that require strict **thread affinity**. Instead, design **PLINQ** queries to execute independently of **thread affinity**, and if necessary, marshal the results back to a specific thread after processing. If parallel execution is required for tasks that demand **thread affinity**, consider using alternative approaches such as parallel loops or custom **TaskScheduler** implementations to ensure correct execution. Parallel loops are discussed in detail in *Chapter 7: Parallel Loops in .Net*. Implementing a custom **TaskScheduler** is covered in *Chapter 9: Advanced Task Management*.

Combining Control Methods

When using fluent syntax in **PLINQ**, control methods apply to the query from the point they are introduced to the end of the query, or until another control method overrides them. Some operations, such as filtering, benefit from parallel execution, while others, such as ordering, inherently require sequential processing for correctness and efficiency.

For example, the following **query** filters one million numbers for those that are divisible by 100,000, then switches to sequential mode to order the numbers, and takes the top five results:

```
var source = Enumerable.Range(1, 1000000);

var results = source.AsParallel()
                .Where(number => number % 100000 == 0)
                .AsSequential()
                .OrderByDescending(number => number)
                .Take(5);

foreach (var result in results)
    Console.WriteLine(result);
```

Since filtering does not require order to be preserved, **AsParallel()** is used before **Where()** to maximize performance. However, ordering operations like **OrderByDescending()** require sequential processing to maintain correctness. By switching to sequential mode with **AsSequential()** before ordering, the **query** avoids unnecessary parallel overhead while ensuring the final output is correctly sorted.

Similarly, **AsOrdered()** and **AsUnordered()** can be combined in a **query** to balance ordering requirements and performance. **AsOrdered()** ensures that elements are processed and emitted in the order of the original sequence after parallel execution, which can be useful when maintaining order is necessary. However, preserving order during parallel processing introduces overhead, as additional synchronization is required to maintain the sequence.

Conversely, **AsUnordered()** removes the requirement to preserve order, allowing subsequent operations to run with greater parallel efficiency. This is particularly useful when ordering is necessary for part of a **query** but can be disregarded later to improve performance. By selectively applying **AsOrdered()** and **AsUnordered()**, developers can fine-tune **PLINQ queries** to balance correctness and efficiency.

Synchronization Considerations

For optimal performance, methods used in **PLINQ** queries should be **pure functions**, which means that they do not access shared resources or cause side effects. Custom operations, such as those in **Select()** or **ForAll()**, should ideally not update shared data or collections, as this can introduce race conditions and undefined behavior.

If aggregation is required, consider using **Aggregate()** or **Sum()**, which are optimized for parallel execution. However, keep in mind that:

- **Sum()** is thread-safe but only applies to numeric operations
- **Aggregate()** follows a three-phase execution:
    1. **Seed initializer** runs once separately for each partition

2. **Function method** runs in parallel within each partition
3. **Combiner method** merges the results across partitions

Design aggregations with these stages in mind to ensure thread safety and avoid unnecessary synchronization.

For custom aggregations, consider using the **`Interlocked`** class for simple atomic updates (e.g. incrementing a counter). When working with shared collections, use thread-safe concurrent collections such as **`ConcurrentBag<T>`** and **`ConcurrentDictionary<TKey, TValue>`**, which allow safe data modifications in parallel **queries**.

Avoid using explicit locks (e.g. **`lock`**, **`Mutex`**, **`Monitor`**) inside **PLINQ**. These can introduce deadlocks and significantly degrade performance. If synchronization is necessary, prefer lock-free approaches such as **`Interlocked`** operations or concurrent collections.

By default, **PLINQ** processes elements in an unordered manner for maximum parallel efficiency. If result ordering is required, the **`AsOrdered()`** operator can be used to maintain the original sequence. However, enforcing order reduces parallel performance by requiring synchronization points between threads. Use **`AsOrdered()`** only when necessary, such as when applying ordered aggregation or producing sorted output, and consider whether a sequential **LINQ** query or using the **`AsSequential()`** method might be more appropriate in such cases.

Error Handling

Proper error handling in **PLINQ** requires catching and handling the **`AggregateException`**, which encapsulates multiple exceptions that may occur during parallel execution. Understanding how to inspect these exceptions and applying appropriate fault tolerance strategies ensures robustness in **PLINQ**-based applications.

Exception Handling in PLINQ

In **PLINQ**, exceptions that occur during **query** execution are aggregated into an **`AggregateException`**, capturing all exceptions that arise across parallel threads. To handle these exceptions properly, developers must catch **`AggregateException`** and inspect the individual exceptions within it. This can be done using the **`InnerExceptions`** property, which provides a collection of all captured exceptions, or by calling the **`Flatten()`** method to merge nested **`AggregateException`** instances into a single list for easier processing. A more in-depth discussion of handling **`AggregateException`** is covered in *Chapter 3: Creating and Running Tasks in C#.*

If the **query** supports cancellation using the **`WithCancellation()`** method, it may throw an **`OperationCanceledException`** when the cancellation token is signaled. Unlike other exceptions in **PLINQ**, **`OperationCanceledException`** is not wrapped in an **`AggregateException`** and should be caught separately in its own catch block.

The entire query should be enclosed in a **`try-catch`** block to properly catch both **`AggregateException`** and **`OperationCanceledException`** at the highest level. Additionally, if **`Select`** or **`Where`** clauses contain logic that could produce errors for individual elements, consider wrapping those sections in **`try-catch`** blocks to prevent failures on a single element from terminating the entire query. This is especially useful when transient errors, such as network timeouts or temporary database unavailability, can occur. In such cases, implementing retry logic with exponential backoff may help maintain query reliability.

At a minimum, exceptions should be logged for debugging purposes. Additionally, depending on the application requirements, developers may consider other strategies, such as adjusting the degree of parallelism using **WithDegreeOfParallelism()**, handling transient failures with retries, or applying graceful degradation techniques to ensure resilience in parallel execution.

Dealing with Non-Deterministic Failures

Failures in **PLINQ** queries can be intermittent or non-deterministic due to the nature of concurrency, where execution order and operation timing are unpredictable. These failures often arise from race conditions, thread scheduling variations, or resource contention. Since intermittent failures can be difficult to detect and debug, it is important to follow best practices to minimize their occurrence and handle them effectively when they arise.

1. **Minimize Locks in Select or Where Clauses**. Avoid using locks inside **Select** or **Where** clauses in **PLINQ** whenever possible, as they can degrade performance and lead to deadlocks. Instead, prefer thread-safe collections such as **ConcurrentDictionary<TKey, TValue>** or **ConcurrentBag<T>** for managing shared state. When atomic updates are required, use the **Interlocked** class to ensure correctness without excessive contention.
2. **Manage Access to Shared External Resources**. Accessing shared resources such as files or databases directly within a **PLINQ** query can introduce race conditions and performance bottlenecks. Instead of modifying shared resources inside **PLINQ**, consider collecting results in memory and performing updates after the **query** completes. If concurrent access is unavoidable, use appropriate synchronization techniques such as **SemaphoreSlim**, **BlockingCollection**, or database transactions to prevent conflicts.
3. **Preserve Processing Order When Necessary**. **PLINQ** processes elements in an unpredictable order, which can impact queries where order matters. If ordering is essential, use **AsOrdered()** to maintain the original sequence while still taking advantage of parallel execution. However, note that **AsOrdered()** may reduce performance by limiting parallelism. If full ordering is required for the final output, consider using **AsSequential()** after processing to restore order while minimizing performance impact.

Non-deterministic failures in **PLINQ** can be challenging to diagnose and resolve, but through these best practices, developers can mitigate common issues and improve the reliability of parallel queries. Careful design choices, such as minimizing shared state, using thread-safe data structures, and managing resource access effectively, allow **PLINQ** to deliver both performance and correctness in multithreaded applications.

Strategies for Fault Tolerance

PLINQ queries should be surrounded by **try-catch** blocks that catch and process **AggregateException**. Since **AggregateException** can contain multiple inner exceptions, each should be logged or handled appropriately to aid debugging and maintenance. Additionally, if the **query** supports cancellation, the **try-catch** block should separately catch and process **OperationCanceledException** to ensure graceful termination when cancellation is requested.

If fault tolerance is a priority, consider the following strategies to make your **query** code more resilient:

- **Efficiently Merging Results**: After parallel processing, results must be merged. Use **WithMergeOptions()** to optimize this process and avoid memory exhaustion, especially for large **queries**. Choose an appropriate mode from the following:
  - **NotBuffered**: Streams results as they become available
  - **AutoBuffered** (default): Uses a moderate buffer to balance performance and memory use
  - **FullyBuffered**: Waits until all results are available before outputting them

- **Handling Failures at the Item Level**: If a failure while processing a single item should not cause the entire **query** to fail, wrap the select logic in a **try-catch** block. The catch block should log the error and return either a default value or an error indicator. If filtering out failed results is acceptable, apply filtering logic such as **`Where(result => result != null)`** afterward.
- **Retrying Transient Errors**: If transient faults could occur in the select logic, implement a retry mechanism with exponential backoff to improve resilience without overwhelming external systems. The retry logic should have a maximum attempt limit and log failures at each stage.

Transient faults most often arise during I/O operations. Including I/O—such as network or disk access—within PLINQ Select logic defeats the purpose of parallelism and should be avoided. However, transient faults can also occur in simulations that emulate I/O using memory constructs, or in unit tests that mock I/O failure scenarios. In rare cases, exceptions may also arise from issues like shared memory race conditions or corrupted deserialized data. In these scenarios, retry logic can still be useful. The following is a simple example that demonstrates how to apply retry logic to handle transient faults in PLINQ.

```
using System;
using System.Linq;
using System.Threading;
using Microsoft.Extensions.Logging;

using var loggerFactory = LoggerFactory.Create(builder =>
    builder.AddSimpleConsole().SetMinimumLevel(LogLevel.Information));
var logger = loggerFactory.CreateLogger("TransientRetry");

var results = Enumerable.Range(1, 20)
    .AsParallel()
    .Select(i => Retry(() => Simulate(i), logger, maxRetries: 3, baseDelayMs:
100))
    .ToList();

results.ForEach(Console.WriteLine);

string Simulate(int value)
{
    if (value % 7 == 0 && Random.Shared.NextDouble() < 0.5)
        throw new InvalidOperationException($"Transient failure for {value}");
    return $"Processed {value}";
}

T Retry<T>(Func<T> action, ILogger logger, int maxRetries, int baseDelayMs)
{
    for (int attempt = 0; ; attempt++)
    {
        try { return action(); }
        catch (Exception ex) when (attempt < maxRetries)
        {
            int delay = baseDelayMs * (1 << attempt);
            logger.LogWarning(ex, "Attempt {Attempt} failed. Retrying in
{Delay} ms...", attempt + 1, delay);
            Thread.Sleep(delay);
        }
        catch
        {
            logger.LogError("All {Max} attempts failed.", maxRetries);
```

```
                throw;
            }
        }
    }
```

In the example, a PLINQ query uses a Select statement that calls a method named `Simulate()`, which may occasionally fail. Failures are simulated by throwing an exception based on random number generation. To handle these transient faults, the `Retry()` method implements retry logic: it catches the exception, waits for an exponentially increasing delay, and retries the operation up to a specified number of attempts.

Each retry attempt and any final failure (after exceeding the retry limit) is logged using **`Microsoft.Extensions.Logging`**. Because failures are randomized, the output can vary between runs. The following is one example of possible output:

```
warn: TransientRetry[0]
      Attempt 1 failed. Retrying in 100 ms...
      System.InvalidOperationException: Transient failure for 14
         at Program.<<Main>$>g__Simulate|0_2(Int32 value) in C:\Users\mcjef\source\repos\Chapter 08\ParallelLinqDemo\RetryFaultsDemo\Program.cs:line 20
         at Program.<>c__DisplayClass0_1.<<Main>$>b__4() in C:\Users\mcjef\source\repos\Chapter 08\ParallelLinqDemo\RetryFaultsDemo\Program.cs:line 12
         at Program.<<Main>$>g__Retry|0_3[T](Func`1 action, ILogger logger, Int32 maxRetries, Int32 baseDelayMs) in C:\Users\mcjef\source\repos\Chapter 08\ParallelLinqDemo\RetryFaultsDemo\Program.cs:line 28
Processed 1
Processed 2
Processed 3
Processed 4
Processed 5
Processed 6
Processed 7
Processed 8
Processed 9
Processed 10
Processed 11
Processed 12
Processed 13
Processed 14
Processed 15
Processed 16
Processed 17
Processed 18
Processed 19
Processed 20
```

By implementing these fault tolerance strategies, **PLINQ** queries can be made more resilient to failures, ensuring that exceptions, resource constraints, and transient errors do not compromise the overall stability of the application. A well-structured approach to error handling, result merging, and retries will enhance reliability while maintaining the performance benefits of parallel execution.

Real-World Example

The following real-world example demonstrates how to leverage **PLINQ** for efficient parallel search operations. To ensure independence from external resources, the dataset will be generated in memory.

Processing a Large Dataset Efficiently

PLINQ can significantly improve query performance for large data sets, particularly when processing over 100,000 elements. However, the actual benefit depends on workload characteristics, such as CPU-bound operations and data partitioning efficiency.

In this example, we will process a dataset of 1,000,000 elements with multiple search criteria. Given the dataset size and complexity, PLINQ appears to be a suitable choice.

To ensure optimal execution time, CPU utilization, and memory usage, we will follow these steps:

1. **Establish a Baseline:** First, run the query using standard LINQ and measure its execution time
2. **Apply PLINQ:** Convert the query to use PLINQ and compare performance against the baseline to confirm a speedup
3. **Profile the Query:** Use Visual Studio Profiler or another profiling tool to analyze CPU usage, thread efficiency, and memory consumption

Profiling and debugging techniques will be covered in greater depth in *Chapter 12, Debugging Parallel Applications Using Visual Studio.* These performance monitoring techniques will help fine-tune the query for optimal performance.

Implementing Parallel Search

In this example, we have a dataset of 1,000,000 people, each with an Id, Name, and Age. To keep the example simple, these objects are generated in memory. Our goal is to find middle-aged people, defined as those between 40 and 59 years old.

The **query** creates the objects using a **`Select()`** statement and filters them using a **`Where()`** clause. Let us examine the implementation:

```
using System.Diagnostics;

var source = Enumerable.Range(1, 1000000);

var middleAged = source.AsParallel()
    .Select(i => new Person { Id = i, Name = $"Person {i}", Age = i % 70 })
    .Where(person => person.Age <= 60 && person.Age > 39);

try
{
    var stopwatch = Stopwatch.StartNew();
    Console.WriteLine($"Number of middle age people = {middleAged.
Count():N0}");
    Console.WriteLine($"Elapsed time: {stopwatch.ElapsedMilliseconds}");
}
catch (AggregateException ex)
{
    foreach (var exception in ex.InnerExceptions)
        Console.WriteLine(ex.Message);
}

class Person
{
```

```
        public int Id { get; set; }
        public string Name { get; set; }
        public int Age { get; set; }
    }
```

We measure **query** performance using the **Stopwatch** class. Running the **query** without **AsParallel()** (standard **LINQ**) results in 71 milliseconds on our test system. Adding **AsParallel()** reduces this to 34 milliseconds, achieving a 2.1x speedup.

The output is as follows:

```
Number of middle age people = 299,996
Elapsed time: 34
```

Note: *Elapsed times may vary based on system hardware configuration, system load, available resources, and operating system scheduling.*

This improvement demonstrates how **PLINQ** can significantly enhance query performance by utilizing multiple CPU cores for data processing.

Measuring Performance

Optimizing **queries** is essential for achieving peak performance. Accurately measuring **query** performance allows developers to fine-tune optimizations and evaluate the effectiveness of performance-tuning actions.

Avoid using **DateTime.Now** to measure performance, as it lacks the necessary precision for short-duration processes. Instead, use the high-resolution **Stopwatch** class from **System.Diagnostics** for more accurate time measurements. When profiling query performance with **Stopwatch**, execute the **query** multiple times and calculate the average time to minimize variability caused by system noise, background processes, or caching effects. Additionally, performing a warm-up run before collecting measurements helps account for JIT compilation overhead.

PLINQ introduces overhead due to parallelization, so it may not always be faster than sequential **LINQ** for small data sets or simple queries. Testing with various data sizes helps determine the break-even point where parallelization becomes beneficial. Computationally expensive queries are more likely to see performance gains. By default, **PLINQ** determines the level of parallelism, but developers can fine-tune it using **WithDegreeOfParallelism(n)**, ensuring CPU resources are used efficiently without excessive context switching.

Using tools like Visual Studio Profiler, PerfView, or JetBrains dotTrace provides deeper insights into CPU utilization, memory allocation, and thread behavior. These profiling tools help assess whether parallelization is yielding meaningful performance improvements.

Effectively measuring **PLINQ** performance is crucial for making informed optimizations. By using high-resolution timers, running multiple iterations, evaluating **query** complexity, and leveraging profiling tools, developers can gain a clear understanding of when and how parallelization benefits their workloads. Careful performance analysis ensures that **PLINQ** is used where it truly adds value, leading to efficient and scalable applications.

Conclusion

Parallel LINQ (PLINQ) extends the power of **LINQ** by seamlessly incorporating parallelism, making it a valuable tool for handling computationally intensive queries or processing large datasets efficiently. By leveraging multiple cores, **PLINQ** can significantly improve query performance, especially when applied correctly with consideration for ordering, exception handling, and merge strategies. However, as with all parallel programming techniques, careful benchmarking and profiling are essential to ensure that parallel execution truly benefits a given workload. When used effectively, **PLINQ** allows developers to harness the full potential of modern multi-core processors, striking a balance between simplicity and performance in data processing.

In the next chapter, we will dive into advanced task management in .NET. You'll learn how to effectively use task continuations, when and why to implement task hierarchies, and how to build a custom task scheduler to optimize performance and control concurrency.

Multiple Choice Questions

1. Which of the following best describes the way **PLINQ** executes queries?
   a. It always executes queries in parallel for maximum performance.
   b. It automatically determines whether parallel execution is beneficial.
   c. It runs **queries** on multiple threads only when explicitly forced.
   d. It executes **queries** in parallel only if the dataset size is greater than 1,000.
2. If a **PLINQ query** does not show performance improvements, what should be checked?
   a. If `AsSequential()` is mistakenly used
   b. If the workload is too small to benefit from parallelization
   c. If too many expensive operations are being performed in parallel
   d. All of the above
3. What does the `AsOrdered()` method do in **PLINQ**?
   a. Forces sequential execution
   b. Ensures that the results preserve the original order of the input sequence
   c. Randomizes the order of execution for better performance
   d. Forces parallel execution regardless of dataset size
4. Which of the following factors can affect **PLINQ**'s performance negatively?
   a. A large number of CPU cores
   b. High computational cost per item
   c. A high degree of data dependency
   d. Processing a large dataset

Answers

1. b
2. d
3. b
4. c

Points to Remember

- **Language Integrated Query (LINQ)** simplifies and standardizes **query** code by making it a part of the C# language itself.
- **Parallel LINQ (PLINQ)** enhances **LINQ** by enabling parallelism for in-memory queries, leveraging multiple CPU cores for improved performance.
- **PLINQ** can speed up **LINQ** queries but introduces overhead, especially for small or simple **queries**. Always profile and test for optimal performance.
- PLINQ provides extension methods for fine-tuning execution, including **`AsOrdered()`** to preserve order, **`WithDegreeOfParallelism()`** to control concurrency, and **`AsSequential()`** to mix parallel and sequential execution as needed.

Questions

1. How does the cost of context switching in **PLINQ** compare to the performance gains of parallel execution? How can you optimize **PLINQ** queries to minimize overhead?
2. How would you implement thread-safe operations in a **PLINQ** query that modifies shared state, and what potential issues could arise from improper synchronization?
3. Consider a scenario where a dataset contains elements that require significantly different amounts of processing time. How would **PLINQ** handle this workload distribution, and what techniques could be used to balance it more effectively?
4. How would you handle exception handling in a **PLINQ query** where different elements might cause different types of failures? Should failures be ignored, retried, or cause the entire **query** to fail? Why?

Key Terms

- **Language Integrated Query (LINQ)**: A standard query language integrated into C# and .NET
- **Parallel LINQ (PLINQ)**: An extension to **LINQ** that enables parallel execution for **LINQ queries**
- **Query**: A declarative language enabling filtering, joining, sorting, grouping, aggregating, and selecting specific fields from data
- **Range Partitioning**: A partitioning strategy that partitions an array or list into smaller contiguous ranges
- **Chunk Partitioning**: A partitioning strategy that partitions an enumerable by allowing a thread to pull a chunk of elements, process them, then retrieve another chunk
- **Hash Partitioning**: A partitioning strategy that partitions an enumerable by calculating a hash for each element. Elements with the same hash are processed on the same partition
- **Thread Starvation**: A performance-degrading phenomenon in parallelism caused by some threads finishing work early while others remain busy
- **Thread Affinity**: A case where a task or operation must consistently execute on a specific thread or set of threads
- **Pure Function**: A method that does not access shared resources or cause side effects

Chapter 9
Advanced Task Management

Introduction

In *Chapter 3, Creating and Running Tasks in C#*, we established the foundational concepts of tasks and task management. We explored how tasks provide a high-level abstraction for executing concurrent operations without requiring direct thread management. While we briefly introduced task scheduling and continuations, we did not explore them in depth.

In this chapter, we will expand our understanding of task management by covering advanced topics. We will delve into fine-tuning continuations and implementing advanced **task chaining**, including complex parent-child relationships. Additionally, we will build a custom **task scheduler** and examine scenarios where custom **schedulers** offer significant benefits.

Structure

In this chapter we will cover the following topics:

- Introduction to Advanced Task Management
  - The Importance of Advanced Task Management
  - Overview of Key .Net Features
- When and How to Use Continuations
  - Understanding `ContinueWith`
  - Using `TaskContinuationOptions`
  - Best Practices for Chaining Tasks
  - Handling Errors in Continuations
- Implementing Complex Task Hierarchies
  - Parent-Child Relationships
  - Using `TaskCreationOptions.AttachedToParent`
  - Managing Nested Lifetimes
  - Handling Exceptions in Hierarchical Structures
- Building a Custom Task Scheduler
  - Understanding Task Scheduler
  - Implementing a Custom Scheduler
  - Controlling Concurrency Levels and Prioritization
  - Optimizing Workloads
  - Testing and Debugging

- Advanced Task Cancellation
  - Cooperative Cancellation
  - Propagating Cancellations
  - Implementing Timeouts
  - Gracefully Handling Cancellations
- Performance Optimization
  - Reducing Overhead with ValueTask
  - Avoiding Common Pitfalls
  - Diagnosing Performance Bottlenecks

Introduction to Advanced Task Management

.NET provides a robust set of tools for managing tasks, enabling developers to execute and coordinate asynchronous operations seamlessly. As applications grow in complexity, advanced task management techniques, such as task continuation, cancellation, synchronization, and fine-grained control over task scheduling, become essential for achieving predictable performance. By leveraging features like **`Task`**, **`TaskFactory`**, and continuations, developers can build scalable, resilient applications that handle task-based concurrency effectively. This chapter covers these advanced concepts, equipping you with the knowledge to maximize the potential of .NET's task-based programming model.

The Importance of Advanced Task Management

Many applications function well with basic tasks and built-in task management. However, as applications grow in complexity, more advanced strategies become essential to maintain efficiency and scalability. Large workloads may require custom scheduling and load balancing to optimize CPU and resource utilization, ensuring even distribution of tasks. Additionally, processing pipelines may need to be designed to efficiently manage complex, hierarchical parallel workflows.

The advanced techniques covered in this chapter will provide practical solutions to these challenges, enabling you to build high-performance, scalable task-based applications in .NET.

Overview of Key .NET Features

In addition to the tools we have learned about in previous chapters, .NET provides the following features for advanced task management:

- **Continuations**: Enable chaining asynchronous operations so that a follow-up task executes automatically when a preceding task completes. These can be configured to run synchronously or asynchronously and support parent-child relationships through **`Task.ContinueWith()`**.
- **Task Schedulers**: Control how tasks are scheduled and executed. While **`TaskScheduler.Default`** uses the .NET thread pool, custom schedulers allow fine-tuned resource management, such as prioritizing specific tasks or restricting concurrency.
- **`ValueTask`**: A lightweight alternative to Task that minimizes heap allocations, making it ideal for high-performance scenarios where avoiding unnecessary object creation improves efficiency. We will cover ValueTasks in *Chapter 10, Asynchronous Programming with Async/Await.*
- **`Task.WhenAll() and Task.WhenAny()`**: **`Task.WhenAll()`** waits for all specified tasks to complete before proceeding, while **`Task.WhenAny()`** completes when the first of the provided tasks finishes, allowing for faster decision-making in asynchronous workflows.

Mastering these features is essential for building efficient, responsive, and scalable task-based applications in .NET.

When and How to Use Continuations

Task continuations, as explained in *Chapter 3, Creating and Running Tasks in C#*, provide a way to chain tasks together so that one task runs only after another completes. When defining a continuation, a delegate is assigned to execute following the completion of an antecedent task. This allows developers to structure task execution in a logical sequence while still leveraging the benefits of asynchronous programming. Multiple tasks can be linked in this way, supporting scenarios where tasks need to run in a specific order while optimizing resource utilization. Additionally, continuations can be configured to run conditionally based on the success, failure, or cancellation of the preceding task.

Task continuations create ordered task chains, an example of which is shown in the following diagram:

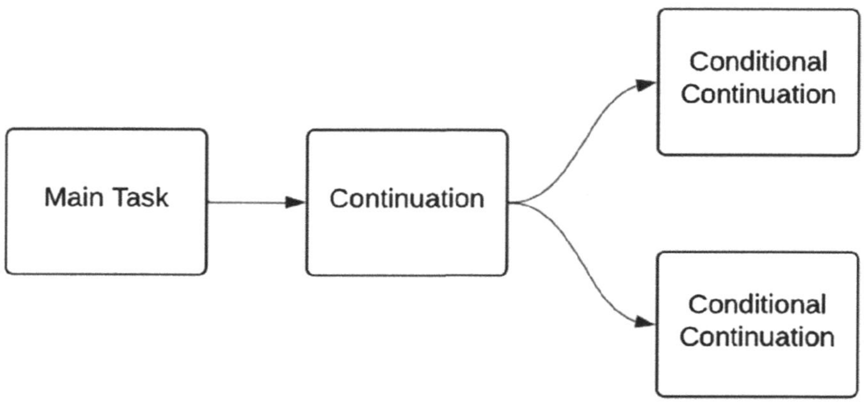

Figure 9.1: *Task Chaining*

Understanding `ContinueWith`

Continuations are typically defined by calling the **`ContinueWith()`** method, as detailed in *Chapter 3, Creating and Running Tasks in C#*. Data that is returned by the antecedent task is passed into the continuation as an input parameter. This allows data to be processed in a pipeline fashion, with different methods performing discrete operations as the chain progresses.

By default, continuations are scheduled by the **task scheduler** after their antecedents and run asynchronously. This means that continuations are not guaranteed to run on the same thread as antecedents. Continuations are tasks themselves and do not block the thread that starts them.

Calling **`ContinueWith()`** assigns a continuation to follow a single antecedent. It is also possible to create continuations that follow multiple antecedents. These are commonly called **multi-task continuations**. The **`TaskFactory`** class provides methods to create such continuations, including:

- **`ContinueWhenAll()`**: Runs after all antecedents have completed
- **`ContinueWhenAny()`**: Runs after any one antecedent completes

The following example demonstrates creating a continuation that will run after all antecedents have completed:

```
Console.WriteLine("Starting tasks...");
var task1 = Task.Run(() =>
{
```

```
        Thread.Sleep(1000);
        Console.WriteLine("Completed task 1.");
    });

    var task2 = Task.Run(() =>
    {
        Thread.Sleep(1000);
        Console.WriteLine("Completed task 2.");
    });

    Task continuation = Task.Factory.ContinueWhenAll([task1, task2], antecedents
    =>
    {
        Console.WriteLine("Completed continuation.");
    });

    continuation.Wait();
    Console.WriteLine("All tasks completed.");
```

The example creates two tasks (**task1** and **task2**) that run asynchronously. The **Task.Factory.ContinueWhenAll()** schedules a continuation to execute after both tasks complete. The continuation receives an array of antecedents as an input parameter but does not aggregate their results. The order in which **task1** and **task2** complete is not deterministic but depends on scheduling. The final output may appear in different sequences, but it will always ensure that the continuation runs only after both tasks are completed. It will show up as:

```
Starting tasks...
Completed task 2.
Completed task 1.
Completed continuation.
All tasks completed.
```

Alternatively, **Task.WhenAny()** or **Task.WhenAll()** can be used to create multi-task continuations. Replacing the **Task.Factory.ContinueWhenAll()** method with **Task.WhenAll(task1, task2).ContinueWith()** will accomplish the same result.

Using TaskContinuationOptions

Continuation behavior can be controlled by passing **TaskContinuationOptions** as a parameter. If no options are specified or **TaskContinuationOptions.None** is used, the continuation executes regardless of the antecedent task's result on the default task scheduler.

TaskContinuationOptions allows control over execution in several ways:

- Influencing scheduling, such as running a continuation synchronously or marking it as a long-running task
- Enforcing conditions, such as executing only if the antecedent task completes successfully, fails, or is cancelled
- Modifying scheduler behavior, such as forcing the use of the default scheduler
- Controlling task hierarchy, such as attaching a continuation to its parent task or preventing child tasks from attaching
- Combining multiple options, except for those that specify contradictory execution behaviors

The conditional options are not valid for multi-task continuations because it is not possible to tell which task should be checked to fulfil the condition.

Now, let us see how **TaskContinuationOptions** can be used to enforce conditions on continuations.

The following example creates a task with two continuations. One executes if the task completes successfully, and the other executes if the task throws an exception.

```
var mainTask = Task.Run(() =>
{
    Thread.Sleep(1000);
    throw new InvalidOperationException("Faulted task.");
});

Task success = mainTask.ContinueWith(antecedent =>
{
    Console.WriteLine("Antecedent succeeded.");
}, TaskContinuationOptions.NotOnFaulted);

Task fail = mainTask.ContinueWith(antecedent =>
{
    Console.WriteLine($"Antecedent faulted with error: {antecedent.Exception.
Message}");
}, TaskContinuationOptions.OnlyOnFaulted);

Console.WriteLine("Started tasks");
try
{
    Task.WaitAll(mainTask, success, fail);
}
catch (AggregateException)
{
}
Console.WriteLine("All tasks completed.");
```

In the example, **mainTask** simulates work by calling **Thread.Sleep()** and then throws an exception. The **success** continuation is added with the option **NotOnFaulted**, meaning it will execute only if **mainTask** completes without throwing an unhandled exception. The **fail** continuation is added with the option **OnlyOnFaulted**, meaning it will execute only if **mainTask** throws an exception. Since **mainTask** always throws an exception, the **fail** continuation always runs, and the **success** continuation never runs.

The output is as follows:

```
Started tasks
Antecedent faulted with error: One or more errors occurred. (Faulted task.)
All tasks completed.
```

Note: *When a continuation executes due to the antecedent task failing, the exception is still processed as normal. The Exception property of a faulted task always contains an* ***AggregateException****, even if only one exception was thrown. This means the exception must be properly caught and processed as an* ***AggregateException****, typically by calling* **Flatten()** *to access the original exception.*

Best Practices for Chaining Tasks

Task chaining is a powerful way to control the order of execution while writing asynchronous code. The following are best practice guidelines to follow when writing chained tasks:

1. Use **ContinueWith()** when fine control is needed, such as conditional execution, handling specific task states, or providing task scheduling hints.

2. Prefer **async/await** when fine control is not needed. **Async/await** is more readable and provides simplified error handling compared to **ContinueWith()**. **Async/await** will be covered in more detail in *Chapter 10, Asynchronous Programming with Async/Await.*

3. Use **Task.WaitAll()** to run multiple independent tasks in parallel and block until they complete. Be cautious, as **Task.WaitAll()** blocks the calling thread, which can lead to deadlocks if used improperly in UI or asynchronous contexts.
4. Use **Task.WaitAny()** to block until the first task completes. This can be useful when you need to process results as soon as one task finishes while other tasks continue running.

   Handle exceptions properly and follow the steps:

   - When using **ContinueWith()**, handle exceptions explicitly by checking **Task.IsFaulted** and accessing **Task.Exception**
   - When using **Task.WaitAll()** or **Task.WaitAny()**, be aware that they throw **AggregateException** if any task fails. Catch and handle exceptions appropriately
5. Avoid unnecessary task nesting to keep the chain simple and reduce complexity
6. Use cancellation tokens to support task cancellation. Pass **CancellationToken** to **Task.Run()**, **ContinueWith()**, and asynchronous methods to allow graceful cancellation

By following these best practices, you can write more efficient, maintainable, and responsive asynchronous code while avoiding common pitfalls such as deadlocks, unnecessary nesting, and unhandled exceptions.

Handling Errors in Continuations

Exceptions in tasks will cause the task to fail if they are not caught within the delegate body. By default, continuations execute regardless of the outcome of their antecedent task when no **TaskContinuationOptions** are specified (i.e., **TaskContinuationOptions.None**). If this behavior is not overridden, a continuation will still run even if the antecedent task has failed.

In this scenario, if the continuation accesses the antecedent's **Result** property, an **AggregateException** will be thrown, containing the original exception that caused the failure. This can lead to cascading failures in chained tasks. Therefore, it is important to check **Task.IsFaulted,** or **Task.Status** before accessing the **Task.Result** property unless **TaskContinuationOptions** are explicitly set to prevent the continuation from processing faulted tasks.

The following **TaskContinuationOptions** ensure that the antecedent did not fault:

- **NotOnFaulted**: The continuation executes only if the antecedent did not fault
- **OnlyOnRanToCompletion**: The continuation executes only if the antecedent completed successfully
- **OnlyOnCanceled**: The continuation executes only if the antecedent was canceled

The following **TaskContinuationOptions** allow execution even if the antecedent has faulted:

- **None** (default): The continuation executes regardless of the antecedent's outcome
- **NotOnRanToCompletion**: The continuation executes only if the antecedent did not complete successfully
- **OnlyOnFaulted**: The continuation executes only if the antecedent faulted
- **NotOnCanceled**: The continuation executes only if the antecedent was not canceled

Note: *Some* **TaskContinuationOptions** *are not conditional and do not affect whether a continuation executes.*

Handling AggregateException

If a task faults, its **Task.Exception** property will contain an **AggregateException**. This exception aggregates all inner exceptions that occurred within the task. If the task did not fail or has not yet failed, this property will return null. To efficiently process multiple exceptions, use **`AggregateException.Flatten()`** to retrieve all inner exceptions in a single collection.

When using blocking methods such as **`Task.Wait()`**, **`Task.WaitAll()`**, **`Task.WaitAny()`**, or accessing **`Task.Result`**, always handle **`AggregateException`** properly to prevent unhandled exceptions. If task cancellation is supported, catch **`OperationCanceledException`** separately in its own handler block to avoid misinterpreting cancellations as failures. Additionally, **`TaskContinuationOptions.OnlyOnCanceled`** can be used to execute specific logic when a task is canceled.

Catching Exceptions in the Delegate Body

Catching exceptions within the task delegate is critical for handling transient faults that should be retried. Implementing structured retry logic, such as exponential backoff or using a resilience library like Polly, helps improve application robustness. Additionally, fine control over exception handling within a task allows for targeted responses based on exception types.

If an exception from a task is never caught, it can lead to unhandled exceptions being thrown at unpredictable times. To mitigate this risk, consider implementing a **`TaskScheduler.UnobservedTaskException`** event handler, as explained in *Chapter 3: Creating and Running Tasks in C#*.

Implementing Complex Task Hierarchies

In .NET, tasks can create and manage other tasks, known as **nested or child tasks**. These **child tasks** maintain a defined relationship with their **parent tasks**, which can influence execution behavior, exception handling, and synchronization. By nesting tasks, complex task hierarchies can be constructed, allowing for more organized and efficient concurrency. This approach is particularly useful when a parent task depends on the completion or result of a child task before proceeding with further processing.

Parent-Child Relationships

In .NET, **parent tasks** can create **child tasks** in one of two relationships: attached or detached. The relationship between the **parent** and **child tasks** determines how they interact, particularly in terms of completion, error propagation, and synchronization.

Attached Child Tasks

Attached child tasks create a dependency between the **parent** and the **child**. A **parent task** will not be considered complete until all its **attached child tasks** finish execution. Additionally, the status of a **parent task** is influenced by the statuses of its **attached child tasks**. If an **attached child task** fails with an exception, the exception propagates to the **parent**, allowing for centralized error handling.

The following diagram illustrates the relationship between **parent tasks** and **attached child tasks**:

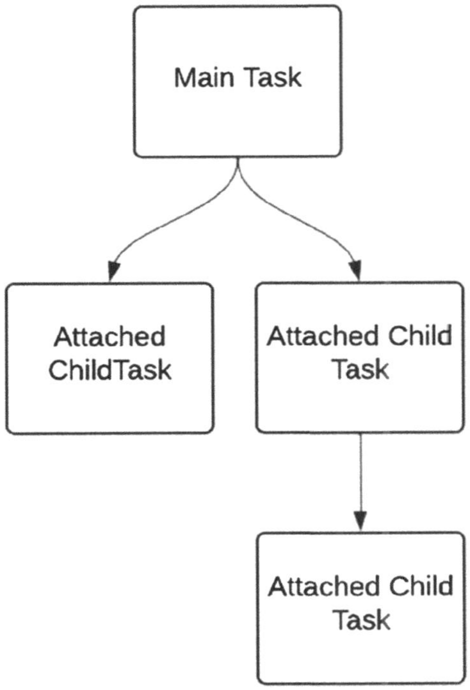

Figure 9.2: *Attached Child Tasks*

To create an **attached child task**, we must explicitly use **`Task.Factory.StartNew()`** with **`TaskCreationOptions.AttachedToParent`**. The following example demonstrates this behavior:

```
Task mainTask = Task.Factory.StartNew(() =>
{
    Task childTask = Task.Factory.StartNew(() =>
    {
        Thread.Sleep(1000);
        Console.WriteLine("Child task completed.");
    }, TaskCreationOptions.AttachedToParent);

    Thread.Sleep(500);
    Console.WriteLine("Main task completed.");
});

mainTask.Wait();
Console.WriteLine("Work completed.");
```

In the prior example, the **child task** is explicitly attached to the **parent** using **`TaskCreationOptions.AttachedToParent`**. As a result, the **parent task** waits for the **child** to complete before it is marked as finished. The output is always as follows:

```
Main task completed.
Child task completed.
Work completed.
```

Even though the main task completes its own work before the **child task** finishes, it must still wait for the **child** before it is considered complete.

Detached Child Tasks

Detached child tasks, on the other hand, operate independently of their **parent**. The **parent** does not wait for **detached child tasks** to complete before finishing execution. Additionally, exceptions in

detached child tasks do not propagate to the **parent**. This means that a **detached child task** can fail silently unless exceptions are explicitly handled within the task delegate body.

The following diagram illustrates the relationship between **parent tasks** and **detached child tasks**:

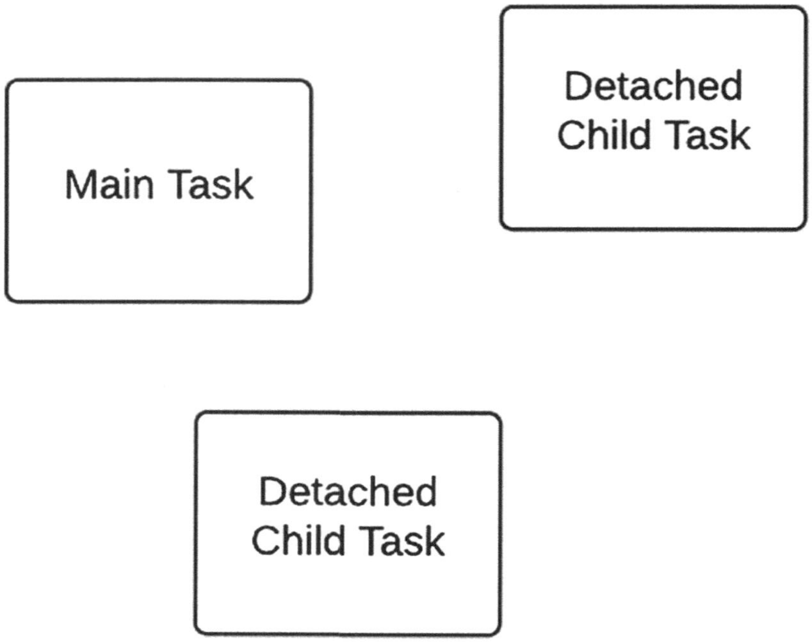

***Figure* 9.3:** *Detached Child Tasks*

By default, when a **child** task is created using **`Task.Run()`**, it is detached. Let us look at an example:

```
var mainTask = Task.Run(() =>
{
    var childTask = Task.Run(() =>
    {
        Thread.Sleep(1000);
        Console.WriteLine("Child task completed.");
    });
    Thread.Sleep(Random.Shared.Next(500, 1500));
    Console.WriteLine("Main task completed.");
});

mainTask.Wait();
Console.WriteLine("Work completed.");
```

In this example:

- The main task creates a child task using **`Task.Run()`**
- Since **`Task.Run()`** only creates **detached child tasks**, the **parent** does not wait for the **child task** to complete
- Depending on the random sleep duration, the **child task** may or may not complete before the application finishes running

Possible outputs include:

```
Main task completed.
Work completed.
```

or

```
Child task completed.
Main task completed.
Work completed.
```

This variability demonstrates that **detached tasks** run independently of their **parent**.

Using `TaskCreationOptions.AttachedToParent`

The `TaskCreationOptions.AttachedToParent` option of `Task.Factory.StartNew()` is used to create a **child task** that is tied to the lifecycle of its parent task. When this option is used, the **parent task** will wait for the completion of all its **attached child tasks** before it completes. However, there are specific conditions regarding how and when this option can be applied, particularly in relation to the way **parent tasks** are created.

When you create a **parent task** using `Task.Factory.StartNew()` it is possible to create **child tasks** that are attached to the **parent**. This means that the **child task** will be bound to the parent's lifecycle, and the **parent task** will not complete until all its **attached child tasks** have completed.

However, if the **parent task** is created using `Task.Run()`, the situation changes. Tasks created with `Task.Run()` are always **detached**, meaning they operate independently of any **parent task**. In this case, even if you attempt to use `TaskCreationOptions.AttachedToParent` for **child tasks**, the option is ignored. The **child tasks** are created as **detached tasks**, and there is no relationship to the **parent task's** lifecycle.

The behavior is similar when a **parent task** is created with `Task.Factory.StartNew()` but with the `TaskCreationOptions.DenyChildAttach` option. **Parent tasks** created in this way explicitly prevent the creation of **attached child tasks**. Even if you try to create child tasks with `TaskCreationOptions.AttachedToParent` in this scenario, the **child tasks** will still be created as **detached tasks**, and the attachment will be disregarded. The `DenyChildAttach` option ensures that no **child tasks** are tied to the **parent's** lifecycle, effectively isolating any **child tasks** from the **parent task's** completion.

In summary, when a **parent task** is created using `Task.Run()`, the task is always detached, and any attempt to create **attached child tasks** will be ignored. Similarly, when using `Task.Factory.StartNew()` with the `TaskCreationOptions.DenyChildAttach` option, the **parent task** cannot create **attached child tasks**, and any **child tasks** created will be **detached** regardless of the `AttachedToParent` option. Both scenarios prevent the use of **attached child tasks**, making the parent-child task relationship non-existent.

Managing Nested Lifetimes

Managing **nested task** lifetimes can be complicated, especially when dealing with **detached tasks**. However, proper lifetime management is critical in task hierarchies to avoid race conditions and unexpected behavior.

Attached child tasks make task lifetime management simpler by ensuring that all **child tasks** complete before the parent task completes. The main thread can then wait for the main task to complete and be assured that all **child tasks** have also completed. This simplicity is a significant advantage when creating task hierarchies and should always be considered when planning **nested task** designs.

In contrast, **detached child tasks** execute independently from their **parent task**, which complicates lifetime management. These **child tasks** must be explicitly waited on to ensure that they complete before the main task finishes. Neglecting to wait for **detached child tasks** can lead to unpredictable behavior. Without proper management, **detached tasks** may never be scheduled or executed.

One way to manage **detached child tasks** is by using a collection, such as **ConcurrentBag<Task>**. The tasks can be added to this collection and then waited on using **Task.WhenAll()**. The following is an example that demonstrates this approach:

```
using System.Collections.Concurrent;

var tasks = new ConcurrentBag<Task>();
tasks.Add(Task.Run(() =>
{
    tasks.Add(Task.Run(() =>
    {
        tasks.Add(Task.Run(() =>
        {
            Thread.Sleep(100);
            Console.WriteLine("Child subtask 1 completed.");
        }));

        Thread.Sleep(100);
        Console.WriteLine("Child task 1 completed.");
    }));

    tasks.Add(Task.Run(() =>
    {
        Thread.Sleep(100);
        Console.WriteLine("Child task 2 completed.");
    }));

    Thread.Sleep(100);
    Console.WriteLine("Main task completed.");
}));

Task.WaitAll(tasks.ToList());
Console.WriteLine("All tasks completed.");
```

In this example, a complex task hierarchy of **detached child tasks** is managed using a **ConcurrentBag<Task>**. The **Task.WhenAll(tasks)** method waits for all tasks to complete before the main thread exits.

Note: *this method may not always work properly in complex task hierarchies due to task scheduling delays. It is possible for the* ***tasks.ToList()*** *snapshot to be called before all tasks have been added, leaving some tasks out of the* ***WaitAll()*** *list. In such circumstances, using attached child tasks is a safer solution.*

Using **attached child tasks** is generally less complex in terms of lifetime, error, and cancellation management compared to **detached tasks**. However, **detached tasks** can offer more flexibility in handling concurrency and independent execution.

Handling Exceptions in Hierarchical Structures

Exception management functions differently in **attached** and **detached child tasks** in .NET, with important implications for how exceptions are handled within task hierarchies.

Attached Child Tasks

When a **child task** is attached to its **parent task** (via the **TaskCreationOptions.AttachedToParent** flag), any unhandled exceptions in the **child task** are automatically propagated to the **parent task**. This behavior consolidates exception handling, simplifying the management of errors in task hierarchies.

In the following example, the main task creates an **attached child task** that throws an exception. The exception is propagated to the main task, and it is caught within the main thread's **`try-catch`** block:

```
Task mainTask = Task.Factory.StartNew(() =>
{
    Task childTask = Task.Factory.StartNew(() =>
    {
        Thread.Sleep(500);
        throw new InvalidOperationException("Child task exception.");
    }, TaskCreationOptions.AttachedToParent);

    Thread.Sleep(100);
    Console.WriteLine("Main task completed.");
});

try
{
    mainTask.Wait();
}
catch (AggregateException ex)
{
    Console.WriteLine(ex.Flatten().Message);
}

Console.WriteLine("All tasks completed.");
```

In this case, the **`InvalidOperationException`** thrown in the **child task** is propagated to the **parent task** and caught by the catch block in the main thread. The **`AggregateException`** is flattened to show the child task's exception.

The output is as follows:

```
Main task completed.
One or more errors occurred. (Child task exception.)
All tasks completed.
```

Detached Child Tasks

On the other hand, **detached child tasks** do not automatically propagate exceptions to their **parent tasks**. This behavior can lead to silent failures, where exceptions in **child tasks** are not observed unless explicitly handled.

Consider the following example where a **child task** throws an exception but is not attached to the **parent**:

```
var mainTask = Task.Run(() =>
{
    var childTask = Task.Run(() =>
    {
        throw new InvalidOperationException("Child task exception.");
    });

    Thread.Sleep(100);
    Console.WriteLine("Main task completed.");
});

try
{
```

```
    mainTask.Wait();
}
catch (AggregateException ex)
{
    Console.WriteLine(ex.Flatten().Message);
}

Console.WriteLine("Work completed.");
```

In this case, the **InvalidOperationException** in the child task goes unobserved, and the exception does not propagate to the **parent task**. Because the **child task** is detached and not awaited or explicitly handled, the exception is not captured by the **try-catch** block for the **mainTask**.

The output is as follows:

```
Main task completed.
Work completed.
```

Unobserved Exceptions

Detached tasks can cause unobserved exceptions if they are not awaited or if there's no explicit handling. By default, unobserved exceptions in tasks can result in unpredictable behavior, including process termination if not dealt with properly. This may trigger the **UnobservedTaskException** event, as discussed in *Chapter 3: Creating and Running Tasks in C#.*

To prevent such issues, it is crucial to ensure that **detached child tasks** are properly waited on or observed. This can be done using methods like **Task.WaitAll()**, **Task.WhenAll()**, or **Task.WaitAny()**, as shown in the following example:

Note: *This example uses a* **ConcurrentBag<Task>**, *which is a thread-safe collection of tasks.* **ConcurrentBag<T>** *and other thread-safe collections are covered in more detail in Chapter 6, Understanding and Using Concurrent Collections.*

```
using System.Collections.Concurrent;

var tasks = new ConcurrentBag<Task>();

tasks.Add(Task.Run(() =>
{
    tasks.Add(Task.Run(() =>
    {
        throw new InvalidOperationException("Child task exception.");
    }));

    Thread.Sleep(100);
    Console.WriteLine("Main task completed.");
}));

Thread.Sleep(100); //ensure all tasks are scheduled.
try
{
    Task.WaitAll(tasks.ToList());
}
catch (AggregateException ex)
{
    Console.WriteLine(ex.Flatten().Message);
}

Console.WriteLine("Work completed.");
```

By using `Task.WhenAll()` or `Task.WaitAll()`, you ensure that exceptions in **detached child tasks** are observed, thus preventing silent failures.

Building a Custom Task Scheduler

The built-in **task scheduler** in .NET is optimized for general use and is sufficient for most scenarios. However, there are cases where building a **custom scheduler** can offer better control over task execution. These scenarios include, but are not limited to:

- Tasks that need to be executed in a specific order due to dynamic dependencies
- Tasks that require custom throttling or assignment to specific resource pools
- Complex cancellation requirements that go beyond what a single `CancellationToken` can manage, including cancellation for different task categories
- Tasks that need to be delayed, run periodically, or scheduled at fixed or custom rates
- Workloads that need to be distributed in a way that prevents `ThreadPool` starvation or overuse of system resources
- Custom prioritization of tasks
- Conditional scheduling of tasks based on certain criteria or events

The default **task scheduler** in .NET is not equipped to handle these specialized scenarios. Fortunately, .NET provides a way to create and use **custom task schedulers**, allowing for fine-grained control over how tasks are managed and executed.

Understanding Task Scheduler

The `TaskScheduler` class, found in the `System.Threading.Tasks` namespace, is responsible for determining when and how tasks are executed in .NET. It ensures that the work contained in each task is eventually run.

The default **task scheduler** provides a robust set of features, such as work-stealing for load balancing, thread pooling, and management via the .NET Thread Pool. This default **scheduler** is optimized for general use cases, providing good throughput and performance for most scenarios.

It is important to note that the default **scheduler** does not directly manage threads. Instead, it coordinates thread management through the `ThreadPool`, which offers advanced features like thread queuing, prioritization, and work stealing. We will delve deeper into the `ThreadPool` in *Chapter 11: Threading and the Thread Pool*.

Tasks can be scheduled to run on a specific thread by calling `TaskScheduler.FromCurrentSynchronizationContext()`. This is especially important in UI frameworks like WinForms or WPF, where UI elements can only be accessed from the thread on which the UI is running.

`TaskScheduler` is an abstract class and serves as the foundation for creating **custom task schedulers**. It provides basic functionality for task scheduling, including support for synchronization contexts and event handling for unobserved task exceptions. By subclassing `TaskScheduler`, you can create **custom schedulers** tailored to specific needs or environments.

Implementing a Custom Scheduler

The `TaskScheduler` class provides an abstract base for **custom schedulers**, and to implement a **custom scheduler**, you must override the following three abstract methods. These methods ensure the proper operation and integration of the scheduler with the Task Parallel Library (TPL) and debuggers:

1. **`QueueTask()`**
    - This method is called when the TPL needs to schedule a task onto the **scheduler**. Your **custom scheduler** is responsible for accepting the task and storing it in some internal data structure, such as a queue or list. The task will then be executed later by a thread that the **scheduler** coordinates or manages
    - The **`QueueTask()`** method is the primary method for accepting tasks and is a critical part of your **custom scheduler**
2. **`TryExecuteTaskInline()`**
    - Executing a task "**`inline`**" means running it immediately on the same thread that requested it, rather than queuing it for execution on a different thread. This can help avoid the overhead of context switching, which occurs when a task is run on a separate thread
    - This method is optional. If your scheduler does not support inline execution, you can simply return **`false`**. If inline execution is supported, the method should attempt to execute the task immediately on the current thread by calling **`TryExecuteTask()`**
    - The **`taskWasPreviouslyQueued`** parameter is true if the task was already queued when **`TryExecuteTaskInline()`** was called. In this case, you may want to skip attempting to process inline
3. **`GetScheduledTasks()`**
    - This method is used to integrate with debuggers. It returns an enumeration (**`IEnumerable<Task>`**) of currently scheduled tasks. This allows debuggers or diagnostic tools to inspect which tasks are pending execution in your custom scheduler
    - The method should return all tasks that have been accepted by the scheduler but have not yet been executed

Example Implementation

To implement a **custom task scheduler**, we derive from **`TaskScheduler`** and override key methods that control task queuing and execution.

1. Define the **scheduler's** purpose and requirements. This will help guide the scope of the **scheduler** and inform the overall design
2. Decide on a mechanism for managing tasks and threads. Tasks can be managed using mechanisms such as **`BlockingCollection<Task>`** or **`ConcurrentQueue<Task>`**. Threads could be started and monitored manually or by using the .NET Thread Pool
3. Implement the **`QueueTask()`** method. This method should accept the task into the internal data structure and make it available to be processed by a thread
4. Implement the **`TryExecuteTaskInline()`** method. This method should check if the task has been queued previously and call **`TryExecuteTask()`**. If inline execution is not supported, this method should simply return **`false`**
5. Implement **`GetScheduledTasks()`** by taking a snapshot of the task list and returning it as an enumeration

In this example we will build a **custom task scheduler** that supports a fixed number of threads in a thread pool. We will manage the thread pool manually by starting threads and storing them in a **`ConcurrentBag<Thread>`** instance. The tasks will be queued for processing using a

BlockingCollection<Task> instance. We will implement **IDisposable** to ensure proper cleanup of the task queue and thread pool. We will name the new **scheduler** class **CustomLimitedScheduler**.

The **QueueTask()** implementation needs to ensure the task is queued for processing. We will use lazy initialization of the thread pool and only start it when tasks are added, so the initialization will be triggered from this method as well. The implementation is as follows:

```
protected override void QueueTask(Task task)
{
    if (!this.taskQueue.IsAddingCompleted)
    {
        this.taskQueue.TryAdd(task);
        if (!this.threadsStarted)
        {
            if (Interlocked.CompareExchange(ref this.threadsStarted, true,
false) == false)
            {
                StartThreads();
            }
        }
    }
}
```

Using **Interlocked.CompareExchange()** ensures **StartThreads()** will be called only once, even in multithreaded environments.

With this design, implementing **GetScheduledTasks()** is straight forward.

```
protected override IEnumerable<Task>? GetScheduledTasks()
{
    return this.taskQueue.IsCompleted ?
      Enumerable.Empty<Task>() : this.taskQueue.ToArray();
}
```

We will support inline task execution with a simple implementation that only supports execution if the task was not previously queued.

```
protected override bool TryExecuteTaskInline(Task task, bool taskWas
PreviouslyQueued)
{
    return !taskWasPreviouslyQueued && TryExecuteTask(task);
}
```

Two private methods are implemented to start the threads in the thread pool and to dequeue and execute tasks.

```
private void StartThreads()
{
    for (var i = 0; i < this.maxThreadPoolSize; i++)
    {
        var thread = new Thread(ExecuteTasks);
        this.ThreadPool.Add(thread);
        thread.Start();
    }
}

private void ExecuteTasks()
{
    while (!this.taskQueue.IsCompleted)
    {
```

```
            if (this.taskQueue.TryTake(out Task? task))
            {
                TryExecuteTask(task);
            }
        }
    }
```

The **StartThreads()** method is called from **QueueTask()** to support lazy thread pool initialization. It starts a number of threads equal to the **maxThreadPoolSize** parameter set when the **scheduler** is constructed. Each thread runs the **ExecuteTasks()** method. This method loops for as long as the **BlockingCollection<Task>** is not completed. It takes a task from the queue and calls **TryExecuteTask()** to execute it.

Finally, the **Dispose()** method of **IDisposable** is used for cleanup.

```
public void Dispose()
{
    this.taskQueue.CompleteAdding();
    foreach (var thread in this.ThreadPool)
        thread.Join();
    this.ThreadPool.Clear();
}
```

The method simply stops the task queue, calls **Join()** on each thread in the pool, and clears the **ConcurrentBag<Thread>** to remove references.

Using a Custom Task Scheduler

Using a **custom scheduler** is done by adding it as a parameter to the **Task.Factory.StartNew()** method, as shown in the following example:

Note: *In this example, the custom scheduler created in the previous section has been implemented in a separate code file in a project called* **LimitedExecutionScheduler**. *The custom implementation is contained in the* **CustomLimitedScheduler** *class.*

```
using LimitedExecutionScheduler;

using (var scheduler = new CustomLimitedScheduler(2))
{
    for (int i = 0; i < 10; i++)
    {
        _ = Task.Factory.StartNew(() =>
        {
            var threadId = Thread.CurrentThread.ManagedThreadId;
            var taskId = Task.CurrentId;
            Console.WriteLine($"Executing task {taskId} on thread:
{threadId}");
        }, CancellationToken.None, TaskCreationOptions.None, scheduler);
    }
}
```

The prior example demonstrates using our **CustomLimitedScheduler** by creating an instance limiting the thread pool size to two threads. The example creates ten tasks and schedules them using the **custom scheduler**. Each task runs on one of the two threads in the thread pool. The output is something like the following. Task ordering is not guaranteed so the output will vary between runs.

```
Executing task 1 on thread: 7
Executing task 2 on thread: 6
Executing task 3 on thread: 6
```

```
Executing task 5 on thread: 6
Executing task 6 on thread: 6
Executing task 4 on thread: 7
Executing task 8 on thread: 7
Executing task 7 on thread: 6
Executing task 9 on thread: 7
Executing task 10 on thread: 6
```

An alternative method for using **custom schedulers** is to create a new instance of `TaskFactory` and pass the scheduler instance into the constructor, then use `StartNew()` to create and schedule tasks.

```
using var scheduler = new CustomLimitedScheduler(2);
var factory = new TaskFactory(scheduler);
var task = factory.StartNew(() => RunTask());
```

Implementing **custom task schedulers** provides fine control over task queueing and thread behavior for specialized situations where the default **scheduler** is not optimized for the situation at hand.

Controlling Concurrency Levels and Prioritization

Custom task schedulers are often implemented to control concurrency levels and enforce task prioritization, which are not directly supported by the default .NET Task Parallel Library (TPL). These capabilities are useful in resource-constrained environments, where multiple tasks compete for limited CPU, I/O, or memory bandwidth.

Controlling Concurrency Levels

In shared environments, limiting concurrency prevents excessive resource contention and ensures that a system remains responsive under high loads. A common approach is to use a fixed pool of worker threads, as demonstrated in the `CustomLimitedScheduler` from the previous section. This ensures that only a set number of tasks execute in parallel.

Other techniques include:

- **Using `SemaphoreSlim`**: Controls how many tasks can run concurrently but does not inherently schedule tasks based on priority
- **Leveraging Bounded `BlockingCollection<Task>`**: Enables controlled task queuing with finer execution constraints
- **Custom Thread Pool-based Schedulers**: Directly managing worker threads to optimize CPU usage

Task Prioritization

.NET's TPL does not natively support prioritizing tasks, so developers must implement their own scheduling mechanisms. This typically involves:

1. **Assigning a priority to tasks at creation**: for example, using `Task.AsyncState` or wrapping tasks in a custom class
2. **Storing tasks in a priority queue**: for example, using `ConcurrentDictionary<int, ConcurrentQueue<Task>>` or a binary heap for fast retrieval
3. **Ensuring high-priority tasks execute first:** by sorting tasks before dequeuing

A **custom scheduler** must override `QueueTask(Task)` to enqueue tasks based on priority and `TryExecuteTaskInline(Task, bool)` to prevent lower-priority tasks from preempting higher-priority ones.

Optimizing Workloads

Custom task schedulers can significantly optimize task workloads by implementing strategies such as controlled concurrency, task prioritization, thread affinity, or other specialized approaches. The best strategy depends on the specific optimization requirements of the application. Some key strategies include:

- **Controlled Concurrency:** Controlled concurrency limits the number of tasks that can run simultaneously, ensuring that system resources are used efficiently and avoiding overload. This can be particularly useful in resource-constrained environments where too many concurrent tasks can degrade performance.
- **Task Batching:** Task batching can reduce the overhead associated with task scheduling, particularly when context switching or shared data is a concern. By grouping smaller tasks into larger batches, you can reduce task queue contention and improve performance. The executing thread pulls multiple tasks from the queue and processes them in a loop, rather than executing them one by one.
- **Task Prioritization:** In scenarios where tasks have varying levels of urgency, task prioritization ensures that higher-priority tasks are executed first. However, task prioritization can sometimes lead to idle threads while tasks wait in lower-priority queues. To mitigate this, a work-stealing algorithm can be employed to ensure fair load distribution across threads.
- **Thread Affinity:** In certain scenarios, tasks may need to run on specific threads to maintain thread-local state or interact with particular resources (e.g., UI threads or I/O-bound tasks). Thread affinity can be implemented by assigning tasks to specific threads, ensuring tasks are always executed on the right thread for correct operation.

It is crucial to ensure that the **scheduler** code itself is highly performant. Inefficient scheduling logic can introduce latency and overhead. Additionally, it is important to account for potential deadlocks and race conditions, especially when tasks share resources or dependencies.

Testing and Debugging

Developing a **custom task scheduler** in .NET requires thorough testing and debugging to ensure reliability, efficiency, and scalability. Effective testing involves validating task execution behavior, debugging pending tasks during development, and monitoring performance under load. By combining unit testing, debugging tools, structured logging, and performance analysis, developers can build robust schedulers that handle concurrent workloads efficiently.

Unit Testing Task Scheduling Behavior

Unit tests play a crucial role in verifying that a **custom task scheduler** behaves as expected. At the core of these tests is ensuring that scheduled tasks execute correctly, adhere to concurrency constraints, and respect thread affinity when required. It is also important to validate execution order, particularly when priority queues or custom dispatch rules are used.

To ensure proper task execution, tests should use methods like `Task.Factory.StartNew()` to create and schedule tasks, followed by assertions to confirm they complete as expected. If a scheduler enforces task prioritization or thread affinity, unit tests should verify that high-priority tasks are executed first and that thread-specific tasks are bound to the correct execution context. Additionally, error handling must be tested to confirm that exceptions propagate correctly without causing deadlocks or orphaned tasks.

Injecting mock dependencies–such as custom queues, locks, or synchronization primitives–allows for fine-grained control over task scheduling behavior, making it easier to isolate specific behaviors in a controlled test environment.

Debugging Scheduled Tasks with Visual Studio

Even with well-written tests, debugging is essential to diagnose complex scheduling behaviors, race conditions, or unexpected performance bottlenecks. One of the most useful tools for debugging **custom task schedulers** is the Visual Studio Tasks window.

By overriding the `GetScheduledTasks()` method in a custom scheduler, developers can expose a list of currently queued tasks. While debugging in Visual Studio, opening Debug > Windows > Tasks allows for real-time inspection of scheduled, running, and completed tasks. This visibility makes it easier to diagnose why certain tasks are stuck or delayed.

Additionally, setting breakpoints inside key methods like `QueueTask()` and task execution methods provides insight into when and how tasks are queued and executed. Conditional breakpoints can further refine debugging, triggering only when specific conditions are met.

Using Logging for Runtime Monitoring

While debugging tools are invaluable during development, real-world issues often require logging to diagnose problems in production environments. Implementing structured logging within a custom task scheduler provides an audit trail of when tasks are queued, executed, and completed.

Logging should capture task IDs, timestamps, and execution duration to help identify potential bottlenecks or unexpected delays. If an exception occurs within a scheduled task, logging the stack trace and associated metadata can be critical for troubleshooting. For structured logging, frameworks like Serilog, Application Insights, or Log4Net provide powerful ways to store and analyze logs efficiently.

By continuously monitoring log data, developers can detect patterns such as **task starvation**, excessive queuing delays, or thread contention, all of which might indicate areas for optimization.

Performance and Stress Testing for Scalability

Beyond functional correctness, a **custom task scheduler** must be tested under realistic workloads to ensure it performs efficiently at scale. Performance testing should measure task throughput, queue latency, and resource consumption under high concurrency.

To simulate production workloads, developers can generate thousands of tasks with varying execution times and monitor how well the scheduler distributes work. Stress testing should evaluate whether lower-priority tasks get executed in a reasonable timeframe or if high-priority tasks monopolize resources.

It is also essential to test different workload types, including CPU-bound tasks that involve intensive computation and I/O-bound tasks that depend on external resources like databases or file systems. Observing CPU and memory usage during these tests helps identify any inefficiencies, such as excessive context switching or resource contention.

Building a Robust Task Scheduler

Testing and debugging a **custom task scheduler** is an iterative process that requires careful validation, continuous monitoring, and performance tuning. By combining unit tests that verify execution behavior, debugging tools like the Visual Studio Tasks window, structured logging for runtime diagnostics, and stress testing to measure scalability, developers can create **schedulers** that handle real-world workloads efficiently.

A well-tested **scheduler** ensures that tasks are processed fairly, efficiently, and without bottlenecks, enabling high-performance applications that can handle complex, concurrent workloads with ease.

Advanced Task Cancellation

Standardized task cancellation using `CancellationTokenSource` and `CancellationToken` is a powerful feature for building robust and responsive concurrent applications. Advanced task cancellation involves propagating cancellation signals, implementing timeouts, designing **cooperative cancellation** mechanisms, and handling exceptions and resource cleanup. Properly implementing cancellation ensures efficient resource management, prevents unnecessary computation, and allows applications to gracefully handle user-initiated or system-driven cancellations.

Cooperative Cancellation

The Task Parallel Library (TPL) cancellation system is cooperative, meaning that code must actively check for cancellation requests and respond accordingly. Properly implementing **cooperative cancellation** ensures that tasks can exit cleanly without unnecessary computation or resource leaks.

To ensure effective cooperation with the cancellation system, follow these guidelines:

- Check for cancellation early using `cancellationToken.IsCancellationRequested`, and exit operations as soon as cancellation is detected
- Use `ThrowIfCancellationRequested()` in long-running operations to immediately halt execution and propagate `OperationCanceledException`
- Pass and respect `CancellationToken` in libraries and shared code, ensuring reusable components correctly support cancellation
- Ensure loops check for cancellation to prevent excessive work. Periodically check `IsCancellationRequested` or use `ThrowIfCancellationRequested()` inside while and for loops
- Gracefully exit upon cancellation, performing any necessary cleanup before stopping execution

By following these cooperative techniques, your application can handle cancellations efficiently and gracefully, improving responsiveness and resource management.

Propagating Cancellations

In .NET, task cancellation is cooperative, meaning that all parts of an application must actively participate in checking and responding to cancellation requests. For this system to work effectively, cancellation tokens must be properly propagated throughout the call hierarchy. Without careful propagation, some tasks may continue running even when they should stop, leading to wasted resources and unresponsive applications.

The first step in proper propagation is ensuring that methods accept and pass `CancellationToken` parameters wherever cancellation might be necessary. This includes custom methods, library calls, and API requests that support cancellation. For example, when making an HTTP request using `HttpClient`, the token should be passed to `SendAsync` so that the request can be aborted if cancellation is triggered. Similarly, when working with long-running operations, passing `CancellationToken` to asynchronous tasks ensures that they do not continue running unnecessarily.

Another important aspect of propagation is managing cancellation token sources properly. When a `CancellationTokenSource` is created, it should be disposed of after use to free system resources and avoid potential memory leaks. Neglecting this step can lead to lingering tokens that may interfere with future operations.

Combining Cancellation Sources

In some cases, a single cancellation trigger may not be enough. For instance, an operation might need to be canceled either if a user explicitly requests cancellation or if a timeout occurs. Instead of handling these conditions separately, .NET provides the **`CreateLinkedTokenSource()`** method, which allows multiple cancellation sources to be combined into a single token. This means that when any of the **linked** sources signals cancellation, the linked token is also canceled.

Consider a scenario where an operation needs to be canceled if it takes longer than 10 seconds or if the user manually stops it. By using a **linked token source**, we can seamlessly merge these conditions:

```
using var userCts = new CancellationTokenSource();
using var timeoutCts = new CancellationTokenSource(TimeSpan.FromSeconds(10));
using var linkedCts =
    CancellationTokenSource.CreateLinkedTokenSource(userCts.Token, timeoutCts.
Token);

CancellationToken linkedToken = linkedCts.Token;

var task = Task.Run(() =>
{
    for (var i = 0; i < 11; i++)
    {
        linkedToken.ThrowIfCancellationRequested();
        Console.WriteLine($"Processing iteration {i}");
        Thread.Sleep(1000);
    }
}, linkedToken);

var userTask = Task.Run(() =>
{
    Console.ReadLine();
    userCts.Cancel();
});

try
{
    task.Wait();
    Console.WriteLine("Operation completed successfully.");
}
catch (AggregateException ex)
when (ex.InnerExceptions.First() is OperationCanceledException)
{
    Console.WriteLine("Operation cancelled.");
}
```

Considerations When Linking Cancellation Sources

While **`CreateLinkedTokenSource()`** is a powerful tool, it should be used thoughtfully. Deep or complex hierarchies of **linked tokens** can become difficult to manage, leading to unintended cascading cancellations that may disrupt other parts of the application. Additionally, **linked token sources** should be properly disposed of to prevent resource leaks.

By consistently passing cancellation tokens, **linking** sources when necessary, and disposing of token sources correctly, developers can ensure that their applications handle cancellation efficiently and predictably. Proper propagation not only improves responsiveness but also helps prevent unnecessary workload and resource consumption, making applications more robust and user-friendly.

Implementing Timeouts

Timeouts can be implemented in several ways using the TPL cancellation system. Cancellation token sources can be set to **timeout** using a **timeout** parameter in the constructor or by calling the `CancelAfter()` method. These sources automatically cancel after the **timeout** period expires.

The cancellation token throws an `OperationCanceledException` regardless of whether the `Cancel()` method is called or a **timeout** occurred. So, it is often important to distinguish between the two for logging and monitoring purposes. To make this distinction, ensure that the **timeout** cancellation token source and a manual cancellation token source are created separately and **linked**. When a cancellation occurs, check the `IsCancellationRequested` property on the tokens for both sources. The property that is true is the one that caused the cancellation.

Another option for implementing **timeouts** is to use `Task.Delay()` to create a **timeout** task and implement a cancellation token source for the operation task. In this case, use `Task.WaitAny()` or `Task.WhenAny()` to wait for both the operation and the **timeout**. These methods return the task that completed first, which can be compared to the operation and **timeout** tasks. If the **timeout** finishes before the operation, cancel the operation using its token source and log the **timeout** or throw a `TimeoutException`.

Gracefully Handling Cancellations

Task cancellations in .NET should not be treated as abrupt failures but as a normal and expected part of a well-designed, responsive application. Since cancellations often occur while an operation is still in progress, it is crucial to ensure that resources are properly cleaned up, partial work is reverted when necessary, and exceptions are handled appropriately.

- **Cleaning Up Resources:** Any operation that allocates resources, such as file handles, network connections, or database transactions, must ensure that these resources are released when cancellation occurs. Failing to do so can lead to memory leaks, resource exhaustion, or unstable application behavior. A well-structured cancellation strategy includes mechanisms that guarantee resource cleanup regardless of how the operation is interrupted. By incorporating proper cleanup techniques, an application can maintain stability and prevent resource-related issues.
- **Undoing Partial Work:** Many operations involve modifying shared state, such as updating a database, writing to a file, or communicating with an external system. When a cancellation request is received mid-process, it is important to ensure that no partial or inconsistent changes remain. This can be achieved by implementing compensating actions, such as rolling back a transaction, deleting partially written files, or resetting in-memory state. By considering cancellation as part of the workflow design, applications can maintain data integrity and avoid leaving operations in an indeterminate state.
- **Handling Cancellations Separately from Errors:** Cancellation is not an error but a controlled mechanism for stopping work when it is no longer needed. It should be handled separately from unexpected failures to avoid unnecessary error logging or misleading diagnostics. A well-structured exception handling approach ensures that cancellation-related exceptions are properly recognized, logged as routine events rather than failures, and propagated correctly to higher levels in the application. This prevents confusion between genuine errors and user-initiated or **timeout**-driven cancellations.
- **Ensuring Proper Cancellation Propagation:** When a task is canceled, it is essential that the cancellation request is propagated correctly throughout the system. Suppressing or mishandling cancellation exceptions can result in incomplete shutdown sequences, lingering background tasks, or inconsistent application states. Ensuring that cancellation flows naturally

through the call stack allows the entire operation to terminate cleanly and predictably, improving both reliability and user experience.

By following these best practices, applications can handle cancellations in a way that is efficient, graceful, and well-integrated into their overall workflow. Proper cancellation management not only improves resource utilization but also enhances application responsiveness and stability.

Performance Optimization

Performance is a critical aspect of any application, and some applications demand a high level of optimization to meet strict performance requirements. The Task Parallel Library (TPL) provides powerful tools and techniques to efficiently manage and optimize task-based applications. By leveraging the right strategies, developers can reduce overhead, improve concurrency, and diagnose bottlenecks to ensure optimal performance.

Avoiding Common Pitfalls

When optimizing performance in task-based applications, it is essential to avoid common mistakes that can degrade performance and lead to unintended issues. The following general guidelines help mitigate such pitfalls:

- **Avoid unnecessary blocking.** Blocking operations can cause deadlocks and reduce application responsiveness. Methods such as **`Wait()`**, **`Result`**, and **`GetAwaiter().GetResult()`** should be used with caution, as they force synchronous execution and may lead to thread pool exhaustion. Instead, consider checking **`IsCompletedSuccessfully`** before accessing the result or designing workflows that minimize blocking.
- **Minimize the creation of very small tasks.** Creating many tiny tasks can introduce significant overhead due to task scheduling and object allocation. In some cases, the cost of creating and scheduling a task may outweigh its actual execution time, negating performance benefits. To improve throughput, consider batching small tasks into larger tasks or using parallel loops where appropriate.
- **Limit the number of concurrent tasks.** Excessive task creation can exhaust system resources, leading to degraded performance. When too many tasks are running simultaneously, contention for CPU and memory can increase latency instead of reducing it. Consider using **custom task schedulers** or thread pool settings to control concurrency levels effectively.
- **Implement proper cancellation for long-running tasks.** Tasks that perform extensive computations or I/O operations should support cancellation tokens to allow graceful termination when no longer needed. Failure to handle cancellation can lead to resource leaks, unnecessary processing, and poor system responsiveness. Additionally, tasks should clean up any allocated resources or incomplete work when canceled.

By following these best practices, developers can build robust, scalable, and performant task-based applications that effectively utilize system resources.

Diagnosing Performance Bottlenecks

When performance bottlenecks occur in task-based applications, identifying the root cause efficiently is essential. The following techniques can help diagnose and resolve performance issues:

- **Use profiling tools to analyze bottlenecks.** Profiling tools such as Visual Studio Profiler, dotTrace, and PerfView provide detailed insights into task execution, thread usage, and system resource consumption. These tools help identify excessive task creation, thread pool saturation, and inefficient task scheduling.

- **Measure execution time using Stopwatch.** The `Stopwatch` class in .NET provides a high-precision way to measure execution time. It can be used to time individual tasks, loops, or sections of code to identify slow operations.
- **Leverage structured logging for execution times and failures.** Implement structured logging using frameworks such as `Serilog`, `NLog`, or `Microsoft.Extensions.Logging` to capture task execution details, including durations, completion statuses, and errors. Logging can help detect long-running tasks, failed operations, and unexpected delays.

By combining these techniques, developers can gain deeper visibility into performance issues, optimize task execution, and ensure efficient resource utilization in task-based applications.

Conclusion

In this chapter, we explored advanced techniques for managing tasks in .NET, focusing on effective task creation, cancellation, and exception handling. We examined the role of `CancellationToken` in building responsive applications and discussed how **custom task schedulers** can optimize workload distribution for specialized scenarios. Additionally, we explored task continuations, demonstrating how they enable better control over execution flow and dependency management in asynchronous workflows. By mastering these advanced task management techniques, you can build highly efficient and scalable applications that leverage concurrency effectively.

With this foundation, we now turn to asynchronous programming with async and await in the next chapter, enabling even greater responsiveness and efficiency in modern .NET applications.

Points to Remember

- Task continuations enable efficient sequencing of operations while preserving the benefits of concurrency.
- Attached child tasks simplify task management in hierarchical structures by consolidating error handling and streamlining task completion.
- Custom task schedulers optimize specialized workloads when the default task scheduler is insufficient.
- Cancellation in the TPL is cooperative, requiring tasks to be explicitly designed to respond to cancellation requests properly.

Multiple Choice Questions

1. What happens if an exception is thrown inside a task and not handled?
   a. The application crashes immediately
   b. The exception is silently ignored
   c. The exception is stored inside the task and can be retrieved later
   d. The exception is logged automatically by .NET
2. Which method is commonly used to attach a continuation to a task?
   a. `Task.Run()`
   b. `Task.WhenAll()`
   c. `Task.Delay()`
   d. `Task.ContinueWith()`

3. What is the primary purpose of a custom task scheduler in .NET?
    a. To increase the priority of certain tasks
    b. To control how and where tasks are scheduled for execution
    c. To automatically cancel long-running tasks
    d. To enforce a fixed number of tasks that can run in an application
4. How can a **`CancellationToken`** improve task management in .NET?
    a. By forcing all tasks to complete within a fixed time
    b. By allowing a task to be paused and resumed
    c. By enabling cooperative task cancellation when requested
    d. By automatically handling all exceptions in a task

Answers

1. c
2. d
3. b
4. c

Questions

1. How can a custom task scheduler be leveraged to improve performance in a high-throughput application? Can you think of scenarios where the default task scheduler might not be optimal?
2. Consider a scenario where multiple interdependent tasks are running, and one of them encounters an error. How would you design a system to gracefully handle such failures while maintaining efficiency?
3. How can you use task continuations to implement a workflow where each step depends on the success of the previous step, but failures need to be handled without stopping the entire process?
4. How would you design a task-based system that optimally balances responsiveness and resource efficiency, especially in a cloud or distributed environment?

Key Terms

- **Task Scheduler**: A class that decides when and how to execute tasks.
- **Custom Task Scheduler**: A task scheduler custom built for specialized task scheduling.
- **Task Chaining**: Structuring tasks with continuations to allow sequencing while still benefiting from concurrency.
- **Multi-task Continuation**: A continuation that has multiple antecedents. one or all of which must complete before the continuation can run.
- **Nested or Child Tasks**: Tasks started by other tasks, which may be attached to their parent task to simplify task management.

- **Parent Tasks**: Tasks that start other tasks. Child tasks may be attached to their parent task to simplify task management.
- **Attached Child Tasks**: Child tasks that create a dependency between the child and the parent task, affecting parent task completion and error handling.
- **Detached Child Tasks**: Child tasks that execute independently of their parent tasks.
- **Task Starvation**: A situation where tasks are delayed significantly or never executed due to resource constraints or scheduling policies.
- **Cooperative Cancellation**: Code designed to actively respond to cancellation requests.
- **Linked Token Source**: A cancellation token that is created as the combination of other cancellation tokens and will cancel if any of its linked tokens cancel.
- **Timeout**: A cancellation token source that is set to cancel after a period of time elapses.

CHAPTER 10
Asynchronous Programming with Async/Await

Introduction

Modern **asynchronous programming** in .NET is built on the Task-based model. We introduced tasks in *Chapter 3, Creating and Running Tasks in C#* and explored advanced task management techniques in *Chapter 9, Advanced Task Management*. Tasks simplify **asynchronous programming** by representing an operation that will be completed in the future, allowing developers to track progress, handle success or failure, and manage concurrent execution.

However, working directly with tasks can be complex. Managing delegates, continuations, and parent-child task relationships requires careful coordination, making the code harder to read and maintain. Additionally, synchronizing task execution with the main thread often involves blocking operations, which can lead to deadlocks and inefficient resource usage.

C# addresses these challenges with the `async` and `await` keywords. These keywords simplify working with tasks by allowing **asynchronous** code to be written in a more natural, **synchronous** style—without blocking threads. In this chapter, we will explore how `async` and `await` make modern **asynchronous programming** in .NET more readable, efficient, and scalable.

Structure

This chapter will focus on the following key topics:

- Introduction to **Asynchronous Programming**
    - Comparing **Synchronous** and **Asynchronous**
    - Key Benefits of **Asynchronous Programming**
    - Common Use Cases
- Using the `async` and `await` Keywords
    - Review of TAP
    - The Role of `Task` and `Task<T>`
    - Converting **Synchronous** to **Asynchronous**
- Creating **Asynchronous Methods**
    - Best Practices for Async Methods
    - Returning `Task`, `Task<T>`, and `ValueTask<T>`
    - Configuring Await

    - Handling Async Operations
- Using Async APIs
    - Working with Built-In APIs
    - Writing Efficient Wrappers
- Handling Exceptions in Async Methods
    - Common Pitfalls
    - Using Try Catch
    - Exception Propagation in Async Code
    - Debugging Async Exceptions
- Enumerations and Disposable
    - Introduction to Async Enumerations
    - Benefits of **Asynchronous Enumeration**
    - Implementing Custom Iterators
    - Using Async Disposable
- Asynchronous Message Passing

Introduction to Asynchronous Programming

Modern **asynchronous programming** in .NET is built on Task-based programming and is greatly simplified by the `async` and `await` keywords. These keywords allow **asynchronous** code to be written in a style like **synchronous** programming while ensuring that execution continues without blocking. Instead of pausing the entire thread, **asynchronous** operations run in the background, resuming when results are ready. This approach improves efficiency by preventing unnecessary thread blocking and reducing the likelihood of deadlocks.

Comparing Synchronous and Asynchronous

The following table highlights the differences between **synchronous** and **asynchronous** programming models.

Aspect	Synchronous Execution	Asynchronous Execution
Thread Blocking	Blocks execution until the task completes.	Does not block, continues executing other tasks.
I/O Performance	Slower I/O performance.	Optimized I/O performance.
UI Responsiveness	UI may freeze while waiting.	UI remains responsive.
Concurrency	One task at a time per thread.	Multiple tasks progress concurrently.

***Table 10.1**: Comparison of Synchronous and Asynchronous Programming*

Key Benefits of Asynchronous Programming

Asynchronous programming provides several advantages over **synchronous** execution, particularly for applications dealing with I/O-bound or CPU-bound workloads. Some key benefits include the following:

- **Improved UI Responsiveness**: In desktop applications, **asynchronous** operations prevent the UI thread from blocking, ensuring a smooth user experience.

- **Better Resource Utilization**: Async programming allows threads to remain free for other tasks instead of idling while waiting for I/O operations such as database queries or network requests, leading to more efficient CPU and memory usage.
- **Scalability**: Server applications, such as ASP.NET Core web APIs, can handle more concurrent requests without increasing the number of threads. This reduces thread contention and improves throughput under high load conditions.
- **Energy Efficiency**: Since async methods do not block threads unnecessarily, CPU cycles are used more efficiently, reducing power consumption, which is especially beneficial for cloud services and battery-powered devices.
- **Better Responsiveness in Web Applications**: In web servers such as ASP.NET Core, async programming prevents thread starvation, allowing the application to handle more requests concurrently and improving overall system responsiveness.
- **Simpler and More Maintainable Code**: The **`async/await`** pattern provides a structured, readable way to write **asynchronous** code, avoiding complex thread management, callbacks, and race conditions that can occur with traditional multi-threading.

By improving responsiveness, scalability, and efficiency while simplifying code, **asynchronous programming** in .NET helps developers build high-performance applications that make better use of system resources.

Common Use Cases

Asynchronous programming is primarily optimized for I/O-bound operations, where avoiding blocking allows threads to remain free for other tasks while waiting for operations to complete. However, CPU-bound workloads can also benefit when parallelism is applied effectively. Some common use cases include the following:

- **Database Access**: Running database queries asynchronously frees up resources while the query executes on the server, improving scalability and responsiveness.
- **Asynchronous Network Requests**: Whether calling a local service or making API requests over the internet, non-blocking access improves efficiency and reduces response times.
- **File I/O Operations**: Reading and writing large files asynchronously prevents UI freezes and improves performance in applications handling multiple file operations.
- **Waiting for Parallel Processes**: Using **`Parallel.ForEachAsync()`** or asynchronous PLINQ queries enables efficient data processing without blocking the calling thread.
- **Asynchronous Web APIs**: In ASP.NET Core, using async controller actions allows web servers to handle more concurrent requests efficiently.
- **Background Tasks and Scheduled Jobs**: **Asynchronous programming** enables non-blocking execution of long-running operations, such as email sending, queue processing, or scheduled tasks.
- **Real-time Applications**: Chat applications, stock tickers, and WebSockets-based systems rely on **asynchronous programming** for real-time updates without excessive resource consumption.
- **UI Operations in Desktop and Mobile Apps**: In Windows Presentation Foundation (WPF), WinForms, and Xamarin/MAUI, async methods keep the UI responsive while performing tasks such as data retrieval or computations.

By applying **asynchronous programming** to I/O-bound operations such as database access, network requests, and file handling, as well as CPU-bound workloads that benefit from parallel processing, developers can create applications that are more scalable, responsive, and efficient.

Using the async and await Keywords

The **async** and **await** keywords simplify **asynchronous programming** in .NET by providing a syntax that closely resembles **synchronous** code. The Task-based Asynchronous Pattern (TAP), which was briefly introduced in *Chapter 3, Creating and Running Tasks in C#*, serves as the foundation for **asynchronous programming** with **async** and **await**.

Review of TAP

The Task-based Asynchronous Pattern (TAP) standardizes asynchronous operations as methods that return either a **Task** instance or a **Task<TResult>** instance. Later .NET versions introduced **ValueTask<TResult>**, which reduces heap allocations for short-lived asynchronous operations.

TAP methods return a **Task**, representing operations that may still be in progress. This allows the operation to finish on a separate thread, independent from the calling thread. Exceptions thrown during **Task** execution are captured and can be handled in the calling code. TAP methods support cancellation by accepting a **CancellationToken**, allowing cooperative cancellation of **asynchronous** operations.

The Role of Task and Task<T>

Task and **Task<TResult>** represent ongoing **asynchronous** operations that will complete in the future.

- **Task** represents an **asynchronous** operation that does not return a value, such as a void method but with better support for error handling and continuation.
- **Task<TResult>** represents an asynchronous operation that produces a result of type **TResult**. For example, **Task<int>** represents an operation that will eventually return an **int**, much like a **synchronous** method returning an **int**.

These classes form the foundation of TAP and enable structured, scalable async workflows in .NET. The **async** and **await** keywords integrate seamlessly with **Task** and **Task<TResult>**, simplifying **asynchronous programming** while maintaining readability and robustness.

Converting Synchronous to Asynchronous

Imagine you need to fetch data from a web API using C#. A straightforward way to do this is by using **HttpClient**, which provides an easy-to-use API for making HTTP requests. However, there is a subtle but significant difference in how you can handle these requests: synchronously or asynchronously. Let us walk through this transformation step by step.

A Synchronous Approach: Blocking the Thread

Consider the following method, which makes an HTTP request and waits for the response:

```
static void GetHttpResponse()
{
    var httpClient = new HttpClient();
    HttpResponseMessage result =
        httpClient.GetAsync("https://httpbin.org/get").Result;
    var content = result.Content.ReadAsStringAsync().Result;
    Console.WriteLine(content);
}
```

At first glance, this seems simple and effective: call **`GetAsync()`**, retrieve the result, and print it to the console. However, there is a hidden cost. The **`Result`** property blocks the main thread while waiting for the HTTP request to complete. This means the program is completely stuck–unable to do anything else–until the response arrives.

In a console application, this might seem like a minor inconvenience, but in UI applications such as WPF or WinForms, blocking the main thread can freeze the entire user interface. Worse, in some cases, it can lead to deadlocks, where the program becomes completely unresponsive.

Embracing **`async/await`**, allows us to perform the same operations without blocking the main thread.

An Asynchronous Approach: Keeping the Thread Free

Let us rewrite the method using **`async/await`**:

```
static async Task GetHttpResponse()
{
    var httpClient = new HttpClient();
    HttpResponseMessage result =
        await httpClient.GetAsync("https://httpbin.org/get");
    var content = await result.Content.ReadAsStringAsync();
    Console.WriteLine(content);
}
```

This version looks quite similar, but there are key differences:

- The method is now marked as **`async`**, allowing it to use the **`await`** keyword.
- The return type has changed from void to **`Task`**, signaling that this method runs asynchronously.
- Instead of **`Result`**, we now use **`await`**, which waits for the operation to complete without blocking the main thread.

With this change, our method can now fetch data in the background while the main thread remains free to perform other tasks. If this were part of a larger application, the UI would stay responsive, and system resources would be used more efficiently.

The impact of this change extends beyond just avoiding thread blocking. By making your code asynchronous, you gain several advantages:

- **Better Performance**: The thread is no longer idle while waiting for an HTTP response. Instead, it can be used for other operations, making the application more efficient.
- **Improved Responsiveness**: In UI applications, this prevents freezing and allows users to continue interacting with the interface while the request is processed.
- **Simpler Exception Handling**: When using **`Result`**, exceptions are wrapped in an **`AggregateException`**, making debugging more cumbersome. With **`await`**, exceptions are thrown naturally, making them easier to handle.

At its core, converting synchronous code to asynchronous is about improving efficiency and responsiveness. By replacing blocking calls with **`await`**, your application can handle more work at once, avoid UI freezes, and make better use of system resources. With **`async/await`**, your code can remain clean, readable, and performant–all while keeping your threads free to do more important work.

Note: *HttpClient is designed to be a long-lived, shared instance rather than created for each request, as shown in these examples. Repeatedly instantiating* **`HttpClient`** *can lead to socket exhaustion, where lingering connections consume system resources. While this book does not cover* **`HttpClient`** *usage in detail, it is important to highlight best practices: in non-ASP.NET applications, a static readonly* **`HttpClient`** *should be used, while ASP.NET Core applications should leverage* **`IHttpClientFactory`** *for* *better resource management. The usage of* `HttpClient` *in these examples is purely for convenience and should not be considered best practice for production code.*

Creating Asynchronous Methods

Asynchronous methods in C# are structured similarly to **synchronous** methods, ensuring consistency and readability. However, they differ in crucial ways. Instead of returning void or a direct result, **asynchronous** methods return `Task` for procedures that do not produce a value and `Task<TResult>` for functions that return a value. While their syntax resembles that of **synchronous** methods, their execution model introduces key differences that impact control flow, performance, and responsiveness.

Best Practices for Async Methods

When designing and writing **asynchronous methods** using `async` and `await`, follow these best practices to ensure efficiency, maintainability, and proper error handling:

- Avoid void return types except for event handlers. **Asynchronous methods** should return `Task` or `Task<TResult>` instead of void, except when implementing an event handler. Methods returning void do not allow exceptions to be captured properly, making error handling difficult.
- Use `ConfigureAwait(false)` in library and service code. When writing library code or background services, use `ConfigureAwait(false)` to avoid capturing the synchronization context, reducing unnecessary overhead. However, do not use `ConfigureAwait(false)` in UI applications (for example, WPF, WinForms) where returning to the original **synchronization context** is necessary to update UI elements.
- Avoid blocking calls (`Result`, `Wait()`). Mixing blocking calls with **asynchronous** code can lead to deadlocks, particularly in UI applications, and can degrade performance in server applications. Instead, use `await` to allow natural **asynchronous** execution.
- Let exceptions propagate naturally. Exceptions in **asynchronous methods** should flow naturally, just as they do in **synchronous** code. Avoid unnecessary `try-catch` blocks unless you have a clear recovery strategy. When using `Task.Run()`, wrap it in `try-catch` only if exceptions need to be logged or handled.
- Make calling methods **asynchronous**. Any method that calls an `async` method should itself be marked `async` to maintain the **asynchronous** flow and prevent blocking. Avoid "sync-over-async" patterns, where an `async` method is called inside a **synchronous** context, as this can lead to deadlocks.
- Use `Task.WhenAll()` and `Task.WhenAny()` for concurrent execution. Use `Task.WhenAll()` to run multiple tasks in parallel and `Task.WhenAny()` to continue execution as soon as one task completes. These methods are preferable to their blocking counterparts (`Task.WaitAll()` and `Task.WaitAny()`), which can cause performance issues.
- Be selective with `async` usage. While **asynchronous methods** improve responsiveness and scalability, overusing them can introduce unnecessary overhead. Use `async` primarily for I/O-bound operations (for example, database queries, HTTP requests) and consider parallelism (for example, `Parallel.ForEach`) for CPU-bound workloads.

Following these best practices ensures that **asynchronous methods** in .NET are efficient, scalable, and maintainable. Properly structuring async code helps prevent deadlocks, improves error handling, and enhances application responsiveness, particularly in UI and server applications.

Returning `Task`, `Task<T>`, and `ValueTask<T>`

In .NET, Task-based Asynchronous Pattern (TAP) methods support three possible return types: `Task`,

Task<TResult>, and **ValueTask<TResult>**. We have previously covered tasks, but in the context of **asynchronous programming**, methods should return **Task** if they are procedural and do not return a value. For functions that return a result of type **TResult**, the best practice is to return **Task<TResult>**, which is optimal for most applications.

However, some applications, such as games, high-frequency trading systems, or real-time applications, have extremely high performance requirements. In such cases, even small optimizations—such as reducing heap allocations—can be significant. To address these performance-sensitive scenarios, .NET introduced **ValueTask<TResult>**, which provides an alternative to **Task<TResult>** that can avoid unnecessary heap allocations when a result is available synchronously.

Using ValueTask<T> Instead of Task<T>

Consider a scenario where data is retrieved from an external source, such as a file or a database, but is then cached in memory. Most of the time, the cached result is returned immediately, and only occasionally is the file accessed. A **Task<TResult>** can be used for this retrieval without blocking, but since **Task<TResult>** is a class, creating one always incurs a heap allocation, which must eventually be collected by the garbage collector.

If the data is usually available in memory, there is no need for the method to complete asynchronously, and the overhead of **Task<TResult>** becomes unnecessary. In high-performance applications, reducing heap allocations can be crucial. This scenario might initially be implemented as follows:

```
using System.Collections.Concurrent;

var cache = new ConcurrentDictionary<string, string>();
var tempFile = Path.GetTempFileName();
try
{
    await File.WriteAllTextAsync(tempFile, "This is some important cached
data.");

    for (var i = 0; i < 10; i++)
    {
        Console.WriteLine(await GetFileData(tempFile));
    }
}
finally
{
    File.Delete(tempFile);
}

async Task<string> GetFileData(string tempFile)
{
    if (cache.TryGetValue(tempFile, out var result))
    {
        return result;
    }

    result = await File.ReadAllTextAsync(tempFile);
    cache.TryAdd(tempFile, result);
    return result;
}
```

In this implementation, **GetFileData()** completes synchronously when the cache has the data but runs asynchronously when it needs to read the file. If cached values are returned most of the time and performance is critical, **ValueTask<TResult>** may improve efficiency.

Optimizing with ValueTask<T>

By changing **GetFileData()** to return **ValueTask<TResult>**, we eliminate unnecessary heap allocations when the result is immediately available:

```
using System.Collections.Concurrent;

var cache = new ConcurrentDictionary<string, string>();

async ValueTask<string> GetFileData(string tempFile)
{
    if (cache.TryGetValue(tempFile, out var result))
    {
        return result;
    }

    result = await File.ReadAllTextAsync(tempFile);
    cache.TryAdd(tempFile, result);
    return result;
}
```

With this change:

- If the cached result is available, **ValueTask<TResult>** directly wraps the value without creating a heap-allocated **Task<TResult>**.
- If the method must perform asynchronous work (reading from the file), it creates a **Task<TResult>** internally and wraps it in a **ValueTask<TResult>**.

Considerations and Best Practices

While **ValueTask<TResult>** can optimize performance in specific scenarios, it has important limitations.

- **Boxing Eliminates Benefits**: Since **ValueTask<TResult>** is a struct, storing it in a variable of type object or passing it to an API expecting **Task<TResult>** results in boxing, negating the performance gains.
- **Cannot be Awaited Multiple Times**: Unlike **Task<TResult>**, a **ValueTask<TResult>** can only be awaited once. If you need multiple awaits, always use **Task<TResult>**.
- **No Support for Multiple Continuations**: **ValueTask<TResult>** does not allow multiple continuations such as **Task<TResult>**, making it unsuitable for event-driven scenarios.
- **Not for Blocking Operations**: Using **ValueTask<TResult>** in synchronous blocking patterns is an anti-pattern and should be avoided.
- **No ValueTask Equivalent to Task**: If an asynchronous method does not return a value, use **Task.CompletedTask** rather than trying to return a **ValueTask**. The reason is that **CompletedTask** is already cached by the compiler and **ValueTask** in most cases does not provide additional optimization. An exception to this rule is **DisposeAsync()** in **IAsyncDisposable**.

Additionally, if a **ValueTask<TResult>** must be used in a context that expects a **Task<TResult>**, you can convert it using **.AsTask()** as follows.

```
ValueTask<string> valueTask = GetFileData(tempFile);
Task<string> task = valueTask.AsTask();
```

Using ValueTask<T>

ValueTask<TResult> can be a useful optimization in high-performance applications, but only if profiling and benchmarking show that heap allocations from **`Task<TResult>`** are a bottleneck. In general:

- Use **`Task<TResult>`** in most cases–it is simpler, supports multiple awaits, and avoids pitfalls.
- Use **`ValueTask<TResult>`** when methods complete synchronously most of the time and performance testing confirms an improvement.

By carefully considering when and where to use **`ValueTask<TResult>`**, you can balance readability, maintainability, and performance in your asynchronous applications

Configuring Await

Asynchronous programming in C# relies on **`async`** and **`await`**, which allow tasks to run in the background while keeping code readable and efficient. However, under the hood, something interesting happens. The compiler transforms **`async`** methods into state machines, breaking them into tasks and continuations. This means that when an **`await`** is encountered, execution pauses, and once the awaited task completes, the continuation–the code following the **`await`**–resumes.

By default, C# tries to be smart about threading. If a **synchronization context** is present, **`await`** will capture it and make sure the continuation resumes on that same context. This behavior is essential in some environments–such as UI applications (WinForms, WPF, MAUI)–where updates must happen on the main thread. If code resumed on a different thread, attempting to modify UI elements would result in runtime exceptions.

.NET solves this problem with the **`SynchronizationContext`** class. UI frameworks such as WinForms and WPF override **`SynchronizationContext`** so that any **asynchronous method** that updates the UI will automatically switch back to the main thread after an **`await`**. This ensures that **`await`** behaves in a way that is intuitive for developers writing UI code.

In older ASP.NET applications (before ASP.NET Core), **`SynchronizationContext`** was also important. It ensured that after an **`await`**, the execution continued on the original request-handling thread, allowing developers to safely interact with **`HttpContext.Current`**. This was necessary because **`HttpContext`** was thread-affine, meaning it could only be accessed from a specific thread.

But while this behavior was useful for UI and web applications, it came with a cost. Resuming execution on a specific thread requires extra coordination and context switching, which introduces overhead. Worse, in some scenarios–especially in server applications that block on **asynchronous methods**–this could lead to deadlocks.

Deadlocks and Overhead

Imagine an ASP.NET application where a developer makes an asynchronous call but then tries to synchronously wait for the result, such as in the following example.

```
public string GetData()
{
    return FetchDataAsync().Result; // Blocks the thread and waits
}

public async Task<string> FetchDataAsync()
{
    return await Task.Delay(1000).ContinueWith(_ => "Hello World");
}
```

This might seem harmless, but it is actually a recipe for a deadlock. This is because the original thread is blocked waiting for the task to complete, while the continuation (the code after **`await`**) is waiting to get back on that same thread—which is already occupied. This circular wait condition causes a deadlock, freezing the application.

To avoid this problem, .NET provides **ConfigureAwait(false)**, a method that allows developers to opt out of **synchronization context** capture, letting continuations run on any available thread rather than waiting to resume on a specific one.

Using ConfigureAwait(false)

Calling **ConfigureAwait(false)** on an awaited task tells .NET to not care about what thread runs the continuation. This can improve performance by reducing thread contention and avoiding unnecessary context switches. Here is how it works in practice.

```
await Task.Delay(500); // Captures the synchronization context (if present)
await Task.Delay(500).ConfigureAwait(false); // Does not capture it
```

For UI applications, avoiding the **synchronization context** using **ConfigureAwait(false)** is dangerous because it could cause UI updates to happen on a non-UI thread, leading to exceptions. But in library code or server applications, skipping synchronization can improve responsiveness and avoid deadlocks.

ASP.NET Core

In older ASP.NET applications, **ConfigureAwait(false)** was critical to avoid blocking request-handling threads. But with ASP.NET Core, this concern largely disappears. Unlike its predecessor, ASP.NET Core does not have a **SynchronizationContext** for requests. This means that **await** already behaves as if **ConfigureAwait(false)** were applied—continuations execute on any available thread automatically.

Because of this fundamental design change, using **ConfigureAwait(false)** in ASP.NET Core applications is often unnecessary unless working with legacy code or libraries that still rely on context-aware execution.

Best Practices

To use **ConfigureAwait(false)** effectively, keep these guidelines in mind:

- Use **ConfigureAwait(false)** in library code where **synchronization context** does not matter. This avoids unnecessary thread switching and potential deadlocks.
- Be cautious in UI applications (WinForms, WPF, MAUI). Avoid **ConfigureAwait(false)** when updating the UI to ensure the code executes on the main thread.
- Understand when it is useful in server applications. For older ASP.NET applications, **ConfigureAwait(false)** can improve scalability by preventing threads from being locked waiting for **synchronous** context switching.
- ASP.NET Core applications do not need it. Since ASP.NET Core has no request-specific **SynchronizationContext**, using **ConfigureAwait(false)** does not provide any performance benefits.

The default behavior of **await**—capturing and restoring the **synchronization context**—makes **asynchronous programming** easier in UI and web applications. But in high-performance scenarios, where reducing thread contention is important, **ConfigureAwait(false)** can be a valuable tool. Understanding when and where to use it is key to writing efficient, scalable, and deadlock-free asynchronous code.

Handling `Async` Operations

CPU bound operations are computations that heavily use the CPU, such as data transformations, image processing, AI model execution, and cryptography. **Asynchronous programming** does not reduce CPU workload or improve raw computation speed. However, it can improve responsiveness by offloading CPU-bound work to background threads.

I/O bound operations are processes that spend time waiting on external resources, such as accessing files and databases, making network requests, and streaming. **Asynchronous programming** is optimized for these types of tasks, ensuring that the time spent waiting does not block threads or keep threads idle while they could be doing other work.

Handling these workloads using **asynchronous** processing requires different strategies.

I/O bound workloads benefit from asynchronous programming using **`async/await`** directly. For example, **`HttpClient.GetAsync()`** is already async enabled and can be awaited.

CPU-bound workloads do not inherently benefit from **`async/await`** but can be integrated into async workflows when needed. These types of methods can be integrated in one of several ways.

- It may be best to just implement these as standard **synchronous methods** and run them synchronously. TAP methods can call **synchronous methods** as well as **asynchronous methods**. If a TAP method can complete synchronously or asynchronously, it can use **`Task.FromResult()`** to return a result synchronously.
- For enumerations, **`Parallel.ForEachAsync()`** or **`Parallel.ForAsync()`** support parallel loops in **TAP methods**, if their use is beneficial. The guidelines for using parallel loops were covered in *Chapter 7, Parallel Loops in .NET*.
- PLINQ does not support **`async/await`** directly, but **`Select()`** statements may contain async operations, which could be processed with **`Task.WhenAll()`**. Async operations may also be applied to enumerating the results of PLINQ queries.
- **`Task.Run()`** should be used for CPU-bound tasks in the background that might otherwise freeze the UI or block an important thread. It is particularly useful in UI applications to keep the main thread responsive. However, in server applications, excessive use of **`Task.Run()`** can reduce scalability by consuming unnecessary thread pool threads.

I/O bound operations directly benefit from **`async/await`** and should be awaited directly. Avoid wrapping I/O operations in **`Task.Run()`** because it adds unnecessary overhead. CPU bound workloads may benefit from **`Task.Run()`** to run them in the background, especially in UI applications. CPU bound workloads may also benefit from parallel loops or PLINQ, which can be integrated with **`async/await`** to avoid blocking.

Using `Async` APIs

Asynchronous programming is essential for building high-performance applications, enabling better scalability, responsiveness, and efficient resource utilization. To support this, .NET provides async-enabled APIs for I/O-bound operations such as file access, networking, and database interactions. Microsoft follows a standard convention of appending "Async" to method names, making it easy to identify asynchronous counterparts of synchronous methods.

Working with Built-In APIs

Most **synchronous** or blocking APIs in .NET also have **asynchronous** counterparts, following the Task-based Asynchronous Pattern (TAP). Using these methods involves defining an **asynchronous method** marked with the **async** keyword and awaiting the operation using the **await** keyword, as we have seen in previous chapters.

For example, earlier we used the **Thread.Sleep()** method to simulate work or introduce a delay. However, **Thread.Sleep()** blocks the calling thread, making it unsuitable for **asynchronous** processing. Instead, TAP-based methods should use **Task.Delay()**, which achieves the same effect without blocking and also supports cancellation.

Using **Task.Delay()** is straightforward, as demonstrated in the following example:

Note: *In this example, the constant number 14,000 is defined using an underscore in place of the comma to improve readability. This feature was introduced in C# 7 specifically to increase readability of numeric constants.*

```
var cts = new CancellationTokenSource(14_000);

for (var i = 1; i < 11; i++)
{
    await Task.Delay(1000);
    Console.WriteLine("Count: " + i);
}

try
{
    while (!cts.IsCancellationRequested)
    {
        await Task.Delay(1000, cts.Token);
        Console.WriteLine("Awaiting cancellation...");
    }
}
catch (OperationCanceledException)
{
    Console.WriteLine("Operation cancelled.");
}
```

In this example, **Task.Delay(1000)** introduces a one-second pause between loop iterations using **await**. The first loop counts from 1 to 10, pausing without cancellation support. The second loop, however, loops indefinitely until the **CancellationTokenSource** signals cancellation. The key distinction between **Task.Delay()** and **Thread.Sleep()** is that **Task.Delay()** does not block the main thread, allowing it to continue processing other tasks during the wait period.

Note: *Unlike many asynchronous methods in .NET,* **Task.Delay()** *does not follow the standard naming convention of appending "Async" to its name. This is because it is inherently part of the Task class and always operates asynchronously.*

Asynchronous File I/O

The **System.IO.File** class also supports **asynchronous programming**. Many of its **synchronous methods**, such as **ReadAllText()**, have **asynchronous** equivalents such as **ReadAllTextAsync()**. Streams in **System.IO** provide similar functionality with methods such as **ReadAsync()** and **WriteAsync()**, enabling non-blocking streaming operations.

For example, reading a file asynchronously can be done as follows:

```
var contents = await File.ReadAllTextAsync(tempFileName);
Console.WriteLine(contents);
```

This method reads the entire file without blocking the calling thread, allowing other tasks to proceed while the file is being read.

Asynchronous Database Access

Modern applications often interact with databases, making **asynchronous programming** crucial for maintaining responsiveness. Entity Framework Core provides **asynchronous methods** for database operations, such as fetching data or saving changes. These methods prevent thread blocking, improve scalability, and support cancellation, making them especially beneficial for high-throughput applications such as web APIs.

Asynchronous Network Access

Network operations, such as making HTTP requests, are inherently slow compared to in-memory computations. The **HttpClient** class in .NET is designed for efficient **asynchronous** network communication, providing methods such as **GetAsync()**, **PostAsync()**, and **SendAsync()**, all of which should be awaited to avoid blocking the calling thread.

For example, retrieving data from a web API asynchronously can be done as follows:

```
using var httpClient = new HttpClient();
string result = await httpClient.GetStringAsync("https://example.com/data");
Console.WriteLine(result);
```

By using **HttpClient** with **async/await**, the application remains responsive while waiting for the network response. This approach is essential for scalable applications, particularly those that make frequent API calls or handle multiple concurrent requests.

Best Practices

When working with asynchronous APIs in .NET, keep the following best practices in mind:

- Avoid blocking calls such as **Wait()** or **Result** in **asynchronous methods**, as these can cause deadlocks or degrade performance. Always use **await** instead.
- Utilize cancellation tokens when supported by an API to allow for graceful cancellation and better resource management.
- Consider **ConfigureAwait(false)** in library code to improve performance by preventing unnecessary synchronization with the calling context, particularly in non-UI applications.

.NET provides a wide range of asynchronous APIs, all following the same fundamental usage pattern. Leveraging these methods in high-performance applications enhances scalability, reliability, and efficiency, making asynchronous programming a key technique for modern software development.

Writing Efficient Wrappers

Some legacy APIs or third-party libraries do not support **async** methods. Using these libraries effectively in TAP methods requires writing a wrapper for the API that follows the TAP pattern. The Task Parallel Library (TPL) provides the **TaskCompletionSource<T>** class to support these scenarios.

TaskCompletionSource<T> creates a **Task<TResult>** that can be manually completed by calling its methods, representing the producer side of an asynchronous operation. **TaskCompletionSource<T>** exposes a **Task** property that represents the consumer side of the operation. Consuming code can await the **Task** returned by this property as they would any other task. **TaskCompletionSource<T>** supports manually setting any task completion state including success, error, or cancellation, giving developers complete control over task completion. This is especially useful for converting legacy APIs that support older asynchronous patters or event-based models.

To see how this works, let us take a .NET API that is not designed for TAP and convert it using **TaskCompletionSource<T>**. The **System.Timers.Timer** class is a simple, event-based API that supports timeouts. It does not support asynchronous programming, however. We will write a wrapper to enable async support.

```
Task WaitForTimerAsync(int milliseconds, CancellationToken token = default)
{
    var tcs = new TaskCompletionSource<bool>();
    var timer = new System.Timers.Timer(milliseconds);

    ElapsedEventHandler? handler = null;
    handler = (sender, e) =>
    {
        timer.Elapsed -= handler!;
        timer.Dispose();
        tcs.TrySetResult(true); // Complete the task
    };

    timer.Elapsed += handler;
    timer.AutoReset = false;
    timer.Start();

    if (token.CanBeCanceled)
    {
        token.Register(() =>
        {
            timer.Elapsed -= handler!;
            timer.Dispose();
            tcs.TrySetCanceled(); // Cancel the task
        });
    }

    return tcs.Task;
}
```

The **System.Timers.Timer** class normally works by registering an event handler that is called when the timer elapses. The prior code wraps this functionality using a **TaskCompletionSource<bool>** instance. The handler is created as a lambda which unregisters the event, disposes the timer, and sets the task result to **true**. This handler is registered with the timer and the **AutoReset** property is set to **false**, indicating that the timer should only fire once. The timer is then started and the **Task** property from the **TaskCompletionSource<bool>** is returned. This wrapper allows the timer to be awaited instead of using the event-based approach.

Cancellation is supported by registering a delegate with the provided cancellation token. The delegate unregisters the handler and cleans up the timer, but then cancels the task by calling **TrySetCanceled()**. This wrapper can be consumed by using **await** as follows.

```
Console.WriteLine("Awaiting event-based timer...");
await WaitForTimerAsync(1000);
Console.WriteLine("Timer expired.");

var cts = new CancellationTokenSource(250);
try
{
    Console.WriteLine("Cancelling...");
    await WaitForTimerAsync(1000, cts.Token);
}
catch (OperationCanceledException)
{
```

```
        Console.WriteLine("Operation cancelled.");
    }
```

The output from the prior example is as follows:

```
Awaiting event-based timer...
Timer expired.
Cancelling...
Operation cancelled.
```

The execution pauses as expected when **`WaitForTimerAsync(1000)`** and **`WaitForTimerAsync(1000, cts.Token)`** are called.

When writing wrappers, remember the following guidelines:

- CPU bound processes do not benefit from asynchronous processing and can be called directly as **synchronous methods** or run in the background using **`Task.Run()`**.
- Prefer wrapping I/O APIs that support **asynchronous** operations natively but use a different approach than **`async/await`**, such as event-based.
- If the I/O API does not expose **asynchronous** operations natively, the synchronous API can be wrapped by queueing the work on a separate thread (**`Task.Run()`** or **`ThreadPool.QueueUserWorkItem()`**). But remember that doing so does not enable **asynchronous** operation and will block the thread during execution. Consider just using the API synchronously in this circumstance unless there is a reason to run it in the background.

Using **`TaskCompletionSource<T>`** is an effective way to integrate legacy or event-based APIs into modern asynchronous workflows. By wrapping such APIs, we can expose them in a way that is compatible with **`async/await`**, improving code readability and maintainability. However, it is important to properly unsubscribe events, handle potential race conditions, and support cancellation when applicable. While wrapping synchronous APIs may sometimes be necessary, it does not inherently provide true asynchronous I/O and should be used with caution. Following these best practices ensures efficient and reliable asynchronous wrappers that seamlessly integrate with the TAP in .NET.

Handling Exceptions in Async Methods

Asynchronous methods in .NET are based on the Task-based Asynchronous Pattern (TAP), meaning their exception-handling behavior is tied to the way tasks work. In a **synchronous method**, when an exception occurs, execution stops immediately, and the exception propagates up the call stack. However, in an **asynchronous method**, exceptions are captured within the returned **`Task`** and are only thrown when the **`Task`** is awaited. This means the handling of exceptions in asynchronous code differs from traditional synchronous exception propagation.

For instance, when calling **`Wait()`** or accessing **`Result`** on a faulted task, the exception is wrapped inside an **`AggregateException`**. However, when using **`await`**, an extra step is taken: **`await`** unwraps the exception from the **`AggregateException`** and rethrows only the original inner exception. This behavior makes error handling in asynchronous code cleaner and more intuitive.

For example, consider a method that throws an **`ArgumentException`**.

```
static async Task ThrowErrorAsync()
{
    throw new ArgumentException("Invalid argument provided.");
}
```

If we use **Wait()** or **Result** to access the task, we get an **AggregateException**.

```
try
{
    ThrowErrorAsync().Wait();
}
catch (AggregateException ex)
{
    Console.WriteLine($"Caught: {ex.GetBaseException().Message}");
}
```

However, using **await**, we directly receive the **ArgumentException**.

```
try
{
    await ThrowErrorAsync();
}
catch (ArgumentException ex)
{
    Console.WriteLine($"Caught: {ex.Message}");
}
```

This design simplifies exception handling, making the code easier to read, maintain, and debug compared to manually handling **AggregateException**. Understanding this behavior is key to properly handling errors in asynchronous .NET applications.

Common Pitfalls

Asynchronous programming in .NET is designed to resemble **synchronous** code in structure, making it easier to read and write. However, beneath the surface, it behaves quite differently. Failing to account for these differences can lead to subtle and sometimes catastrophic issues. Let us explore some of the most common pitfalls developers encounter when handling exceptions in asynchronous code and how to avoid them.

Unobserved Task Exceptions: The Silent Failures

One of the biggest mistakes developers make is calling an **asynchronous method** without awaiting it. When a task is started but never awaited, any exceptions it throws are effectively ignored. These are known as **unobserved task exceptions**, and they can be particularly troublesome because they often do not appear until it is too late—causing unpredictable behavior or even crashing the application.

To avoid this, always **await asynchronous methods**. If a task does not need to be awaited directly, consider storing it and handling exceptions later using **ContinueWith()** or a global exception handler.

For extra safety, .NET provides the **TaskScheduler.UnobservedTaskException** event, which can help catch these silent failures before they cause havoc. We discussed this mechanism in *Chapter 3, Creating and Running Tasks in C#*—a valuable tool for debugging.

Blocking Calls: The Deadlock Trap

Another common mistake is using blocking calls such as **Wait()**, **Result**, or **GetAwaiter().GetResult()** to force an **asynchronous method** to complete immediately. While this may seem like a quick workaround, it can lead to deadlocks in UI-based applications and ASP.NET environments that rely on synchronization contexts.

Again, the proper approach is to always use **await** when dealing with **asynchronous methods**. For non-UI applications, blocking calls might not always result in a deadlock, but they can still reduce performance and responsiveness. In general, it is best to embrace **async/await** fully and avoid mixing **synchronous** and **asynchronous** code.

A Hidden Trap

In most cases, **asynchronous methods** should return a **Task**, allowing the caller to **await** them and handle exceptions properly. However, the compiler also allows **async void** methods. This feature exists for one specific reason–supporting event handlers in UI applications. Using this pattern in other contexts is a hidden trap.

An **async void** method cannot be awaited, which means any exception it throws is **unobserved** and can crash the application. The rule here is simple: only use **async void** for event handlers in UI code. For everything else, stick to **async Task** to ensure exceptions are properly handled.

Asynchronous programming is a powerful tool, but it comes with unique challenges that can lead to hard-to-debug issues if not handled correctly. By always awaiting tasks, avoiding blocking calls, and being cautious with async void methods, you can write more stable and maintainable asynchronous code.

Keeping these pitfalls in mind will not only prevent frustrating bugs but also help you design applications that are more responsive, scalable, and resilient.

Using Try Catch

Handling exceptions in **asynchronous methods** works much like in **synchronous** code–by wrapping calls in a **try-catch** block. However, exceptions from **asynchronous methods** can only be caught if the **Task** is awaited. If an **asynchronous method** is called but not awaited, any exceptions it throws will go **unobserved**, potentially causing instability in the application.

Let us consider an example where an **asynchronous method**, **ThrowErrorAsync()**, raises an **ArgumentException**. The following code correctly catches the exception because the method is properly awaited.

```
try
{
    await ThrowErrorAsync();
}
catch (ArgumentException ex)
{
    Console.WriteLine($"Caught: {ex.Message}");
}
```

However, if we call the method without awaiting it, the exception will not be caught, even though we have a **try-catch** block.

```
try
{
    ThrowErrorAsync(); //No await
}
catch (ArgumentException ex)
{
    Console.WriteLine("Exception will not be caught.");
}
```

Here, the exception is thrown inside **ThrowErrorAsync()**, but because the method is not awaited, the catch block never gets a chance to handle it. This results in an **unobserved exception**, which could crash the application or cause unexpected behavior. Therefore, always await **asynchronous methods** to ensure exceptions are properly handled.

One challenge arises when working with UI frameworks such as Windows Forms or WPF, where event handlers cannot return a **`Task`**—they must have a void return type. This means the caller cannot **`await`** them, and exceptions cannot be propagated up the call stack.

To handle this properly, wrap the entire method in a **`try-catch`** block so that any exceptions are caught within the method itself.

```
private async void button2_Click(object sender, EventArgs e)
{
    try
    {
        this.label1.Text = await FetchDataAsync();
    }
    catch (Exception ex)
    {
        MessageBox.Show(ex.Message, "Error",
            MessageBoxButtons.OK, MessageBoxIcon.Error);
    }
}
```

Here, **`button2_Click`** is an event handler and cannot return a **`Task`**, so it must handle exceptions internally. This prevents crashes and ensures that errors are properly reported to the user.

By following these best practices, you can ensure that **`try-catch`** blocks work as expected, providing stable and robust exception handling in **asynchronous** code.

Exception Propagation in Async Code

Unlike **synchronous** code, where exceptions propagate immediately up the call stack, asynchronous exceptions are captured within faulted tasks and are only thrown when the task is awaited. This behavior provides flexibility in handling errors, particularly for scenarios where tasks run independently or in parallel.

Handling Exceptions in Fire-and-Forget Tasks

In some cases, an **asynchronous method** might be launched without being awaited, often referred to as a fire-and-forget task. Since unawaited tasks do not propagate exceptions in the usual way, you must explicitly handle errors to prevent them from being lost. One approach is to use a continuation with **`ContinueWith()`**, which allows you to inspect and handle any errors:

```
FireAndForgetAsync().ContinueWith(task =>
{
    if (task.IsFaulted)
    {
        Console.WriteLine(task.Exception.Message);
    }
});

await Task.Delay(1000);
Console.WriteLine("Done");

static async Task FireAndForgetAsync()
{
```

```
        await Task.Delay(500);
        throw new InvalidOperationException("An invalid operation occurred.");
    }
```

In this example, **FireAndForgetAsync()** runs in the background without being awaited. The **ContinueWith()** method ensures that if an exception occurs, it is detected and logged instead of being silently ignored.

Exception Handling with Task.WhenAll()

When working with multiple tasks, **Task.WhenAll()** is commonly used to wait for all tasks to complete without blocking the main thread. However, if multiple tasks throw exceptions, they are aggregated into an **AggregateException**.

By default, **await** unwraps the **AggregateException** and throws only the first exception, potentially causing other errors to be lost. To properly handle all exceptions, inspect the **Exception** property of the faulted task and use **Flatten()** to retrieve all inner exceptions.

```
Task resultTask = null!;
try
{
    resultTask = Task.WhenAll(
        ThrowErrorAsync(),
        ThrowErrorAsync(),
        ThrowErrorAsync(),
        Task.Delay(500)
        );
    await resultTask;
}
catch (Exception)
{
    Console.WriteLine($"Caught: {resultTask.Exception?.Flatten().Message}");
}

static async Task ThrowErrorAsync()
{
    throw new ArgumentException("Invalid argument provided.");
}
```

In this example, defining **resultTask** outside the **try-catch** block ensures that, if an exception occurs, we can still access **resultTask.Exception** to retrieve all the faults. This method prevents exception loss and ensures that all errors are properly reported.

Handling Exceptions with Task.WhenAny()

The **Task.WhenAny()** method waits for only the first task to complete, regardless of whether it succeeds or fails. However, the remaining tasks continue running in the background, and any exceptions they throw may go **unobserved**, leading to instability.

To properly handle all exceptions, you can use continuations to capture errors from the remaining tasks after **Task.WhenAny()** completes.

```
List<Task> tasks = [.. new[] {ThrowErrorAsync(),
    ThrowErrorAsync(),
    ThrowErrorAsync(),
    Task.Delay(500)}];

Task<Task> whenAnyTask = null!;
```

```
try
{
    whenAnyTask = Task.WhenAny(tasks);
    await whenAnyTask.Unwrap();
}
catch (Exception ex)
{
    Console.WriteLine($"Caught: {ex.Message}");
}

var remainingTasks = tasks.Where(t => t != whenAnyTask.Result).ToList();
await Task.WhenAll(remainingTasks).ContinueWith(task =>
{
    foreach (Task remainingTask in remainingTasks)
    {
        if (remainingTask.IsFaulted)
        {
            Console.WriteLine($"Caught: {remainingTask.Exception?.Flatten().
Message}");
        }
    }
});
```

The output of the prior example is as follows:

```
Caught: Invalid argument provided.
Caught: One or more errors occurred. (Invalid argument provided.)
Caught: One or more errors occurred. (Invalid argument provided.)
```

Here, **`Task.WhenAny()`** completes when the first task finishes (successfully or with an error), but the remaining tasks continue running. To ensure that their exceptions are also handled, we use **`Task.WhenAll()`** with a continuation. This way, no exceptions go **unobserved**, improving application stability.

Alternatively, if the tasks support cancellation, the remaining tasks could be cancelled instead of awaiting them.

When using **`Task.WhenAny()`**, the returned task is a wrapper task that represents the first completed task from the provided list. However, this wrapper task does not automatically propagate exceptions from the inner completed task. This means that simply awaiting the result of **`Task.WhenAny()`** does not throw the exception from the actual completed task, which can lead to **unobserved exceptions**.

To ensure that exceptions propagate correctly, we use the **`Unwrap()`** method. This method extracts the inner task from the wrapper task and allows us to **`await`** it properly. By using **`Unwrap()`** the awaited result reflects the true outcome of the completed task, not just the wrapper task.

By understanding and addressing these nuances in async exception propagation, you can build robust and fault-tolerant asynchronous applications in .NET.

Debugging Async Exceptions

Asynchronous exception handling in **TAP methods** differs from traditional **synchronous methods**, which can sometimes make debugging more challenging. While many exceptions will be visible and easily caught—especially if best practices are followed—some may remain **unobserved** or otherwise difficult to detect.

Detecting Unobserved Exceptions

One common issue in **asynchronous programming** is **unobserved task exceptions**, which can fail silently or cause unexpected crashes. To catch these, implement the **TaskScheduler.UnobservedTaskException** event, as covered in *Chapter 3, Creating and Running Tasks in C#*. This event allows you to log exceptions that would otherwise go unnoticed, making it easier to identify and fix potential issues.

Using the Tasks Window in Visual Studio

Visual Studio provides a Tasks Window that displays active and faulted tasks. You can access this window via **Debug** > **Windows** > **Tasks.**

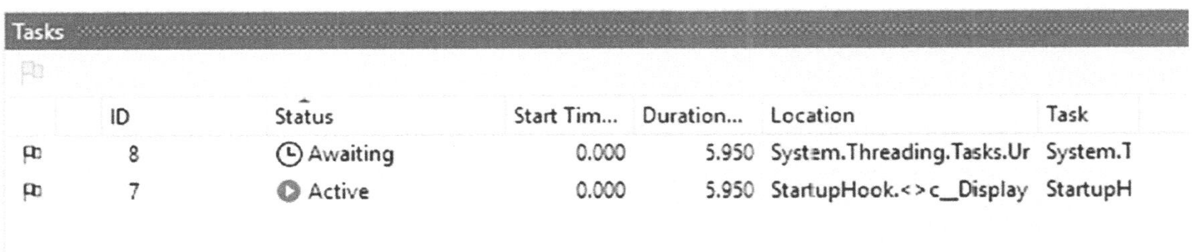

Figure 10.1: *Visual Studio Tasks Window*

This tool is particularly useful for monitoring long-running or background tasks, quickly identifying those that are in a faulted state, and determining if additional handling is necessary.

Enabling First-Chance Exceptions

To ensure you catch exceptions as they occur, enable First-Chance Exceptions in Visual Studio:

1. Go to **Debug** > **Windows** > **Exception Settings**.
2. Expand **Common Language Runtime Exceptions**.
3. Check the box to enable breaking on all exceptions.

This setting forces the debugger to pause immediately when an exception is thrown, even before it is caught. This can be invaluable for diagnosing async exceptions that might otherwise be lost or swallowed by faulty error-handling logic.

By combining these techniques—event logging, task monitoring, and first-chance debugging—developers can effectively track and resolve even the most elusive async exceptions.

Enumerations and Disposable

Enumerations in .NET are typically implemented using **IEnumerable<T>** and **IEnumerator<T>**, which are designed for iterating over in-memory data sets synchronously. While this approach works well for collections stored in memory, it becomes inefficient when dealing with I/O-bound operations such as database queries, file access, or network requests. In such cases, blocking operations can degrade performance and scalability.

To address this, .NET introduces **IAsyncEnumerable<T>** and **IAsyncEnumerator<T>**, which enable asynchronous iteration, allowing data to be retrieved efficiently without blocking execution.

Introduction to Async Enumerations

Imagine executing a database query that returns a large result set. To keep things simple, you would want to process each record in the result set in a foreach loop. Before the introduction of **asynchronous enumerations**, you would typically use **`IEnumerable<T>`** to enable foreach support. However, this approach requires the entire result set to be loaded into memory before iteration can begin.

In a single-user desktop application, this may not pose a significant issue. However, in highly scalable service applications, loading large datasets into memory can lead to high memory consumption and potential memory starvation, reducing the efficiency of the application. This makes **`IEnumerable<T>`** with foreach a less desirable solution for large, I/O-bound operations.

.NET addresses this challenge with **`IAsyncEnumerable<T>`**, which enables asynchronous streaming of data using **`await foreach`**. When combined with **`yield return`**, this approach allows database results to be processed one record at a time as they arrive from the server, rather than being fully loaded into memory before iteration. This significantly reduces memory footprint and improves responsiveness.

The benefits of **`IAsyncEnumerable<T>`** extend beyond database queries. It is also useful for:

- **Processing large files** asynchronously to avoid blocking I/O.
- **Streaming data across networks**, such as fetching paginated API results.
- **Interacting with cloud services**, such as querying large object storage or streaming logs.

By leveraging **`IAsyncEnumerable<T>`**, developers can write scalable, memory-efficient applications that process data as it becomes available rather than waiting for the entire dataset to load.

Benefits of Asynchronous Enumeration

Asynchronous enumeration provides a powerful way to process large or unpredictable data sources efficiently. Unlike traditional **`IEnumerable<T>`**, which requires loading all data into memory before iteration, **`IAsyncEnumerable<T>`** enables applications to consume data as it becomes available, reducing memory pressure and improving performance.

One of the most significant advantages is non-blocking execution, which allows applications to stay responsive while waiting for data. When using **`await foreach`**, the calling thread remains free to handle other tasks instead of sitting idle. This is especially valuable in high-throughput environments, such as web APIs and background services, where optimizing thread usage is critical for scalability. By preventing thread starvation, **asynchronous enumeration** ensures that applications can handle more concurrent operations with fewer resources.

Another key benefit is optimized memory usage. Instead of allocating large buffers to store entire datasets, applications can process one item at a time, keeping memory consumption low. This is particularly useful for database queries that return thousands of rows, processing massive log files, or streaming real-time event data. Rather than holding an entire result set in memory, an application can handle each record as it arrives, improving efficiency and reducing the risk of memory exhaustion.

Beyond performance, **asynchronous enumeration** integrates seamlessly with Task-based asynchronous programming (TAP) in .NET. Because it works naturally with await, it fits well with other async operations, such as database queries (**`AsAsyncEnumerable()`** in Entity Framework Core), file I/O, and network requests. This means developers can write clean, non-blocking code that scales well under heavy workloads.

Asynchronous enumeration also plays a vital role in data processing pipelines, where data is fetched, transformed, and processed in stages. This is particularly useful for event-driven architectures, such as real-time log monitoring, message queue consumers, and ETL workflows. By processing data incrementally, applications can react as soon as new information arrives, improving overall responsiveness and efficiency.

In UI applications, **IAsyncEnumerable<T>** can prevent UI freezes by incrementally loading and displaying data rather than waiting for an entire dataset to be retrieved. This enhances the user experience in scenarios such as loading search results dynamically, progressive media streaming, or handling large data lists in desktop and mobile apps.

Additionally, **IAsyncEnumerable<T>** supports lazy evaluation, meaning it only retrieves and processes data as needed. This helps minimize computational overhead, especially when working with expensive or slow data sources such as remote APIs, sensor data streams, or database queries that require sorting and filtering. Instead of preloading all available data, results are fetched on demand, improving efficiency and responsiveness.

Another critical benefit is cancellation support, which allows applications to stop iteration early if needed. By leveraging **CancellationToken**, developers can gracefully exit long-running loops when a request times out or a user cancels an operation. This is particularly useful in web applications, background tasks, and long-running data streams, where stopping work early can save resources and improve responsiveness. Implementing cancellation properly ensures that system resources are not wasted on unnecessary processing.

Finally, **IAsyncEnumerable<T>** works well with **asynchronous disposal** mechanisms through **IAsyncDisposable**. Many async enumerators involve I/O-bound operations that require proper resource cleanup—such as closing database connections, releasing network resources, or disposing of file streams. Using **asynchronous disposal** ensures that resources are released as soon as they are no longer needed, preventing potential memory leaks and improving application stability.

By enabling non-blocking execution, efficient memory management, seamless async integration, support for data pipelines, UI responsiveness, lazy evaluation, cancellation support, and proper resource cleanup, **IAsyncEnumerable<T>** provides a modern, scalable solution for handling large-scale or real-time data processing efficiently. Whether you are working with databases, network streams, or file processing, asynchronous enumeration helps build applications that are faster, more responsive, and highly scalable.

Implementing Custom Iterators

.NET contains many APIs that support **IAsyncEnumerable<T>**, which can be used with **await foreach**. Let us see how it works with **File.ReadLinesAsync()**.

```
await foreach (var line in File.ReadLinesAsync(tempFileName))
{
    await Task.Delay(1000);
    Console.WriteLine(line);
}
```

In this example, we read all lines from the file **tempFileName** and write them one at a time, with a small delay between each line. Note that **await foreach** allows **ReadLinesAsync()** to read a line at a time from the file asynchronously, preventing thread blocking while data is being retrieved.

Adding Cancellation Support

Long-running loops should support cancellation to improve efficiency. We can pass a **CancellationToken** to **File.ReadLinesAsync()**.

```
await foreach (var line in File.ReadLinesAsync(tempFileName, cts.Token))
{
    await Task.Delay(1000, cts.Token);
```

```
        Console.WriteLine(line);
    }
```

If the cancellation token is signaled, reading from the file is stopped, and the file is closed. This allows for responsive and interruptible processing.

Implementing a Custom Async Iterator

We can implement **`IAsyncEnumerable<T>`** in a custom iterator using **`yield return`**.

```
static async IAsyncEnumerable<int> GenerateNumbersAsync(int limit)
{
    for (var i = 0; i < limit; i++)
    {
        await Task.Delay(100);
        yield return Random.Shared.Next(100);
    }
}
```

This example simulates asynchronously fetching data by using **`Task.Delay()`** before yielding random numbers up to the given limit. The compiler transforms this into a state machine that enables efficient asynchronous iteration.

Using **`IAsyncEnumerable<T>`** is a powerful approach for processing data streams efficiently. It is particularly useful when dealing with:

- Large datasets that should be processed incrementally instead of loading into memory all at once.
- Streaming data from external sources, such as APIs, databases, or real-time event streams.
- Asynchronous processing of collections where items arrive over time rather than being available all at once.

By leveraging async enumerable APIs, developers can build scalable, responsive applications that efficiently handle asynchronous data processing.

Using Async Disposable

Classes that implement **`IDisposable`** allow for efficient resource cleanup, ensuring that memory and system resources are freed when no longer needed. However, **`IDisposable`** only supports synchronous cleanup, which can block threads when dealing with external resources such as streams, database connections, or network clients.

To address this limitation, .NET provides **`IAsyncDisposable`**, which enables **asynchronous** resource cleanup using **`DisposeAsync()`**. This prevents unnecessary thread blocking and improves scalability in high-performance applications.

The following example demonstrates a class that implements **`IAsyncDisposable`** to clean up resources asynchronously:

```
public class AsyncResource : IAsyncDisposable
{
    private bool _disposed;

    public async ValueTask DisposeAsync()
    {
        if (!this._disposed)
        {
            await Task.Delay(100);
```

```
                Console.WriteLine("Async resources cleaned up.");
                this._disposed = true;
            }
        }

        public async Task<string> GetDataAsync()
        {
            await Task.Delay(100);
            return "Retrieved data.";
        }
    }
```

In this example:

1. **DisposeAsync()** is an **asynchronous method** returning **ValueTask**, ensuring efficient cleanup without unnecessary heap allocations.
2. **GetDataAsync()** simulates retrieving data asynchronously.

To use an **IAsyncDisposable** instance, you should use **await using**, which ensures proper disposal when the variable goes out of scope:

```
await using var resource = new AsyncResource();
Console.WriteLine("Using async resource...");
Console.WriteLine(await resource.GetDataAsync());
```

The expected output is as follows.

```
Using async resource...
Retrieved data.
Async resources cleaned up.
```

Using **IAsyncDisposable** allows applications to clean up external resources asynchronously, improving efficiency and avoiding unnecessary thread blocking. This is particularly beneficial in high-performance and scalable applications that rely on asynchronous workflows.

Asynchronous Message Passing

In *Chapter 6, Understanding Concurrent Collections*, we introduced the producer-consumer model using **BlockingCollection<T>**. While **BlockingCollection<T>** enables threads to produce and consume work, it can cause consumers to block while waiting for data and producers to block when the collection reaches capacity. To avoid blocking, a more scalable approach is needed.

Channel<T> provides an efficient way to pass messages between threads asynchronously. It consists of a writer (**Writer**) and a reader (**Reader**), making it useful for producer-consumer patterns, streaming data, and message passing.

To use a channel, create an instance and write to it asynchronously:

```
var channel = Channel.CreateBounded<int>(5);

static async Task ProduceAsync(ChannelWriter<int> writer, int producerId,
CancellationToken token)
{
    try
    {
        while (!token.IsCancellationRequested)
        {
            var item = Random.Shared.Next(100);
            await writer.WriteAsync(item, token);
```

```
                Console.WriteLine($"Producer {producerId} produced: {item}");
                await Task.Delay(Random.Shared.Next(500, 1000), token);
            }
        }
        catch (OperationCanceledException) { }
        finally
        {
            Console.WriteLine($"Producer {producerId} stopped.");
        }
    }
```

Readers process messages using **ReadAllAsync()**:

```
static async Task ConsumeAsync(ChannelReader<int> reader, int consumerId,
CancellationToken token)
{
    try
    {
        await foreach (var item in reader.ReadAllAsync(token))
        {
            Console.WriteLine($"Consumer {consumerId} consumed: {item}");
            await Task.Delay(700, token);
        }
    }
    catch (OperationCanceledException) { }
    finally
    {
        Console.WriteLine($"Consumer {consumerId} stopped.");
    }
}
```

Each time **ProduceAsync()** or **ConsumeAsync()** is called, a new producer or consumer is created:

```
var producers = new List<Task>
        {
            ProduceAsync(channel.Writer, 1, cts.Token),
            ProduceAsync(channel.Writer, 2, cts.Token)
        };

var consumers = new List<Task>
        {
            ConsumeAsync(channel.Reader, 1, cts.Token),
            ConsumeAsync(channel.Reader, 2, cts.Token)
        };
```

These tasks execute asynchronously, and calling **channel.Writer.Complete()** signals consumers that no more data will be written:

```
await Task.WhenAll(producers);
channel.Writer.Complete();
await Task.WhenAll(consumers);
```

By using **Channel<T>**, applications can efficiently implement producer-consumer workflows without blocking, improving scalability and responsiveness in concurrent applications.

Conclusion

Asynchronous programming with **async/await** in .NET 9 provides a powerful and efficient way to handle concurrency, improving responsiveness and scalability while simplifying code structure. By leveraging **Task**, **ValueTask**, **Channel<T>**, and other asynchronous constructs, developers can write high-performance applications that efficiently utilize system resources. However, with great power comes responsibility–understanding pitfalls such as deadlocks, excessive thread creation, and synchronization issues is crucial for writing robust and maintainable code. As we move forward, the principles of **asynchronous programming** will continue to play a vital role in modern software development, enabling applications to handle increasing workloads with efficiency and grace.

In the next chapter, we will explore the .NET Thread Pool, a fundamental component for managing and optimizing multithreaded workloads. We will examine how it efficiently handles background tasks, dynamically scales to meet demand, and reduces the overhead of thread creation and destruction. Understanding the Thread Pool's behavior and tuning its settings appropriately can significantly enhance application performance, especially in high-concurrency scenarios.

Points to Remember

Here are some key things to remember about asynchronous programming in .NET.

- The **async/await** pattern allows developers to write non-blocking, **asynchronous** code in a more readable and easy-to-maintain manner compared to older callback-based approaches.
- Using **Task** and **ValueTask** enables better CPU and I/O bound task management, preventing unnecessary thread blocking and improving application responsiveness.
- Deadlocks, excessive thread creation, and improper use of **ConfigureAwait(false)** can introduce performance bottlenecks or unintended behavior, making it essential to understand best practices.
- The **Channel<T>** class provides a robust mechanism for implementing producer-consumer patterns, enabling efficient data processing in highly concurrent applications.

Multiple Choice Questions

1. What is the primary benefit of using **async/await** in .NET?
   a. It speeds up code execution by running everything in parallel.
   b. It makes asynchronous code more readable and maintainable.
   c. It prevents all race conditions and deadlocks.
   d. It ensures that all tasks complete in a predictable order.
2. What is the key advantage of using **ValueTask** instead of **Task**?
   a. It allows synchronous completion without heap allocation.
   b. It automatically runs in parallel.
   c. It forces immediate execution on the caller's thread.
   d. It avoids the need for exception handling.

3. What happens if you do not await an asynchronous method in .NET?
   a. The method runs synchronously and blocks the calling thread.
   b. The method executes but any exceptions may be lost or **unobserved**.
   c. The method does not execute at all.
   d. The method automatically runs on the Thread Pool.
4. Which of the following statements about async void methods is true?
   a. They should be used for all async methods to improve performance.
   b. They can be awaited safely within other asynchronous methods.
   c. They are typically used only for event handlers.
   d. They are required when using await inside a synchronous method.

Answers

1. b
2. a
3. b
4. c

Questions

1. How does **asynchronous programming** with `async/await` differ from parallel execution with `Parallel.For()` or `Task.Run()`? In what scenarios would you choose one over the other?
2. What are some real-world examples where improper use of `async/await` could lead to deadlocks? How can you design your code to avoid them?
3. The `ThreadPool` automatically manages worker threads for async operations. How can excessive async operations overload the `ThreadPool`, and what are some best practices to prevent performance degradation?
4. What are some real-world examples where improper use of async/await could lead to deadlocks? How can you design your code to avoid them?

Key Terms

- **Asynchronous Programming**: A technique that allows a program to perform other tasks while waiting for long-running operations such as I/O.
- **Synchronous Programming**: A sequential execution model where each operation must complete before the next one starts, potentially causing the program to wait during long-running tasks.
- **Asynchronous Methods/TAP Methods**: Methods that create and return `Task` or `Task<T>` and are designed to complete sometime in the future.
- **Synchronous Methods**: Methods that execute operations immediately waiting for each operation to complete before the next one begins.

- **Asynchronous Enumeration**: Iterating over data streams asynchronously, enabling non-blocking retrieval of items.
- **Synchronization Context**: An abstraction in .NET that manages how asynchronous tasks resume execution, ensuring that the code runs on the appropriate thread or context.
- **Unobserved Task Exceptions**: Exceptions that are never caught or handled, often leading to lost exceptions or instability.
- **Asynchronous Enumerations**: Enumerations that support awaiting for I/O between each iteration in an **`async foreach`** loop.
- **Asynchronous Disposal**: A method of disposing resources asynchronously without blocking the calling thread by using **`await using`**.

CHAPTER 11
Threading and the Thread Pool

Introduction

Underlying technologies such as ASP.NET Core, the Task Parallel Library (TPL), and event-driven APIs like `System.Threading.Timer` are the .NET thread pool. Found in `System.Threading.ThreadPool`, the thread pool efficiently manages a pool of background **worker threads**, optimizing resource usage for **short-lived**, concurrent tasks. It abstracts away the complexity of thread lifetime management and task scheduling, providing a simple yet powerful API for queuing and executing work asynchronously. This chapter will explore the design, operation, and best practices for using the thread pool effectively.

Structure

In this chapter, we will cover the following topics:

- Introduction to the Thread Pool
  - Thread Management
  - Usage Advantages
  - Scenarios where Thread Pool is Beneficial
- Using the Thread Pool
  - Queueing Work
  - Passing Parameters
  - Handling Exceptions
- Optimizing Performance
  - Configuration Settings
  - Best Practices
- Tasks and the Thread Pool
  - Scheduling Tasks
  - Tasks versus Work Items
  - Converting Work Items to Tasks
- Managing Long Running Tasks
  - Creating Long Running Tasks
  - Alternative Approaches
  - Choosing the Right Approach

- Thread Pool versus Dedicated Threads
    - Performance Implications
    - Choosing the Right Model

Introduction to the Thread Pool

Most applications benefit from concurrency, whether handling I/O operations, processing large datasets in parallel, managing timers, or executing background CPU-bound tasks. While these jobs require threads to run concurrently, manually creating and managing threads for **short-lived** tasks can be inefficient due to the overhead of thread creation, scheduling, and lifecycle management. The .NET thread pool provides an optimized solution by dynamically managing a pool of **worker threads**, allowing applications to efficiently execute **short-lived** tasks without the complexity of manual thread management.

Thread Management

In a modern .NET application, managing threads efficiently is crucial to achieving high performance without overwhelming system resources. Fortunately, .NET provides an intelligent, self-regulating mechanism for handling threads: the **thread pool**, represented by the `System.Threading.ThreadPool` class.

At its core, the **thread pool** is responsible for managing two distinct types of threads: **worker threads** and **I/O completion threads**. Each serves a unique role in optimizing application performance.

Worker Threads: The Backbone of General Task Execution

Worker threads are the workhorses of the thread pool. They are designed to handle CPU-bound operations and general-purpose tasks that developers explicitly queue using methods, such as `ThreadPool.QueueUserWorkItem()` or higher-level abstractions including `Task.Run()`.

One important characteristic of **worker threads** is that they are created as background threads—meaning they will not prevent an application from exiting if all foreground threads have completed. The thread pool does not pre-allocate a fixed number of **worker threads**. Instead, it dynamically manages them based on demand, ensuring that enough threads are available to handle workloads efficiently while preventing unnecessary thread creation that could degrade performance.

I/O Completion Threads: Handling Asynchronous Operations

Unlike **worker threads**, which actively process tasks, **I/O completion threads** play a different role. They are not responsible for performing I/O operations themselves but rather for handling the completion of asynchronous I/O tasks.

When an asynchronous I/O operation—such as reading from a file, making a network request, or querying a database—is initiated, the .NET runtime delegates the task to the operating system, rather than using a managed thread to wait for the operation to complete. On Windows, this is made possible through **I/O Completion Ports (IOCP)**, a highly efficient mechanism that allows the OS to handle I/O in the background.

Once the operation is completed, the OS signals its completion, and an **I/O completion thread** picks up the callback to process the result. If additional computation is required beyond the initial callback, the work may be manually scheduled onto a **worker thread** to continue execution. This separation ensures that managed threads are not needlessly blocked while waiting for I/O, leading to better scalability and responsiveness.

The Role of `async/await` in Efficient Thread Management

In modern .NET applications, asynchronous programming using **`async`** and **`await`** further enhances thread efficiency. When you await an asynchronous method—such as **`FileStream.ReadAsync()`** or **`HttpClient.GetAsync()`**—the calling thread does not sit idle, waiting for the operation to complete. Instead, it is released back to the thread pool, allowing other tasks to execute while the I/O operation continues in the background.

When the operation completes, the thread pool schedules the continuation of the async method, either on a **worker thread** or—if the application is running in a UI context like WPF or WinForms—back on the original synchronization context to ensure UI updates happen safely.

Usage Advantages

Using the .NET **thread pool** provides key advantages over manually managing threads with the **`Thread`** class. The **thread pool** maintains a dynamic pool of **worker threads**, reducing the overhead of creating and destroying threads manually. It is optimized for **short-lived**, background tasks and reuses threads to minimize excessive context switching, improving application scalability and performance.

The **thread pool** dynamically adjusts the number of threads to match workload and system resources, creating and releasing threads as needed. It queues work efficiently and, when used with the Task Parallel Library (TPL), benefits from work-stealing algorithms to balance workloads across CPU cores. This makes it well-suited for high-concurrency scenarios where many tasks need execution.

Unlike manually created threads, **thread pool** threads are automatically managed and cleaned up when no longer needed. This simplifies resource management and reduces the risk of thread leaks.

Using **thread pool** threads is straightforward. Developers can use **`ThreadPool.QueueUserWorkItem()`** for lightweight background tasks or **`Task.Run()`** for tasks that require TPL features such as cancellation, continuations, and work-stealing. Since the **thread pool** is tightly integrated with **`async/await`**, it serves as the foundation for scalable, responsive applications in modern .NET development.

Scenarios Where Thread Pool is Beneficial

The **thread pool** is beneficial for scenarios where **short-lived** asynchronous or background processing is needed without the overhead of manually creating and managing threads. Ideal use cases include:

- Short-running asynchronous tasks, such as reading from large files, accessing databases, or making network requests. These tasks should be performed asynchronously (**`async/await`**) to avoid blocking **thread pool** threads.
- Offloading CPU-bound operations to multiple background threads, such as image or video processing, complex mathematical calculations, or parallel encoding operations. However, for CPU-intensive workloads, **`Parallel.For()`**, **`Parallel.ForEach()`**, or **dedicated threads** may provide better performance.
- Reducing request pipeline blocking in ASP.NET applications by offloading work such as logging, caching data, sending emails, or generating reports. These tasks should be executed asynchronously to prevent request threads from being tied up.
- Implementing event-driven or scheduled tasks, such as those executed via **`System.Threading.Timer`**, **`Task.Run()`**, or event callbacks, which rely on the **thread pool** for efficient execution.
- Executing thousands of lightweight concurrent operations, such as handling chat messages in a real-time messaging application or processing high volumes of incoming API requests.

- Managing batch jobs in worker services efficiently, such as periodically aggregating and processing sales data. These tasks should avoid blocking **thread pool** threads for extended periods to prevent thread starvation.

In general, any asynchronous, **short-lived**, or CPU-bound job that does not require **dedicated threads** and should run in the background is a good candidate for thread pool processing.

Using the Thread Pool

The **thread pool** is a core component of .NET's concurrency model and serves as the foundation for the Task Parallel Library (TPL). It is utilized by high-level parallel programming constructs such as **`Parallel.For()`**, **`Parallel.ForEach()`**, and PLINQ, which manage **thread pool** threads automatically. Developers can also use the **thread pool** directly when more control is needed. For simple background work, **`ThreadPool.QueueUserWorkItem()`** provides a lightweight way to execute tasks. However, for more advanced scenarios requiring features such as task continuations, cancellation, or work-stealing, **`Task.Run()`**—which leverages the TPL—is the preferred approach.

Queueing Work

Because work is processed by a pool of reusable threads rather than **dedicated threads**, it must be queued before execution. The default task scheduler in the Task Parallel Library (TPL) uses the **thread pool** to schedule tasks, adding advanced features such as cancellation, continuations, and work-stealing as part of the scheduler. However, the thread pool itself does not provide these higher-level features. If cancellation, continuations, or other task-based features are required, use **`Task.Run()`** to queue work to the thread pool. We have covered **`Task.Run()`** extensively in prior chapters.

For lightweight background jobs that do not require task-based features, **`ThreadPool.QueueUserWorkItem()`** can be used to queue work directly to the **thread pool**. This method accepts a **`WaitCallback`** delegate, which is a method that takes an optional state object as its parameter. The following example demonstrates how to queue work using **`QueueUserWorkItem()`**:

```
var mainThreadId = Thread.CurrentThread.ManagedThreadId;
ThreadPool.QueueUserWorkItem(ProcessWork);
Thread.Sleep(100);
Console.WriteLine($"Completed main thread: {mainThreadId}.");

static void ProcessWork(object? state)
{
    var threadId = Thread.CurrentThread.ManagedThreadId;
    Console.WriteLine($"Hello World from ThreadPool thread: {threadId}");
}
```

In this example, the **`ProcessWork()`** method implements the **`WaitCallback`** delegate signature. It is passed to **`QueueUserWorkItem()`**, which queues the delegate as a thread pool work item. The main thread then sleeps briefly before printing a completion message and exiting.

The **`Task.Delay(100)`** ensures that the background thread has an opportunity to execute before the main thread terminates. Because **thread pool** threads are background threads, they do not keep the application running. If the main thread exits before the work item runs, the application will terminate before the background work is complete.

An example of the output is as follows:

```
Hello World from ThreadPool thread: 6
Completed main thread: 1.
```

Passing Parameters

The **WaitCallback** delegate allows passing an optional state object as a parameter. This object can be set by adding it as an argument to **QueueUserWorkItem()**. We can modify our previous example to pass a state object to the worker thread, shown as follows:

```
var mainThreadId = Thread.CurrentThread.ManagedThreadId;
ThreadPool.QueueUserWorkItem(ProcessWork, "Hello there!");
await Task.Delay(100);
Console.WriteLine($"Completed main thread: {mainThreadId}.");

static void ProcessWork(object? state)
{
    var threadId = Thread.CurrentThread.ManagedThreadId;
    Console.WriteLine($"{state} from ThreadPool thread: {threadId}");
}
```

This example passes the string **"Hello there!"** as the state object, which is received by **ProcessWork()** when it executes on a **worker thread**. A string is passed in this example, but any object can be passed. A sample output might be:

```
Hello there! from ThreadPool thread: 6
Completed main thread: 1.
```

Type Safety with Action

The default **WaitCallback** delegate lacks type safety, as it accepts an **object?** parameter. To address this, **QueueUserWorkItem()** provides an overload that accepts an **Action<TState>**, ensuring type safety:

```
var mainThreadId = Thread.CurrentThread.ManagedThreadId;

ThreadPool.QueueUserWorkItem((string state) =>
{
    Console.WriteLine($"{state} using Action<TState>.");
}, "Hello there!", false);

await Task.Delay(100);
Console.WriteLine($"Completed main thread: {mainThreadId}.");
```

This example uses a type-safe lambda that directly accepts a string parameter. A class method could also be used instead. The expected output is as follows:

```
Hello there! using Action<TState>.
Completed main thread: 1.
```

Passing Multiple Parameters

QueueUserWorkItem() does not support multiple parameters directly. However, if a method is part of a class, its properties can be used to store additional data needed by the worker thread.

```
var multiplier = new Multiplier { Factor = 10 };
var amount = 10;
var done = new ManualResetEventSlim(); // Ensure completion

ThreadPool.QueueUserWorkItem(
    (int amount) =>
    {
        multiplier.Multiply(amount);
        done.Set(); // Signal completion
```

```
    }, amount, false);

done.Wait(); // Wait for Multiply to finish

Console.WriteLine(
    $"The result of {amount} * {multiplier.Factor} is {multiplier.Product}");

public class Multiplier
{
    public int Factor { get; set; }
    public int Product { get; set; }

    public void Multiply(int amount)
    {
        Product = amount * Factor;
    }
}
```

When working with thread pool delegates, passing multiple parameters requires a different approach since **`QueueUserWorkItem()`** only accepts a single state object. In this example, the **`Multiplier`** class is introduced to encapsulate the necessary parameters and computation results. Instead of passing multiple values separately, we use a combination of a class instance and an integer argument to achieve the desired behavior.

To ensure the **`worker thread`** completes execution before the main thread accesses the computed value, we introduce **`ManualResetEventSlim`**. This synchronization mechanism allows the main thread to pause execution until the worker thread signals that it has finished its task. Without this safeguard, the **`Console.WriteLine()`** statement might execute before **`Multiply()`** completes, potentially leading to incorrect or unexpected results due to race conditions.

By structuring the code this way, we create a clean and thread-safe approach for passing multiple parameters to a thread pool delegate while avoiding common pitfalls in multithreaded programming.

Handling Exceptions

The **thread pool** has no built-in exception handling. Therefore, exceptions occurring in **thread pool work item** delegates must be handled within the delegate itself.

Unhandled exceptions in **thread pool** threads do not crash the application (unlike exceptions on foreground threads) but are lost unless explicitly handled. The following example demonstrates an unhandled exception in a thread pool work item:

```
ThreadPool.QueueUserWorkItem((state) =>
{
    throw new InvalidOperationException("This will be unhandled.");
});
```

Since the thread pool does not handle exceptions, wrap work items in a **`try-catch`** block to prevent silent failures:

```
ThreadPool.QueueUserWorkItem((state) =>
{
    try
    {
        throw new InvalidOperationException("This will be caught.");
    }
    catch (Exception ex)
    {
```

```
            Console.WriteLine("Exception caught: " + ex.ToString());
        }
    });
```

Since exceptions are not propagated back to the caller, logging them inside the delegate is essential for debugging and maintenance. Use a logging framework such as ILogger, NLog, or Serilog instead of console output in production.

Reporting Exceptions to the Calling Thread

Since **`ThreadPool.QueueUserWorkItem()`** does not propagate exceptions to the main thread, an explicit mechanism is required to capture and retrieve exceptions. One approach is to use a **`BlockingCollection<Exception>`** or **`ConcurrentQueue<Exception>`** to consolidate error reporting:

```
var exceptionQueue = new BlockingCollection<Exception>();

ThreadPool.QueueUserWorkItem((state) =>
{
    try
    {
        throw new InvalidOperationException("Exception for main thread.");
    }
    catch (Exception ex)
    {
        exceptionQueue.Add(ex);
    }
    exceptionQueue.CompleteAdding();
});

Exception exception = exceptionQueue.Take();
Console.WriteLine($"Processed exception: {exception}");
```

If more robust error handling is required, consider using **`Task.Run()`** with **`await`** or **`ContinueWith()`**, which provide built-in exception propagation. Additionally, **`Parallel.Invoke()`** will propagate exceptions by wrapping them in an **`AggregateException`**, allowing structured error handling. When exception propagation is necessary, these higher-level abstractions reduce code complexity while ensuring robust error handling.

Optimizing Performance

The **thread pool** in .NET optimizes thread usage by efficiently creating and reusing threads to handle transient workloads. Initially, threads are created as needed until the minimum thread count is reached, ensuring a baseline level of concurrency. Once this threshold is met, additional threads are introduced gradually, with a slight delay before each new thread is added. This delay prevents unnecessary thread creation during short workload spikes. If the workload continues to grow and the maximum thread count is reached, new **work items** are queued until an existing thread becomes available. This adaptive approach helps optimize resource utilization while preventing excessive thread growth that could degrade system performance.

However, in high-performance scenarios, profiling may reveal that the **thread pool** is a bottleneck–either due to a delay in scaling (leading to slow task execution) or an insufficient maximum thread count (limiting concurrency). In such cases, the default settings may need to be adjusted to reduce scaling lag or allow a higher thread limit. The **`ThreadPool`** class provides methods to fine-tune these parameters for better performance.

Configuration Settings

The .NET **thread pool** plays a crucial role in managing the execution of background tasks, automatically handling the creation and reuse of **worker** and **I/O completion threads**. While the default settings are often sufficient, there are times when fine-tuning these values can improve performance for high-throughput applications.

To examine the current thread limits, you can call the **`ThreadPool.GetMaxThreads()`** and **`ThreadPool.GetMinThreads()`** methods. These methods return two values: the number of **worker threads** and the number of **I/O completion threads** that the **thread pool** can utilize. The following example demonstrates how to retrieve these values:

```
var maxWorkerThreads = 0;
var maxIoCompletionThreads = 0;
var minWorkerThreads = 0;
var minIoCompletionThreads = 0;

ThreadPool.GetMaxThreads(out maxWorkerThreads, out maxIoCompletionThreads);
ThreadPool.GetMinThreads(out minWorkerThreads, out minIoCompletionThreads);

Console.WriteLine($"Max worker: {maxWorkerThreads:N0}; max I/O: {maxIoComple-
tionThreads:N0}");
Console.WriteLine($"Min worker: {minWorkerThreads:N0}; min I/O: {minIoComple-
tionThreads:N0}");
```

When executed, this might produce output like the following:

```
Max worker: 32,767; max I/O: 1,000
Min worker: 20; min I/O: 1
```

These values represent the upper and lower bounds for how many threads the **thread pool** can allocate. However, depending on your application's workload, you may need to adjust these settings to optimize resource utilization.

Modifying Thread Pool Limits at Runtime

If your application requires a larger **thread pool** to handle increased parallel workloads, you can modify these limits dynamically using the **`ThreadPool.SetMaxThreads()`** and **`ThreadPool.SetMinThreads()`** methods. For example, the following code increases the minimum number of **worker threads** by 20 and the maximum number of **I/O completion threads** by 10:

```
ThreadPool.SetMinThreads(minWorkerThreads + 20, minIoCompletionThreads);
ThreadPool.SetMaxThreads(maxWorkerThreads, maxIoCompletionThreads + 10);

ThreadPool.GetMaxThreads(out maxWorkerThreads, out maxIoCompletionThreads);
ThreadPool.GetMinThreads(out minWorkerThreads, out minIoCompletionThreads);

Console.WriteLine($"Max worker: {maxWorkerThreads:N0}; max I/O: {maxIoComple-
tionThreads:N0}");
Console.WriteLine($"Min worker: {minWorkerThreads:N0}; min I/O: {minIoComple-
tionThreads:N0}");
```

After running this code, the updated configuration might look like this:

```
Max worker: 32,767; max I/O: 1,010
Min worker: 40; min I/O: 1
```

While **`SetMaxThreads()`** and **`SetMinThreads()`** provide flexibility for adjusting thread counts at runtime, these changes only persist for the lifetime of the application. If you want to establish a consistent baseline for **worker threads** across application runs, you can configure them in the project's settings.

Configuring Worker Threads in the Project File

For scenarios where you need to ensure a specific minimum number of **worker threads**, .NET allows you to define this setting in the **`.csproj`** file. Adding the following configuration ensures that the application always starts with at least 40 worker threads:

```
<PropertyGroup>
  <ThreadPoolMinThreads>40</ThreadPoolMinThreads>
  <ThreadPoolMaxThreads>32000</ThreadPoolMaxThreads>
</PropertyGroup>
```

It is important to note that once the **worker thread** count is set this way, it can no longer be changed at runtime using **`SetMinThreads()`** or **`SetMaxThreads()`**. However, this restriction applies only to **worker threads**–**I/O completion threads** must still be configured at runtime if adjustments are necessary.

Choosing the Right Configuration Approach

- If your application needs to dynamically scale based on workload conditions, modifying **thread pool** settings at runtime using **`SetMaxThreads()`** and **`SetMinThreads()`** provides the flexibility to optimize performance on demand.
- If you want a consistent **worker thread** configuration across application runs, defining thread settings in the project file is a better choice.
- Since **I/O completion threads** do not have a corresponding .csproj setting, they must always be configured using **`SetMaxThreads()`** and **`SetMinThreads()`**.

By understanding these configuration options, you can fine-tune the **thread pool** to better suit your application's performance needs, ensuring efficient execution of background tasks without unnecessary resource constraints.

Tasks and the Thread Pool

.NET provides a robust threading model that includes both the **thread pool** and the Task Parallel Library (TPL) for managing concurrency. The **thread pool** is a pool of **worker threads** managed by the runtime, designed to efficiently handle short-lived and background operations. On top of this, the TPL introduces tasks, which provide a higher-level abstraction for concurrent programming.

Tasks in .NET are scheduled using task schedulers, as covered in *Chapter 9, Advanced Task Management*. By default, the standard task scheduler uses the **thread pool** to execute tasks on **worker threads**. However, if a task is marked as long-running using **`TaskCreationOptions.LongRunning`**, it is executed on a **dedicated thread** instead of a **thread pool worker**.

Using tasks is the preferred way to schedule work on the **thread pool** because they offer important features such as cancellation, result handling, exception propagation, and better workload distribution. However, for very lightweight operations that do not require these advanced features, direct use of the **thread pool** may be an alternative.

Scheduling Tasks

Tasks in .NET are scheduled when created using **`Task.Run()`**, **`Task.Factory.StartNew()`**, or when returned from an async method. By default, if **`Task.Run()`** is used or no custom scheduler is specified with **`Task.Factory.StartNew()`**, the default task scheduler queues the task on a **thread pool worker thread**.

Tasks scheduled this way benefit from the **thread pool**'s automatic thread reuse and load balancing, as well as work-stealing and scheduling fairness from the task scheduler. However, because the default scheduler leverages the **thread pool**, task **worker threads** do not support explicit priority adjustments like manually created threads.

The **thread pool** actively monitors workload and may inject additional **worker threads** to prevent starvation and optimize CPU utilization. However, excessive task creation can overwhelm the **thread pool**, leading to **thread pool exhaustion**—a state where too many pending tasks cause increased queuing delays, degrading performance. Proper task management strategies are essential to prevent overloading the **thread pool** and ensure efficient parallel execution.

One effective strategy to prevent **thread pool** overload is **task batching**. If the **thread pool** is overwhelmed by too many small, **short-lived** tasks, batching work by combining multiple operations into a single **`Task.Run()`** call can reduce thread contention. This approach minimizes the overhead of frequent context switching by using fewer threads for slightly longer durations, which can significantly improve performance in high-load scenarios. By reducing the number of enqueued tasks, batching also helps maintain better thread pool efficiency and prevents excessive queuing delays.

Tasks versus Work Items

Tasks are a high-level abstraction that provide cancellation, result processing, continuations, structured exception handling, and integration with **`async/await`**. By default, they are scheduled and processed on **thread pool worker threads**, gaining the benefits of the **thread pool** while maintaining their higher-level features. Therefore, tasks are preferred for most general-purpose background and asynchronous processing.

Work items (delegates scheduled using **`QueueUserWorkItem()`**) are more lightweight, providing only basic scheduling and load balancing. Unlike tasks, they do not support exception propagation, return values, or structured concurrency. While not ideal for general use, they are well-suited for fire-and-forget background work due to their low overhead.

The following table compares tasks versus work items:

Features	**Tasks**	**Work Items**
Uses Thread Pool	Yes	Yes
Supports Return Values	Yes, with `Task<TResult>`	No
Multiple Parameters	Yes	No, must be handled by class properties or closures
Exception Handling	Yes, with `await`	No, must be handled manually
Continuations	Yes, with `ContinueWith()` or `await`	No
Long Running	Yes, with `Task.Factory.StartNew()`	No
Supports Cancellation	Yes, with `CancellationToken`	No
Performance Overhead	Slightly Higher	Lower

Table 11.1: *Tasks versus Work Items*

In modern .NET development, tasks are the preferred choice for most asynchronous and background operations due to their flexibility, built-in exception handling, and integration with **`async/await`**. However, for simple, non-blocking fire-and-forget scenarios where overhead must be minimized,

work items remain a lightweight and efficient alternative. Choosing the right approach depends on the complexity, error handling needs, and performance considerations of your workload.

Converting Work Items to Tasks

As codebases mature, operations that once worked well as work items may require more advanced functionality provided by tasks. Unlike **work items**, tasks support multiple parameters, return values, exception propagation, and cancellation. In these cases, converting from **work items** to tasks becomes necessary.

Basic conversion of an existing **work item** is straightforward. The following example replaces **`ThreadPool.QueueUserWorkItem()`** with **`Task.Run()`**, ensuring the work runs asynchronously while supporting modern task-based programming patterns.

```
//Old work item
ThreadPool.QueueUserWorkItem(_ =>
{
    Console.WriteLine("Old work item.");
});

await Task.Delay(100);

//Converted to task
await Task.Run(() =>
{
    Console.WriteLine("Converted to new task.");
});
```

Handling Return Values and Parameters

If the new task requires return values or multiple parameters, the **work item** logic can be extracted into a separate method. This method can then be executed via **`Task.Run()`**, ensuring type safety and structured exception handling.

```
//Old work item
var amount = 42;
ThreadPool.QueueUserWorkItem(state =>
{
    var square = amount * amount;
    Console.WriteLine(square);
}, amount, true);

await Task.Delay(100);

//New task
var result = await Task.Run(() => ComputeSquare(amount));
Console.WriteLine(result);

static int ComputeSquare(int amount)
{
    return amount * amount;
}
```

Converting to Asynchronous I/O

If the new functionality involves asynchronous I/O, consider converting the operation into an async method. Note that async methods run synchronously unless an **`await`** statement is present in their execution path. This may cause the process to run on the calling thread unless explicitly executed with **Task.Run()**.

For example, converting a **work item** that performs file I/O:

```
//Old work item
ThreadPool.QueueUserWorkItem(fileName =>
{
    File.AppendAllText(fileName, "Old work item.\n");
}, tempFile, true);

await Task.Delay(100);

//New task
await WriteLogAsync(tempFile, "New task.");
Console.WriteLine(File.ReadAllText(tempFile));

static async Task WriteLogAsync(string logFilePath, string message)
{
    await File.AppendAllTextAsync(logFilePath, message);
}
```

Using **Task.Run()** ensures that CPU-bound work is scheduled on a separate thread. However, for pure async I/O operations, calling await directly without **Task.Run()** is usually preferable, as async methods do not block the thread.

Converting **work items** to tasks modernizes legacy code by integrating with the **async/await** model, enabling better error handling, cancellation support, and improved code maintainability. While **Task.Run()** provides an easy transition for CPU-bound workloads, asynchronous I/O operations should leverage async methods directly to avoid unnecessary thread usage. By adopting these patterns, developers can ensure that their applications remain scalable, efficient, and aligned with modern .NET best practices.

Managing Long Running Tasks

The .NET **thread pool** is optimized for executing **short-lived** tasks that complete quickly, allowing **worker threads** to be efficiently reused. This design works well for asynchronous I/O operations and CPU-bound tasks that do not require prolonged execution.

However, some operations require continuous or **long-running** execution, such as background data processing, logging, telemetry collection, health checks, real-time streaming, scheduled jobs, and IoT device communication. Running these types of tasks on **thread pool** worker threads can lead to resource contention, thread starvation, or delays in executing other queued tasks.

To avoid these issues, **long-running** tasks should be executed outside the **thread pool** using alternative approaches, such as **dedicated threads**, background services, or scheduled jobs, depending on the specific requirements of the application.

Creating Long Running Tasks

In .NET, **long-running** tasks are often necessary for background processing, continuous monitoring, or periodic operations. The task scheduler provides built-in support for such tasks using **TaskCreationOptions.LongRunning**, which signals the scheduler to create a **dedicated thread** rather than relying on the **thread pool**. This is particularly useful when a task is expected to run indefinitely or for an extended duration without yielding back to the system.

A simple example of a **long-running** task is shown in the following code, where a task continuously performs work at fixed intervals:

```
Task.Factory.StartNew(() =>
{
    while (true)
    {
        Thread.Sleep(1000);
        Console.WriteLine("Processed work iteration.");
    }
}, TaskCreationOptions.LongRunning);

Console.WriteLine("Press a key to exit.");
Console.ReadKey();
```

This approach ensures that the task does not compete for resources in the **thread pool**, as the runtime creates a **dedicated thread** for its execution. Additionally, in .NET 9 and earlier versions, threads created with **`TaskCreationOptions.LongRunning`** are automatically set as background threads. This means they will not prevent the application from exiting once all foreground threads have completed. However, developers should still ensure proper task management and cancellation to avoid unintended resource consumption.

Supporting Cancellation in Long-Running Tasks

In many cases, a long-running task should be able to gracefully shut down when it is no longer needed. To achieve this, a **`CancellationToken`** can be used to signal the task to stop execution:

```
var cts = new CancellationTokenSource();
Task<Task> backgroundTask = Task.Factory.StartNew(async () =>
{
    while (!cts.Token.IsCancellationRequested)
    {
        Thread.Sleep(1000);
        Console.WriteLine("Processed work iteration.");
    }
}, cts.Token, TaskCreationOptions.LongRunning, TaskScheduler.Default);

Console.WriteLine("Press a key to exit.");
Console.ReadKey();

cts.Cancel();
await backgroundTask.Unwrap();

Console.WriteLine("Background task exited.");
```

By using a cancellation token, the task can periodically check for a stop request and exit cleanly. This approach is particularly useful for applications that need to shut down tasks predictably rather than relying on abrupt termination.

Handling Async Long-Running Tasks

Working with asynchronous operations in **long-running** tasks differs from handling synchronous tasks. When an asynchronous task calls **`await`**, the executing thread is not blocked; instead, it is released back to the **thread pool** to handle other tasks. Because of this, asynchronous **long-running** tasks do not monopolize a thread and are well-suited for execution on **thread pool** threads.

These tasks can be started by directly calling an asynchronous TAP (Task-based Asynchronous Pattern) method or by using **`Task.Run()`**, as shown in the following example:

```
var cts = new CancellationTokenSource();
var backgroundTask = Task.Run(async () =>
{
    while (!cts.Token.IsCancellationRequested)
    {
        await Task.Delay(1000, cts.Token);
        Console.WriteLine("Processed work iteration...");
    }
});

Console.WriteLine("Press a key to exit.");
Console.ReadKey();

cts.Cancel();
try
{
    await backgroundTask;
}
catch (OperationCanceledException)
{
}

Console.WriteLine("Background task exited.");
```

By using **`Task.Run()`**, the task executes asynchronously within the **thread pool**. When **`await`** is called, the task suspends execution without blocking a thread, resuming later on another available **thread pool** thread. This pattern ensures efficient resource usage while allowing the task to run continuously for an extended duration. As a result, **`Task.Run()`** is the preferred method for **long-running** asynchronous tasks.

Creating **long-running** tasks using **`Task.Factory.StartNew()`** provides a structured approach to managing processes that run indefinitely or for extended durations. By incorporating **`TaskCreationOptions.LongRunning`**, the task runs on a dedicated background thread, preventing interference with the **thread pool**. Meanwhile, for asynchronous **long-running** tasks, **`Task.Run()`** is preferable as it efficiently utilizes **thread pool** resources without monopolizing a **dedicated thread**. Adding cancellation support ensures that tasks can be cleanly terminated when necessary, and proper asynchronous handling allows for efficient execution without unnecessary thread blocking. Together, these approaches provide powerful and flexible options for managing long-running operations in .NET applications.

Alternative Approaches

While **`Task.Factory.StartNew()`** is a widely used method for running **long-running** operations, it may not always be the best approach. In most cases, it works well within the **thread pool**, automatically managing resources and optimizing task scheduling. However, certain scenarios require more control over how and where a task executes.

For example, in a hosted environment such as ASP.NET Core, background tasks should be integrated with the application's lifecycle to ensure they start and stop appropriately. Additionally, some applications require fine control over a thread's priority, something the default task scheduler does not provide. In these cases, alternative approaches become necessary.

Manually Creating a Thread for Fine-Grained Control

There are times when an application needs to ensure that a background task runs at a lower priority than other processes. The **thread pool** does not provide built-in support for setting thread priority, so if an operation should consume fewer CPU cycles or yield to higher-priority tasks, a manually created thread is the best option.

Consider the following scenario: an application needs to run a background process that performs low-priority work, such as periodic logging or cache cleanup. This task should run in the background without interfering with more critical operations. The best way to achieve this is by creating a **dedicated thread** with a lower priority.

The following example demonstrates how to accomplish this:

```
var cts = new CancellationTokenSource();

var backgroundThread = new Thread(() =>
{
    while (!cts.Token.IsCancellationRequested)
    {
        Thread.Sleep(1000);
        Console.WriteLine("Handling low priority processing.");
    }
})
{
    Priority = ThreadPriority.BelowNormal,
    IsBackground = true
};
backgroundThread.Start();

Console.WriteLine("Press any key to exit.");
Console.ReadKey();
cts.Cancel();

backgroundThread.Join();
Console.WriteLine("Background thread stopped.");
```

Here, a new thread is explicitly created and assigned **`ThreadPriority.BelowNormal`**, ensuring that it runs at a lower priority than other threads. The **`CancellationTokenSource`** provides a mechanism to gracefully stop the thread when the application shuts down. Calling **`backgroundThread.Join()`** ensures the main application waits for the background task to finish before exiting.

This approach works well when precise control over thread execution is necessary. However, it comes at the cost of manual thread management, which is generally less efficient than leveraging the **thread pool**.

Using `BackgroundService` for Hosted Environments

In an ASP.NET Core application, executing **long-running** background processes is a common requirement, but manually creating threads is not the best approach in this context. Instead, the preferred method is to integrate background tasks into the hosting environment by implementing a **`BackgroundService`**.

A **`BackgroundService`** is a special type of hosted service that runs in the background while the application is running. It provides built-in support for dependency injection and automatic lifecycle management, ensuring that tasks start and stop with the application. **`BackgroundService`** is a part of the **`Microsoft.Extensions.Hosting`** NuGet package.

To define a background service, create a class that inherits from **BackgroundService** and override the **ExecuteAsync()** method:

```
using Microsoft.Extensions.Hosting;
using Microsoft.Extensions.Logging;

namespace BackgroundServiceDemo;
internal class BackgroundWorkerService : BackgroundService
{
    private readonly ILogger logger;

    public BackgroundWorkerService(ILogger<BackgroundWorkerService> logger)
    {
        this.logger = logger;
    }

    protected override async Task ExecuteAsync(CancellationToken stoppingTo-
ken)
    {
        this.logger.LogInformation("Background service starting.");

        while (!stoppingToken.IsCancellationRequested)
        {
            try
            {
                await Task.Delay(5000, stoppingToken);
                this.logger.LogInformation($"Background service processing at
{DateTime.Now}.");
            }
            catch (OperationCanceledException) { }
            catch (Exception ex)
            {
                this.logger.LogError("Background service error: " + ex.To-
String());
            }
        }

        this.logger.LogInformation("Background service stopping.");
    }
}
```

In this implementation, the service runs indefinitely until the application shuts down. The **stoppingToken** ensures that the process exits cleanly when cancellation is requested. Logging is added to provide visibility into when the service starts, executes, encounters errors, and stops.

To register this background service with the application, it must be added to the **ConfigureServices()** method during application startup:

```
using BackgroundServiceDemo;
using Microsoft.Extensions.DependencyInjection;
using Microsoft.Extensions.Hosting;
using Microsoft.Extensions.Logging;

IHostBuilder builder = Host.CreateDefaultBuilder(args)
    .ConfigureServices((hostContext, services) =>
    {
        services.AddLogging();
```

```
            //Register hosted service
            services.AddHostedService<BackgroundWorkerService>();
        })
        .ConfigureLogging(logging =>
        {
            logging.AddConsole();
        });

    IHost host = builder.Build();
    await host.RunAsync();
```

This configuration ensures that the background service starts when the application begins running and stops gracefully when the application shuts down. Since the service is managed by the hosting environment, it benefits from dependency injection, structured logging, and clean shutdown handling—all of which make it the preferred approach for **long-running** background tasks in ASP.NET Core.

Choosing the Right Approach

When designing **long-running** tasks, selecting the right execution model is crucial for balancing performance, control, and integration with the application lifecycle. While **`Task.Factory.StartNew()`** with **`TaskCreationOptions.LongRunning`** is often the preferred approach—signaling to the runtime that a task should run on a **dedicated thread** rather than within the **thread pool**—it is not the only option. Some scenarios require even finer control, while others demand seamless integration with a hosting environment.

For general-purpose **long-running** tasks, using **`TaskCreationOptions.LongRunning`** provides a straightforward way to ensure that work is offloaded from the thread pool, reducing contention for shared resources. However, this option does not allow direct control over thread priority or guarantee a specific execution context.

In cases where precise control over execution characteristics is required—such as setting thread priority or ensuring a task remains isolated from the **thread pool**—manually creating a thread is a viable alternative. This approach is particularly useful when background work should run at a lower priority than other tasks, something that **`TaskCreationOptions.LongRunning`** does not address. The trade-off, however, is increased complexity in managing the thread's lifecycle and ensuring a clean shutdown.

For applications running in a hosted environment such as ASP.NET Core, background tasks should integrate with the application's lifecycle rather than being manually managed. The **`BackgroundService`** class provides a structured approach, ensuring that tasks start and stop alongside the application while benefiting from dependency injection, logging, and lifecycle management. This makes it the preferred choice for background processing in web applications and other hosted services.

Ultimately, while **`TaskCreationOptions.LongRunning`** is a powerful and often appropriate tool for managing long-running tasks, it is not a one-size-fits-all solution. Developers must consider the specific requirements of their workload—whether it is execution control, priority management, or lifecycle integration—to choose the best approach for their application.

Thread Pool versus Dedicated Threads

The **thread pool** provides a dynamically managed pool of threads that the system optimizes for reuse. It is suitable for **short-lived** tasks and automatically adjusts the number of active threads based on workload demand. **Thread pool** threads are always background threads, meaning they do not prevent process termination, and their lifecycle is entirely managed by the system. The system recycles threads to reduce the overhead of frequent thread creation.

Dedicated threads are explicitly created using the **`Thread`** class or indirectly via **`Task.Factory.StartNew()`** with **`TaskCreationOptions.LongRunning`**. Unlike **thread pool** threads, **dedicated threads** provide full control over priority, scheduling, and lifetime, at the cost of greater complexity and resource overhead. Manually created threads can be either foreground or background threads and are ideal for **long-running** or blocking tasks that should not interfere with the **thread pool**.

Performance Implications

Thread pool threads and **dedicated threads** are optimized for different use cases, as illustrated in the following table:

Aspect	Thread Pool	Dedicated Thread
Resource Efficiency	Optimized for reuse, reducing memory and CPU overhead.	Incurs creation overhead and requires manual scheduling.
Scalability	Automatically adapts to workload changes.	Excessive threads can degrade performance due to context switching.
Context Switching	Reduces context switching by reusing existing threads.	The more **dedicated threads**, the greater the context switching overhead.
Latency Considerations	Can introduce a slight delay when the pool is exhausted, as new threads are created conservatively.	Avoids thread creation delays but increases system load.

***Table 11.2**: Thread Pool versus Dedicated Thread Performance*

Choosing the Right Model

Selecting between **thread pool** threads and **dedicated threads** depends on the nature of the workload and the level of control required.

For most applications, the **thread pool** is the preferred choice because it efficiently manages thread reuse, reducing the overhead of frequent thread creation and destruction. It is particularly well-suited for **short-lived**, I/O-bound, or CPU-bound tasks where automatic thread management is beneficial. Tasks such as handling web requests, processing background jobs, and running parallel loops or asynchronous operations are ideal candidates for the **thread pool**. Since the system dynamically adjusts the number of available threads, it helps maintain scalability and prevents excessive resource consumption.

However, there are scenarios where **dedicated threads** are the better option. If an operation is **long-running** or blocking, using a **dedicated thread** prevents it from occupying a **thread pool** thread, which could otherwise be used for more frequent, **short-lived** tasks. **Dedicated threads** also provide greater flexibility, allowing for custom scheduling, priority adjustments, and thread affinity, which may be necessary for certain high-performance applications or real-time processing.

Another key consideration is thread-local storage. The **thread pool** does not reset **`ThreadLocal<T>`** values when reusing threads, which can lead to unexpected behavior if tasks rely on thread-specific data. In such cases, using **dedicated threads** ensures better isolation and prevents unintended data persistence across different executions.

In summary, the **thread pool** is the best choice for most concurrent workloads due to its efficiency and scalability. **Dedicated threads** should be used when fine-grained control over execution is necessary, particularly for **long-running** tasks, custom scheduling, or strict thread isolation requirements.

Best Practices

The .NET **thread pool** is designed to be highly efficient, automatically managing threads to maximize performance for most applications. In many cases, its default behavior is optimal, requiring little manual intervention. However, following a few best practices can help ensure that your application makes the best use of available resources, improving both scalability and responsiveness.

- One of the most important considerations when working with the **thread pool** is the nature of the tasks you schedule. **Short-lived** tasks are ideal, as they allow the pool to quickly reuse threads and maintain responsiveness. **Long-running** operations, on the other hand, can lead to thread starvation, reducing overall system throughput. If a task needs to run for an extended period, consider using a **dedicated thread** or configuring it with **`TaskCreationOptions.LongRunning`** to prevent it from consuming thread pool resources.
- For lightweight, fire-and-forget tasks where tracking completion is unnecessary—such as logging, telemetry collection, or background cleanup jobs—**`QueueUserWorkItem()`** can be a good choice. It avoids the overhead of creating a full **`Task`** object, making it more efficient for simple workloads. However, when structured scheduling, exception handling, or result retrieval is needed, **`Task.Run()`** is generally the better approach. It provides better integration with the Task Parallel Library (TPL), supports continuations, and propagates exceptions more effectively.
- When using **`QueueUserWorkItem()`**, an often-overlooked optimization is enabling local queueing by passing **`true`** for the **`preferLocal`** parameter. This ensures that tasks are first attempted on a queue local to the current thread before being distributed to the global queue, reducing contention and improving performance in high-throughput scenarios.
- Another common performance pitfall is scheduling an excessive number of small tasks, leading to frequent context switching and thread contention. In these cases, batching tasks can be beneficial. Using **`ConcurrentQueue<T>`** to aggregate small workloads or leveraging **`Parallel.ForEach()`** to process collections in parallel can significantly reduce overhead and improve efficiency.
- To ensure your application is making the most of the **thread pool**, regular monitoring is essential. Tools such as dotnet-counters, dotnet-trace, and **`EventSource`** can provide valuable insights into thread availability and workload distribution. The **`ThreadPool.GetAvailableThreads()`** method can also help detect potential exhaustion before it becomes a bottleneck.
- In highly parallel applications, a custom task scheduler may be necessary to achieve finer-grained control over task execution. This can be especially useful in scenarios that require priority-based scheduling or workload balancing beyond what the default **thread pool** provides. Custom schedulers and advanced task management techniques are covered in *Chapter 9, Advanced Task Management*.
- Finally, exception handling should never be an afterthought. Unhandled exceptions in **thread pool** tasks can lead to silent failures, making debugging difficult. Whether using **`Task.Run()`** or **`QueueUserWorkItem()`**, wrapping tasks in **`try-catch`** blocks and logging errors using structured logging frameworks such as Serilog or ILogger ensures that failures are properly captured and addressed.

By following these best practices, you can ensure that your application scales effectively while maintaining high performance. The **thread pool** is a powerful tool, and with careful tuning, it can help maximize the efficiency of multithreaded workloads without unnecessary overhead.

Conclusion

The .NET **thread pool** provides an efficient and scalable way to manage concurrency in applications, reducing the overhead of manual thread creation while optimizing system resource utilization. By leveraging the **thread pool** for **short-lived** tasks, background processing, and asynchronous operations, developers can improve application performance and responsiveness. However, it is essential to understand its limitations–such as its unsuitability for **long-running** or highly specialized threading scenarios–where **dedicated threads** may be more appropriate. By applying best practices, monitoring thread pool performance, and choosing the right threading model for each scenario, developers can build high-performance, concurrent applications that fully utilize modern hardware capabilities.

Debugging parallel applications presents unique challenges, from tracking race conditions to diagnosing deadlocks and understanding asynchronous execution flow. In the next chapter, we will explore how Visual Studio's powerful debugging tools–such as the Parallel Stacks window, Parallel Watch window, and Concurrency Visualizer–help simplify the debugging process. We will also cover essential strategies for identifying and resolving issues in multithreaded applications, including deadlocks, race conditions, and debugging task-based asynchronous code.

Points to Remember

- The .NET **thread pool** is implemented in the `ThreadPool` class and provides a managed pool of **worker** and **I/O completion threads**.
- It is designed for **short-lived**, lightweight tasks and dynamically adjusts the number of threads based on workload.
- Developers should avoid blocking **thread pool** threads (for example, using `Thread.Sleep()` or waiting on locks) because this reduces **thread pool** efficiency.
- The Task Parallel Library (TPL) internally leverages the **thread pool** for task execution.
- **Long-running** tasks should be run on **dedicated threads** either manually created or by using `TaskCreationOptions.LongRunning`.

Multiple Choice Questions

1. Which method is used to queue work directly to the **thread pool**?
   a. `Task.Run()`
   b. `ThreadPool.QueueUserWorkItem()`
   c. `Task.Factory.StartNew()`
   d. `Thread.Sleep()`
2. What type of threads does the **thread pool** manage?
   a. **Worker threads** and foreground threads.
   b. **Worker threads** and **I/O completion threads**.
   c. Foreground threads and background threads.
   d. Background threads and I/O threads.
3. Which of the following is a scenario where the **thread pool** is beneficial?
   a. **Long-running** operations.
   b. **Dedicated threads** for CPU-bound operations.
   c. Blocking request pipeline in ASP.NET applications.
   d. Short-running asynchronous tasks.

4. How does the **thread pool** handle exceptions?
   a. It has built-in exception handling.
   b. Exceptions are not allowed in the **thread pool**.
   c. Exceptions must be handled within the delegate itself.
   d. Exceptions are propagated back to the caller.

Answers

1. b
2. b
3. d
4. c

Questions

1. Why is manually managing threads often inefficient compared to using the .NET **thread pool**?
2. What are some potential pitfalls of using `ThreadPool.QueueUserWorkItem()`, and how can they be avoided?
3. What strategies can you use to prevent **long-running** tasks from degrading the performance of the **thread pool**?
4. How can you monitor and tune **thread pool** behavior in a production environment?

Key Terms

- **Thread Pool**: A managed pool of worker and I/O completion threads for efficiently executing **short-lived** tasks.
- **Worker Threads**: Threads from the **thread pool** used for CPU-bound or general background tasks.
- **I/O Completion Threads**: Special threads in the **thread pool** that handle the completion of asynchronous I/O operations.
- **Dedicated Threads**: Threads that are created outside the **thread pool** to service specific tasks.
- **I/O Completion Ports (IOCP)**: A highly efficient mechanism in Windows that allows the operating system to handle I/O in the background.
- **Short-Lived**: A unit of work that completes quickly, typically within milliseconds to a few seconds.
- **Long-Running**: A unit of work that runs indefinitely or for an extended period, typically longer than a few seconds.
- **Work Item**: A delegate queued to the **thread pool** to be processed on a **worker thread**.
- **Thread Pool Exhaustion**: A state where too many pending tasks cause increased queueing delays, degrading performance.

CHAPTER 12
Debugging Parallel Applications Using Visual Studio

Introduction

Debugging parallel applications presents distinct challenges, such as race conditions, deadlocks, and unpredictable execution orders. Without the right tools, identifying and resolving these issues can be time-consuming and frustrating. Fortunately, Visual Studio offers a comprehensive suite of parallel debugging tools designed to simplify this process. In this chapter, we will explore these tools, along with best practices and strategies, to help you efficiently diagnose and fix issues in parallel applications.

Structure

In this chapter, we will cover the following topics:

- Debugging Parallel Applications
    - Overview of Debugging Parallel Applications
    - Challenges of Parallel Applications
- Visual Studio Overview and Setup
    - Tools Overview
    - Debugger Setup
- Using the Parallel Stacks Window
    - Viewing Threads and Tasks
    - Navigating Execution Paths
    - Diagnosing Issues
- Using the Parallel Watch Window
    - Monitoring Variables
    - Comparing Values
    - Identifying Inconsistent States
- Thread and Task Management
    - Using the Threads Window
    - Suspending, Resuming, and Switching Threads

    - Using the Tasks Window
    - Debugging Affinity and Scheduling
- Using Breakpoints
    - Setting and Using Breakpoints
- Using the Concurrency Visualizer
    - Analyzing Execution Timelines
    - Identifying Bottlenecks
    - Visualizing Lock Contention

Debugging Parallel Applications

Debugging parallel applications is significantly more complex than debugging single-threaded applications. Each thread has its own call stack and executes independently, often running the same code blocks concurrently. This behavior can impact even basic debugging tools such as breakpoints and watches, making issues such as race conditions and deadlocks harder to diagnose. To be effective, developers need robust debugging tools and well-defined strategies to handle concurrency-related challenges.

Overview of Debugging Parallel Applications

Debugging parallel applications requires a different approach than debugging sequential programs due to the complexities introduced by multiple threads or tasks executing concurrently. Unlike sequential code, where execution follows a predictable order, parallel programs can exhibit non-deterministic behavior, making issues such as race conditions, deadlocks, and synchronization errors difficult to reproduce and diagnose. Effective debugging involves carefully inspecting thread interactions, monitoring shared state changes, and employing techniques such as logging, breakpoints, and thread visualization. Additionally, understanding execution timing and how parallel workloads are scheduled is crucial, as debugging itself can influence program behavior. By using structured debugging strategies and tools designed for concurrency, developers can identify and resolve issues while ensuring optimal performance and correctness in multi-threaded applications.

Challenges of Parallel Applications

Debugging parallel applications presents unique challenges due to the unpredictable nature of thread execution. Unlike sequential programs, where execution follows a predictable path, parallel applications are subject to variations in execution order caused by operating system thread scheduling, the .NET runtime, and hardware factors such as CPU core availability. This variability can make bugs intermittent and difficult to reproduce. A defect may appear in one execution and disappear in the next, depending on how threads interact with shared resources. Even debugging tools themselves, such as breakpoints and stepping through code, can influence thread scheduling, potentially masking or exposing different behaviors than those encountered during normal execution.

Each thread in a parallel application maintains its own call stack and local variables, even when multiple threads execute the same code. This can lead to significant confusion when interpreting watch values, as different threads may be at different points in execution. Debugging parallel code requires tracking multiple execution paths simultaneously, a task further complicated by frequent context switching. Developers must mentally reconstruct the program's state across multiple threads, often leading to errors in diagnosing issues.

Breakpoints, a fundamental debugging tool in sequential programs, behave differently in multithreaded applications. By default, a breakpoint typically suspends only the currently executing thread while allowing others to continue running. This selective suspension can make it difficult to inspect the system holistically, as the program state continues to evolve while the debugger is paused. Additionally, pausing a single thread can disrupt normal scheduling, introducing artificial delays that make reproducing race conditions and timing-sensitive bugs more difficult. Careful configuration of the debugger is necessary to ensure that breakpoints provide meaningful insights rather than inadvertently altering program behavior.

Parallel execution also increases the risk of race conditions, where multiple threads access shared data concurrently without proper synchronization. These conditions can result in inconsistent states, corrupted data, or unpredictable behavior. Debugging such issues requires careful analysis of thread interactions and the use of synchronization mechanisms such as locks, mutexes, and atomic operations. Deadlocks present another challenge, occurring when multiple threads become stuck waiting for resources that are held by each other. Diagnosing and resolving deadlocks requires examining thread states, stack traces, and resource dependencies to identify the exact conditions that led to the impasse.

Exception handling in parallel applications introduces additional complexity. Unlike single-threaded programs, where an unhandled exception typically terminates execution or triggers a clear error message, exceptions in multithreaded code may occur in different threads and go unnoticed if not explicitly caught. In some cases, an exception may terminate a thread while allowing the rest of the application to continue running, potentially leading to silent failures or an inconsistent state. Debugging these issues requires special techniques, such as monitoring first-chance exceptions in Visual Studio, setting up thread exception handlers, and logging unhandled task exceptions using mechanisms such as **`TaskScheduler.UnobservedTaskException`**.

Logging is another critical tool for diagnosing parallel execution issues, but it comes with its own challenges. In multithreaded applications, log messages from different threads can become interleaved, making it difficult to reconstruct the actual execution flow. Without proper structuring, logs can quickly become unreadable. To maintain clarity, logs should include timestamps, thread identifiers, and log levels. Advanced correlation techniques, such as activity tracing and distributed context propagation, may be necessary when debugging asynchronous code that spans multiple execution contexts. Managing and filtering logs effectively requires specialized tools to group and analyze related events, ensuring that useful insights can be extracted from large volumes of log data.

Given these complexities, effective debugging of parallel applications requires specialized tools and techniques. Visual Studio provides a suite of powerful debugging features designed to address these challenges, making it easier to analyze, diagnose, and resolve parallel execution issues. Mastering these tools will greatly enhance the efficiency and reliability of your debugging sessions, enabling you to develop high-performance, robust multithreaded applications.

Visual Studio Overview and Setup

The first step to effective debugging using Visual Studio is to understand its debugging tools and how they can be applied to efficiently debug parallel and asynchronous applications. The debugger includes options that influence breakpoint behavior, and understanding these settings is essential for properly inspecting running threads. Proper debugger configuration is crucial for an effective debugging experience in Visual Studio.

Note: *While other IDEs support .NET development and may offer similar debugging tools, this book focuses specifically on debugging with Visual Studio, the premier .NET IDE.*

Tools Overview

Visual Studio offers a robust toolset for debugging parallel and asynchronous applications. These tools are accessible during a debugging session:

Tool	Menu Item / Shortcut	Description
Parallel Stacks Window	`Debug` > `Windows` > `Parallel Stacks` / *Ctrl+Shift+D, S*	Displays call stack information for threads and tasks, allowing developers to visualize execution flow and pivot call stacks on selected methods.
Parallel Watch Window	`Debug` > `Windows` > `Parallel Watch` (1–4) / *Ctrl+Shift+D, 1–4*	Enables monitoring and comparing expression values across multiple threads simultaneously.
Threads Window	`Debug` > `Windows` > `Threads` / *Ctrl+Shift+D, H*	Displays all active threads in the application, providing options to **freeze**, **thaw**, or switch between them.
Tasks Window	`Debug` > `Windows` > `Tasks` / *Ctrl+Shift+D, K*	Lists active tasks in asynchronous code, allowing developers to track task status, parent-child relationships, and execution order.
Concurrency Visualizer	`Analyze` > `Concurrency Visualizer`	Provides performance insights into thread execution, CPU utilization, and contention hotspots to optimize parallel processing.

Table 12.1: *Visual Studio Parallel Debugging Tools*

Breakpoints for Precise Debugging

Visual Studio supports various types of breakpoints to provide precise control over debugging:

- **Conditional Breakpoints**: Trigger only when a specified condition is met.
- **Function Breakpoints**: Activate when a specific function is called.
- **Data Breakpoints**: Halt execution when a monitored variable or object property changes.
- **Dependent Breakpoints**: Fire only after a related breakpoint has been hit.
- **Temporary Breakpoints**: Trigger once and then automatically disable themselves.

Mastering these tools enhances efficiency when debugging complex parallel and asynchronous code. By leveraging the **Parallel Stacks** and **Parallel Watch** windows, developers can gain insight into thread execution and variable states across multiple contexts. The Threads and **Tasks** windows provide fine-grained control over the thread and task management, making it easier to diagnose synchronization issues and unexpected behaviors. Additionally, the **`Concurrency Visualizer`** helps identify performance bottlenecks and thread contention, allowing for better optimization. Combined with precise breakpoint strategies, these tools form a powerful debugging framework that enables developers to analyze, troubleshoot, and optimize parallel execution with confidence.

Debugger Setup

There are several Visual Studio options that control aspects of debugging, particularly useful for parallel debugging. These settings are available after debugging starts. Use these settings to fine-tune the debugger's behavior to meet your specific needs:

Option	Menu Item	Description
Enable Just My Code	`Debug` > `Options` > `General`	Skips system and third-party libraries to focus on user-written code. Disable this if stepping into a framework or dependency code is required.

Break all processes when one process breaks	`Debug` > `Options` > `General`	Suspends execution across **all processes** when a breakpoint is hit in any process. Useful when debugging distributed or multi-process applications.
Enable breakpoint filters	`Debug` > `Options` > `Debugging`	Allows breakpoints to be applied selectively based on thread ID, process ID, or other criteria.
Exception Settings	`Debug` > `Windows` > `Exception Settings`	Under **`Common Language Runtime`**, select exceptions to break on. Consider enabling **`OperationCanceledException`** and **`AggregateException`** to ensure exceptions in parallel tasks are properly handled.
Source Symbols	`Debug` > `Options` > `Symbols`	Enable **`Microsoft Symbol Servers`** and disable **`Just My Code`** to debug framework-level parallel execution. Enable local caching to improve performance.

Table 12.2: *Debugger Settings*

By properly configuring these settings and tools, Visual Studio is optimized for debugging parallel applications efficiently.

Using the Parallel Stacks Window

The **Parallel Stacks Window** is designed to show call stack information in parallel applications. It has two main views: Thread View and Task View. The thread view visualizes the call stacks for all running threads in the application. Task view shows the call stacks for all Task instances in the application. The **Parallel Stacks Window** can only be accessed during a debug session, via **`Debug`** > **`Windows`** > **`Parallel Stacks`**.

Viewing Threads and Tasks

The **Parallel Stacks Window** can be used to view active threads and active tasks in the application, depending on the view used. The view is controlled by selecting the desired view from the View dropdown in the middle of the toolbar at the top of the window.

Viewing Threads

The Thread View shows the running threads in the application. It shows all threads both managed and unmanaged, and the call relationships between them. The following figure shows the Thread View with two managed threads running.

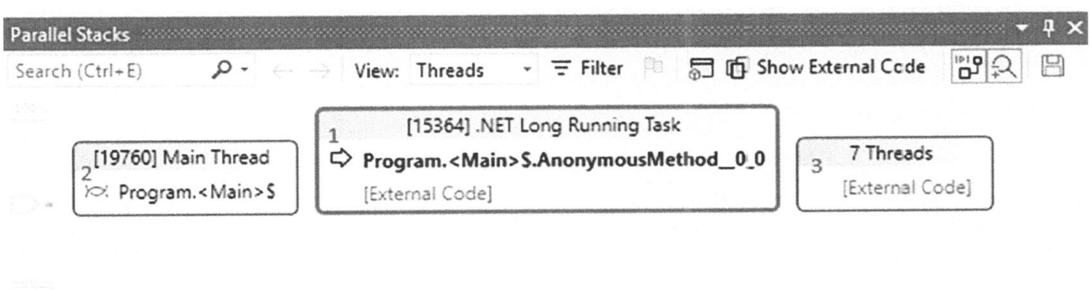

Figure 12.1: *Parallel Stacks Thread View*

This view shows the main thread and a long-running thread created by calling **`Task.Factory.StartNew()`**. The window shows the following details, indicated by the red numbers.

- The current location is in the current thread. The current thread in this case is named "**`.NET Long Running Task`**" and is highlighted in blue. The current call stack location is identified by the arrow icon.

- The main thread appears suspended, as indicated by the grey color. The current call stack location in the main thread is shown by the non-current thread active location icon.
- This box indicates seven other threads running external code in this application. These threads are managed by the .NET hosting environment.

The code being debugged is shown in the following figure.

Figure 12.2: *Code Window Debugging View*

Lines 1 through 8 define the long-running background task and lines 9 through 11 define the main thread. The current location in the current active thread is on line 5. This corresponds to the arrow at number 1 in *Figure* 12.1. The main thread is waiting for user input on line 11. This corresponds to number 2 in *Figure* 12.1.

Hovering the mouse over one of the thread boxes in this view will show a detailed call stack tooltip, as shown in the following figure.

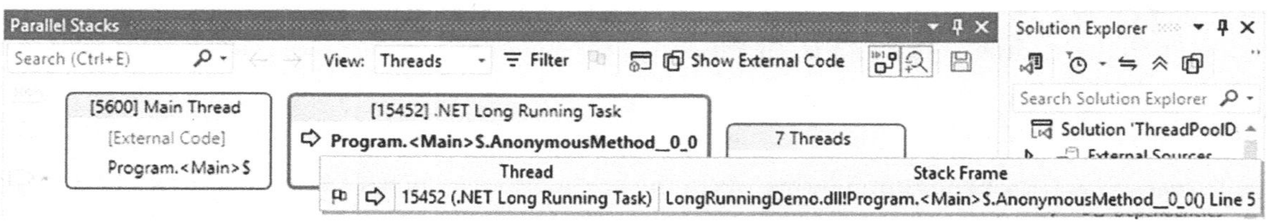

Figure 12.3: *Thread View Call Stack Tooltip*

The call stack tooltip shows the currently running thread ID and name, along with the active stack frame and source line number.

Viewing Tasks

The Task View shows the logical stacks of all active tasks (**`System.Threading.Tasks.Task`**) in the application, instead of threads. Call stacks are a part of threads, but considering **`async/await`** and continuations, tasks can run on multiple threads. Therefore, the **`Task View`** shows Async Logical Stacks instead of call stacks.

Switching to **`Task View`** for our program shows the following.

Note: *The code being debugged in this instance is the same code shown in Figure 12.2. The view is just being switched from Threads view to Tasks view.*

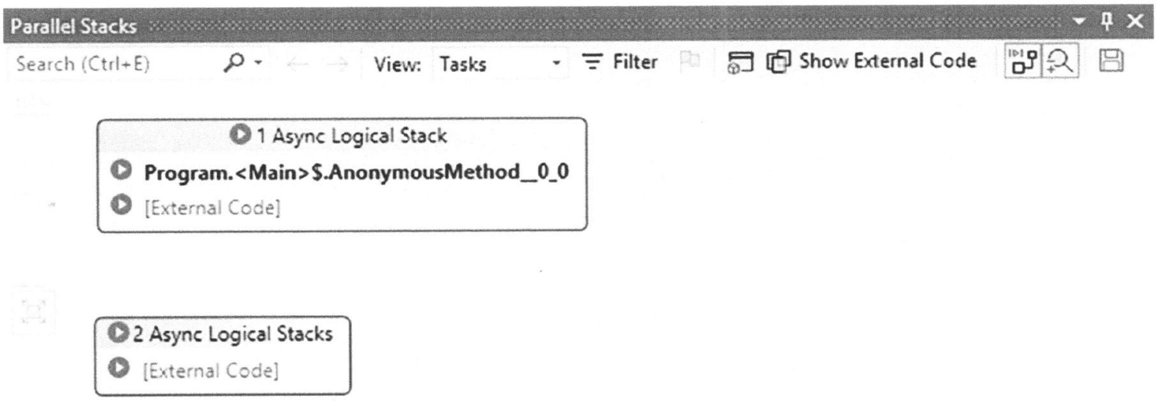

Figure 12.4: *Parallel Stacks Task View*

The long-running task is shown in a single Async Logical Stack because it runs its own independent loop. There are two other Async Logical Stacks that are external code associated with the .NET hosting environment. In this program, the main thread does not run any tasks, so it is not shown.

Hovering the mouse over Async Logical Stack nodes in the `Task View` shows a tooltip with task information including the **`task ID`**, **`thread ID`** and **`name`**, **`task status`**, and **`active stack frame`**.

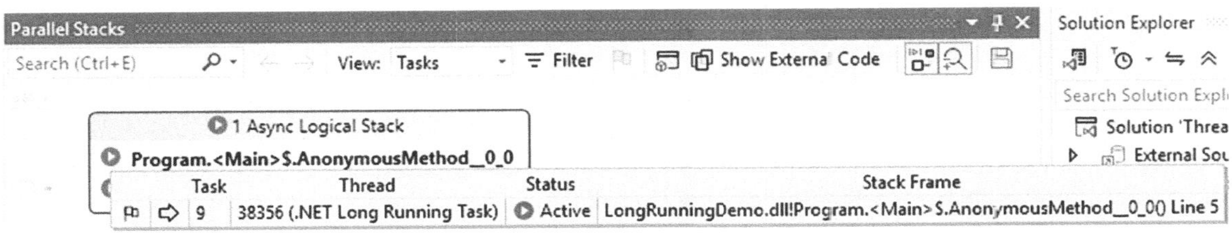

Figure 12.5: *Task View Tooltip*

These different views allow developers to visualize the thread and task contexts in the running application and view the interaction of threads and tasks.

Navigating Execution Paths

The **Parallel Stacks Window** is designed to help you efficiently navigate the execution paths in your application using the following features:

1. Double-clicking a call stack frame will navigate to the corresponding source code in the debugger, allowing you to quickly inspect execution locations.
2. Use the appropriate icons in the call stack box to expand or collapse execution paths for better clarity.
3. Look for synchronization primitives such as **`lock`** statements, **`Monitor.Wait()`**, **`SemaphoreSlim.Wait()`**, **`Task.Wait()`**, or **`await`** statements to determine where execution is paused. This can help identify potential deadlocks or bottlenecks.
4. The **`Thread View`** shows actual call stacks for each thread. The **`Task View`** shows logical execution stacks for asynchronous operations. Since tasks can execute across multiple threads due to **`await`**, the **`Task View`** is essential for correctly visualizing task execution.
5. Stacks are grouped if they share common execution paths. Grouped stacks are shown with a count greater than 1. This helps identify patterns, such as multiple threads executing the same function concurrently, which is common in parallel loops.

6. Hierarchical task relationships, such as those created using **`Task.Run()`** or **`Task.Factory.StartNew()`**, are represented with arrows connecting parent and child tasks, as shown in *Figure* 12.6. This allows you to trace how tasks were created and executed.

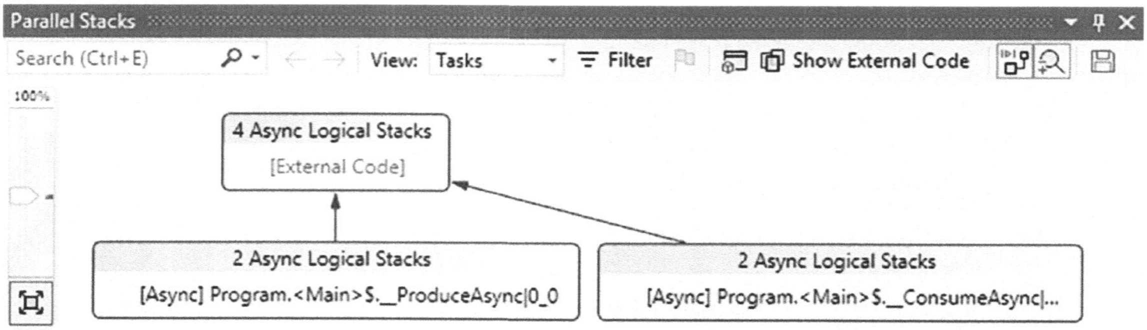

***Figure* 12.6:** *Arrows Indicating Parent-Child Relationships*

7. Use the zoom controls to adjust the visualization in complex scenarios. Click and drag to reposition the view when debugging large applications.
8. Hover over a thread or task node to view additional debugging details, including thread ID, task ID, status, and active stack frame information.
9. External code is hidden by default. Show external code by clicking the *Show External Code* button. This is useful for identifying issues dealing with library or .NET framework code.

By using these features, you can efficiently explore execution paths, even in complex applications, while maintaining a clear visualization of how threads and tasks interact.

Diagnosing Issues

While the **Parallel Stacks Window** is a powerful tool for debugging multithreaded and asynchronous applications, certain challenges may arise. The following are common issues and ways to resolve them.

1. Missing Threads or Tasks in the View
    - **Issue:** Some threads or tasks do not appear in the **Parallel Stacks Window**.
    - **Possible Causes and Solutions:**
        - The debugger may be filtering out external or system-managed threads. Enable the display of all threads by checking the appropriate option in the **Threads Window** (*Ctrl + Alt + H*).
        - The task may not be active or scheduled yet. Ensure the task has started executing before pausing the debugger.
        - The application might be optimized by the JIT compiler, making some stack frames unavailable. Try running the application in Debug mode (**`Debug`** > **`Options`** > **`Suppress JIT Optimization`**).
2. Call Stacks Appear in External Code
    - **Issue:** The call stack includes [External Code] entries, making it difficult to trace execution.
    - **Possible Causes and Solutions:**

- The debugger hides non-user code by default. Enable external code display by clicking `Show External Code` in the `Call Stack` window.
- If your code is making asynchronous framework calls, consider switching to the Task View to follow logical execution instead of raw thread execution.

3. Difficulty Tracing Asynchronous Code
   - **Issue:** Execution seems to "*jump*" between different threads unexpectedly.
   - **Possible Causes and Solutions:**
     - This is expected behavior for `async/await` since tasks resume on different threads. Use the Task View instead of the Thread View to follow logical execution flow.
     - Ensure you have debug symbols loaded (.pdb files) for third-party libraries if stepping through external async code.
4. Deadlocks or Hanging Execution
   - **Issue:** The application appears to be frozen, with some threads stuck in `Monitor.Wait()` or `Task.Wait()`.
   - **Possible Causes and Solutions:**
     - Look for synchronization primitives in the call stack. These may indicate contention or circular dependencies.
     - Use the Tasks View to check for tasks that are waiting indefinitely for an event to complete.
     - Try breaking execution (`Debug` > `Break All`) and examine blocked threads to identify the source of the deadlock.
5. Navigating Large Thread/Task Counts Becomes Confusing
   - **Issue:** The **Parallel Stacks Window** is cluttered with too many threads or tasks, making debugging difficult.
   - **Possible Solutions:**
     - Use filtering options in the **Threads Window** to focus on relevant threads (*Ctrl + Alt + H*).
     - Collapse similar call stacks by using the grouping feature in **Parallel Stacks**.
     - Zoom in and pan the window to get a clearer view of execution paths.

By recognizing and addressing these common issues, you can make the most of the **Parallel Stacks** Window and effectively debug complex, multithreaded applications.

Using the Parallel Watch Window

Most developers are familiar with the concept of watches in debugging. A watch is an expression that a developer monitors while stepping through code during a debugging session. It can be as simple as a variable or property reference or as complex as a computed expression. The Watch Window in Visual Studio provides a way to view and manage these watches efficiently.

Debugging parallel applications introduces additional complexity. Multiple threads may execute the same code block simultaneously, and shared data can be modified by different threads, making it difficult to track variable states accurately. To address this challenge, Visual Studio provides the `Parallel Watch` Window, a specialized tool for managing watches in parallel debugging scenarios.

The `Parallel Watch` Window allows developers to observe expressions across multiple threads simultaneously. Instead of manually switching between threads to check values, developers can view and compare the same expression across different threads in one place. This feature helps in identifying race conditions, unexpected data modifications, and synchronization issues, ultimately simplifying the debugging of multithreaded applications.

Monitoring Variables

The **Parallel Watch** Window is displayed by choosing **`Debug`** > **`Windows`** > **`Parallel Watch`** and then choosing a watch window to display. Up to four watch windows can be opened at any given time. The following window will be shown.

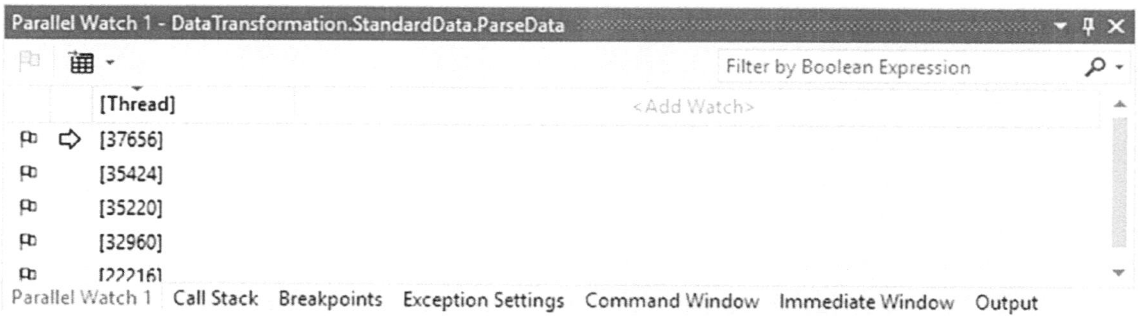

Figure 12.7: *Parallel Watch Window*

The top toolbar contains a button to toggle filtering by flagged threads, export the data in the window to Excel, and filter by a Boolean Expression. Each row in the grid represents a different active thread, identified by thread ID and name. Threads can be flagged by clicking the flag icon in the left column, marking the thread as interesting to the developer and allowing other threads to be filtered by clicking the button in the top left of the toolbar. The yellow arrow indicates the currently executing thread at the breakpoint.

Watches are added to the grid by clicking the **`Add Watch`** column and defining the watch expression. This adds a new column to the grid that shows the watch value in each thread. Multiple watch columns may be added using this method.

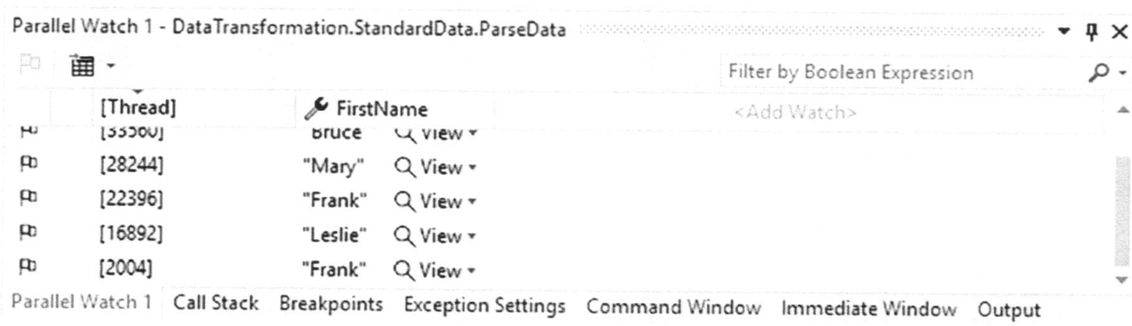

Figure 12.8: *Added Watch Column*

In *Figure* 12.8, a new watch has been added for the **`FirstName`** property of a class being processed by multiple threads. The window shows the current value of this property for each of the threads. As the developer steps through the code, the latest values will be displayed for each of the threads. Rows can be sorted by column values by clicking on the column header.

Comparing Values

As values change, the modified value is displayed in a red-colored font, as shown in the following figure.

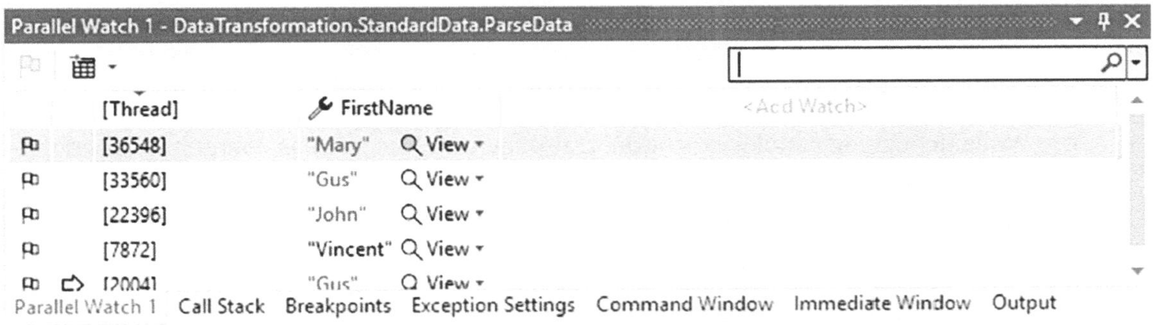

Figure 12.9: *Changed Data in Red*

This makes it easier to spot unexpected changes that could lead to inconsistent states. Tracking these changes helps in identifying potential threading issues, such as race conditions or unintended modifications to shared data.

The sorting feature allows the grid to be sorted by any column, grouping values together for easier identification of outliers that may indicate undesired behavior. Additionally, using the filter expression or filtering flagged threads can help focus attention on problem areas, further isolating and diagnosing issues. Filters support expressions, enabling conditions such as filtering by specific thread IDs or variable values.

Adding multiple watch columns for related variables that interact enables visualization of thread behavior as these variables change. This is particularly useful for spotting issues with shared data, counters, or lock states. The following figure shows multiple related watch columns.

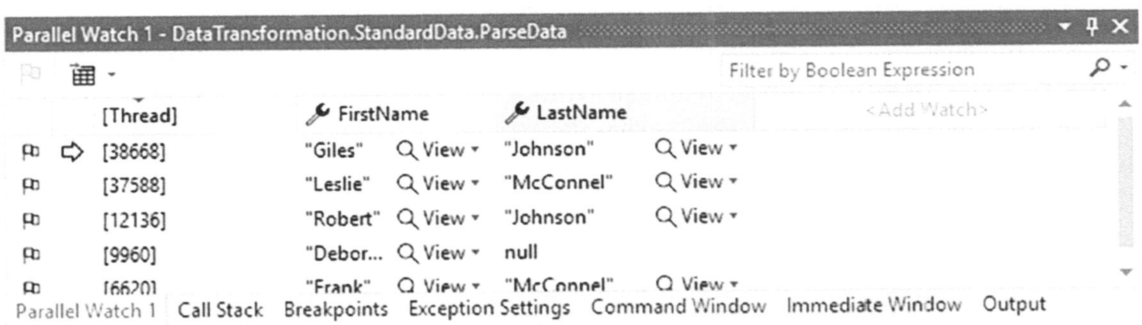

Figure 12.10: *Multiple Watch Columns*

For complex debugging scenarios where different aspects of thread execution need to be monitored, multiple **`Parallel Watch`** windows can be opened, up to a maximum of four. Each window can focus on different flagged threads, watch columns, filtering criteria, or sorting preferences.

Sometimes, it is useful to take snapshots of values to compare between breakpoints, before and after variable updates, or across debugging sessions. Since the **`Parallel Watch`** Window does not have a built-in snapshot mechanism, manual snapshots must be taken when needed. Copying values to Excel using the *Export to Excel* toolbar item, taking screenshots, or manually copying data to an external source such as *Notepad* are all viable options for capturing snapshots.

Identifying Inconsistent States

Concurrency issues can lead to subtle, hard-to-reproduce bugs, and the **`Parallel Watch`** Window is an invaluable tool for identifying these problems. The following are strategies for using the **`Parallel`**

`Watch` Window to detect and resolve anomalies, race conditions, and inconsistencies by comparing values across threads.

1. Detecting Unexpected Value Changes
   - While debugging parallel execution, track key variables such as counters, collections, or state flags.
   - Look for unexpected or inconsistent values between threads. For example:
     - A variable that should be read-only changes unexpectedly.
     - A counter that should be incrementing sequentially suddenly skips or duplicates values.
     - A flag should be set once but appears in different states across threads.
   - **Practical Example:** A shared **`totalOrdersProcessed`** variable that should be the same across all threads instead is different. This may indicate a race condition.
2. Identifying Race Conditions
   - Values are observed to change inconsistently across threads.
   - Compare values at breakpoints before and after a suspected race condition to see if they change unexpectedly.
   - **Practical Example:** Two or more threads update a **`jobQueue`** queue but some jobs are duplicated or lost as observed in the **`Parallel Watch` Window**. This may indicate improper locks or other synchronization issues.
3. Monitoring Thread-Specific Anomalies
   - Observe variables that should be local to threads but appear to be modified by multiple threads.
   - Check for null values or uninitialized data appearing randomly. This may indicate an initialization problem or unintended shared data.
   - **Practical Example:** If a thread-local collection is updated by multiple threads, it might indicate improper thread-local storage.
4. Detecting Deadlocks and Incorrect Synchronization
   - If a thread appears to be stuck while others are executing, it could indicate a deadlock.
   - Compare lock states of synchronization primitives such as **`SemaphoreSlim`**, **`Monitor`**, or **`Mutex`** across threads to determine if a resource is being held indefinitely, leading to a deadlock.
   - **Practical Example:** If one thread is waiting on a **`ManualResetEvent`** that is never signaled, the flag might show false across all threads.

By carefully comparing values across threads in the **`Parallel Watch`** Window, you can detect race conditions, shared resource issues, deadlocks, and other concurrency bugs that might otherwise be difficult to identify. Using breakpoints, snapshots, and filters, you can efficiently pinpoint where and how anomalies occur in your multi-threaded application.

Thread and Task Management

Threads and tasks are fundamental to parallel programming in .NET, enabling concurrent execution and efficient resource utilization. Visual Studio provides dedicated debugging tools—the **Threads Window** and the **Tasks Window**—to help developers monitor, manage, and troubleshoot multithreading and asynchronous execution. These tools offer insights into thread states, task scheduling, and execution flow, making it easier to diagnose concurrency issues and optimize performance.

Using the Threads Window

The **Threads** Window in Visual Studio is available during debugging sessions and provides a real-time view of all threads in the executing application. It can be accessed via **Debug** > **Windows** > **Threads**. The following figure illustrates the **Threads** Window:

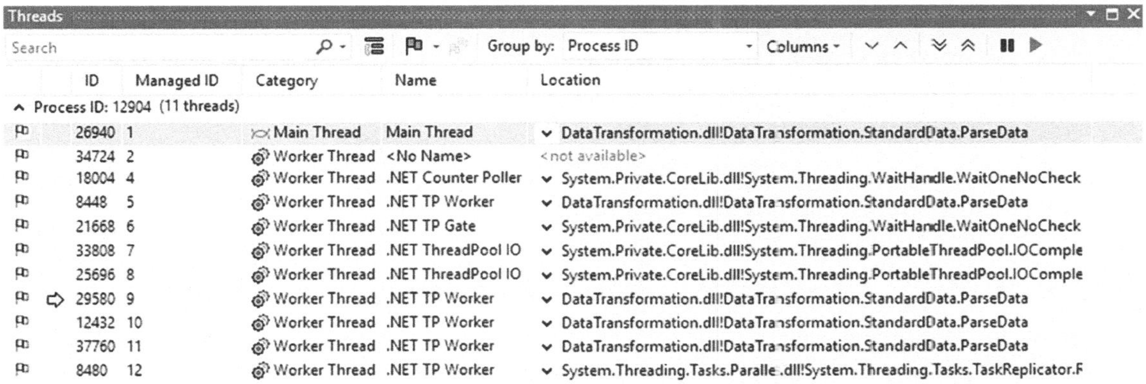

Figure 12.11: *Threads Window*

Toolbar Features

The top toolbar includes several controls for managing and filtering threads:

- **Search box**: Filters threads based on search criteria. A toggle button to the right extends the search to include thread call stacks.
- **User code filtering**: Flags threads that contain Just My Code (user code only) or threads running code from specific loaded modules.
- **Flagged thread filtering**: Toggles filtering to show only flagged threads.
- **Grouping dropdown**: Changes how threads are grouped. By default, threads are grouped by Process ID (PID).
- **Column selection dropdown**: Allows customization of the displayed columns.
- **Expand/collapse buttons**: Expands or collapses thread call stacks and grouped threads.
- **Freeze/thaw buttons**: Allows developers to pause (**freeze**) or resume (**thaw**) selected threads for debugging analysis.

Thread Details and Customization

The **Threads Window** displays key information about each thread in columns, with the following default columns:

- **Operating System Thread ID (OS Thread ID)**
- **Managed Thread ID** (for threads managed by the .NET runtime)
- **Thread Category**
- **Thread Name** (if set)
- **Stack Frame L**(showing where the thread is currently executing)

The current thread is highlighted with a yellow arrow. Clicking on a column header sorts the rows based on that column.

Threads can be renamed using the context menu, which helps improve readability during debugging. While runtime-generated threads typically have names, manually created threads may not.

Call Stack and Location Column

The Location column displays the call stack for each thread, which can be expanded or collapsed. Hovering over the Location column also reveals the call stack in a tooltip.

- The collapsed view shows the current stack frame (where the thread is paused).
- The expanded view shows the entire call stack, with the top frame representing the most recent execution point.

These call stacks help developers understand where each thread is paused, aiding in debugging deadlocks, race conditions, and thread execution flow.

Suspending, Resuming, and Switching Threads

The **Threads Window** allows manual control over thread execution during debugging. By selecting the threads to be affected and using the `Freeze/Thaw` buttons in the toolbar or choosing `Freeze` or `Thaw` from the context menu, you can pause or resume individual threads. *Figure 12.12* shows the `Freeze` and `Thaw` options in the Threads Window context menu.

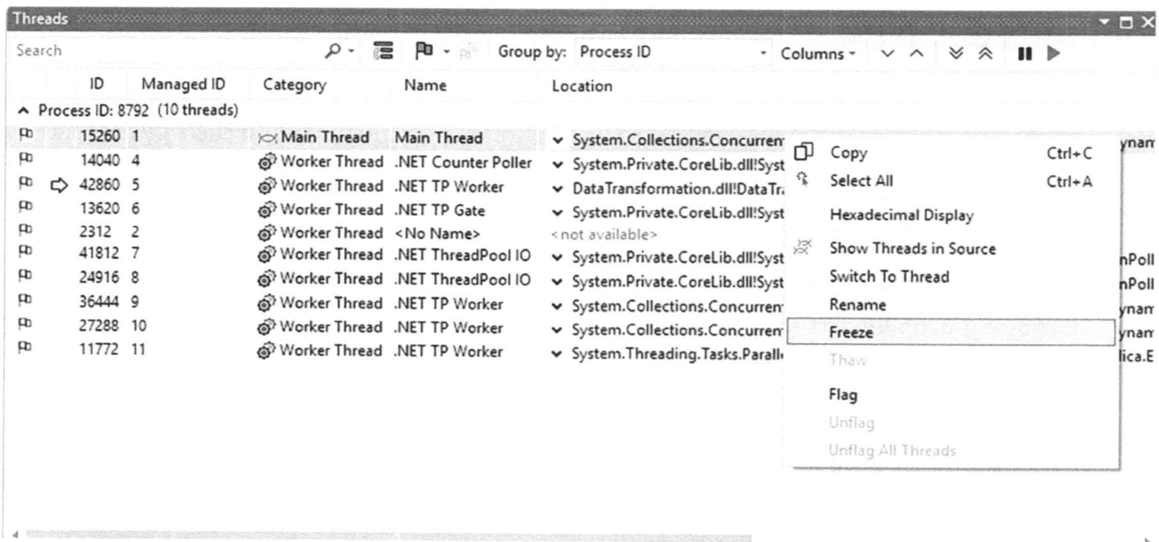

Figure 12.12: *Freeze and Thaw in Thread Window Context Menu*

- **Freezing (Suspending) a thread**: **Freezing** a thread pauses its execution, but other threads can continue running. The frozen thread stays in its current state, and you can interact with the other threads while the frozen one is paused.
- **Thawing (Resuming) a thread**: **Thawing** a thread reverses the **freeze**, allowing it to continue execution from where it left off as if nothing had interrupted its flow.

Freezing and **thawing** threads are invaluable tools for debugging issues related to thread synchronization. Here are some scenarios where **freezing** and **thawing** are particularly useful:

- **Race Conditions**: If two or more threads are involved in a race condition, **freezing** one thread while allowing the others to continue can confirm the issue. This allows you to observe how the other threads behave in a controlled sequence, helping you identify and address the problem.

- **Deadlocks**: In a deadlock scenario, **freezing** a thread that is waiting for a lock enables you to focus on another thread that holds the lock. This helps you examine where the circular dependency or waiting chain is occurring.
- **Inspecting Critical Code Points**: **Freezing** a thread at a specific point in the code allows you to inspect important variables, check the call stack for inconsistencies, and analyze its state more thoroughly.
- **Performance Bottlenecks**: If you suspect a thread is causing unnecessary context switching or performance issues, **freezing** that thread and observing the other threads helps verify this and provides insights into how to optimize the thread's execution.
- **Complex Multithreaded Applications**: In large applications with multiple threads, it can be difficult to keep track of everything simultaneously. **Freezing** certain threads allows you to isolate and focus on specific operations, making the debugging process more manageable.
- **Intermittent Bugs**: Timing issues between threads often cause intermittent bugs. **Freezing** threads can help you control the timing of thread interactions and isolate the specific conditions under which the bug occurs.
- **Thread Priorities and Scheduling**: **Freezing** threads can also be used to investigate how different thread priorities are affecting thread execution and performance.

In addition to the **Threads Window**, **freezing** and **thawing** threads can also be done in the **Parallel Watch Window** via the context menu, offering another way to manage thread execution.

Switching Threads

You can switch between threads by double-clicking on a thread in the **`Threads` Window**. This action updates the Source Code, Call Stack, Autos, Locals, and Watch windows accordingly, allowing you to view and debug the selected thread's execution context within the source code. Switching threads in this way helps you visualize the thread's activity and better understand its role in the overall execution flow. Switching threads in this way is also available in the **`Parallel Watch` Window**.

Using the Tasks Window

Because tasks are a higher-level abstraction that uses threads to manage concurrency, they require a different debugger view. The **`Tasks` Window**, accessed via **`Debug`** > **`Windows`** > **`Tasks`** from the main menu, allows developers to view and manage tasks in the application.

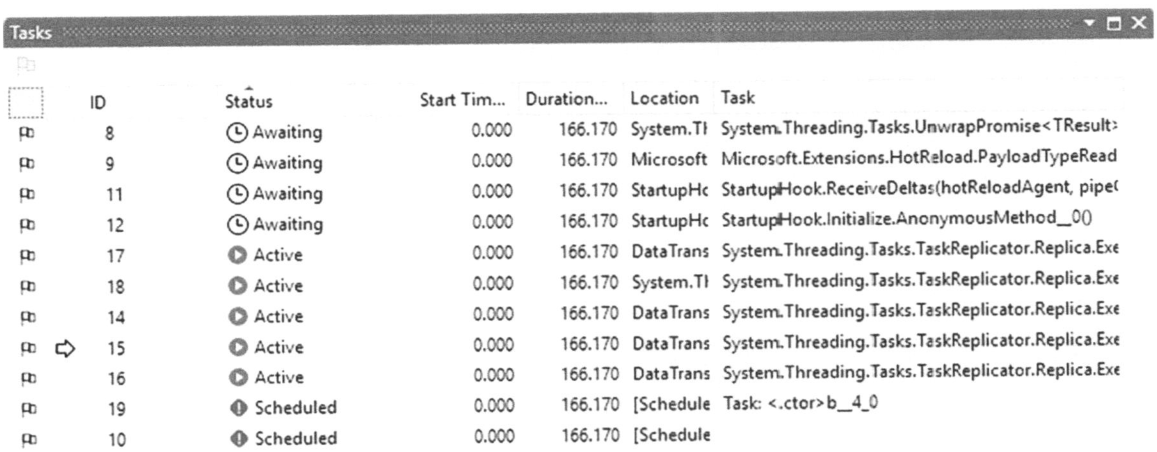

Figure 12.13: *Tasks Window*

The top toolbar in the **Tasks Window** contains a button to toggle showing only flagged tasks.

The default columns are as follows:

- **Flagged Task**: Indicates flagged tasks and allows users to flag or unflag a task.
- **Current Task**: Displays a yellow arrow next to the currently executing task.
- **ID**: The system-generated, unique task ID (within a process).
- **Status**: The execution state of the task.
- **Start Time**: The time in seconds since the application started when the task became active.
- **Duration**: The total time in seconds the task has been active.
- **Location**; The current active stack frame in which the task is executing.
- **Task:** Displays the method that initiated the task, including its name and parameters.

Additional optional columns for managed code include:

- **Completion Time:** The time when the task completed execution.
- **Parent**: The ID of the task that created this task (blank if there is no parent).
- **Thread ID**: The ID and name of the thread currently executing the task.
- **AppDomain**: The application domain in which the task is running.
- **Process**: The process ID in which the task is running.

Task States and Debugging

The Status column helps track a task's execution state. The possible states are:

Task State	Description
`Scheduled`	The task is scheduled but has not yet run. Tasks in this state do not have assigned threads, call stacks, or related information.
`Active`	The task is currently executing before hitting a breakpoint.
`Blocked`	The task is waiting for an event to be signaled or a lock to be released.
`Awaiting`	The task is asynchronously waiting on an operation (such as an await call).

Table 12.3: *Task States*

Note: *The* **Tasks** *Window supports additional states applicable only to native code, which are not covered in this book.*

Hovering over a task in the **Awaiting** state displays a tooltip with additional information about the awaited operation, as shown in *Figure 12.14*.

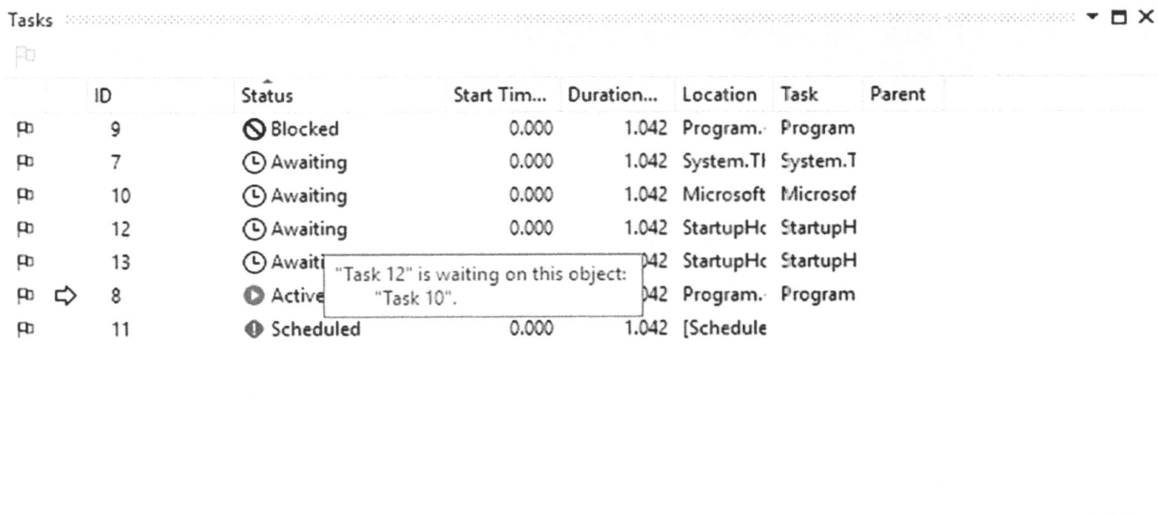

***Figure 12.14:** Additional Await Info Tooltip*

Sorting and Grouping Tasks

Tasks can be sorted by clicking any column header and toggling between ascending and descending order. Sorting persists across debugging sessions.

Tasks can also be grouped by any column, including hidden ones. To group tasks:

1. Right-click a column header.
2. Select **`Group By`** and choose the desired column.

When tasks are grouped, two new buttons appear in the toolbar:

- **`Expand All`**: Expands all grouped categories.
- **`Collapse All`**: Collapses all grouped categories.

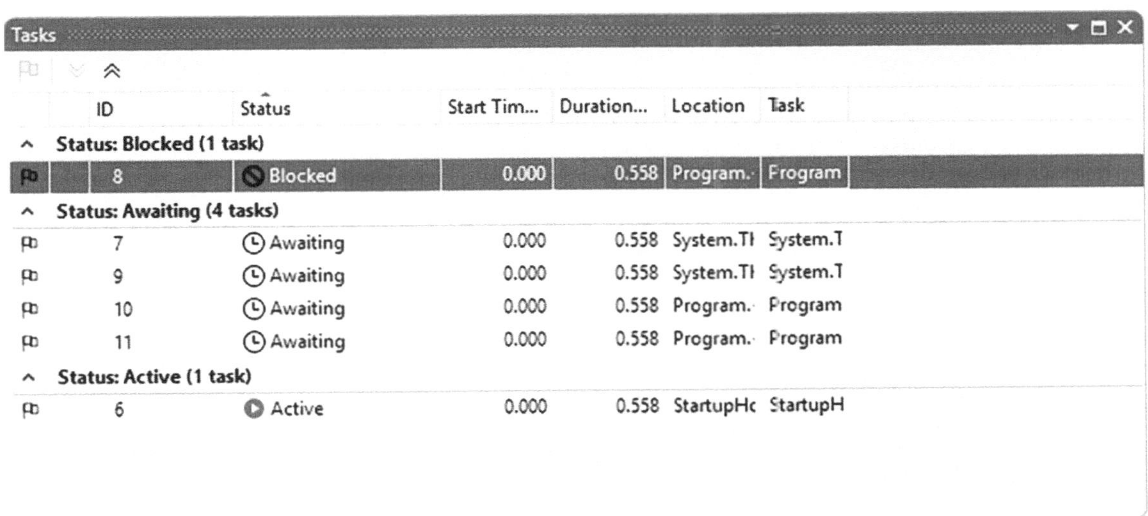

***Figure 12.15:** Grouped Tasks*

Flagging, Freezing, and Thawing Tasks

Tasks can be flagged by clicking the flag icon in the first column. This marks the underlying thread executing the task. Flagged tasks can be filtered by clicking the **`Show Only Flagged`** button in the toolbar.

Note: *Tasks without an assigned thread, such as Awaiting or Scheduled tasks, cannot be flagged.*

The context menu provides options to **freeze** and **thaw** tasks:

- **Freezing** a task suspends the execution of its associated thread.
- **Thawing** a task resumes the execution of a previously frozen thread.

Tasks in the **`Awaiting`** or **`Scheduled`** states cannot be **frozen** or **thawed**, as they do not have an active thread.

Debugging Affinity and Scheduling

We covered task scheduling in detail in *Chapter 9, Advanced Task Management*. As a review, tasks are scheduled to run on a Thread Pool thread by the .NET Task Scheduler, which uses a work-stealing queue to balance the load across multiple CPU cores. In some cases, the scheduler may execute a task inline (on the same thread that started it) if it determines this is the most efficient approach.

For many applications, this behavior does not cause issues. However, in UI applications, thread affinity is critical because UI controls can only be accessed by the main thread. If a task switches between threads unexpectedly, it may lead to race conditions, crashes, or UI **freezes**. The Thread ID column in the Tasks Window helps track a task's movement between threads, making it useful for diagnosing synchronization issues. For applications that require strict thread affinity, this column is essential for ensuring that the synchronization context is properly captured and restored.

Tasks may wait indefinitely if too many long-running tasks occupy the Thread Pool, leading to thread starvation. This often manifests as tasks stuck in the Scheduled or Blocked states for extended periods. Additionally, deadlocks can occur if a task is waiting for a UI or thread-bound operation that never completes–for example, when a UI thread is blocked waiting for a task that, in turn, needs the UI thread to proceed. Using the **`Parallel Stacks` Window** alongside the **`Tasks` Window** allows developers to visualize task dependencies, execution paths, and thread usage to identify and resolve such issues.

The default Task Scheduler does not guarantee execution order, which can be problematic for real-time applications, games, and simulations that rely on precise timing. When debugging timing-sensitive applications, developers should use breakpoints, logging, and the **`Tasks` Window** to monitor execution orders and detect unexpected delays. Additionally, the **`Parallel Stacks` Window** provides a higher-level view of task interactions, helping to identify scheduling bottlenecks and optimize concurrency.

Using Breakpoints

Breakpoints are a fundamental tool for debugging, allowing developers to pause execution and inspect variables, call stacks, and other runtime information. In single-threaded applications, a standard breakpoint that pauses execution whenever it is hit is often sufficient. However, debugging multithreaded and parallel applications requires more advanced breakpoint options due to increased complexity.

Visual Studio provides several specialized breakpoints to give developers fine control over when and how execution is paused.

Setting and Using Breakpoints

Visual Studio supports multiple breakpoint types, each suited for specific debugging scenarios.

Conditional Breakpoints

A **conditional breakpoint** pauses execution only when a specified condition is met. These are useful for stopping execution when a variable reaches a specific value or when a specific thread hits a breakpoint.

For example, to pause execution only when the thread ID is 5, a condition can be set to `Thread.CurrentThread.ManagedThreadId == 5`.

How to Set:

1. Right-click on an existing breakpoint.
2. Select **`Conditions`** from the context menu.
3. Enter an expression that must evaluate to true for the breakpoint to trigger.

Data Breakpoints

A data breakpoint pauses execution whenever the value of a specific variable changes, regardless of which thread modifies it.

This is useful when debugging unexpected modifications to shared variables. **Data breakpoints** are available in .NET Core 3 and later, with full support for managed objects introduced in .NET 6.

How to Set:

1. Locate the variable in the **`Autos`**, **`Locals`**, or **`Watch`** window.
2. Right-click and select **`Break when value changes`**.

Dependent Breakpoints

A dependent breakpoint pauses execution only after another breakpoint has been hit first. This is useful when debugging sequential issues in parallel applications.

For example, if a breakpoint is set inside a parallel loop, execution can be paused only after another breakpoint in the initialization phase has been triggered.

How to Set:

1. Open **`Breakpoint Settings`** (right-click a breakpoint).
2. Select **`Only enable when the following breakpoint is hit`** and choose the dependent breakpoint.

Hit Count Breakpoints

A **hit count breakpoint** allows execution to continue until a breakpoint has been hit a specified number of times. This is useful for debugging loops, where pausing on every iteration would be impractical.

For example, to pause execution only on the 10th iteration of a loop, a hit count of 10 can be set.

How to Set:

1. Open **`Breakpoint Settings`** (right-click a breakpoint).
2. Select **`Hit Count`** and enter the desired value.

Function Breakpoints

A **function breakpoint** allows execution to pause when a specific function is called, even if its location in the code is unknown. This is particularly useful when debugging large projects with multiple function calls.

To narrow the breakpoint to a specific overload, parameter types can be specified. For example, **`ProcessData(int, string)`** ensures that only the correct method signature is targeted.

How to Set:

1. Go to **`Debug`** > **`New Breakpoint`** > **`Function Breakpoint`**.
2. Enter the function name.
3. (Optional) Specify parameter types.

Thread-Specific Breakpoints

Thread-specific breakpoints allow execution to pause only when a designated thread reaches a breakpoint, preventing unnecessary stops on other threads.

For example, if multiple threads execute the same method, execution can be paused only when Thread 7 reaches a certain line of code.

How to Set:

1. Open **`Breakpoint Settings`** (right-click a breakpoint).
2. Select *Filter* and enter **`ThreadId == 7`**.

Tracepoints

In highly parallel applications, stopping execution may not be ideal. A **tracepoint** logs a custom message to the Output window instead of pausing execution. This is useful for tracking function calls or variable values without disrupting the program's flow.

For example, a **tracepoint** can log each time a function is called, providing insight into execution order without interrupting execution.

How to Set:

1. Right-click on a breakpoint.
2. Select **`Actions`** and enter a message to log.
3. Uncheck **`Pause execution`** to ensure execution continues.

Using the right type of breakpoint minimizes debugging disruption and helps track down race conditions, unexpected data modifications, and execution order issues in complex parallel applications. Visual Studio's advanced breakpoint options provide the flexibility needed to debug efficiently without excessive manual stepping.

Using the Concurrency Visualizer

The Visual Studio Performance Profiler is a suite of tools designed to help developers optimize software performance and diagnose performance issues. One of these tools is the **`Concurrency Visualizer`**, which provides insights into how an application utilizes CPU cores and threads. It helps identify inefficiencies in parallelism and concurrency, such as thread contention, excessive context switching, and underutilized CPU cores.

The **`Concurrency Visualizer`** is available as a free extension to Visual Studio. Installing it adds a **`Concurrency Visualizer`** option under the *Analyze* menu. Use this menu to start **`Concurrency Visualizer`**.

Unlike traditional debugging tools, **`Concurrency Visualizer`** analyzes an application as it runs outside the debugger to avoid interference with normal execution. For the most accurate performance insights, it is recommended to profile a release build instead of a debug build, as the latter may introduce additional overhead and distort performance data.

Using `Concurrency Visualizer`

To begin profiling with **`Concurrency Visualizer`**, open the Performance Profiler and select one of the following options:

- **Start with Current Process**: Profiles the application that is started by the debugger.
- **Launch a New Process**: Opens a dialog to select an executable file to run and profile.
- **Attach to Process**: Allows profiling of an already running process.

Once profiling starts, the **`Concurrency Visualizer`** will begin collecting data while the application runs. To obtain meaningful results, the application should execute realistic workloads, particularly those involving multithreading, parallel loops, or asynchronous operations.

After profiling is complete, closing the application or stopping the profiler will begin the analysis phase, during which Visual Studio processes the collected data. Depending on the complexity of the application and the amount of data collected, analysis may take a significant amount of time. Once complete, the **`Concurrency Visualizer`** will display various views to help identify bottlenecks and optimization opportunities.

Analyzing Execution Timelines

After Visual Studio completes its analysis, the **`Concurrency Visualizer`** report window appears. The report provides multiple views that help developers examine CPU utilization, thread activity, and core distribution over time.

Utilization View

The default view in **`Concurrency Visualizer`** is the **`Utilization`** View (refer to *Figure* 12.16).

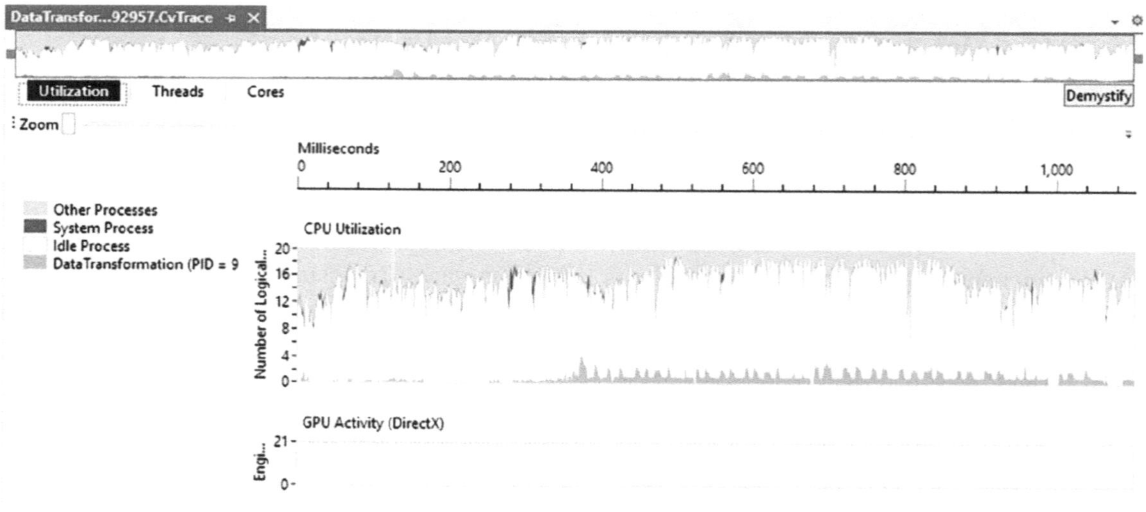

Figure 12.16: *Concurrency Visualizer*

This graph displays CPU usage over time, placing the application's execution in the context of overall system activity.

- The X-axis represents execution time (for example, milliseconds).
- The Y-axis represents the number of logical CPU cores used.
- The green area in the graph shows how many CPU cores the application utilized at any given moment.

This view helps identify CPU-bound performance patterns, such as spikes in core utilization. For example, *Figure 12.16* shows a sudden increase in CPU usage before the 400-millisecond mark, followed by periodic spikes, suggesting the application has bursty CPU usage patterns.

The zoom function allows developers to focus on specific time periods with high CPU activity or analyze system-wide CPU consumption during key execution phases.

Threads View

The **Threads** View (refer to *Figure 12.17*) provides the most detailed breakdown of thread activity as the application executes.

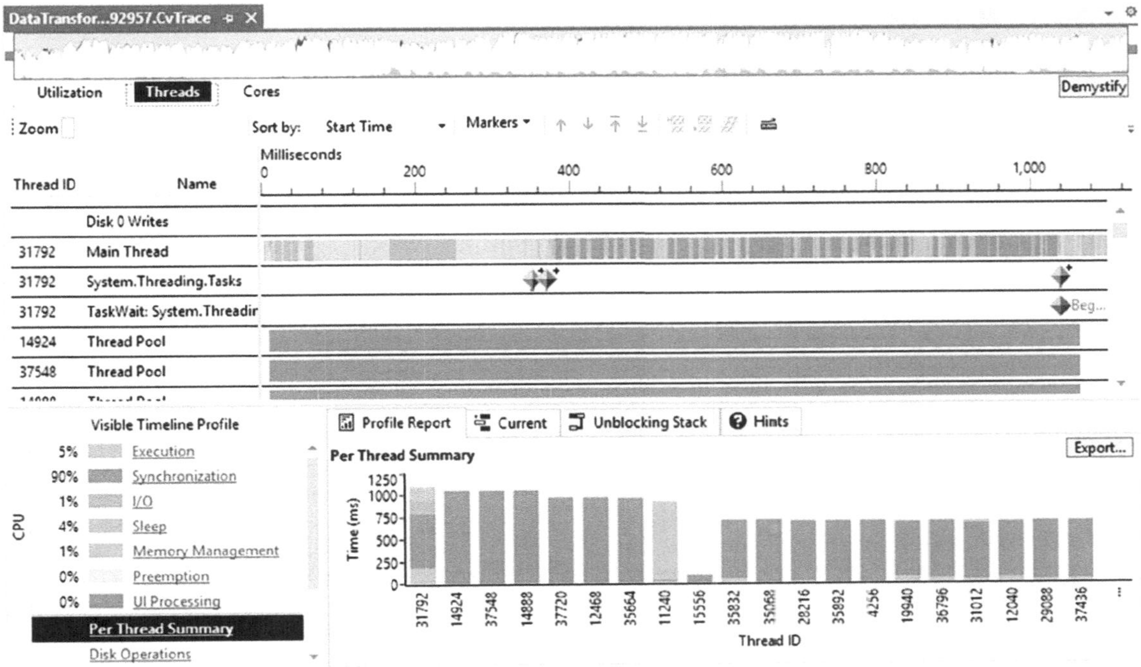

Figure 12.17: *Threads View*

Some key features of the **`Threads`** View are as follows:

- Application Timeline (Upper Panel)
  - Displays all threads, including physical disk activity and GPU engine activity.
  - Threads are sorted by creation order but can be rearranged using the *Sort by* dropdown.
  - Each thread's timeline is color-coded based on its execution state (visible in the Timeline Profile key).
- Thread State Analysis
  - Hovering over a section of a thread displays a tooltip with details, such as:
    - **`Category`** (**`Running`**, **`Waiting`**, **`Blocked`**, and so on).
    - **`Start Time`** (relative to application start).
    - **`Delay Duration`** (how long it was in a particular state).
  - Clicking on a segment opens the **`Call Stack`** (*Current tab*), revealing what code was executing at that moment.
  - If a thread is blocked, the viewer shows:
    - The blocking API (for example, a lock, synchronization primitive, or I/O operation).
- Detecting Thread Dependencies
  - The Threads View highlights dependencies between threads, making it easier to diagnose lock contention and inter-thread signaling.
  - Clicking a blocked thread segment draws a visual connection between the blocking and unblocking threads.
  - The Unblocking Stack tab displays the call stack of the unblocking thread, helping developers pinpoint bottlenecks caused by locks or resource contention.

Cores View

The **Cores** View (refer to *Figure 12.18*) provides insights into how threads are distributed across CPU cores and how context switching impacts performance.

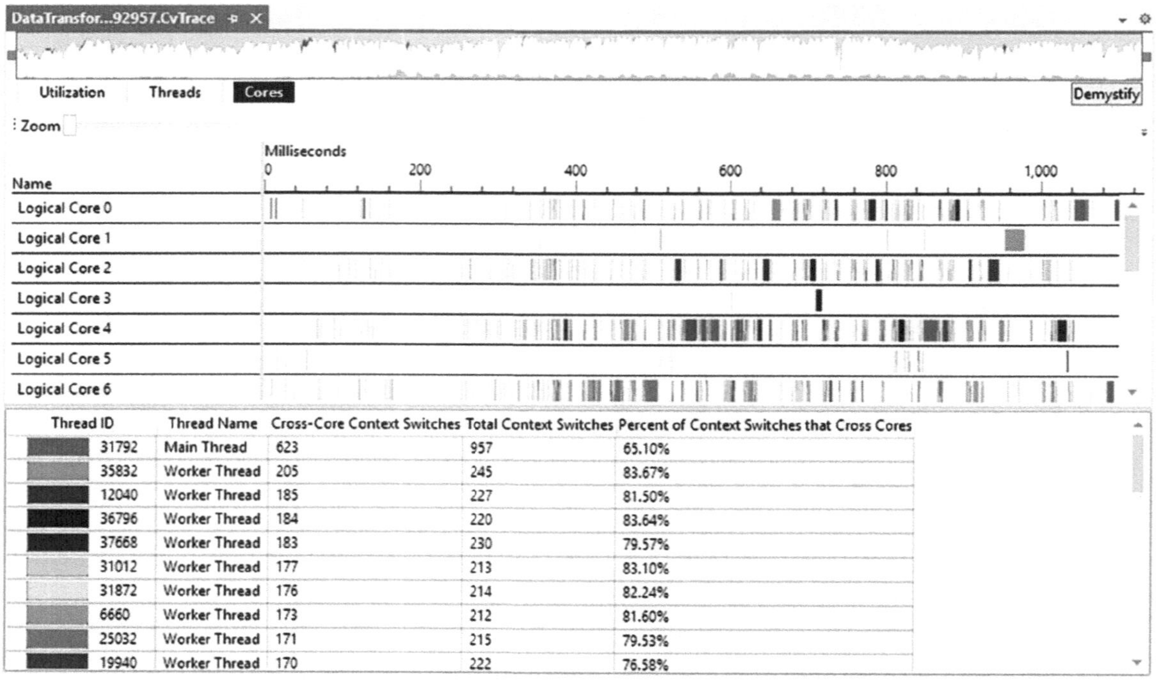

Figure 12.18: *Cores View*

The key features of the **Cores** View are as follows:

- Thread Execution on Logical Cores
  - The upper panel shows all logical cores in the system and how threads are scheduled across them over time.
  - Threads are color-coded, and their execution can be traced across cores.
  - This helps identify imbalances where some cores are overloaded while others remain underutilized.
- Context Switching Analysis
  - The bottom panel provides data on thread context switches.
  - Frequent context switching (excessive yellow segments) may indicate thread scheduling inefficiencies or CPU contention.
  - Hovering over any point in the timeline displays a tooltip with details about the executing thread at that moment.

The **Concurrency Visualizer** is a powerful tool for diagnosing and optimizing parallel and concurrent applications. By analyzing execution timelines, developers can:

- Identify CPU bottlenecks and underutilization issues.
- Detect thread contention and lock delays.
- Optimize thread distribution across CPU cores.
- Reduce context switching overhead for better efficiency.

By leveraging these insights, developers can significantly improve application scalability, responsiveness, and performance.

Identifying Bottlenecks

A bottleneck occurs when a specific resource or operation limits overall application performance. In multithreaded applications, bottlenecks often arise due to excessive CPU usage, inefficient thread management, poor workload distribution, or delays from I/O operations. Identifying and resolving these bottlenecks is critical for ensuring application scalability, responsiveness, and efficient resource utilization.

`Concurrency Visualizer` is a powerful tool for detecting performance bottlenecks by providing detailed insights into CPU usage, thread execution, and system activity. The following sections describe common bottlenecks and how to detect them using **Concurrency Visualizer**.

Excessive CPU Utilization

High CPU usage without a corresponding performance improvement may indicate inefficient parallelization or excessive thread contention. If some CPU cores show sustained high usage while others remain idle, the application may not be distributing workloads effectively.

To detect this issue, examine the Utilization View to identify prolonged CPU saturation, especially on a single logical core. The Threads View may reveal a single thread running continuously with frequent preemptions, indicating an uneven workload distribution.

Possible solutions include improving parallel execution using `Parallel.For()`, `Parallel.ForEach()`, or PLINQ, optimizing algorithms to reduce redundant computations and using asynchronous execution to prevent blocking the main thread with CPU-bound work.

Thread Starvation and Imbalance

When some threads remain idle for extended periods while others are heavily loaded, the application may be experiencing thread starvation. This is often caused by insufficient worker threads, excessive blocking, or inefficient scheduling.

Thread starvation can be detected in the `Threads` View, where some threads remain in a waiting state while others execute continuously. Long gaps of inactivity may indicate a shortage of available worker threads, preventing tasks from progressing.

To address this issue, ensure that blocking operations do not tie up worker threads by using asynchronous programming techniques. If necessary, adjust the thread pool settings to increase the number of available worker threads, but only after identifying the root cause of the imbalance.

Excessive Context Switching

Frequent thread switching increases CPU overhead and reduces efficiency. If a thread repeatedly switches between cores without making significant progress, performance may suffer due to excessive context switching.

In the `Cores` View, frequent migrations of threads across cores and a high number of context switches indicate inefficiencies in CPU scheduling. If the number of active threads exceeds the number of logical cores, context switching may be limiting performance.

Reducing the total number of active threads, batching small tasks, and ensuring that threads complete meaningful work before switching can help mitigate this issue. In some cases, binding high-priority threads to specific cores can reduce migration overhead.

Synchronization and I/O Delays

Performance bottlenecks can also arise from slow I/O operations, including disk reads, network requests, and database queries. These delays cause threads to remain idle while waiting for external resources, reducing CPU utilization.

In the Utilization View, periods of low CPU usage despite an active workload may indicate I/O bottlenecks. The Threads View can reveal long waiting periods for threads blocked on I/O operations, such as file access or network communication.

Mitigating these delays may involve using asynchronous I/O with async/await to free up worker threads while waiting for operations to complete. Other solutions include caching frequently accessed data to minimize repeated expensive operations and batching or streaming large data sets to reduce wait times.

Visualizing Lock Contention

When multiple threads compete for the same shared resources, they may spend significant time waiting to acquire a lock, a phenomenon known as lock contention. Lock contention can degrade performance by increasing thread wait times, reducing CPU utilization, and causing excessive context switching. The **`Concurrency Visualizer`** in Visual Studio provides tools to analyze and mitigate these issues by revealing thread states, synchronization events, and blocking dependencies.

Identifying Symptoms of Lock Contention

Common symptoms of lock contention include:

- Threads repeatedly spending long durations in a waiting state while attempting to acquire a lock.
- A high number of threads blocked on the same resource, leading to reduced parallel efficiency.
- Frequent context switching, where threads rapidly transition between running and waiting states, increasing overhead.

The **`Threads`** view and **`Cores`** view in the **`Concurrency Visualizer`** are particularly useful for diagnosing these issues.

Analyzing Lock Contention in the Threads View:

- Blocked threads appear in a distinct category and color, indicating they are waiting for a resource.
- Hovering over a blocked thread displays details such as blocking API, start time, and wait duration.
- Clicking on a blocked thread reveals:
  - The call stack of the blocked thread, showing where it was attempting to acquire the resource.
  - The call stack of the unblocking thread, identifying which thread held the resource.
  - A visual connection between the blocked and unblocking threads, making it easier to track dependencies.

Using the `Cores` View to Detect Underutilization

The **`Cores`** view provides a high-level perspective of how threads are distributed across logical processors. It can highlight:

- Long idle periods where CPU cores are underutilized due to excessive thread blocking.

- Patterns of low core usage despite high thread activity, indicating synchronization bottlenecks rather than CPU-bound execution.
- Context switching spikes, suggesting inefficiencies caused by frequent lock acquisitions and releases.

Optimizing to Reduce Lock Contention

To mitigate lock contention and improve concurrency efficiency:

- **Use finer-grained locks**: Replace broad locks such as `Monitor.Enter()` with finer-grained locks such as `SemaphoreSlim` to allow more granular control.
- **Optimize read-heavy workloads**: When there are significantly more readers than writers, use `ReaderWriterLockSlim` to minimize contention.
- **Adopt lock-free alternatives**: Consider `Interlocked`, `ConcurrentDictionary`, or `ConcurrentQueue` to reduce dependency on explicit locking.
- **Minimize critical section size**: Ensure that locks are held for the shortest possible duration to reduce contention.
- **Use `TryEnter()` for contention-sensitive sections**: `Monitor.TryEnter()` allows threads to check for lock availability before blocking, improving responsiveness.

By leveraging the **Concurrency Visualizer**, developers can detect synchronization inefficiencies, analyze execution bottlenecks, and implement strategies to improve parallel execution and responsiveness in multithreaded applications.

Conclusion

Debugging parallel applications presents unique challenges, but with the right tools and techniques, identifying and resolving issues becomes much more manageable. Visual Studio provides powerful debugging features, such as **Parallel Stacks**, **Tasks**, and Threads, that help developers gain deep insights into their multithreaded code. By leveraging breakpoints, **tracepoints**, and performance profiling tools, you can diagnose deadlocks, race conditions, and inefficiencies more effectively. Mastering these debugging strategies ensures that your parallel applications run reliably and perform optimally under real-world conditions.

While debugging helps identify and fix issues in parallel applications, achieving high performance requires a proactive approach to optimizing your code. In the next chapter, we will explore practical performance challenges that arise in real-world applications and how to address them effectively. We will cover strategies for handling CPU-bound workloads, mitigating I/O bottlenecks, managing excessive memory usage in multithreaded environments, and optimizing data access and loops. By understanding these challenges and their solutions, you will be better equipped to build high-performance, scalable applications that fully leverage the power of parallelism.

Points to Remember

- Visual Studio provides specialized debugging tools such as **Parallel Stacks**, **Tasks**, and **Parallel Watch** windows to help visualize thread execution and dependencies.
- Use breakpoints, **tracepoints**, and logging to detect synchronization issues such as race conditions, deadlocks, and thread contention.
- The **Threads Window** in Visual Studio allows you to inspect the state of each thread, helping to diagnose unexpected behavior in multithreaded applications.

- Use the **`Concurrency Visualizer`** to identify inefficiencies in thread scheduling, excessive context switching, and resource contention.

Multiple Choice Questions

1. Which Visual Studio tool provides a graphical representation of threads and their relationships in a parallel application?
    a. Threads Window
    b. Parallel Stacks Window
    c. Call Stack Window
    d. Watch Window
2. Which debugging feature in Visual Studio allows you to track logical execution flow across multiple threads?
    a. Immediate Window
    b. Threads View
    c. Task View
    d. Solution Explorer
3. What is the primary cause of a deadlock in a multithreaded application?
    a. A thread consuming too much CPU time.
    b. Excessive memory usage in parallel loops.
    c. A task failing to complete due to an exception.
    d. Multiple threads waiting indefinitely for resources held by each other.
4. How can the **`Concurrency Visualizer`** in Visual Studio help improve application performance?
    a. It provides a detailed breakdown of thread execution and synchronization behavior.
    b. It automatically fixes race conditions.
    c. It stops deadlocks from occurring.
    d. It replaces the need for breakpoints and logging.

Answers

1. b
2. c
3. d
4. a

Questions

1. The **`Concurrency Visualizer`** in Visual Studio provides insights into thread execution, context switching, and synchronization issues. How can developers use this tool to make informed decisions about optimizing performance, rather than just fixing bugs?
2. The **`Tasks`** and **`Parallel Stacks`** windows in Visual Studio provide different views of multi-threaded execution. In what scenarios would one be more useful than the other? How can developers use them together to gain deeper insights into their applications?
3. The **`Parallel Watch` Window** allows monitoring variable values across multiple threads. How can this feature help identify data inconsistencies and race conditions? What challenges might arise when interpreting the values in a highly dynamic multithreaded environment?
4. The **`Tasks` Window** is designed to track asynchronous operations, such as those using **`Task.Run()`** or **`async/await`**. How does debugging using the **`Tasks` Window** differ from debugging traditional multi-threaded code, and what are the limitations of this approach?

Key Terms

- **Parallel Stacks Window**: Displays call stacks for all threads in a parallel application, helping developers visualize and analyze thread interactions.
- **Parallel Watch Window**: Allows inspection of variables across multiple threads simultaneously, making it easier to detect inconsistencies in parallel execution.
- **Tasks Window**: Shows active and scheduled tasks in a Task-based parallel application, aiding in understanding task execution and dependencies.
- **Concurrency Visualizer**: A profiling tool that provides insights into thread execution, CPU utilization, and synchronization overhead, helping diagnose performance bottlenecks.
- **Data Breakpoints**: A feature that pauses execution when a specific variable's value changes, useful for tracking unexpected modifications in shared memory.
- **Conditional Breakpoints**: Trigger only when a specified condition evaluates to true, helping to isolate issues that occur under specific circumstances.
- **Function Breakpoints**: Pause execution when a specific function is entered, allowing for debugging of function calls across multiple threads.
- **Hit Count Breakpoints**: Trigger when a breakpoint has been hit a specified number of times, useful for debugging loops and iterative parallel operations.
- **Tracepoints**: A type of breakpoint that logs messages to the output window instead of pausing execution, aiding in non-intrusive debugging of parallel applications.
- **Threads Window**: Displays all active threads, their current state, and stack information, aiding in identifying blocked or stalled threads.
- **Freezing**: Manually suspending the execution of a specific thread during debugging, allowing developers to analyze its state without interference from other running threads.
- **Thawing**: Manually resuming the execution of a previously **frozen** thread, allowing it to continue running as part of the program's normal execution flow.

CHAPTER 13
Practical Performance Challenges and Solutions

Introduction

Parallel and concurrent applications promise greater throughput and responsiveness, but they also introduce increased complexity. When dealing with **CPU-bound** computations, **I/O-bound** operations, or **memory-intensive workloads**, poor design choices can lead to thread starvation, excessive memory consumption, and underutilized hardware resources. In this chapter, we will explore common performance pitfalls in multithreaded .NET applications and walk through practical, actionable solutions. Through focused examples and case studies, we will learn how to identify bottlenecks, optimize data access patterns, manage memory efficiently, and apply best practices for parallel loops and asynchronous operations. By the end of this chapter, you will have the tools to transform problematic concurrent code into efficient, scalable solutions.

Structure

This chapter will cover the following topics.

- Defining Performance Challenges
  - Differences Between **Workloads**
  - Key Optimization Considerations
- Optimizing **CPU-Bound** Applications
  - Recognizing Symptoms
  - Profiling Techniques
  - Optimizations
- Dealing with **I/O-Bound** Issues
  - Common Bottlenecks
  - Profiling Options
  - Optimizations
- Managing Excessive Memory Usage
  - Causes of Memory Issues
  - Diagnostic Tools
  - Optimizations
- Optimizing Data Access and Loops
  - Inefficient Data Patterns
  - Optimizations

- Case Study
    - Example Application
    - Profiling the Application
    - Applying Solutions

Defining Performance Challenges

Performance challenges in parallel and concurrent applications can be broadly categorized into **CPU-bound workloads**, **I/O-bound** operations, and **memory-related issues** such as memory pressure and contention. Each category presents distinct symptoms and requires targeted optimization strategies. **CPU-bound workloads** typically suffer from high processor utilization and thread contention. **I/O-bound** operations, such as disk or network access, often experience latency and throughput limitations. **Memory issues** can arise from high allocation rates, excessive garbage collection, or contention over shared memory resources. Recognizing these categories and understanding their specific characteristics is essential for writing and optimizing efficient multithreaded and parallel code.

Differences between Workloads

Workloads that are limited primarily by the speed of computations are referred to as **CPU-bound workloads**. These include applications that perform heavy data processing, complex mathematical calculations, cryptographic operations, and video encoding or processing. **CPU-bound workloads** typically exhibit high CPU utilization with minimal I/O wait times.

In contrast, **workloads** where performance is constrained by input/output operations rather than computations are called **I/O-bound workloads**. Examples include reading from or writing to disk, network communications, database queries, and file transfers. These **workloads** often display low or idle CPU usage while threads wait for I/O operations to complete.

Some **workloads** place significant demands on memory resources, leading to performance degradation due to excessive memory pressure. These **memory-intensive workloads** often involve complex object graphs, in-memory caching systems, or processing large datasets held in memory. Symptoms of **memory-bound workloads** include high memory usage, frequent garbage collection cycles, increased paging or swapping, and in extreme cases, out-of-memory exceptions. Additionally, they may suffer from limited memory bandwidth, where processors are starved for fast memory access.

The key differences between these workloads are summarized in the following table:

Aspect	CPU-Bound	I/O-Bound	Memory-Bound
Resource Utilization	High CPU core utilization	High disk or network utilization	High RAM usage, potential memory bandwidth saturation
Scalability	Scales with more CPU cores	Scales with faster I/O or asynchronous models	Benefits from efficient memory usage and faster memory access
Thread Behavior	Threads are computation-heavy	Threads wait for I/O completion	Threads may pause during garbage collection or paging
Indicators	High CPU usage	Disk or network latency	Paging, high memory usage, frequent garbage collection

Table 13.1: *Workload Key Differences*

It is important to understand that **workloads** can shift dynamically during an application's lifetime. For example, an application performing data ingestion may initially be **I/O-bound**, but as data is processed, it could become **CPU-bound** or **memory-bound**. Effective optimization often requires addressing multiple types of workloads at different stages of application execution.

Key Optimization Considerations

Before diving into specific techniques for optimizing .NET applications, it is essential to step back and understand the broader principles that guide performance tuning. Effective optimization is rarely about a single change or isolated improvement. Instead, it requires a holistic view of your application's behavior, environment, and **workload** patterns. Without this context, it is easy to fall into the trap of premature optimization or waste effort on changes that deliver little actual benefit.

The following are key considerations to keep in mind as you approach performance tuning. These principles will help you prioritize your efforts, make informed decisions, and avoid common pitfalls.

- **Understand Your Workload:** Begin by accurately identifying whether your application is **CPU-bound**, **I/O-bound**, **memory-bound**, or a mixture. Understanding the nature of the **workload** ensures that optimization efforts target the actual bottlenecks.
- **Measure Before and After:** Performance improvements must be data-driven. Use reliable measurement tools to establish a baseline and confirm that your changes have the intended impact. Avoid relying on intuition alone.
- **Focus on Bottlenecks:** Not every part of your codebase needs to be highly optimized. Focus on the components that most significantly affect overall performance, as identified through profiling and monitoring.
- **Balance Trade-offs:** Optimization often involves trade-offs between performance, maintainability, scalability, and resource consumption. Be mindful of these trade-offs to avoid sacrificing long-term stability for short-term gains.
- **Design for Scalability:** Aim for solutions that not only improve performance now but also scale as your application grows in usage and complexity. Scalability considerations are crucial for long-term success.
- **Avoid Premature Optimization:** Resist the urge to optimize code before it is necessary. Early optimization can introduce complexity without clear benefit and may even obstruct future improvements.
- **Iterate and Validate:** Optimization is an ongoing, iterative process. Regularly validate your assumptions, revisit past optimizations, and remain responsive to changes in usage patterns and system behavior.

As we progress through this chapter, we will explore how these considerations apply in practical scenarios. By keeping these principles in mind, you will be well-equipped to make informed decisions and systematically improve your application's performance, rather than relying on guesswork or ad hoc fixes.

Optimizing CPU-Bound Applications

CPU-bound applications are limited by the speed of computation, not external factors like disk or network I/O. Tasks such as complex calculations and processing large data sets can quickly overwhelm CPU cores, causing thread contention and degraded performance. Recognizing **CPU-bound** workloads early is essential for applying effective optimization strategies. In this section, we will look at how to identify CPU bottlenecks, measure processor utilization, and apply parallelism to distribute work efficiently.

Recognizing Symptoms

Slow performance in a **CPU-bound** application is often accompanied by clear technical indicators. You may observe high and sustained CPU utilization, slow or inconsistent responsiveness as load increases, and typically low I/O activity. Applications might perform adequately at lower loads, masking underlying inefficiencies until throughput demands grow – at which point CPU saturation reveals itself through sharply declining responsiveness and throughput.

CPU utilization often remains consistently high, approaching or exceeding 90–100% on one or more cores, even when an even distribution of work across multiple cores is expected. In severe cases, prolonged heavy CPU usage can cause thermal throttling, where the system reduces CPU frequency to manage heat, further degrading performance.

Profiling tools frequently reveal these issues through signs such as thread contention, increased context switching, and significant time spent in specific computational hotspots. These hotspots commonly include tight loops, serialization or deserialization processes, complex algorithms, or inefficient data transformations. At the same time, I/O activity, including disk and network usage, typically remains normal or even low during periods of degraded performance – confirming that the bottleneck is within the CPU rather than in external resource access.

When the thread pool is involved, you may notice exhaustion of available threads, with tasks queuing for extended periods before execution. This queuing generally results from the CPU being overwhelmed rather than from blocking I/O, which further emphasizes that CPU constraints are the primary cause.

To aid in detection, the following checklist can help confirm **CPU-bound** behavior:

1. Measure sustained high CPU usage, often near 100%, especially on specific cores.
2. Observe performance degradation as workload increases, indicating poor scalability.
3. Profile the application to locate methods consuming excessive CPU time, such as intensive loops or computational routines.
4. Monitor the thread pool for signs of exhaustion and queued work items waiting for CPU availability.
5. Check for elevated context switching, which can point to thread contention or oversubscription of CPU cores.
6. Verify that disk, network, and other I/O metrics remain low while CPU usage stays high.
7. Investigate system logs or hardware monitoring tools for signs of thermal throttling under load.

Despite clear indicators, developers sometimes make common mistakes when diagnosing **CPU-bound workloads**. One frequent error is confusing CPU saturation with memory pressure. While both can impact performance, **CPU-bound** applications show high CPU metrics without corresponding spikes in memory usage. Another mistake is assuming asynchronous programming models will resolve CPU bottlenecks – asynchronous code improves scalability for **I/O-bound** tasks but does not reduce CPU **workload**. Over-reliance on visual CPU graphs without deeper profiling can also lead to misdiagnosis, as these graphs often lack the granularity needed to identify specific problem areas. Additionally, it is important not to attribute slow performance solely to thread pool exhaustion; this is typically a symptom of CPU overload, not the root cause. Finally, neglecting to run scaling tests under realistic load conditions can allow CPU limitations to go unnoticed until the application is in production.

Understanding these symptoms is only the first step. To accurately pinpoint and quantify CPU bottlenecks, we need to go beyond observation and apply structured profiling techniques.

Profiling Techniques

Recognizing symptoms of CPU saturation is crucial, but to move from observation to resolution, we need precise, data-driven insights. Profiling tools provide visibility into how an application utilizes CPU resources, exposing the methods, threads, and code paths responsible for excessive consumption. In this section, we will explore effective profiling strategies to uncover CPU hotspots, analyze thread behavior, and distinguish between genuine computational workload and inefficiencies, such as unnecessary context switching or thread contention. By learning to interpret profiling data accurately, you will be equipped to target optimizations where they will have the greatest impact.

Visual Studio provides one of the most powerful and accessible profiling tools available for .NET applications: **Visual Studio Profiler**. It allows you to analyze how your application uses CPU resources, providing insights into which functions and threads consume the most resources.

Key Benefits of Visual Studio Profiler for CPU-Bound Issues

- **Real-Time Profiling: Visual Studio Profiler** allows you to analyze performance in real-time while the application runs, giving immediate feedback on CPU usage and dynamically identifying performance issues as users interact with the application.
- **Sampling versus Instrumentation:** Sampling captures CPU usage data periodically with minimal overhead, making it ideal for long-running applications. Instrumentation, on the other hand, offers deeper insights into method calls but may impact performance. Instrumentation involves using an SDK and making changes to your application to capture deep profiling data. A full discussion of instrumentation is beyond the scope of this book.
- **Call Tree and Flame Graphs:** These visual tools help visualize function usage and call stacks, enabling you to identify where the application spends the most time and uncover performance bottlenecks.
- **Thread Profiling:** By tracking thread execution, **Visual Studio Profiler** pinpoints synchronization problems such as thread contention or starvation.

These tools, combined with the `Concurrency Visualizer` and debugging windows introduced in *Chapter 12, Debugging Parallel Applications Using Visual Studio*, provide a powerful and comprehensive set of analysis tools to help diagnose and resolve **CPU-bound** issues.

Profiling for CPU Usage with Visual Studio Profiler

1. **Load the Application:** Start by opening your application in Visual Studio.
2. **Set to Release Mode:** Ensure that the application is in Release mode to get more accurate performance data.
3. **Launch Profiler:** Go to `Debug` > `Performance Profiler`. If this option is not available, make sure the profiler is installed. The following window will be displayed:

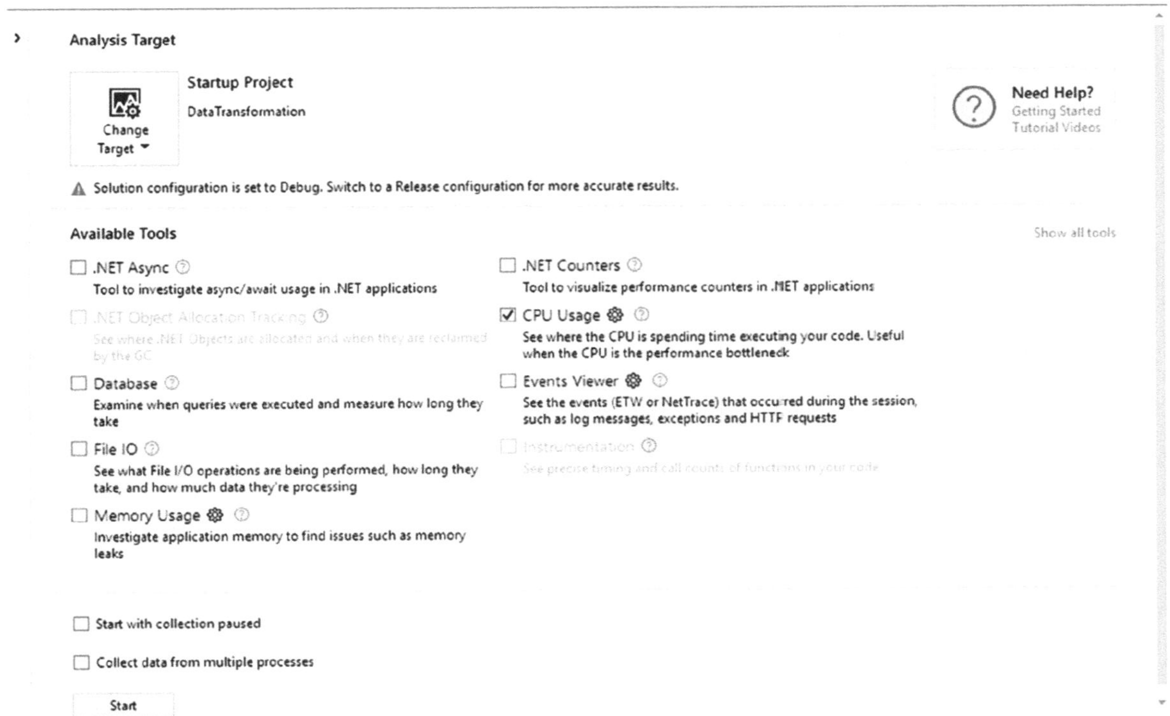

Figure 13.1: *Visual Studio Profiler*

1. **Select the Target Application:** Confirm the correct application is selected for profiling. The default target is typically the startup project, but you can change this by clicking the **`Change Target`** button.
2. **Select CPU Usage:** In the checklist, choose **`CPU Usage`** to begin profiling CPU consumption. You can also adjust the sampling rate and enable collection of call counts. Lower sampling rates are best for long-running processes to reduce data size without sacrificing key insights. Call counts can help isolate methods that are called very frequently, highlighting potential bottlenecks. These settings are accessed by clicking the *Settings* icon.
3. **Start Profiling:** Click *Start* to begin profiling. Optionally, enable **`Database/File I/O analysis`** to confirm the application is **CPU-bound** rather than **I/O-bound**.

As your application runs, be sure to simulate realistic workloads and user interactions to replicate performance issues. Once finished, either exit the application normally or click *Stop* on the profiler to analyze the results.

Interpreting the Results

Once profiling is complete, you will see a **`CPU Analysis Summary`** screen. This includes a timeline of the application's performance and a graph showing CPU percentage usage. Hovering over the graph will display key time points during the application lifecycle. Clicking and dragging the graph zooms in on a time range, offering a more granular view of CPU usage during high-load periods.

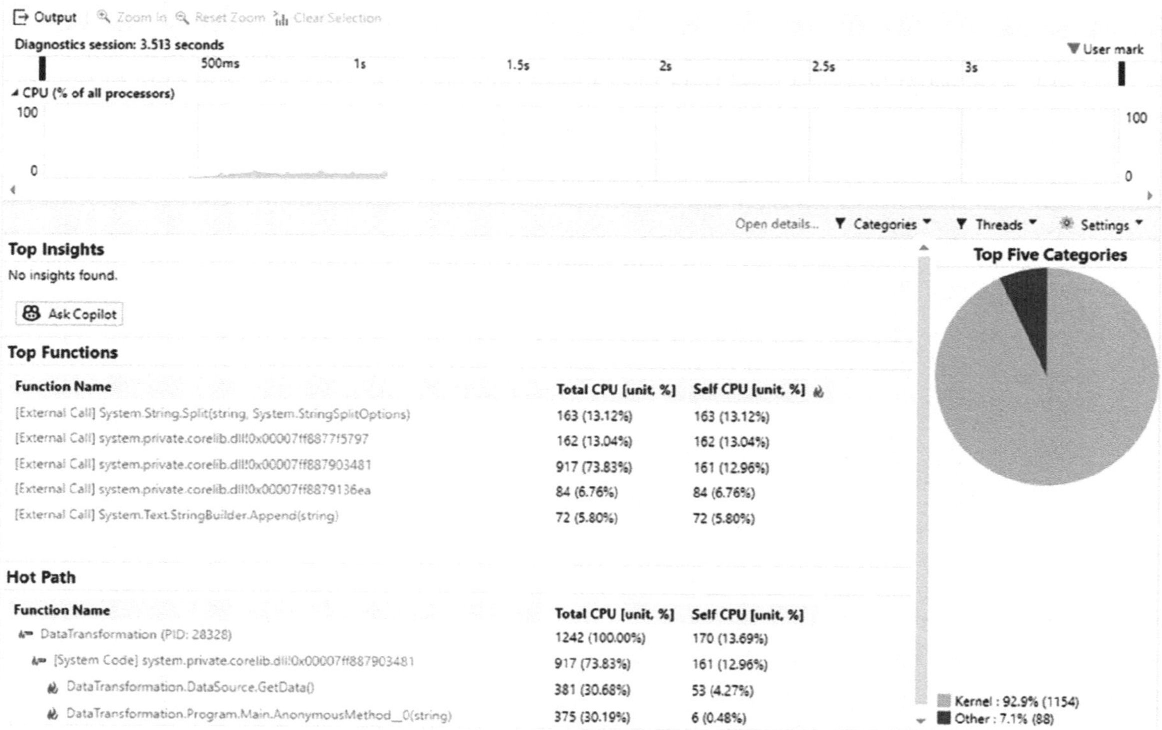

Figure 13.2: *CPU Analysis Summary*

- `Top Insights` **Section:** This section provides AI-driven analysis of the results, helping speed up the review process and highlight potential issues.
- `Top Categories` **Pie Chart:** This visual shows the top five categories of code using the most CPU time, helping you quickly identify which areas of your application are responsible for CPU consumption.
- `Top Functions` **List:** This list shows the specific functions consuming the most CPU time in the selected time range. These functions are strong candidates for optimization.
- `Hot Path` **Section:** This is where you'll find the most critical data. Methods that use the most CPU are marked with flame icons, indicating they are "*hot paths*" and potential performance bottlenecks. Clicking on these functions opens a *Call Tree* and *Source View* that shows the function name, CPU time, and the breakdown of CPU usage across different lines of code.

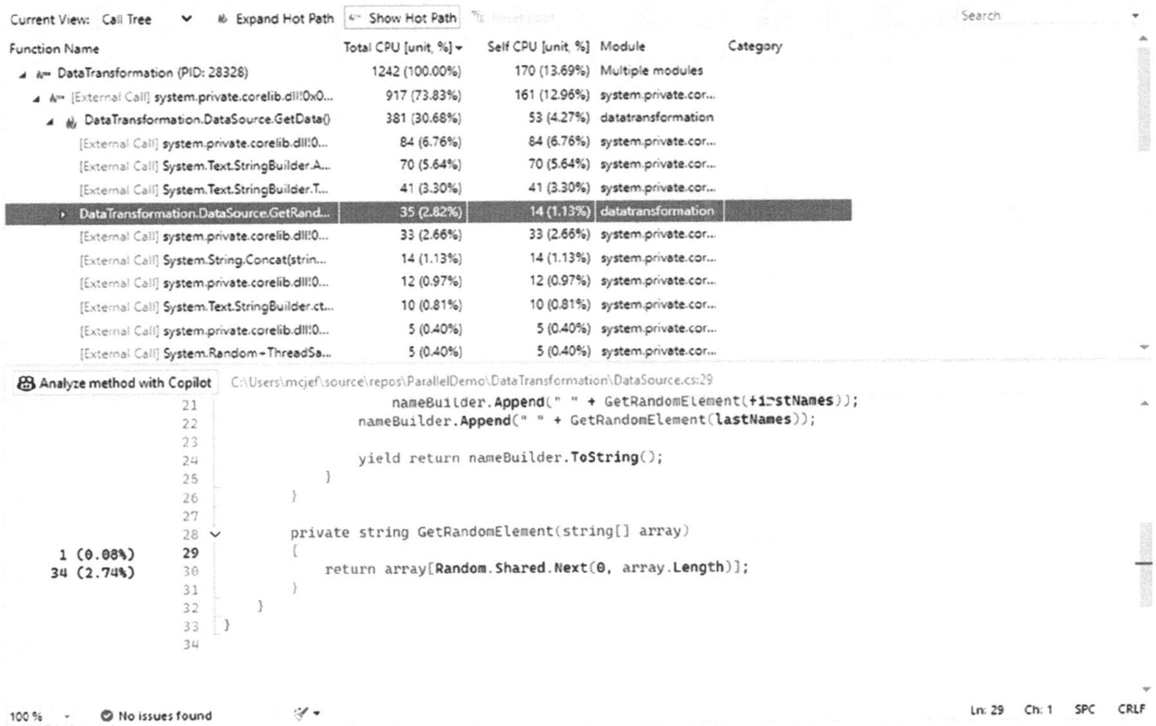

Figure 13.3: *Call Tree and Source View*

Visualizing Performance with Call Tree and Source View

In the *Call Tree* view, the first column shows the name of the function executing, the second column displays the total CPU time for that method in milliseconds, and the third column shows the time spent executing user code (excluding external calls). Additional columns indicate the module the method is in and the category of the method (for example, computation, external calls).

In the *Source View*, methods are listed in the left margin with the number of milliseconds they consume, along with the percentage of CPU utilization in parentheses. This data corresponds to the CPU time reported in the `Call Tree` view, offering a detailed breakdown of CPU usage at the source code level. Navigating the hot path in this view will help identify how frequently methods are called and how their workload could be optimized.

Additional Tools for Profiling and Performance Analysis

While Visual Studio Profiler is a robust tool for analyzing CPU utilization, there are other specialized tools that can provide deeper insights or are more suited for different analysis scenarios. For example, `PerfView` is a powerful performance tool that can be deployed in production or user testing environments, capturing performance data as the application runs in real-world conditions. This makes it particularly useful for identifying hard-to-reproduce issues or those occurring in production environments. Another valuable tool is `BenchmarkDotNet`, which is excellent for establishing performance baselines and comparing various versions of an application to understand the impact of different optimizations. Using a combination of these tools alongside `Visual Studio Profiler` can provide a comprehensive view of performance, enabling you to fine-tune your application more effectively.

By analyzing these key areas, you can identify high-CPU usage methods and threads that can be optimized. The `Call Tree` and `Source View` views provide detailed insights that will guide you in choosing the best optimization strategies.

Optimizations

Once bottlenecks in a **CPU-bound** application have been identified through profiling, the next step is to apply targeted optimizations to improve performance. These optimizations focus on maximizing CPU utilization, reducing thread contention, and efficiently distributing **workloads**. By leveraging parallel algorithms, minimizing synchronization overhead, utilizing hardware acceleration through **SIMD**, and fine-tuning task execution, developers can significantly enhance the responsiveness and scalability of their applications.

While no single solution fits every scenario, the following optimization strategies target some of the most common sources of CPU inefficiency. These techniques can help improve performance in a wide range of **CPU-bound** applications.

Use Parallel Loops Effectively

Parallel loops such as **`Parallel.For()`** and **`Parallel.ForEach()`** provide an accessible way to parallelize iterations, offering substantial performance improvements for computationally intensive tasks that can be broken down into independent units of work. These constructs were covered extensively in *Chapter 7, Parallel Loops in .NET.*

Parallel loops are most effective when applied to compute-heavy **workloads** that can be partitioned into smaller, independent units of execution. Patterns that benefit from parallel loops include:

- Independent operations such as processing rows in a dataset, batch operations, or applying transformations to large collections of objects.
- CPU-intensive tasks, including complex mathematical computations, scientific algorithms, encryption routines, or simulations.
- Processing large datasets, such as bulk data transformations or large-scale file processing tasks.

When applied appropriately, parallel loops can yield significant performance gains. To maximize their benefits, consider the following best practices:

- Avoid making units of work too small, as the overhead of managing parallelism can outweigh the performance benefits. Conversely, overly large tasks can result in suboptimal CPU utilization. Aim for balanced workloads and re-profile your application after adjustments to verify efficient resource usage.
- Ensure that workloads are evenly distributed across threads to prevent idle threads and bottlenecks. Leverage task schedulers that support work-stealing and other dynamic load-balancing techniques to maintain efficiency.
- Be mindful of exception handling in parallel loops. Exceptions thrown within individual tasks do not stop the entire loop by default, and proper aggregation and handling of these exceptions are essential. Refer to *Chapter 7, Parallel Loops in .NET* for guidance on managing exceptions effectively in parallel loops.

Reduce Contention with Lock Free Data Structures

Lock contention occurs when multiple threads attempt to acquire the same lock simultaneously, causing thread blocking and resulting in performance degradation. If profiling reveals that lock contention is a bottleneck, consider using lock-free data structures to minimize or eliminate the need for locks during synchronization. Lock-free alternatives include:

- Concurrent collections such as **`ConcurrentBag`** and **`ConcurrentDictionary`**, which provide thread-safe operations without the explicit use of locks. These collections were covered extensively in *Chapter 6, Understanding Concurrent Collections.*

- Atomic operations provided by the **Interlocked** class, which enable efficient, low-level thread-safe updates to shared variables. The details of the **Interlocked** class were introduced in *Chapter 4, Data Sharing and Synchronization*.

Lock-free data structures are specifically designed to prevent performance degradation caused by synchronization contention. By allowing multiple threads to operate on shared data without blocking, these structures help maintain high throughput and responsiveness in concurrent applications.

Leverage SIMD Operations

The **System.Numerics** namespace contains classes, structs, and interfaces designed to support advanced mathematical operations. Among these are structs specifically designed to leverage modern CPUs' capabilities for parallel computations: **Vector<T>**, **Matrix3x2**, and **Matrix4x4**. These structs support a CPU feature called **Single Instruction, Multiple Data (SIMD)**, a form of data-level parallelism where the CPU executes a single instruction across multiple data elements simultaneously. **SIMD** operations are highly efficient, making optimal use of CPU caching while minimizing instruction overhead. They are well suited to operations that need to be consistently applied across large sets of numeric data.

Matrix operations are supported by the **Matrix4x4** and **Matrix3x2** structs. These operations are critical for transformations such as brightness adjustments or rotation in image processing, physics simulations, games, and graphics processing. The matrix structs optimize these operations by applying **SIMD** acceleration to large matrix computations.

Vector<T> can be used to apply operations across all elements in an array using **SIMD** instructions. The size of **Vector<T>** is hardware-dependent and fixed for each supported data type, so it should be used as a building block for high-performance operations rather than as a general-purpose collection.

For example, consider a loop that multiplies every element in an array by 10 using a standard approach:

```
for (i = 0; i < source.Length; i++)
{
    result[i] = source[i] * 10;
}
```

A vectorized version of the same operation looks like this:

```
var length = source.Length;
var vectorSize = System.Numerics.Vector<double>.Count;
for (i = 0; i < length - vectorSize; i += vectorSize)
{
    var vector = new System.Numerics.Vector<double>(source, i);
    (vector * 10).CopyTo(result, i);
}

//Process remaining elements
for (; i < length; i++)
{
    result[i] = source[i] * 10;
}
```

While the vectorized code is more complex, the performance improvement is substantial.

```
Standard Loop Time: 00:00:00.0002052
Vectorized Loop Time: 00:00:00.0000623
```

In this example, the vectorized loop is more than three times faster than the standard version. While this example demonstrates the potential of **SIMD** operations, full coverage of **SIMD** programming with **Vector<T>** and matrix operations is beyond the scope of this book. For advanced scenarios such as complex physics simulations, 3D graphics rendering, or custom numerical algorithms, further study of **SIMD** techniques and hardware capabilities is recommended.

Fine - Tune the Thread Pool

Tuning the .NET thread pool can provide significant performance benefits, especially in **CPU-bound** scenarios. While the default thread pool settings are sufficient for most applications, adjusting the minimum and maximum number of worker threads may be necessary for specific workloads that require higher throughput. As discussed in *Chapter 11, Threading and the Thread Pool*, you can configure these settings to match the demands of your application, such as increasing the minimum number of threads to ensure faster response times during periods of high activity. However, it is important to carefully profile the application to ensure that such changes do not lead to resource contention or unnecessary performance degradation.

In **CPU-bound** scenarios, using `Task.Run()` can be an effective way to offload work from the main thread, allowing computationally intensive tasks to run asynchronously without blocking the UI or other important operations. However, overusing `Task.Run()` can lead to thread pool saturation, which can negatively impact performance by consuming excessive threads. Be mindful of the **workload** size and how it interacts with thread pool resources.

This approach ensures that the CPU-intensive task runs in the background, allowing the main thread to remain responsive. When tuning the thread pool or using `Task.Run()`, always rely on profiling data to guide adjustments, ensuring optimizations align with the application's needs. For a deeper exploration of thread pool tuning, refer to *Chapter 11, Threading and the Thread Pool.*

Dealing with I/O Bound Issues

Many high-performance applications encounter limitations not in CPU or memory, but in I/O throughput. Common sources of I/O bottlenecks include disk reads and writes, network calls to external services, and database queries. Unlike **CPU-bound** work, **I/O-bound** operations spend much of their time waiting for external resources to respond.

The first step in optimizing I/O performance is to ensure your code uses asynchronous programming with `async` and `await`. Asynchronous methods allow threads to return to the thread pool while waiting for I/O to complete, preventing thread starvation and keeping the application responsive under load. Without this, I/O operations can easily exhaust the thread pool, especially under heavy concurrency.

Common Bottlenecks

I/O bottlenecks generally fall into a few predictable categories. Disk access is one of the most obvious: reading large files, writing logs, or performing heavy file operations can slow down your application, especially on slower storage media or in cloud environments with variable latency.

Network calls are equally common sources of delay. External API requests, microservices communication, and third-party integrations introduce unpredictable latency due to network conditions and the responsiveness of the remote endpoint. Long-running HTTP requests or a high volume of small, chatty network calls can quickly overwhelm the application.

Database queries, however, are perhaps the most frequent and insidious culprits. Poor query design, missing indexes, and inefficient access patterns can grind performance to a halt. Problems such as the **N + 1 query issue** – where data retrieval in a loop generates many redundant database hits – exacerbate latency and increase load on both the application and the database server.

Even in asynchronous applications, pitfalls remain. Blocking calls to **`Result`** or **`Wait()`** on async methods can effectively serialize what should be non-blocking work, leading to thread pool starvation. These kinds of mistakes often hide in plain sight until the system is placed under production-level stress.

Profiling Options

Before making changes, it is essential to build a clear picture of how your application behaves under load. Visual Studio offers excellent profiling tools that help uncover I/O-related performance issues early in the development cycle. The .NET Async tool in **Performance Profiler** is designed specifically to profile asynchronous activity.

Using .NET Async Profiler

1. **Open Performance Profiler**: In Visual Studio, go to the top menu and select **`Debug`** > **`Performance Profiler`**.
2. **Select Profiling Tools**: In the profiler window, check the box for .NET Async. Optionally, also select **`.NET CPU Usage`** and **`Events Viewer`** to capture more context.
3. **Start the Profiler**: Click **`Start`** and run your application through typical workloads – especially the parts you suspect of being I/O heavy (database queries, file uploads, API calls).
4. **Review Async Activity**: Once you stop profiling, Visual Studio will present a timeline of asynchronous tasks. The columns are: task name, occurrence count in the selected timeline, start time, end time, and total time.

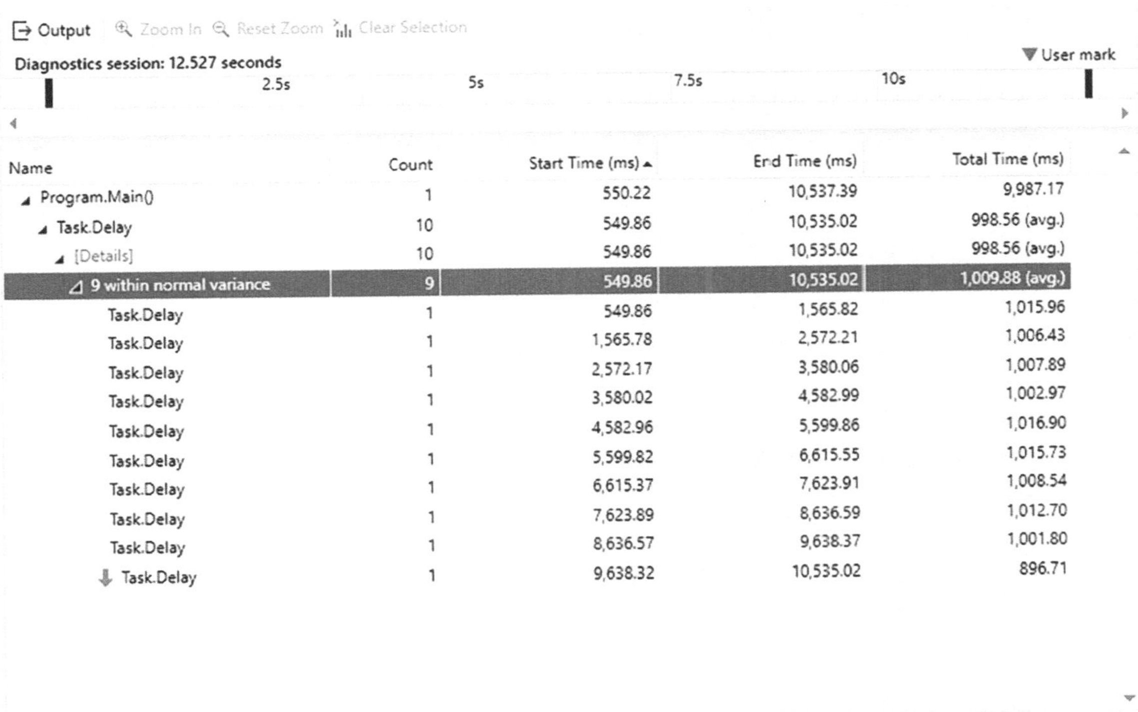

Figure 13.4: *.NET Async Profiler*

5. **Look for the following**:
   - Tasks with long durations.
   - Delays between task creation and execution.

- Common I/O operations such as **`HttpClient.SendAsync`**, **`Stream.ReadAsync`**, or database provider async methods.

6. **Inspect Call Stacks**: Drill into slow operations to see where they are called from. Look for blocking calls that might be holding up progress unnecessarily.
7. **Check Thread Pool Activity**: If async operations are slow to start, inspect thread pool usage to spot potential starvation or thread exhaustion.

For production environments, tools such as **Azure Application Insights**, dotnet-counters, and **`EventSource`** provide real-time telemetry. **Application Insights** can break down dependency calls (HTTP, SQL, etc.) and highlight operations with high latency or failure rates. Distributed tracing tools, such as **OpenTelemetry**, give you an end-to-end view of request flows across services, helping detect cascading I/O delays and external system dependencies.

Optimizations

Once I/O bottlenecks have been identified, there are several strategies to improve performance and efficiency:

- **Embrace asynchronous patterns:** Always prefer asynchronous APIs over synchronous counterparts for I/O operations. This keeps threads free and available for other tasks, improving scalability.
- **Leverage `ValueTask<T>` and `IAsyncEnumerable<T>`:** For high-frequency or streaming scenarios, these types reduce allocations and improve throughput. These were covered in detail in *Chapter 10, Asynchronous Programming with Async/Await.*
- **Implement effective batching:** Group multiple I/O operations into a single batch to reduce round trips. For databases, this may involve using IN clauses or bulk insert/update methods. For APIs, consider batching requests where supported.
- **Use caching strategically:** Memory caches such as **`MemoryCache`** or distributed caches including Redis can dramatically reduce the need for repetitive I/O operations. Combine caching with sensible expiration policies and background refresh to maintain data freshness without overwhelming data sources. For example, a background task can be added to an ASP. Net Core application to refresh cached data periodically or in response to application events.
- **Avoid the N + 1 problem:** In data access code, ensure that you are not inadvertently issuing one query to fetch a list of items and then separate queries for each related item. Use eager loading techniques such as **`Include()`** in Entity Framework, or fetch related data in fewer, more efficient queries.
- **Optimize query design:** Ensure indexes support the query patterns used in your application. Monitor query execution plans and refactor queries to minimize full scans and expensive joins.
- **Connection management:** Use connection pooling and ensure that connections are opened as late as possible and closed (or disposed) as early as possible. Mismanaged connections can lead to contention and resource exhaustion.
- **Consider Producer Consumer:** In some cases, offloading I/O work to a background task by implementing the producer/consumer model can make the application more responsive. Consider **`Channel<T>`** to implement producer/consumer without blocking. This class was introduced in *Chapter 10.*
- **Minimize external dependencies where possible:** Evaluate whether some external I/O operations can be eliminated or reduced. For example, maintain local read replicas for databases that are geographically distributed, or pre-load configuration data at startup.

Note: *Profiling tools can help spot* **N + 1** *issues by revealing unusually high numbers of similar database queries in a short period. Use the timeline view or production telemetry to watch for repetitive patterns.*

With these strategies in place, applications can handle I/O demands more gracefully and remain responsive under load. Importantly, always validate optimizations with measurement – both pre- and post-change – to confirm their effectiveness in your specific environment.

Managing Excessive Memory Usage

In parallel applications, memory consumption can quickly become a limiting factor, especially as the number of threads, tasks, or parallel operations increases. The simultaneous execution of multiple tasks leads to a larger memory footprint and, if not managed properly, can result in excessive memory usage, fragmentation, or even memory leaks. Identifying and addressing these **memory issues** early is crucial for maintaining both the efficiency and scalability of your application.

Causes of Memory Issues

Excessive memory usage in parallel applications can arise from a variety of causes, some of which are unique to concurrent programming. Here are some common sources of memory-related issues in parallel applications:

1. **Memory Fragmentation**: As threads allocate and release memory independently, fragmentation can occur, where small unused chunks of memory accumulate over time. This can increase memory usage and reduce the overall efficiency of memory utilization.
2. **Unmanaged Object References**: Holding references to large objects (such as collections or buffers) across multiple tasks can prevent the garbage collector from reclaiming memory. This issue is exacerbated in parallel programs, where references might be inadvertently retained in multiple places due to the complex flow of asynchronous tasks or multithreaded operations.
3. **Thread-local Storage**: When using thread-local variables (for example, `ThreadLocal<T>`), memory is allocated per thread. In a parallel application with a large number of threads, this can result in excessive memory usage, particularly when many threads are created dynamically.
4. **Large Object Heap (LOH) Usage**: The LOH is where objects larger than 85,000 bytes are allocated. While efficient in some scenarios, high memory usage on the LOH can lead to fragmentation and delayed garbage collection, especially when objects are frequently allocated and deallocated.
5. **Improper Use of Collections**: Parallel applications often use concurrent collections (such as `ConcurrentDictionary` or `ConcurrentBag`) to ensure thread safety. However, these collections may grow uncontrollably under high contention, leading to excessive memory consumption.
6. **Memory Leaks**: Memory leaks occur when objects are not properly disposed of or released, and they accumulate over time. In parallel applications, memory leaks can be particularly tricky to detect because memory is being allocated and freed by different threads or tasks, sometimes making it difficult to identify the root cause.

Diagnostic Tools

To manage and optimize memory usage, it is crucial to first identify where the issues lie. Visual Studio offers a range of diagnostic tools specifically designed to help you analyze memory usage in parallel applications.

Using Visual Studio Memory Profiler

1. **Open the Performance Profiler**: In Visual Studio, navigate to `Debug` > `Performance Profiler...` from the menu bar.

2. **Select Memory Usage**: In the **`Performance Profiler`** window, choose the **`Memory Usage`** option. This tool allows you to track memory allocations, identify high memory usage patterns, and pinpoint areas where excessive allocations occur.
3. **Start Profiling**: Click **`Start`** to launch the profiler. The profiler window will appear.

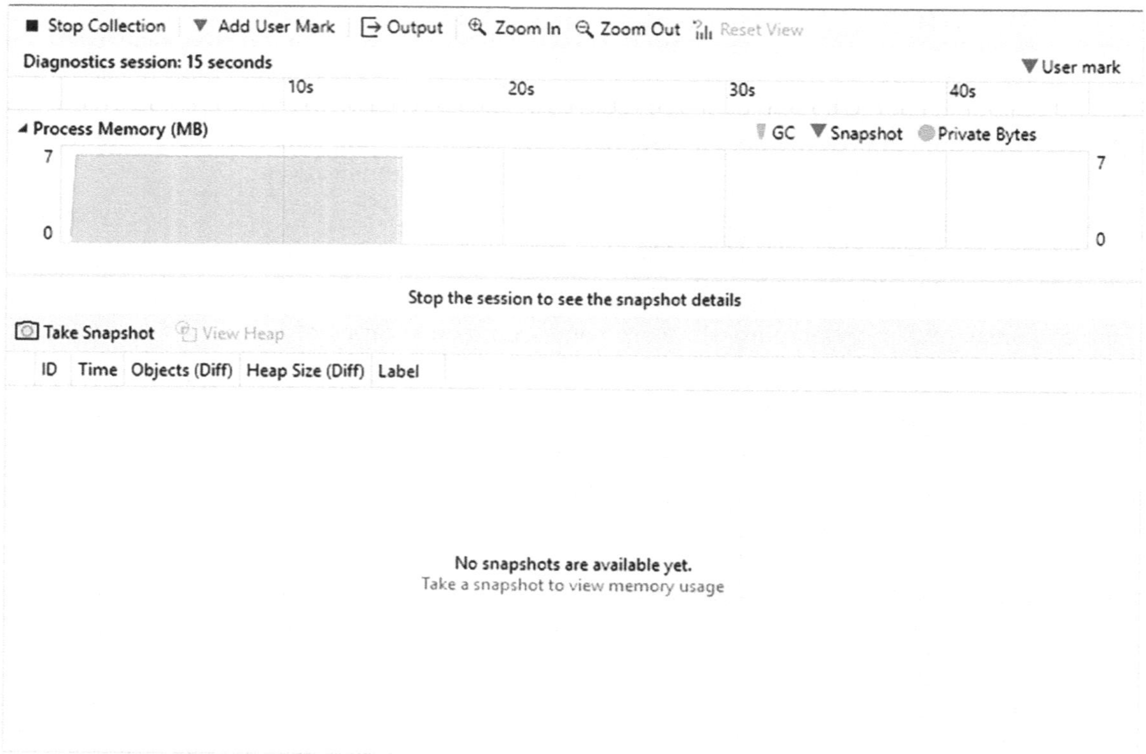

***Figure 13.5**: .NET Memory Profiler*

4. **Use the Application:** Run your application through typical workflows, particularly those that stress memory usage – such as those involving high levels of concurrency or parallel operations.
5. **Review Memory Usage Over Time**: Once profiling is complete, the profiler will display a timeline showing memory usage throughout the application's runtime. Look for the following key indicators:
   - Spikes in memory usage that correspond with specific actions, such as creating threads or loading large datasets.
   - Memory growth trends that don't return to baseline levels, indicating potential memory leaks.
   - The number and size of objects in memory at different points in the application's lifecycle.
6. **Inspect Allocated Objects**: You can take snapshots of memory usage at specific points in time to compare memory allocations before and after certain operations or stages of your application. To take a snapshot:
   - Click **`Take Snapshot`** in the **`Memory Usage`** window during profiling.
   - After taking the snapshot, run the application through specific memory-intensive tasks (such as batch operations or large dataset processing).
   - After the task completes, take another snapshot.

- Compare the snapshots to identify which objects were allocated and how memory usage changed between snapshots.

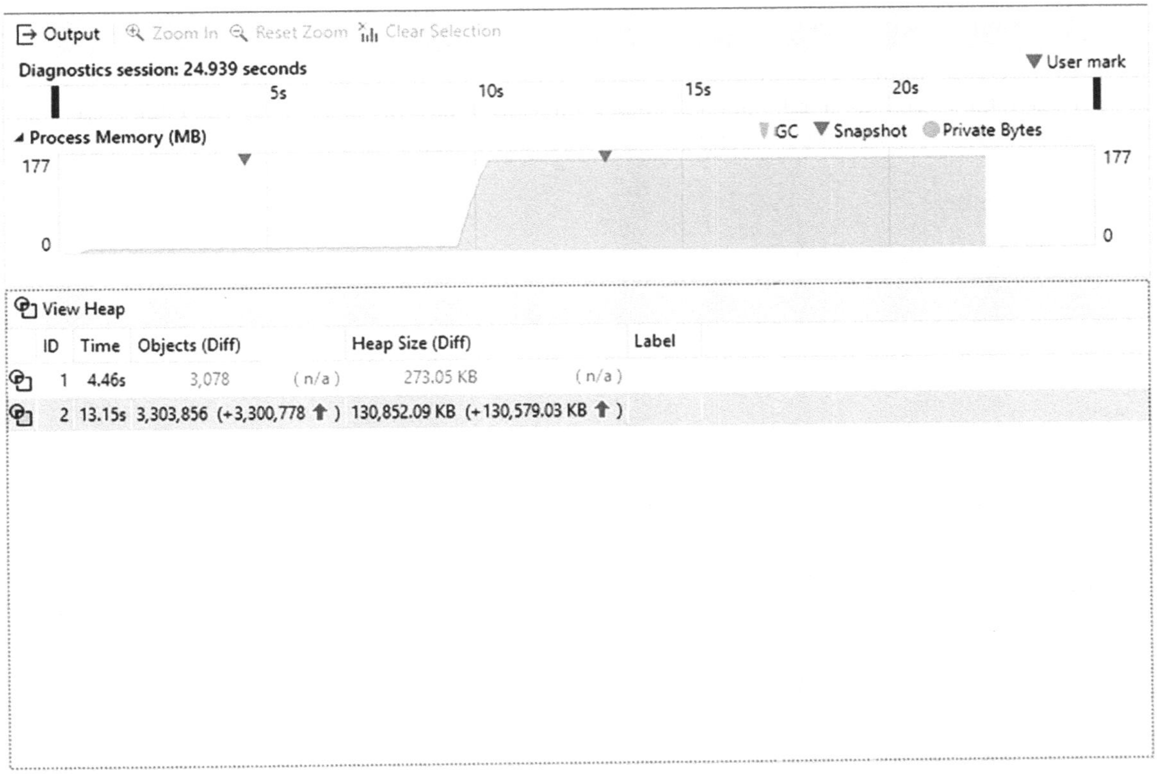

***Figure 13.6:** Memory Usage*

7. **Analyze Snapshot Data**: By clicking on links in the **`Objects`** or **`Heap Size`** column, Visual Studio will display a detailed view of objects allocated in memory, including their size and references.

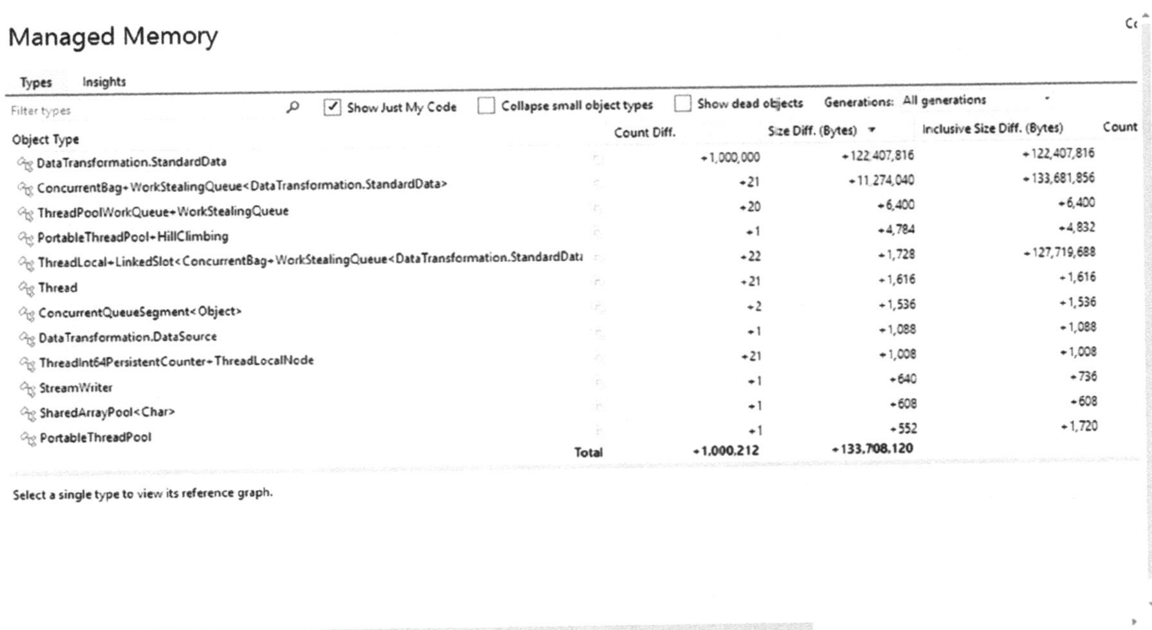

***Figure 13.7:** Managed Memory Types*

The **`Managed Memory`** window is divided into two tabs: **`Types`** and **`Insights`**. The **`Types`** tab displays memory usage by classes within the application, offering insight into how class allocations are impacting overall memory usage. The bottom pane shows a reference graph that visualizes how types are allocated and held in memory.

The **`Insights`** tab highlights potential memory issues that could affect the application, such as duplicate strings or sparse arrays. While the insights provided are not necessarily critical problems, they serve as areas to consider when optimizing memory usage.

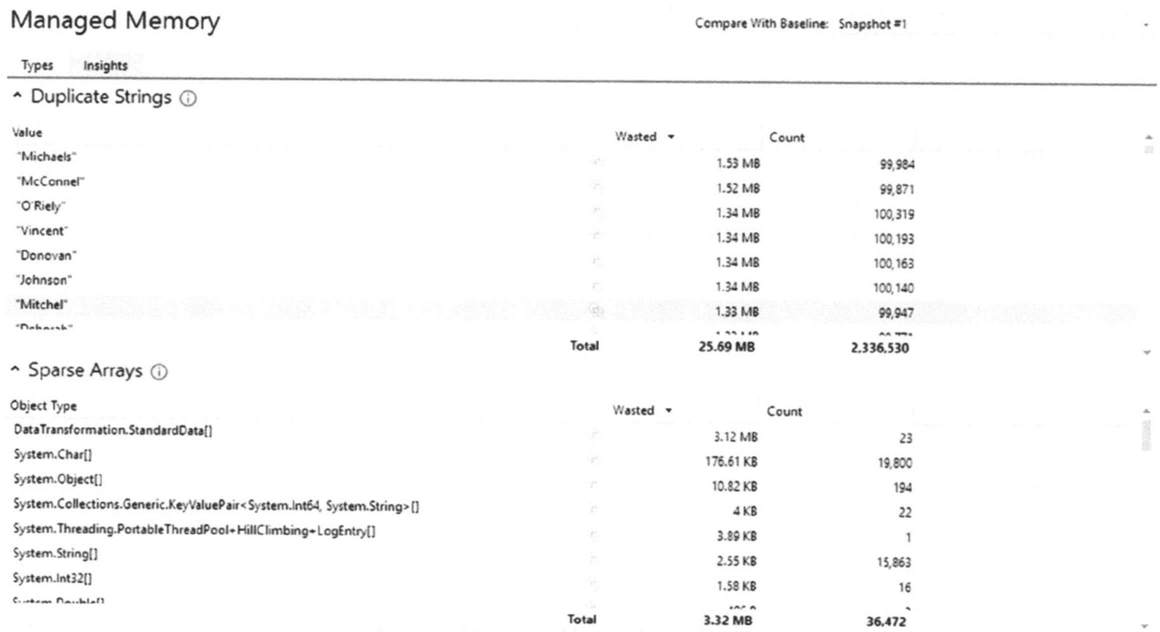

Figure 13.8: *Managed Memory Insights*

8. **Look for the following key indicators**:
   - Large allocations or spikes in the number of objects.
   - Unexpected object retention – this can help pinpoint memory leaks or objects that are not being disposed of correctly.
9. **Track Garbage Collection Events**: Use the GC Allocations markers in the timeline window to track how often garbage collection (GC) occurs, and whether it is effectively reclaiming memory. Frequent GC pauses or high memory fragmentation can indicate inefficiencies in memory management.

Note: *Frequent garbage collections can indicate that an algorithm is allocating too many objects. If you suspect this, use the .NET Object Allocation Tracking tool in the Visual Studio Performance Profiler. This tool tracks object allocations and garbage collection (GC) activity, helping you visualize where memory allocations occur and identify opportunities to reduce both allocations and GC frequency. Optimizing object allocation patterns can lead to improved application performance and reduced GC overhead.*

Optimizations

Once you have identified excessive memory usage, several optimization strategies can help mitigate the impact and improve overall efficiency. Many of these optimizations are particularly important in parallel applications, where memory is being allocated and accessed simultaneously by multiple threads or tasks.

- **Optimize Collection Usage**: Choose the appropriate collection type based on your use case. For example, prefer immutable collections such as `ImmutableList<T>` or `ImmutableDictionary<TKey, TValue>` when the collection does not need to be modified concurrently. Use `ConcurrentDictionary<TKey, TValue>` only when there is a need for thread-safe operations with frequent updates.
- **Reduce Memory Allocation Overhead**: Allocate memory in large chunks or pools to reduce the frequency of garbage collection. Using memory pools, such as `ArrayPool<T>`, can greatly reduce the number of allocations and deallocations, especially in high-performance applications that need to manage large arrays of data concurrently.
- **Minimize Thread-local Storage**: When working with thread-local variables (for example, `ThreadLocal<T>`), ensure that they are disposed of or reused as efficiently as possible. If many threads are being created, consider using a shared memory model or task-based parallelism that can reduce the need for excessive memory allocations.
- **Avoid Large Object Heap Fragmentation**: Ensure that large objects are managed efficiently by reducing the number of allocations that exceed 85,000 bytes. This can help avoid fragmentation of the LOH. Use `ArrayPool<T>` or consider splitting large objects into smaller components.
- **Implement Memory Pooling**: Use memory pooling to manage memory for frequently allocated objects. A `MemoryPool<T>` allows you to reuse memory blocks, reducing the need for frequent allocations and garbage collection, particularly for large or complex objects used in parallel processing.
- **Carefully Manage Task and Thread Lifecycles**: Be cautious about creating too many short-lived tasks or threads that allocate large objects. Tasks can hold onto memory until they are fully completed, leading to unnecessary memory usage in parallel applications. Use thread pools and task scheduling to efficiently manage memory usage across concurrent tasks.
- **Use `ValueTask<T>` for High-Frequency Operations**: `ValueTask<T>` is a value type that can be used for async operations that are completed synchronously. It reduces heap allocations, which is particularly useful in high-frequency parallel operations.
- **Dispose of Objects Properly**: Always ensure that objects implementing `IDisposable` are properly disposed of in parallel workflows. Use `using` statements, or implement manual disposal patterns to free up memory when objects are no longer needed.

By incorporating these optimizations, you can significantly reduce excessive memory usage and prevent common pitfalls associated with memory management in parallel applications. Regular profiling and continuous monitoring, especially in production environments, will ensure that memory remains well-managed as your application scales.

Optimizing Data Access and Loops

Efficient data access and loop optimization are key factors in improving the performance of parallel applications. Suboptimal data access patterns and inefficient loops can quickly become bottlenecks that diminish the potential benefits of parallelism. This section explores common data access patterns that can lead to performance issues and offers actionable strategies to optimize them.

Inefficient Data Patterns

Inefficient data access patterns are one of the primary causes of performance degradation in parallel applications. The way data is accessed—whether from memory, databases, or external resources—

plays a significant role in how well an application can scale. Here are some common inefficient data access patterns to look out for:

- **Frequent Disk Access**: Reading and writing data from the disk can introduce significant latency, especially if the application repeatedly accesses the disk during operations that can be handled in memory.
- **Unoptimized Database Queries**: Inefficient queries or queries that retrieve more data than necessary can slow down applications that depend on database access. This includes the **N + 1 query problem**, where many small queries are executed in sequence instead of retrieving all the needed data in a single, efficient query.
- **Poorly Structured Data Iteration**: Iterating over large datasets inefficiently in loops can lead to excessive overhead. For example, using nested loops for operations that could be handled in parallel or in a more memory-efficient way (such as using LINQ) can severely impact performance.
- **Excessive Locking on Shared Data**: When accessing shared data across multiple threads, improper synchronization can lead to excessive locking, which diminishes the benefits of parallelism. This often results in thread contention and high latency.

Profiling Options

To identify inefficient data access patterns, profiling tools such as **Visual Studio Performance Profiler** can help track long-running operations and memory issues.

- **CPU Usage and Memory Usage in Visual Studio**: Use the `Performance Profiler` in Visual Studio to identify methods that may be inefficiently accessing or modifying large datasets, particularly focusing on functions dealing with disk or database access.
- **Managed Memory View**: Use the `Managed Memory` view to examine how memory is allocated across your classes and identify inefficient object creation or memory usage patterns, especially for large collections or arrays.
- **Concurrency Visualizer**: Look for signs of thread contention in parallel applications. Thread contention can occur when multiple threads are waiting to acquire locks, which negatively impacts performance.

Optimizations

Once profiling has revealed the problematic data access and loop patterns, it is time to implement optimizations. The following strategies can help reduce memory and CPU overhead, improving performance and scalability in parallel applications:

1. **Efficient Data Access Patterns**
    - **Batch Processing**: Reducing the number of I/O operations by grouping smaller requests into batch operations can significantly improve performance. For database operations, this might involve executing bulk queries or stored procedures instead of multiple individual queries. For disk or network I/O, consider buffering reads and writes to minimize overhead.
    - **Avoiding the N + 1 Problem**: The **N + 1 query problem** occurs when the application issues a large number of small, sequential database queries instead of a single, optimized query. To solve this, always aim to fetch all required data in as few queries as possible, ideally by using joins or batch-fetching mechanisms. Ensure that ORM frameworks are configured to minimize unnecessary round trips to the database, such as lazy loading in Entity Framework.

- **Optimizing Data Retrieval**: Fetch only the data you need from databases or other external resources. Select specific columns instead of using `SELECT *`, and apply appropriate filtering in the query to avoid bringing back unnecessary data. This reduces memory usage and improves performance by minimizing the amount of data processed.
- **Using Caching**: Caching frequently accessed data, either in memory or using distributed caches (such as, Redis or Memcached), can reduce the need for repeated expensive database queries or disk accesses. Use caching techniques to store the results of common queries or data operations, making them quickly accessible when needed.

2. **Optimizing Loops and Iterations**
   - **Parallelizing Loops**: For CPU-bound operations in loops, consider parallelizing the workload using `Parallel.For()` or `Parallel.ForEach()`. This can help distribute the work across multiple threads and take advantage of multi-core CPUs. However, ensure that the data being processed is independent and that no shared resources are being accessed simultaneously.
   - **Using LINQ**: Language Integrated Query (LINQ) can sometimes help improve the readability and performance of data transformations. LINQ operations can often be optimized to run in parallel and can replace inefficient foreach loops or nested loops for operations such as filtering, grouping, or transforming data.
   - **Minimizing Nested Loops**: Nested loops can lead to performance issues when working with large datasets. Look for opportunities to flatten nested iterations or use more efficient algorithms (such as hash-based lookups or binary search) to reduce the need for nested loops.
3. **Reducing Lock Contention**
   - **Using Lock-Free Data Structures**: For applications with multiple threads accessing shared data, lock contention can significantly slow down execution. Using thread-safe collections such as `ConcurrentDictionary` or `ConcurrentQueue` can help minimize locking. These collections allow multiple threads to access data concurrently without blocking each other.
   - **Atomic Operations**: Where possible, use atomic operations (for example, `Interlocked.CompareExchange`) to update shared variables without the need for locks. These operations can improve performance in highly concurrent applications.

By analyzing the data access and loop patterns in your application and applying these optimizations, you can significantly reduce memory usage and improve the overall performance of your parallel applications. Profiling tools such as **Visual Studio Performance Profiler**, and *Concurrency Visualizer* provide the insights needed to pinpoint areas for improvement and validate the effectiveness of your optimizations.

Case Study

In this case study, we will apply the tools and techniques from this chapter to a real-world parallel application. You will see how to identify common performance issues, interpret profiling data, and implement practical optimizations to improve throughput and efficiency. This step-by-step example will show how diagnostics translate into meaningful improvements.

Example Application

The following application calculates the final amount of principal and interest for a large list of account records. To improve performance, the original developer chose to use parallel loops to process the data concurrently. However, despite this, users have been reporting that the application runs very slowly.

The current implementation is as follows:

```
using System.Diagnostics;

object lockObject = new object();
var tempFileName = Path.GetTempFileName();
try
{
    var data = LoadData(100_000);
    var stopwatch = Stopwatch.StartNew();

    Parallel.ForEach(data, record =>
    {
        string result = PerformComputation(record);
        lock (lockObject)
        {
            File.AppendAllText(tempFileName, result + Environment.NewLine);
        }
    });

    stopwatch.Stop();
    Console.WriteLine($"Processing time (inefficient): {stopwatch.ElapsedMilli-
seconds} ms");
}
finally
{
    File.Delete(tempFileName);
}

static string[] LoadData(int count)
{
    var data = new string[count];
    for (int i = 0; i < count; i++)
    {
        data[i] = $"Record {i}";
    }
    return data;
}

static string PerformComputation(string input)
{
    double principal = 1000;
    double rate = 0.05;
    int periods = 10000;
    double amount = principal;

    for (int i = 0; i < periods; i++)
    {
        amount *= (1 + rate);
    }

    return $"{input.ToUpper()} - Final Amount: {amount:F2}";
}
```

According to the output, in its current form the application takes about 13 seconds to run.

```
Processing time (inefficient): 13601 ms
```

At first glance, there are some questionable choices in this code, such as the use of a **`lock`** statement within the parallel loop to handle file writes. However, rather than make assumptions, we want to take a data-driven approach to optimization. Before making any changes, we will begin by profiling the application to understand where the real performance bottlenecks lie.

Profiling the Application

Since the use of the lock statement in the parallel loop is a likely suspect for performance issues, we will begin by using the **`Concurrency Visualizer`** to determine if thread contention is causing significant wait times.

The **`Threads`** View indicates that threads are indeed spending a significant amount of time waiting for locks to be released, confirming our initial suspicion.

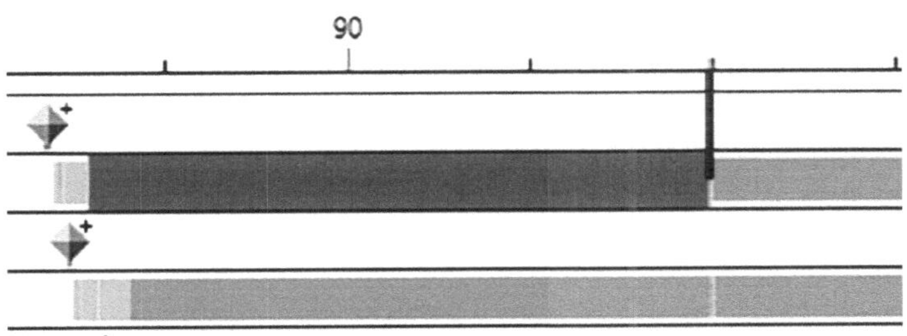

Figure 13.9: *Concurrency Visualizer - Thread Waiting*

Switching to the *Current* tab further confirms this finding. It shows that the threads are waiting on other threads, indicating lock contention.

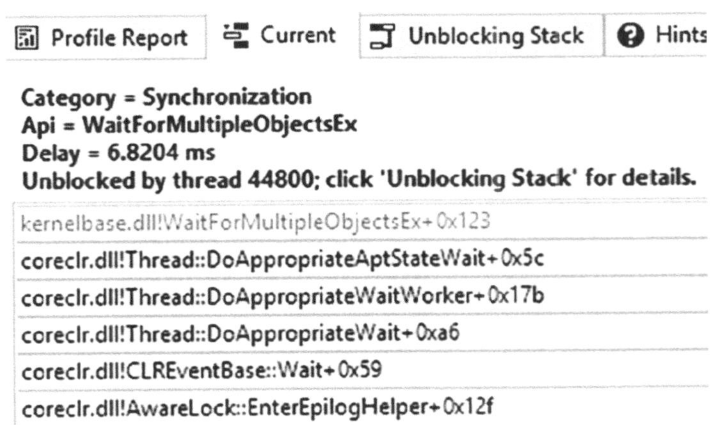

Figure 13.10: *Concurrency Visualizer - Current Tab*

Next, we profile the application using **`Visual Studio Performance Profiler`** with both the **`CPU Usage`** and **`.NET Async`** tools enabled. The **`CPU Usage`** tab reveals another major contributor to the performance issue: the **`System.IO.WriteToFile()`** method is consuming over 67% of the CPU time. Additionally, the **`PerformComputation()`** method accounts for around 11%.

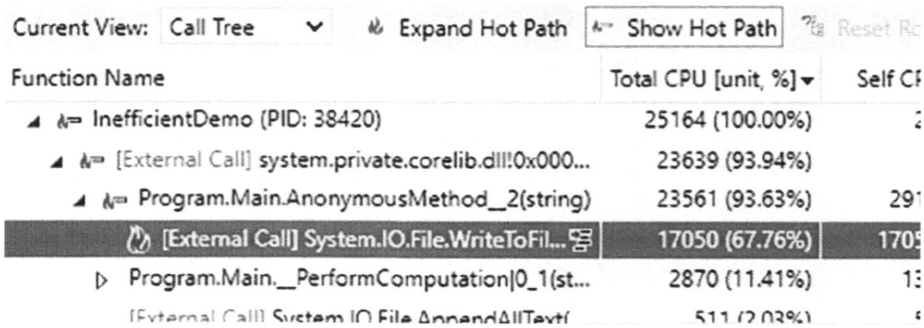

Figure 13.11: *CPU Usage Hot Path*

Meanwhile, the **Async Activities** tab shows that work is being evenly distributed across the thread pool tasks created by the parallel loop. There's no apparent bottleneck at the task scheduling level, as each task completes in roughly the same amount of time.

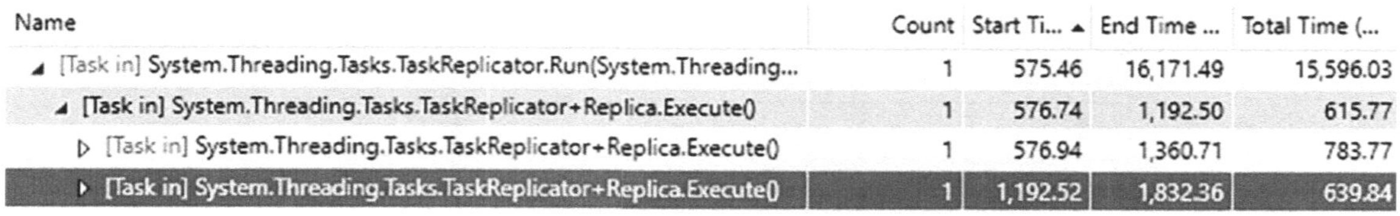

Figure 13.12: *Async Activity Evenly Distributed*

With this profiling data in hand, we are now well-positioned to make informed decisions about how to optimize the application.

Applying Solutions

The profiling data clearly identifies the lock statement as a major bottleneck to parallelism. Although **`File.AppendAllText()`** is thread-safe, it internally locks the file for each write operation, meaning that when multiple threads attempt to write simultaneously, they contend for exclusive access. This is likely the reason the lock statement was originally used. However, a better solution is to use a **`StreamWriter`** to append data asynchronously, which allows for more efficient, buffered writes.

To fully optimize the parallel loop and let it focus solely on computation, we can apply the producer/consumer model to offload file writing to a separate task. By using a **`Channel<string>`**, we can cleanly separate computation from I/O, improving throughput and scalability.

After applying these improvements, the parallel loop is refactored to the following:

```
var channel = Channel.CreateUnbounded<string>();
var writerTask = WriteToFileAsync(channel);

Parallel.ForEach(data, record =>
{
    string result = PerformComputation(record);
    channel.Writer.TryWrite(result);
});

channel.Writer.Complete();
await writerTask;
```

The new **`WriteToFileAsync()`** method handles writing to the file asynchronously:

```
static async Task WriteToFileAsync(Channel<string> channel)
{
    await using var writer = new StreamWriter("output.txt", append: true,
encoding: Encoding.UTF8);
    await foreach (var line in channel.Reader.ReadAllAsync())
    {
        await writer.WriteLineAsync(line);
    }
}
```

Re-profiling the application after these changes shows a significant performance improvement. The total runtime drops to around 350 milliseconds, and the CPU *Usage* view highlights a new hotspot: the float formatting operation within **`PerformComputation()`**. Since formatting the float is a necessary part of the output, there are no optimizations to apply here.

However, inspecting the source view of this hotspot uncovers another opportunity:

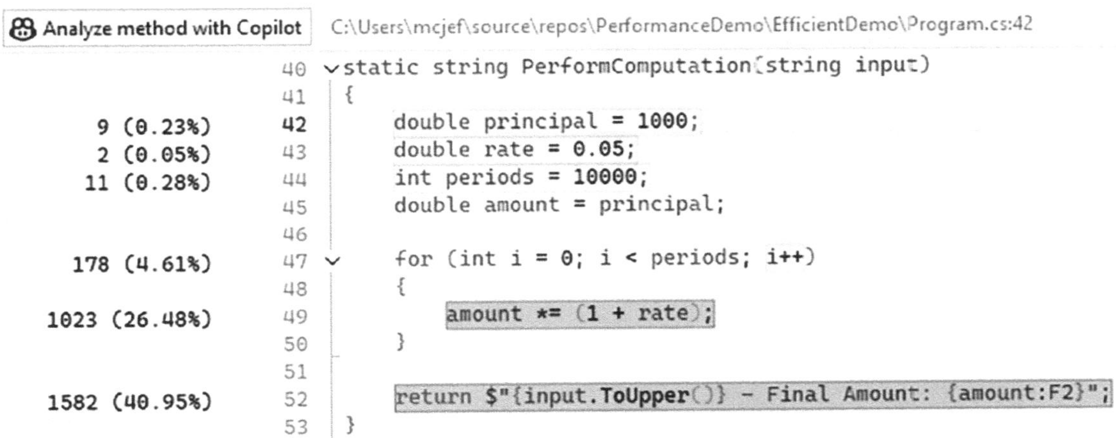

Figure 13.13: *Source View*

The formula for calculating the total loan amount has been implemented using a loop, which is unnecessarily consuming CPU time inside **`PerformComputation()`**. Upon reviewing the requirements, we determine that the calculation can be simplified by using **`Math.Pow()`**:

```
amount = principal * Math.Pow(1 + rate, periods);
```

Applying this optimization brings the runtime down further to approximately 280 milliseconds.

With these optimizations in place, we have transformed a heavily bottlenecked process into an efficient, well-balanced pipeline. By eliminating contention points and separating computation from I/O, we achieved a substantial performance gain. This demonstrates the power of profiling and iterative refinement in building high-performance applications.

Conclusion

Performance tuning is not a one-time task but a continuous discipline of identifying bottlenecks, analyzing behavior under load, and applying targeted improvements. In this chapter, we examined the typical pitfalls of parallel applications, from thread pool saturation and I/O delays to excessive memory consumption and inefficient data access patterns. With the right combination of profiling tools and code-level optimizations, even complex issues can be unraveled and resolved, leading to faster, more scalable applications.

In the next chapter, we will move from theory to practice with a hands-on case study: building a responsive chat application. You'll learn how to design both the client and server components, implement real-time communication, and apply performance techniques covered so far. Along the way, we will highlight practical lessons learned from building a high-performance system under real-world conditions.

Points to Remember

- **Performance tuning is iterative**: Continuously profile, analyze, and refine – especially in parallel applications where issues often emerge under load.
- **Keep thread pool use efficient**: Efficient use of the thread pool is essential. Avoid flooding it with unnecessary work and be mindful of thread starvation and long-running tasks.
- **Async/await is critical for I/O-bound operations**: Use asynchronous patterns to prevent blocking threads and improve scalability.
- **Watch for excessive memory use**: Leverage Visual Studio Memory Profiler snapshots to understand allocations, lifetimes, and potential leaks.
- **Favor efficient data access and looping patterns**: Minimize redundant data processing, avoid locking where unnecessary, and use local variables to reduce contention.

Multiple Choice Questions

1. Which Visual Studio tool can help you capture and analyze asynchronous call stacks to diagnose I/O bottlenecks?
   a. CPU Usage tool
   b. Memory Usage tool
   c. .NET Async tool
   d. IntelliTrace
2. When profiling memory in Visual Studio, what does the "`Insights`" tab of the Managed Memory view show?
   a. Only confirmed memory leaks
   b. Performance counters
   c. Common patterns and potential issues, such as duplicate strings
   d. CPU-intensive functions
3. Which of the following is a sign of excessive memory usage in a parallel application?
   a. Gradual increase in memory consumption over time
   b. High CPU usage with stable memory consumption
   c. Frequent thread pool scaling events
   d. Decreased disk I/O

4. What is a good first step when encountering unexplained application slowdowns in production?
    a. Increase server hardware
    b. Use profiling and monitoring tools to gather diagnostic data
    c. Rebuild the application in release mode
    d. Disable logging to improve performance

Answers

1. c
2. c
3. a
4. b

Questions

1. When diagnosing performance issues in a parallel application, how do you decide whether to start with CPU profiling, memory analysis, or thread pool diagnostics? What factors influence this decision?
2. Consider a situation where profiling shows high CPU usage but low application throughput. What steps would you take to investigate the root cause? How would you differentiate between genuine workload and inefficiencies?
3. This chapter discussed the N+1 problem and other inefficient data access patterns. How might you proactively detect and prevent these issues during development, rather than during production troubleshooting?
4. Visual Studio and other tools offer powerful insights, but they also require interpretation. What are the risks of relying solely on profiling data without understanding the application context?

Key Terms

- **CPU-bound:** Workload that are limited primarily by the speed of computations.
- **I/O-bound**: Workloads where performance is constrained by input/output operations rather than computations.
- **Memory-intensive, Memory Issues, Memory-Bound**: Workload that heavily relies on memory allocations and usage, potentially leading to excessive garbage collection and out-of-memory conditions if not managed properly.
- **Workload**: The total amount of computational tasks and operations that an application performs during its lifetime.
- **Visual Studio Performance Profiler**: A comprehensive toolset in Visual Studio for profiling application performance.

- `PerfView`: A performance tool that can be deployed in production or test environments to capture performance data in real-time.
- `BenchmarkDotNet`: A tool that can be used to establish performance baselines during testing.
- **Azure Application Insights**: A monitoring tool for production environments that can capture performance data in real-time.
- `OpenTelemetry`: A distributed tracing tool that provides end-to-end views of request flows across services.
- **Single Instruction, Multiple Data (SIMD)**: A form of data-level parallelism where the CPU executes a single instruction across multiple data elements simultaneously.
- **N + 1 Query Problem**: A problem in data access code where a single query obtains a list, and then subsequent queries obtain the detail data.

CHAPTER 14
Building a Chat Application

Introduction

Building a chat application may sound like a simple assignment, but it quickly becomes a proving ground for real-time communication, responsive interfaces, and clean architecture. In this chapter, we will walk through the process of creating a desktop chat app using **Windows Presentation Foundation (WPF)** and **WebSockets**—one that supports multiple chat rooms, lets users create and manage those rooms, and handles live messaging with minimal delay. This is the kind of project that forces us to think about threading, connection management, and UI updates all at once. More importantly, it gives us a chance to apply the performance principles we have explored throughout this book in a hands-on, practical way.

Structure

In this chapter, we will cover the following topics:

- Introduction and Goals
  - Key Features
  - Technologies Used
- The Assignment
  - Functional Requirements
  - Non-Functional Requirements
  - Constraints
- Structuring the Client
  - WPF and MVVM
  - UI Components
  - ViewModel Behavior
  - WebSocket Integration
- The Server Architecture
  - WebSocket Server Overview
  - Message Routing
  - Real-Time Broadcasting
  - User Lifecycle
  - Room Management
  - Threading and Async Flow

- Implementing the Solution
    - Server Implementation
    - Client Implementation
- Lessons Learned
    - Real-World Challenges
    - Performance Considerations
    - Additions for Production

Introduction and Goals

The goal of this chapter is to walk through the design and implementation of a fully functional chat application, a familiar yet technically demanding project that brings together many of the principles and strategies explored throughout this book. The application will support real-time messaging with low latency and will feature a modern desktop user interface built with **Windows Presentation Foundation (WPF)**. This exercise highlights the key aspects of high-performance development, including asynchronous communication, efficient UI updates, and scalable server design. You can download the complete source code for this chapter's application at:

https://github.com/ava-orange-education/Ultimate-C-for-High-Performance-Applications/tree/main/Chapter%2014

Key Features

This chat application is designed to demonstrate how to build a responsive, real-time messaging system using modern .NET technologies. While intentionally simple in some areas to maintain focus on architectural clarity and performance, it includes several important features found in production systems:

- **Multiple Chat Rooms**: Users can be added to existing rooms or create new ones dynamically, allowing for separate conversations across different topics or groups.
- **User Management**: Each room maintains its own list of active participants, with the ability to add or remove users in real time.
- **Real-Time Messaging**: All messages are delivered over **WebSockets**, enabling low-latency, bidirectional communication without polling.
- **WPF Desktop Client**: A rich, responsive user interface built using **Windows Presentation Foundation**, following the **Model-View-ViewModel (MVVM)** pattern for testability and maintainability.
- **Asynchronous Communication**: Both the client and server use asynchronous programming techniques to handle multiple users and rooms efficiently, without blocking threads or degrading performance.
- **Extensible Protocol Design**: A simple, text-based message protocol using JSON ensures easy integration and future enhancement, such as support for persistence, authentication, or file attachments.

Together, these features provide a solid foundation for exploring how performance-conscious design decisions play out in a realistic, interactive desktop application.

Technologies Used

This project brings together a mix of client-side and server-side technologies to demonstrate a complete, high-performance chat system:

- **Windows Presentation Foundation (WPF):** The desktop client is built using WPF, which provides a powerful framework for creating responsive and visually rich Windows applications. The **MVVM** pattern is used to separate UI, logic, and state management, making the application easier to test and maintain.
- **WebSockets (`System.Net.WebSockets`):** Real-time communication between the client and server is handled via **WebSockets**, allowing for low-latency, bidirectional messaging without the overhead of HTTP polling or long-poll techniques.
- **ASP.NET Core:** The server is implemented as an ASP.NET Core application, which provides a lightweight and efficient platform for handling **WebSocket** connections, managing state, and routing messages between clients.
- **Dependency Injection:** Both the client and server projects use dependency injection to manage component lifetimes, reduce coupling, and make the system easier to configure, extend, and test.
- **C# 13 and .NET 9:** The latest features of the C# language and the .NET runtime are used to demonstrate best practices in asynchronous programming, memory management, and concurrency.
- **JSON Messaging Protocol:** All messages exchanged between the client and server use a custom JSON-based protocol. This keeps the communication format simple, human-readable, and easy to extend.

This combination of technologies strikes a balance between performance, developer productivity, and clarity, making it ideal for demonstrating real-world application design in a focused, educational setting.

The Assignment

Before diving into code, it is important to clearly understand the scope and goals of the application we are about to build. The assignment is to create a multi-room chat application that delivers a fast, fluid user experience on the desktop using **WPF**, while supporting real-time communication through a **WebSocket**-based backend. Users should be able to create and join chat rooms, exchange messages instantly, and see updates, such as new users joining or leaving, in real time. While the feature set is intentionally focused, the design must be clean, scalable, and aligned with high-performance development practices. This section lays out the essential requirements that will guide the implementation in the sections that follow.

Functional Requirements

At its core, the chat application must support real-time, multi-user communication across multiple chat rooms. To keep the scope focused while still demonstrating meaningful complexity, the application will include the following core features:

- **User Connection and Identity:** When a user launches the application, they should be able to connect to the chat server and choose a display name that identifies them to others in the system.
- **Room Management:** Users can view a list of chat rooms they are participating in, create new rooms, and add or remove users from rooms at will. Each user may only be active in one room at a time, but they can switch rooms freely.

- **Messaging:** Once inside a room, users can send and receive messages in real time. All messages are broadcast to all users currently in the room, and message delivery should appear instantaneous.
- **User Presence Updates:** Users should be able to see who else is currently present in the room. The user list should update automatically as users join or leave.
- **Client Responsiveness:** The user interface should always remain responsive, even during message bursts or rapid room switching. UI operations should not block the main thread.

These requirements ensure that the application covers critical aspects of concurrency, real-time communication, and user experience, making it a practical demonstration of high-performance application design.

Non-Functional Requirements

Beyond the core features, the application must also meet several non-functional requirements that reflect real-world expectations for responsiveness, maintainability, and scalability:

- **Low Latency:** Message delivery between users should feel instantaneous. Network and processing delays must be kept to a minimum, with real-time updates delivered via WebSockets rather than slower polling mechanisms.
- **Thread Safety:** Both the client and server must be designed to handle concurrent operations safely. Shared resources–such as user lists or message buffers–must be protected using appropriate synchronization techniques.
- **Scalability:** The server architecture should be capable of supporting multiple concurrent users and rooms without performance degradation. This includes efficient handling of WebSocket connections and message routing.
- **Extensibility:** The system should be structured in a modular way, allowing future features, such as authentication, chat history, or file sharing, to be added with minimal rework.
- **Testability:** Key components should be designed with testability in mind, using patterns such as dependency injection and clear separation of concerns to allow for unit and integration testing.
- **Error Handling:** The application should gracefully handle unexpected events, such as dropped connections or malformed messages, without crashing or locking up the user interface.

Meeting these non-functional requirements is just as important as getting the core features right, especially when the goal is to build a system that performs well under real-world conditions.

Constraints

To keep the scope of the project focused and aligned with the learning objectives of this book, several deliberate constraints have been placed on the implementation:

- **No External Frameworks for Real-Time Messaging:** While libraries such as SignalR offer significant productivity gains, this project uses raw **WebSockets** to expose the underlying communication mechanics and give readers a better understanding of how real-time systems operate at a lower level.
- **In-Memory State Only:** The server will maintain active user and room information in memory only–there is no persistence layer for chat history, user authentication, or long-term room storage. This allows us to focus on architectural and performance concerns without the overhead of database integration.

- **Single Server Instance:** The application assumes a single server process, without distributed clustering or load balancing. This simplifies connection and state management while remaining realistic for small to mid-sized deployments.
- **Unsecured Communication:** For simplicity, the chat system does not include authentication, encryption, or transport-layer security (TLS). These would be essential in a production setting but are omitted here to reduce complexity and focus attention on performance fundamentals.
- **Desktop-Only Client:** The client is implemented exclusively using **WPF**. While many chat applications today are web- or mobile-based, focusing on a native desktop UI allows us to explore UI responsiveness, threading, and **MVVM** design patterns in the context of high-performance application design.

These constraints reflect real trade-offs made during the design of any system. By working within them, we focus on the key learning areas: performance, responsiveness, and clarity of architecture, without diluting the educational impact with unrelated complexities.

Structuring the Client

Designing a responsive and maintainable desktop chat client begins with a clear separation of responsibilities, both in terms of code architecture and communication flow. In this application, we use a hybrid communication model: HTTP is used for request/response interactions (such as creating or joining rooms), while WebSockets handle real-time updates and messaging (such as receiving new chat messages or being notified when users enter or leave a room). This approach allows us to simplify the implementation of user-driven actions using familiar, stateless HTTP requests, while leveraging **WebSockets** for low-latency, persistent communication where immediacy is critical. On the client side, this means building two complementary pathways: one for initiating state changes and another for subscribing to updates. The design also emphasizes WPF best practices, such as the MVVM pattern, to ensure a responsive and testable user interface.

WPF and MVVM

Windows Presentation Foundation (WPF) is a well-established UI framework for building rich, responsive desktop applications on Windows. It uses a declarative XML-based language called eXtensible Application Markup Language (XAML) to define the layout and visual elements of the user interface. Visual Studio provides deep, integrated support for **WPF** development, including visual designers, real-time XAML editing with IntelliSense, and robust data binding features. These built-in tools make **WPF** especially productive for developing a desktop UI with minimal setup.

While modern cross-platform frameworks such as .NET MAUI and Uno Platform are available for building UI applications across desktop and mobile operating systems, **WPF** remains a strong choice when targeting Windows-only environments, particularly when time-to-value and tooling support are key concerns. In this example, **WPF** was chosen because the chat client does not require multi-platform support, and Visual Studio's native tooling offers a smooth development experience out of the box.

Though **WPF** supports event-driven programming through tightly coupled event handlers, relying on this approach can quickly lead to brittle code that is difficult to maintain and test. UI behavior—such as updating visual state, managing user input, and interacting with backend systems—benefits greatly from a clean separation of concerns. This is where the **Model-View-ViewModel (MVVM)** pattern excels.

MVVM divides the application into three key components:

- **View**: The user interface, defined in XAML and concerned only with presentation.
- **ViewModel**: A non-UI class that serves as the binding target for the **View**. It encapsulates UI

behavior, commands, and data properties, and acts as a mediator between the **View** and the **Model**.

- **Model**: A set of classes that represent application state and logic, including the code responsible for communication with backend services via HTTP and **WebSockets**.

This pattern improves testability, code organization, and long-term maintainability by keeping UI concerns separate from business logic and data operations. In this chapter, we will consistently apply the **MVVM** pattern to demonstrate how it helps simplify even moderately complex interfaces such as a multi-room chat application.

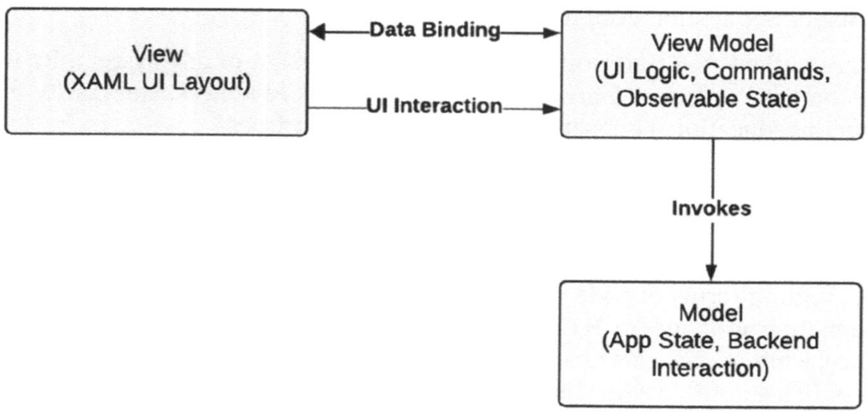

Figure 14.1: *The MVVM Pattern*

Although a full treatment of **WPF** and **MVVM** is beyond the scope of this book, readers will see how these principles are applied in practice to build a responsive and well-structured desktop application.

UI Components

The user interface of the chat application is structured to support multiple chat rooms, real-time messaging, and responsive user interactions. To keep the design focused and maintainable, the UI is composed of modular components that each serve a specific role. These components are implemented using XAML and are bound to corresponding **ViewModel** classes to follow the **MVVM** pattern.

The main UI components include:

- **Main Window**: Acts as the application shell. It hosts the application controls and dynamic content, such as the list of available chat rooms and the currently selected room.
- **Room List Panel**: Displays a list of all chat rooms in which the user is participating. Users can select a room to view or create a new one. This panel also reflects message receipts in unselected rooms in real time.
- **Message Panel**: Shows the message history for the active chat room. It includes a message input field and a send button. Incoming messages are displayed immediately via **WebSocket** updates.
- **User List Panel**: Displays the users currently in the selected chat room. Updates dynamically when users join or leave.
- **Room Management Popups**: Popups for creating rooms, renaming rooms, or managing users (such as inviting or removing participants). Popups are used instead of dialogs for a more modern look and feel.

Each of these components is backed by a `ViewModel` that exposes bindable properties and commands.

For example, the Create Room Popup **ViewModel** contains a **RoomName** property, which is bound to the room name **TextBox** and defines a command called **CreateRoomCommand** that creates the room when the user clicks "Create."

By designing the UI in this modular way, we make the application easier to test, maintain, and extend, whether we are adding user presence indicators, typing notifications, or additional room settings in the future.

ViewModel Behavior

In the **MVVM** pattern, the **ViewModel** serves as the bridge between the user interface and the underlying application logic. It exposes data to the **View** via bindable properties and responds to user actions through commands. In this chat application, **ViewModels** are responsible for managing user input, updating UI-bound data collections, and interacting with the backend services that support messaging and chat room management.

Each major UI component has a corresponding **ViewModel**. These **ViewModels** use observable collections (**ObservableCollection<T>**) and property change notifications (**INotifyPropertyChanged**) to ensure that the user interface automatically reflects changes in state. For example:

- The **ChatRoomsPanelViewModel** maintains a list of available chat rooms and exposes commands to join or create a new room.
- The **MessagesPanelViewModel** tracks the current conversation, including a collection of messages and the input text for new messages. It handles sending messages and updating the conversation when messages are received via WebSocket.
- The **UsersPanelViewModel** monitors the users present in a selected room and updates in real time as users enter or leave.

To manage interactions between **ViewModels** and backend services, the application uses a combination of service classes and dependency injection. For instance, the **IChatRoomApiClient** interface abstracts room management logic, so the **ViewModels** can remain testable and free from direct socket or HTTP logic.

Command objects (usually implemented with **ICommand**) are bound to UI controls such as buttons or menu items. When a user clicks "**Send**" or "**Create Room**," the corresponding command executes the business logic defined in the **ViewModel**, such as validating input, sending a message, or invoking a backend service call.

This separation of logic ensures that the **ViewModels** remain loosely coupled to both the **View** and the data layer, making the application easier to test, debug, and extend. For example, unit tests can validate message handling logic without involving any UI elements or network dependencies.

WebSocket Integration

To support real-time communication between clients and the server, this chat application uses **WebSockets**, a low-latency, full-duplex communication protocol ideal for scenarios like messaging where instantaneous updates are expected. Unlike traditional HTTP, which operates on a request/response cycle, **WebSockets** allow the server to push updates to the client as they occur, such as incoming messages or room participant changes.

In this application, **WebSockets** are primarily used to handle:

- **Broadcasting new messages** to all participants in a chat room.
- **Notifying clients** when users join or leave a room.

- **Reflecting room creation** events across connected clients.

A single **WebSocket** connection is opened when the application starts and remains open for the session duration. The client listens for incoming events using a lightweight message dispatcher that routes messages to the appropriate `ViewModel` handlers. For example, when a new message is received on the socket, the `MessagePanelViewModel` updates its bound message collection accordingly.

To keep things simple and educational, **WebSockets** are used strictly for chat message handling and push-based events. All request/response-style operations–such as creating a room, joining a room, or modifying user participation–are handled via standard HTTP calls to the server's RESTful API. After these operations complete successfully, the server broadcasts changes to affected clients via **WebSockets** to ensure consistent state.

This hybrid approach strikes a balance between modern real-time responsiveness and the maintainability of classic REST patterns. It also helps to clearly demonstrate the distinct roles of request/response and event-driven communication models in a distributed application.

The Server Architecture

A well-structured server architecture is essential to supporting a responsive and scalable chat application. In this chapter, we examine the architectural principles behind the server design, focusing on how different responsibilities, such as user management, message routing, and real-time updates, are cleanly separated and coordinated. Rather than diving into code, this section provides a conceptual overview of how the system is organized, how components interact, and how communication flows through the application.

The server is built on ASP.NET Core and is designed to support a hybrid communication model: HTTP is used for command-oriented interactions such as creating chat rooms or managing participants, while **WebSockets** enable real-time communication between clients. This combination provides clarity, flexibility, and performance, especially in scenarios involving frequent updates and multiple concurrent users.

The following architectural concepts will be explored to illustrate how the server supports real-time chat across multiple rooms while maintaining clean separation of concerns and efficient resource management.

WebSocket Server Overview

The **WebSocket** server in this application is designed with a clear separation of responsibilities: it manages low-level socket connections and provides real-time communication services to the rest of the server, but it does not handle user logic directly. Each **WebSocket** connection is tracked and associated with a user via a unique user ID, while a separate service manages the user lifecycle, including authentication, profiles, and room participation. This separation is intentional and strategic. It allows the connection infrastructure to evolve independently of the user management logic, promoting maintainability, testability, and adherence to the single responsibility principle.

This architecture also provides flexibility for future enhancements. For example, supporting multiple simultaneous connections per user, migrating to distributed connection handling, or swapping out the transport layer entirely could be done without significant changes to the business logic. The **WebSocket** server exposes connection events and messaging interfaces in a clean and focused way, enabling other parts of the application to respond to connection-level changes without being tightly coupled to the transport layer.

Understanding how **WebSockets** work is important context for the implementation discussed later in this chapter. Unlike traditional HTTP, which follows a request/response model, **WebSockets** establish a long-lived, bidirectional communication channel. Once a **WebSocket** handshake is complete, the connection remains open until explicitly closed by the client or server, or until an error or timeout occurs.

To maintain the connection and allow the server to process incoming messages, a receive loop must run continuously for each active connection. This loop reads incoming frames from the client and reacts to control signals like disconnection or ping/pong keep-alive messages. Without this loop, the server cannot receive messages or detect a dropped connection, and the real-time aspect of the chat application breaks down.

Note: *The receive loop is not optional. It is the heart of the real-time communication model. It must be kept running to ensure the connection remains alive and responsive.*

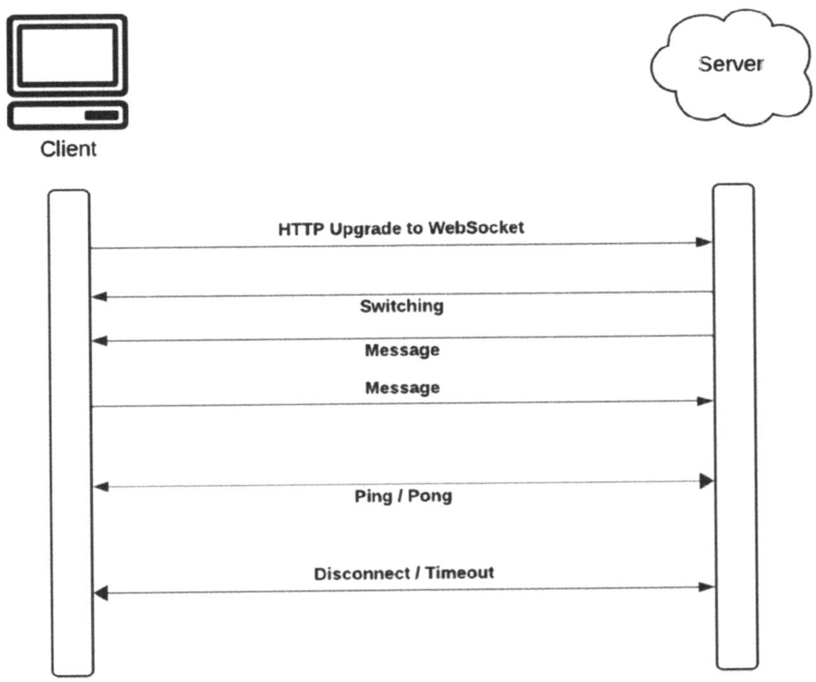

Figure 14.2: *WebSocket Communication Flow*

This persistent, asynchronous communication model enables the chat server to immediately push updates to all connected clients, such as new messages, changes to room membership, or user presence updates. By abstracting the socket-level handling into a dedicated component, the application can scale and adapt without being locked into a specific protocol or tightly coupled implementation.

This design reflects sound architectural thinking, balancing the demands of real-time responsiveness with the need for a clean, modular, and extensible system.

WebSocket Communication Constraints in .NET

While the **WebSocket** protocol is full-duplex and supports simultaneous message flow in both directions, the .NET implementation using **`System.Net.WebSockets.WebSocket`** introduces some practical constraints. Specifically, only one **`SendAsync`** operation can run at a time per connection. Attempting concurrent sends will result in exceptions or undefined behavior. To ensure correctness, send operations must be synchronized using a lock, a semaphore, or a queue with background processing. On the receive side, a dedicated task or loop must continuously run to read incoming messages and maintain the connection. These constraints do not limit the protocol itself but reflect safe usage patterns enforced by the .NET runtime. Understanding and respecting these patterns is essential to building a reliable real-time communication system.

Message Routing

In a real-time chat application, routing messages to the appropriate recipients is essential for responsiveness and correctness. In this implementation, message routing is performed server-side, where it connects user interactions with the appropriate **WebSocket** connections. The routing layer ensures that when a message is sent by a user, it is delivered to all other users in the correct chat room.

In this design, the client application is responsible for tracking the user's current room. Each time a message is sent, the client includes the associated room ID in the message payload. The server uses this room ID, along with the sender's connection and user ID, to determine the appropriate set of recipients.

The server maintains an internal mapping of active **WebSocket** connections, associated users, and their room memberships. When a message arrives, the server looks up the room ID provided by the client and broadcasts the message to all other users currently connected to that room.

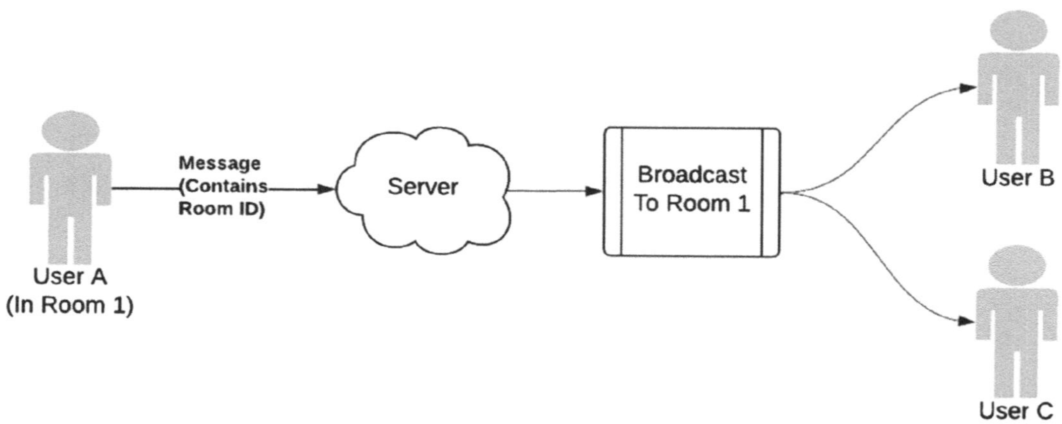

Figure 14.3: *Example Message Routing Flow*

Figure 14.3 shows a simplified routing flow. A message sent by User A from Room 1 is broadcast by the server to all users currently connected to that room (User B and User C). The server relies on the room ID supplied in the message to determine the correct broadcast targets.

This architecture supports scalable and maintainable communication. Future enhancements–such as direct messaging, message archival, or moderated rooms–can be layered onto the existing routing framework without requiring structural redesign.

This implementation deliberately avoids the additional complexity of direct (private) user-to-user messaging. While such functionality could be implemented by extending the routing logic and user directory, the current focus is on room-based messaging to keep the design clear and the implementation accessible.

Real-Time Broadcasting

Once messages are routed to the appropriate recipients, the next architectural responsibility is broadcasting them efficiently over the active **WebSocket** connections. This is a core strength of **WebSockets**: enabling low-latency, real-time updates to multiple clients simultaneously with minimal overhead.

In the context of this chat application, real-time broadcasting is used not only for chat messages but also for notifying clients when users join or leave rooms, and when new rooms are created. This ensures that all connected users receive timely updates and that the UI can react appropriately without requiring explicit polling or refresh actions.

Broadcasting is handled by a dedicated messaging service on the server that receives structured message payloads and dispatches them to the WebSocket connections associated with the relevant users. The service considers the following factors:

- **Room membership**: Messages are only broadcast to users currently joined to the room identified in the message.
- **Connection status**: Only users with active **WebSocket** connections are considered for message delivery.
- **Message type**: Different types of messages—such as chat content, system notices, and user updates—may be handled differently by the client. These distinctions are encoded in the payload structure to enable appropriate handling on the receiving end.

This broadcasting service also acts as a point of abstraction between the message origin and delivery. For instance, even if a message is triggered by an HTTP request (such as a user joining a room), the broadcasting still flows through the same real-time channel used for chat.

Because **WebSockets** are full-duplex, each connection can independently receive messages at any time. However, as noted earlier, care must be taken to serialize message sending and receiving on each connection to avoid conflicts. The server handles outgoing messages in a thread-safe, asynchronous manner to ensure smooth delivery without blocking other operations.

This model keeps the client responsive and synchronized in real time with the server state, while remaining scalable and extensible. Future enhancements such as delivery acknowledgments, private message queues, or message filtering could be added to this layer without impacting the routing or connection logic.

User Lifecycle

Managing a user's lifecycle within the chat application involves coordinating user identity, connection status, and room participation through a cleanly decoupled architecture. This design separates the concerns into three main services: the **WebSocket** service (for maintaining active connections), the User service (for handling user identity and profiles), and the Chat Room service (for tracking room membership and message history).

The typical user lifecycle includes the following stages:

1. **Connection Establishment**: The client initiates a **WebSocket** connection to the server and sends a user identification message. The **WebSocket** service maps this connection to the provided user ID.
2. **User Identification**: The user ID is passed to the User service, which verifies the user and associates it with the active connection.
3. **Room Participation**: Room membership is managed through standard HTTP requests (for example, to join, leave, or create rooms). These are handled by the Chat Room service, which updates its internal tracking and history records accordingly.
4. **Real-Time Notifications**: When users join or leave rooms, the Chat Room service issues notifications to the **WebSocket** service, which pushes real-time updates to affected clients in the room.
5. **Disconnection and Cleanup**: On disconnection, the **WebSocket** service informs both the User and Chat Room services. Any associated state (such as room participation) is cleaned up, and other users are notified of the departure.

6. **Scalability Considerations**: This service-oriented lifecycle allows for future enhancements such as multi-device sessions, offline messaging, and recovery features, while preserving clean separation of responsibilities.

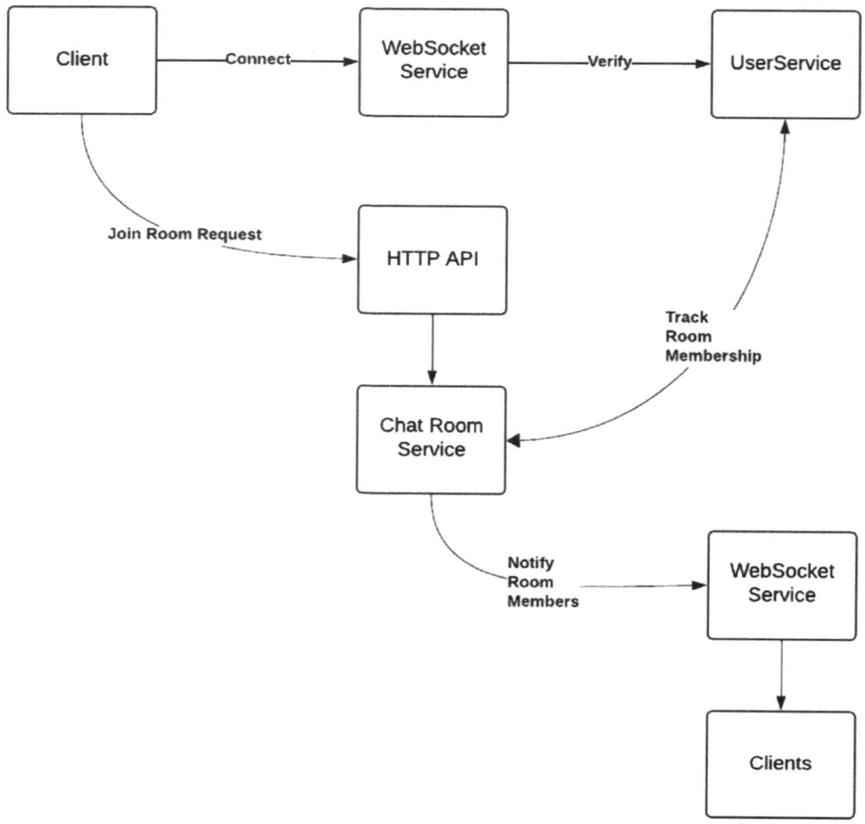

Figure 14.4: *User Lifecycle Flow*

This diagram illustrates the flow from the client's initial connection through registration, room participation, and real-time update delivery. Each service plays a well-defined role, ensuring flexibility, testability, and the potential for future growth.

Room Management

In a multi-room chat application, maintaining a reliable and scalable room system is crucial. In this implementation, room-related concerns are encapsulated in a dedicated Chat Room Service. This design ensures that the logic for room creation, membership tracking, and message history is isolated from other parts of the application, making it easier to evolve, test, and maintain independently.

Each room in the system has a unique identifier, a name, a list of current members (by user ID), and a message history buffer. This buffer allows the application to optionally support limited message persistence or display recent messages when a user joins a room.

Room membership is managed explicitly by the Room Service in response to HTTP requests such as:

- `CreateRoom`: Registers a new room and assigns it a unique ID.
- `JoinRoom`: Adds a user to a room's membership list.
- `LeaveRoom`: Removes a user from a room.

- `GetRoomList`: Returns the list of active rooms for the UI.

Although most room actions are initiated via HTTP, updates that affect real-time state, such as users joining or leaving, trigger broadcast events. These are sent through the **WebSocket** Manager to notify connected clients of the change, ensuring the UI stays in sync across participants.

This decoupled design allows the Room Service to scale independently or incorporate enhancements, such as:

- Access control or roles within rooms (for example, moderators).
- Room-level settings (for example, max user count, visibility).
- Message history persistence with database integration.

The Room Service collaborates closely with the **WebSocket** Manager and User Service, but it does not directly handle connections or user identity. Instead, it receives user IDs and delegates communication back through the **WebSocket** system.

Threading and Async Flow

Handling multiple simultaneous users in a real-time chat application requires a thoughtful approach to concurrency and asynchronous programming. The **WebSocket** server must support many open connections at once, with each connection needing its own logic to receive messages, send messages, and respond to server-initiated broadcasts—all without blocking or slowing down the rest of the system.

This implementation uses `async` and `await` patterns throughout the **WebSocket** handling logic. Each client connection is managed independently via an asynchronous receiver loop. This loop continuously listens for new messages on the socket without blocking the thread, allowing hundreds or thousands of concurrent clients to be handled efficiently.

When a message is received from a client, it is processed asynchronously, routed through services such as the Room Service, and followed by a call to the broadcasting logic, which also operates asynchronously. By relying on asynchronous I/O rather than spawning new threads for each connection, the server avoids excessive resource usage and maintains scalability.

Task-based concurrency ensures the server remains responsive, even under load. Any potentially long-running operations (such as room history updates or message dispatches) are handled without blocking the receiver loop, which is critical because blocking a receiver loop could cause the connection to time out or behave unpredictably.

In this architecture, careful attention is paid to ensure that:

- Shared state (such as user and room data) is accessed through thread-safe services.
- Long-running operations are awaited properly.
- The server never blocks on a single user's slow client or bad connection.

This threading model supports robust, scalable communication without introducing the complexity of low-level thread management. Readers familiar with earlier chapters on `async/await` and concurrent collections will find these concepts put into practice here.

Implementing the Solution

With the architecture laid out in the previous section, we now turn to the implementation details of the chat application. This section walks through the concrete steps taken to build the solution, connecting each architectural component to the code that brings it to life. We will explore how the WPF client interface is wired up to the `ViewModel` layer, how user input is processed and dispatched, and how the server handles messages, connections, and broadcasts using the **WebSocket** and HTTP APIs.

Rather than presenting a full listing of the code, this section focuses on key parts of the implementation that demonstrate how to apply high-performance design principles in a real-world context. Each component—client and server—will be examined with an emphasis on structure, communication patterns, separation of concerns, and responsiveness.

By the end of this section, you should have a solid understanding of how the system works from end to end and be prepared to customize or extend the application for more advanced use cases.

Server Implementation

The server implementation for the chat application is structured around a set of modern design principles aimed at ensuring modularity, testability, and responsiveness. The architecture uses explicit separation of concerns, asynchronous messaging, and in-memory storage to create a lightweight but powerful platform for real-time communication.

At the core of the server's request/response handling is the **Command Query Responsibility Segregation (CQRS)** pattern. **CQRS** is a design approach that separates read operations (queries) from write operations (commands). This separation simplifies the mental model of each operation type and allows them to evolve independently. Queries are focused on returning data, while commands are used to perform actions that change the system state. In this application, **CQRS** also makes it easier to handle message flow asynchronously and cleanly.

To implement **CQRS** and decouple the handling of operations from their invocation, the server uses the open-source MediatR library. MediatR provides a lightweight in-process messaging mechanism that allows commands, queries, and notifications to be dispatched to their appropriate handlers without the sender needing to know who will handle them. This results in a highly maintainable and testable system, where logic is organized by intent and responsibilities are clearly defined.

MediatR is also used for internal event-driven communication. Some commands generate domain events after processing. For example, when a user joins a room, the join command triggers room update events and broadcasts that notify other connected clients of the change. This use of events reflects a broader event-driven architecture approach, making it easier to extend or modify behaviors later (e.g., logging, analytics, or auditing).

Real-time communication with clients is managed by the **`UserSocketService`**, which tracks and coordinates all active **WebSocket** connections. Each **WebSocket** is associated with a user ID and runs a persistent receive loop. Incoming messages are deserialized and passed into the system via MediatR as either events or notifications. Outgoing messages—both individual responses and system-wide broadcasts—are queued using a **`Channel<string>`** to ensure non-blocking, ordered delivery.

User state and room state are maintained in memory using concurrency-safe structures. These are encapsulated in two core services: **`UserStore`** and **`ChatRoomStore`**. These services manage user profiles, room memberships, and chat message histories, respectively. Both use **`ConcurrentDictionary`** to ensure thread safety and enforce identity uniqueness without relying on a database.

This overall approach reflects a modular and scalable design, where subsystems such as connection management, user tracking, and room state are implemented independently. As the application evolves, this makes it easier to add new features such as authentication, message persistence, or private messaging, without disrupting existing functionality.

`SharedContracts` Library

To promote reuse, maintain consistency, and simplify deployment between the server and client components of the application, all shared message types and constants are defined in a dedicated **SharedContracts** library. This library is a .NET class library project that contains strongly typed representations of the messages exchanged between clients and the server, as well as other cross-cutting abstractions and enumerations.

By isolating contracts into their own library, the implementation avoids duplication of serialization structures or reliance on brittle string-based message formats. Instead, both the server and client refer to a single source of truth for message definitions. This makes the system easier to evolve and maintain over time—adding a new message type or extending an existing one becomes a localized, intentional change that benefits from full IDE support, including IntelliSense and compile-time validation.

The **SharedContracts** library contains:

- **Notification Contracts**: Used for broadcast messages sent to clients when events occur (e.g., **UserJoinedChatNotification**, **UserLeftChatNotification**).
- **Event Types**: Used to represent domain-specific events that may trigger other processing or notifications (e.g., **ChatMessageReceivedEvent**).
- **Commands**: Used to represent actions that change the state of the system in some way (e.g. **SendChatMessageCommand**).
- **Enumerations**: Such as message types or room status codes, ensuring that string-based constants are avoided in favor of strongly typed identifiers. The current implementation contains a **MessageType** enumeration.
- **Responses**: **CQRS** query responses with room and message information.

This approach not only improves development productivity but also facilitates versioning and testing. **SharedContracts** can be versioned independently, and test fixtures can use real production types without recreating mocks or stubs unnecessarily.

In summary, the **SharedContracts** library is the glue that ensures the client and server remain in sync, enabling clear, reliable communication between distributed components.

Dependency Injection and Service Registration

In .NET 9 applications, Dependency Injection (DI) is a core feature that facilitates loose coupling, improves testability, and optimizes the management of object lifetimes. This implementation leverages ASP.NET Core's built-in DI container to manage the lifecycle of services and their dependencies, promoting a clean and maintainable architecture.

The main services of the server, such as **UserSocketService**, **UserStore**, and **ChatRoomStore**, are registered in the DI container during application startup. This allows services to declare their dependencies without needing to manually manage object creation or lifecycle. For example, **UserSocketService** depends on **UserStore** for user tracking and **ChatRoomStore** for room membership management. Rather than explicitly creating these dependencies, the DI container is responsible for resolving and injecting them when needed.

In the **Program.cs**, services are registered as follows:

```
var builder = WebApplication.CreateBuilder(args);
// Add services to the container.
builder.Services.AddControllers();
builder.Services.AddHttpContextAccessor();
builder.Services.AddMediatR(config =>
    config.RegisterServicesFromAssemblies(typeof(Program).Assembly,
    typeof(SendChatMessageCommand).Assembly));
```

```
builder.Logging.ClearProviders();
builder.Logging.AddDebug();
builder.Logging.AddConsole();
builder.Logging.AddConfiguration(builder.Configuration.GetSection("Logging"));

//Services that store state are registered as singletons
builder.Services.AddSingleton<IUserSocketService, UserSocketService>();
builder.Services.AddSingleton<IUserStore, UserStore>();
builder.Services.AddSingleton<IChatRoomStore, ChatRoomStore>();

//Services that do not store state are registered as transient
builder.Services.AddTransient<IBroadcastService, BroadcastService>();

var app = builder.Build();
```

`AddSingleton` ensures that each service is instantiated once and shared across the application, which is ideal for stateful services such as **`UserStore`** and **`ChatRoomStore`** that persist data across requests.

`AddMediatR` integrates MediatR with the DI container, enabling the dispatching of commands, queries, and notifications across the application.

`AddTransient` instantiates services on demand, which is ideal for services such as **`BroadcastService`**, which does not maintain state and can be instantiated as needed.

Dependency injection provides several benefits to applications, such as:

- **Testability**: By using DI, services can easily be unit tested by injecting mock implementations of their dependencies, making the testing process straightforward.
- **Separation of Concerns**: Services are decoupled from their dependencies, allowing them to focus on their specific logic without worrying about how dependencies are instantiated.
- **Scalability**: Adding new services (such as a persistence layer or logging service) to the application is simple. New dependencies can be registered with minimal changes elsewhere in the application.
- **Centralized Configuration**: The DI container provides a centralized location for configuring and managing the lifetime of services, which makes it easy to adjust the behavior of services globally (e.g., switching from an in-memory store to a database-backed implementation).

By utilizing ASP.NET Core's DI container in .NET 9, the server maintains clean boundaries between components, allowing the system to grow and evolve without unnecessary complexity.

Command and Query Handling with MediatR

In this implementation, we follow **Command Query Responsibility Segregation (CQRS)** to separate the responsibilities of reading data (queries) from writing data (commands). This architecture improves scalability and maintainability by allowing these two types of operations to evolve independently.

We use MediatR, a lightweight library, to implement this pattern. MediatR acts as the dispatcher, routing commands, queries, and notifications to their respective handlers. This decouples the sender and receiver, making the system more modular and easier to maintain.

- **Commands**: These are requests to modify the system state, such as sending a chat message or updating user status.
- **Queries**: These are requests to retrieve data without causing side effects, such as fetching the list of users in a chat room.

- **Events**: These are used to broadcast events to multiple listeners, such as notifying users of a new message in a room.

Using **CQRS** with MediatR allows us to implement clear boundaries between different operations, reducing complexity and improving code maintainability. Commands and queries are handled by separate handlers, while events are broadcast to all interested listeners, ensuring that the system is both efficient and scalable.

A typical processing flow is shown in the following diagram:

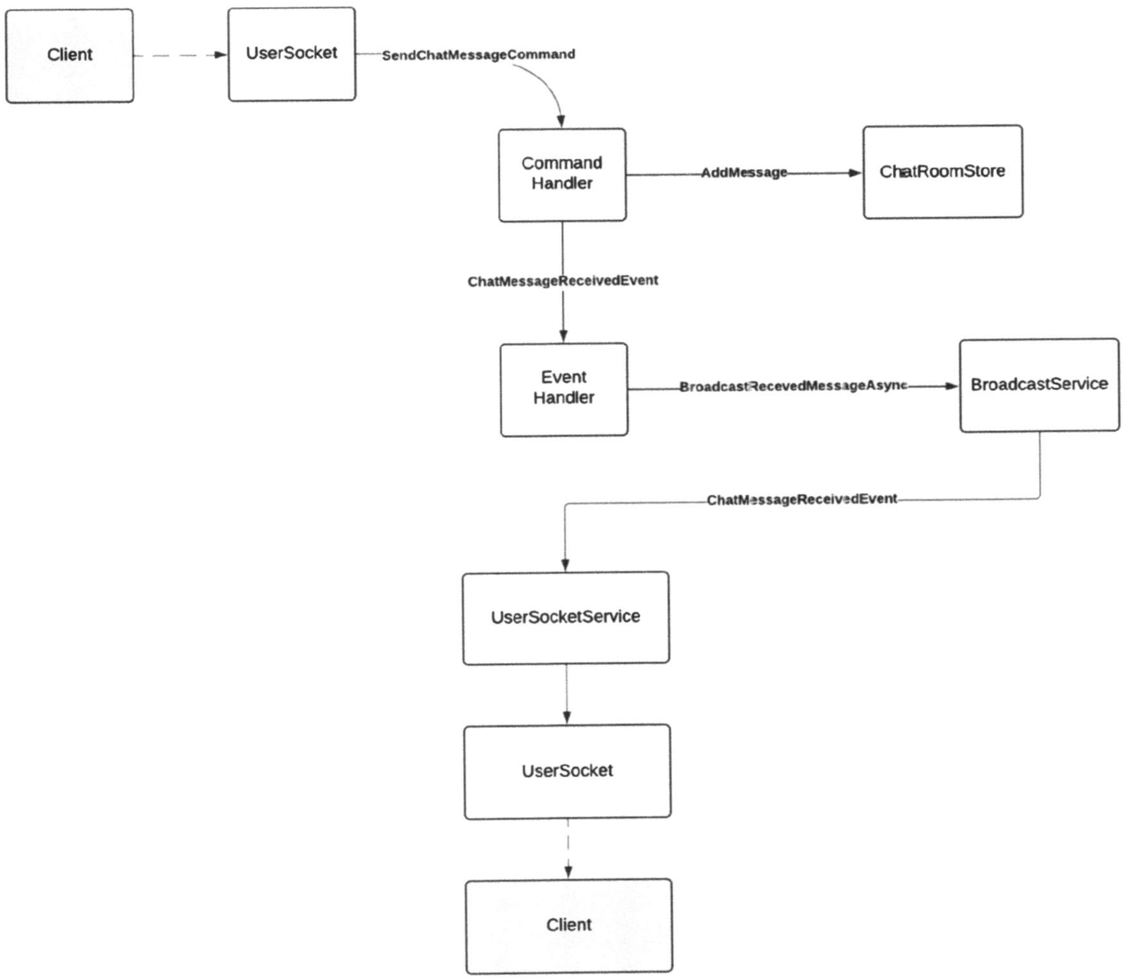

***Figure 14.5**: Processing Flow for SendChatMessageCommand*

New chat messages are sent from the client to the server over the **WebSocket** connection in the form of a **`SendChatMessageCommand`**. The **`UserSocket`** receives the command and forwards it to MediatR for processing. MediatR locates the registered **`SendChatMessageCommandHandler`** and dispatches the command to it.

The command handler uses the **`ChatRoomStore`** to persist the message in the appropriate room, identified by the **`RoomId`** property in the command. After storing the message, the handler raises a **`ChatMessageReceivedEvent`** via MediatR to indicate that a new message has been successfully handled.

MediatR then dispatches the event to all registered event handlers for **ChatMessageReceivedEvent**. One such handler uses the **BroadcastService** to distribute the message to all users in the corresponding chat room.

The **BroadcastService** interacts with the **UserSocketService**, which maintains the list of active **WebSocket** connections. For each user in the room, the service enqueues the **ChatMessageReceivedEvent** onto that user's outbound channel.

Each **UserSocket** runs a background loop that dequeues messages from this channel and transmits them over the **WebSocket** connection back to the respective clients.

This loosely coupled design, enabled by **CQRS**, provides several important benefits. By decoupling senders from receivers, **CQRS** allows each component, such as the **WebSocket** layer, command handlers, event handlers, and broadcasting logic, to evolve independently. This makes the system more maintainable and extensible, as changes to one part of the processing flow (for example, how messages are stored or broadcast) do not require modifications to other parts. Additionally, new behaviors can be added, such as logging, auditing, or analytics, by simply registering additional handlers for existing commands or events. This level of flexibility and modularity is especially valuable in real-time systems, where responsiveness and scalability are critical.

Threading Considerations with WebSockets

WebSocket communication introduces specific threading concerns, particularly in a concurrent, event-driven architecture. Each active **WebSocket** connection is encapsulated in a **UserSocket** instance, which is responsible for managing both incoming and outgoing communication in a thread-safe, asynchronous manner.

The receive loop is an essential part of the **UserSocket** and must remain active to keep the **WebSocket** connection alive. It listens for new messages from the connected client and immediately deserializes and dispatches them using MediatR. Since this loop operates asynchronously, it avoids blocking the calling thread and allows the server to efficiently handle multiple concurrent connections.

```
public async Task ReadMessagesAsync()
{
    var buffer = new byte[1024 * 4];
    WebSocketReceiveResult result;
    while (webSocket.State == WebSocketState.Open)
    {
        try
        {
            result = await webSocket.ReceiveAsync(new ArraySegment<byte>
(buffer), readerCts.Token);
            await ProcessReceivedMessageAsync(buffer, result);
        }
        catch (OperationCanceledException)
        {
            logger.LogDebug("Socket canceled: {message}", "Operation
canceled");
            await CloseSocketConnectionAsync();
        }
        catch (WebSocketException ex)
        {
            if (ex.WebSocketErrorCode == WebSocketError.ConnectionClosed
Prematurely)
            {
```

```
                logger.LogWarning("WebSocket connection closed prematurely:
{message}", ex.Message);
                await CloseSocketConnectionAsync();
            }
            else
            {
                logger.LogError(ex, "An error occurred while processing
messages: {message}", ex.Message);
                await CloseSocketConnectionAsync();
            }
        }
    }
}
```

To handle outgoing messages, each **UserSocket** maintains a **Channel<string>**, which acts as a queue for outbound communication such as broadcasts and system notifications. A separate asynchronous write loop reads from this queue and sends messages to the client, ensuring that only one write operation occurs at a time, which is critical for maintaining the integrity of the **WebSocket** stream, which does not support concurrent writes.

```
private async Task SendMessagesAsync(CancellationToken cancellationToken)
{
    await foreach (var message in channel.Reader.ReadAllAsync(cancellation
Token))
    {
        logger.LogDebug("Sending message: {message}", message);
        var buffer = Encoding.UTF8.GetBytes(message);
        if (webSocket.State == WebSocketState.Open)
        {
            await webSocket.SendAsync(new ArraySegment<byte>(buffer),
                WebSocketMessageType.Text,
                true,
                cancellationToken);
        }
    }
}
```

This separation of concerns—isolated read and write loops—provides a natural concurrency boundary that avoids race conditions without requiring explicit locks. As messages are received and processed, commands are sent to MediatR, and responses or broadcast events are queued via the write loop. Shared services such as **UserSocketService** and **ChatRoomStore** use thread-safe data structures (**ConcurrentDictionary**, and so on) to safely track active sockets and manage shared application state.

By adopting this pattern, the implementation ensures that:

- Each socket operates independently and safely.
- The system scales effectively with increasing connection counts.
- Core **CQRS** principles remain unimpeded by transport-layer concurrency issues.

Client Implementation

In this section, we turn our attention to the implementation details of the chat application's client. Built using **WPF** on .NET 9, the client is responsible for rendering the user interface, maintaining a live connection to the server via **WebSockets**, and coordinating the exchange of messages between the user and the server.

The client acts as a thin, responsive front end that sends commands such as chat messages and listens for events such as message broadcasts. It relies on shared message contracts (defined in the **SharedContracts** library) to maintain consistent communication with the server, ensuring that both systems interpret messages the same way.

The architecture of the client is deliberately layered. The UI components (**Views**) bind to **`ViewModels`** that encapsulate interaction logic. These **`ViewModels`** interact with a **WebSocket** client component that handles message transmission and reception. This separation of concerns allows for easy maintenance, testing, and future evolution of the user interface or transport layer.

Connection Lifecycle and Initialization

The **WebSocket** connection is established after the user has identified themselves through the login popup. When the application launches, the user is prompted to enter a username. Once the username is provided, the client proceeds to initialize the **WebSocket** connection, associating that connection with the supplied user identity.

In this implementation, the **`WebSocketClient`** is instantiated via dependency injection (DI) and injected where needed within the application. The DI container, which is maintained in **`App.xaml.cs`**, ensures that the **`WebSocketClient`** is properly managed throughout the application's lifecycle. After the user provides their username, the **`WebSocketClient`** is used to establish the connection with the server.

The **`ChatRoomManagerModel`** interacts with the injected **`WebSocketClient`** to manage the **WebSocket** connection lifecycle. Once the connection is initialized, a receive loop is started on a background task to continuously listen for incoming messages. This loop must remain active to maintain the connection and ensure proper message delivery.

If the connection is lost due to network disruptions or server-side restarts, the client will inform the user of the disconnection error.

A simplified flow of the connection lifecycle is as follows:

1. The **`MainWindow`** view prompts the user for their username. The **`MainWindowViewModel`** receives the input and proceeds with the login sequence.
2. The **`MainWindowViewModel`** calls the **`ChatRoomManagerModel`**, which calls **`ChatRoomApiClient.LoginUserAsync`** to register or re-establish the user ID with the server. Users can reconnect using the same username after disconnection.
3. The **`ChatRoomManagerModel`** calls **`WebSocketsClient.ConnectAsync`** using the user ID obtained from the server to initiate a **WebSocket** connection.
4. **`WebSocketsClient.ConnectAsync`** establishes the connection to the server and starts the receive loop by invoking **`ReceiveMessagesAsync`**. This background task is stored in the **`receiveTask`** field.
5. Messages received from the server are deserialized and published through the **`Messenger`** class to notify relevant **`ViewModels`** or services.
6. When the application exits, the **`MainWindowViewModel`** calls the **`ChatRoomManagerModel`**, which calls **`WebSocketsClient.DisconnectAsync`**, which stops the receive loop and closes the **WebSocket** connection.

Messages received from the server are deserialized into strongly-typed events (defined in the **`SharedContracts`** library) and dispatched to the appropriate **`ViewModel`** or client-side service. This design cleanly separates connection management from message handling, keeping the architecture modular and easy to maintain.

Sending Commands to the Server

In this implementation, commands are sent to the server using two transport mechanisms: **WebSocket** for real-time operations and HTTP for more conventional request/response actions. Both types of commands are strongly typed and defined in the SharedContracts library to maintain consistency between client and server.

Real-time commands, such as **`SendChatMessageCommand`**, are sent over the WebSocket connection using **`WebSocketsClient`**. When the user submits a new chat message, the **`MessagePanelViewModel`** calls **`ChatRoomManagerModel.AddMessageAsync`**, which constructs a **`SendChatMessageCommand`** and passes it to **`WebSocketsClient.SendCommandAsync`**. This method serializes the command into JSON and writes it to the open **WebSocket** connection. Since multiple parts of the client may attempt to send concurrently, the client serializes access to the connection to avoid message collisions or partial writes. A **`Channel<string>`** instance is used to ensure serial processing, just as the server implementation uses.

Other commands, such as logging in or joining a room, are sent via HTTP using the **`ChatRoomApiClient`**, which wraps standard **`HttpClient`** calls. For example, the login process uses **`LoginUserAsync`** to create or restore a user session with the server, while room listing or user listing commands also follow a traditional REST pattern.

This hybrid approach leverages the strengths of each protocol: HTTP is used for reliable, discrete operations with well-defined responses, while **WebSocket** supports low-latency, bidirectional communication for ongoing chat activity. Internally, the server routes each command according to its type and handles them using MediatR and the **CQRS** pattern.

This separation allows for a clean division of responsibilities on the client and provides flexibility for scaling or evolving the server-side infrastructure over time.

Receiving and Handling Events

Once the **WebSocket** connection is established, the client enters a continuous receive loop that listens for incoming messages from the server. These messages represent events such as new chat messages, user join or leave notifications, and other broadcasted updates defined in the **`SharedContracts`** library.

The receive loop is implemented in the **`ReceiveMessagesAsync`** method of the **`WebSocketsClient`** class. Each message received is deserialized from JSON into a strongly-typed object and dispatched to the rest of the application using the **`Messenger`** class, which supports loose coupling between components.

This design allows different parts of the client, such as the message panel, user list, or room display, to subscribe only to the message types they are interested in. For example, when a **`ChatMessageReceivedEvent`** is received, the message panel can update its display, while the user panel can ignore it.

To ensure responsiveness and thread safety, the **`Messenger`** raises notifications on the UI thread when needed, allowing **ViewModels** to safely update bound properties and collections.

This event-driven, publish-subscribe mechanism enables a clean and scalable way to react to incoming data, and makes the system easier to extend with new event types in the future.

`ViewModel` and UI Integration

The client follows the **Model-View-ViewModel (MVVM)** pattern to maintain a clean separation between UI and application logic. **`ViewModels`** serve as intermediaries between the views (UI) and underlying services, including the **WebSocketsClient**, **ChatRoomApiClient**, and the **Messenger**-based event system.

All **ViewModels** are instantiated via dependency injection and receive their dependencies, including services, through their constructors. This approach ensures modularity and simplifies unit testing.

Key **ViewModels** include:

- **MainWindowViewModel**: Coordinates application-level behavior, such as login and logout, initializing the WebSocket connection, and managing navigation between views.
- **ChatRoomsPanelViewModel**: Handles the list of available chat rooms, receives updates when users join or leave, and supports room switching.
- **MessagePanelViewModel**: Manages the display of incoming messages and the composition and sending of new messages.
- **UsersPanelViewModel**: Displays the list of active users and responds to events that update user presence.

Each **ViewModel** subscribes to relevant events using the **Messenger** system. For instance, **MessagePanelViewModel** listens for **ChatMessageReceivedEvent** messages, while **UsersPanelViewModel** handles **UserJoinedChatNotification** or **UserLeftChatNotification**. When an event is published, the **Messenger** ensures it reaches all subscribed **ViewModels**, enabling them to update their state and, by extension, the UI.

The integration with the WPF UI is done through data binding and observable properties. Each **ViewModel** exposes bindable collections and commands that respond to user input, making the UI reactive and consistent with the application state.

This layered structure reinforces loose coupling and testability, and allows developers to extend or modify individual UI components without disrupting the entire client.

SharedContracts and Serialization

To ensure consistency and type safety between the client and server, this implementation uses a shared library named **SharedContracts**. This library defines the core communication contracts used across both layers, including:

- Command and event message types, such as **SendChatMessageCommand** and **ChatMessageReceivedEvent.**
- Data models for users, messages, and chat rooms.

All messages sent over the WebSocket connection inherit from a common abstract base class, **MessageBase**, which is annotated with the **JsonPolymorphic** attribute from the **System.Text.Json** namespace. This enables polymorphic serialization and deserialization without requiring custom converters or manual envelope handling.

```
[JsonPolymorphic]
[JsonDerivedType(typeof(SendChatMessageCommand), (int)MessageType.SendChat
MessageCommand)]
[JsonDerivedType(typeof(ChatMessageReceivedEvent), (int)MessageType.Chat
MessageReceivedEvent)]
[JsonDerivedType(typeof(UserJoinedChatNotification), (int)MessageType.User-
JoinedChatNotification)]
[JsonDerivedType(typeof(UserLeftChatNotification), (int)MessageType.UserLeft-
ChatNotification)]
public class MessageBase
{
}
```

Each message type derives from **`MessageBase`** and is tagged with a unique discriminator value using the **`JsonDerivedType`** attribute. When a message is serialized, the **`$type`** discriminator is automatically embedded in the JSON. During deserialization, **`System.Text.Json`** uses this discriminator to instantiate the correct concrete type.

This design provides several key advantages:

- **Extensibility**: Adding new message types only requires defining a new subclass and updating the discriminator list in **`MessageBase`**.
- **Consistency**: Both client and server rely on the same polymorphic structure, eliminating mismatches and simplifying versioning.
- **Simplicity**: The need for wrapper envelopes or manual type resolution is removed, reducing boilerplate and potential sources of error.
- **Strong Typing**: Messages are deserialized into their appropriate .NET types, allowing handlers to work with clear, strongly-typed objects.

Serialization and deserialization are handled entirely by the built-in **`System.Text.Json`** mechanisms, which ensure high performance and broad compatibility across platforms.

This approach contributes to a clean and modular architecture, with a clear separation between the transport layer and the message processing logic, while maintaining type safety and flexibility.

Lessons Learned

Building the chat application provided valuable insights into the practical realities of developing real-time, event-driven software using modern .NET technologies. While the focus was on creating a clear and educational reference implementation, the process revealed common challenges, design trade-offs, and areas where additional work would be needed for a production-ready system. In this section, we briefly summarize some of the real-world considerations encountered during development, with notes on performance, scalability, and future improvements.

Real-World Challenges

While this application is designed for instructional purposes, its development surfaced several challenges that are common in production environments and offered valuable lessons in how to address them effectively.

One key challenge was managing asynchronous message handling over WebSockets without introducing thread contention or resource leaks. To address this, the application isolates WebSocket communication within a dedicated **`WebSocketsClient`** class that manages the receive loop on a background thread using **`async/await`**. This approach ensures that message processing remains responsive and non-blocking, while also simplifying error handling and shutdown procedures.

Maintaining type-safe communication between client and server was another important concern. The use of a shared **`SharedContracts`** library provided a single source of truth for all command and event types, helping prevent mismatches and versioning issues. Rather than implementing a custom message envelope system, the solution leverages NET's **`System.Text.Json`** with the **`JsonPolymorphic`** attribute and a **`MessageBase`** class. This built-in polymorphic deserialization mechanism streamlines message parsing while preserving strong typing, reducing boilerplate and improving maintainability.

Incorporating the **CQRS** pattern introduced additional complexity around how and where to process different responsibilities. The implementation addressed this by clearly separating command sending (for user actions) from event handling (for server updates), and by centralizing routing logic on the client through the **`Messenger`** system. This kept the **ViewModels** focused on their primary roles and made it easier to test and extend specific behaviors independently.

Finally, dependency injection in a **WPF** context required care to maintain clean separation of concerns and consistent component lifetimes. By configuring the DI container in App.xaml.cs and injecting dependencies into the **`ViewModels`**, the application avoids service locator patterns and ensures testability and composability of services such as **`WebSocketsClient`**, **`ChatRoomApiClient`**, and **`Messenger`**.

These solutions reflect practical patterns for building real-time, message-driven applications and demonstrate how architectural discipline can mitigate complexity even in small-scale projects.

Performance Considerations

Although the application is relatively lightweight, designing with performance in mind helped ensure that the architecture would scale gracefully under more demanding conditions. Several key decisions contributed to this goal.

First, asynchronous programming was used consistently to prevent UI thread blocking and to improve responsiveness. All network operations—including WebSocket message handling and HTTP API calls—are performed using **`async/await`**, which allows the application to remain responsive even when waiting on I/O-bound operations. Specifically, the receive loops in both the **`WebSocketsClient`** on the client side and the **`UserSocket`** on the server side are handled asynchronously. By leveraging **`async/await`**, these receive loops do not require dedicated background threads, reducing thread contention and optimizing resource usage while ensuring continuous message processing without blocking the main execution flow.

Second, message dispatching via the **`Messenger`** pattern decouples message receipt from message handling on the client. This reduces contention and allows each component (such as **ViewModels**) to react only to the messages it cares about. This separation avoids bottlenecks and enables future optimizations, such as message filtering or prioritization if needed.

Another key performance improvement is the use of message queuing with **`Channel<T>`** for message serialization. Both the **`WebSocketsClient`** and **`UserSocket`** utilize **`Channel<T>`** to queue outgoing messages, ensuring they are sent in an orderly manner. This queuing mechanism serves two purposes: it protects against potential race conditions when sending messages and enhances performance by managing asynchronous message dispatch. By offloading the task of queuing and serializing messages into a channel, the system can efficiently handle multiple messages without overwhelming the socket connection or introducing delays due to simultaneous send operations.

The use of strongly typed, shared contracts across client and server reduces runtime overhead related to dynamic type handling or complex reflection. With **`System.Text.Json`**'s **`JsonPolymorphic`** support and a well-defined **`MessageBase`** hierarchy, messages can be deserialized efficiently with minimal ambiguity or overhead. This reduces latency in message processing and simplifies the serialization code path.

Finally, unnecessary allocations and UI updates are minimized by ensuring **ViewModels** update only in response to relevant events. For example, chat room and user lists are only refreshed when the server sends updated state, avoiding excessive UI refreshes and preserving application responsiveness under load.

While the current implementation is not benchmarked for high-throughput environments, these foundational choices align with practices used in production-grade applications and provide a clear path to further optimization if needed.

Additions for Production

As the application is prepared for production, several key enhancements should be considered to ensure reliability, scalability, and ease of maintenance.

- **Error Handling and Logging**: Robust error handling and logging mechanisms should be introduced to capture exceptions and provide meaningful feedback for debugging and maintenance. This includes using libraries such as Serilog or NLog for logging, along with structured logging to capture error details and operational metrics. Proper error handling would also ensure that the application can gracefully handle unexpected failures, such as network interruptions or server-side issues, without crashing or losing state.
- **Resilience and Retry Logic**: While the client can handle WebSocket disconnections and server failures, in production, a more sophisticated resilience strategy would be needed. This could include automatic reconnection mechanisms, exponential backoff for retries, and the ability to failover to alternate servers or endpoints. Tools such as Polly could be integrated for this purpose to provide a more fault-tolerant system. SignalR offers built-in automatic reconnection features, making it a more production-ready solution in this regard.
- **Authentication and Authorization**: The current application assumes that a user is identified via the login screen, but production applications must securely manage user authentication and authorization. Implementing industry-standard protocols such as OAuth2, OpenID Connect, or JWT-based authentication would be essential to secure the communication channels and ensure that only authenticated and authorized users can access the system.
- **SignalR for Scalable WebSocket Connections**: While **WebSockets** were chosen for educational purposes to illustrate low-level communication, SignalR would be the ideal choice in production environments. SignalR abstracts the complexities of managing **WebSocket** connections and provides automatic fallback mechanisms for environments that don't support **WebSockets**. It handles connection management, reconnection, scaling, and more, making it an optimal solution for production chat applications.
- SignalR's backplane support allows for scaling across multiple servers while maintaining consistent user connections, an essential feature for handling high traffic. Furthermore, SignalR simplifies the process of broadcasting messages to connected clients, reducing the need for manual message queuing and delivery logic that was implemented with **WebSockets** in this educational version.
- **Scaling and Load Balancing**: With SignalR, scaling becomes easier as it offers built-in mechanisms for scaling out **WebSocket** connections across multiple servers. Using Azure SignalR Service or other cloud-based SignalR backplanes can automatically handle connection distribution and load balancing. This is essential for production systems that need to support a high number of concurrent users, ensuring that the application can scale horizontally without requiring manual intervention.
- **Performance Optimization**: In addition to the improvements already implemented, further performance optimization might be necessary for production environments. This could involve implementing message batching or prioritizing high-priority messages to reduce latency in high-traffic scenarios. Monitoring and profiling tools such as Application Insights or New Relic could provide ongoing performance metrics to track and optimize resource utilization.
- **Security Considerations**: Ensuring that the communication is secure is critical in production. With SignalR, secure communication via WebSocket Secure (WSS) can be configured out of the box. Additionally, securing API endpoints with SSL/TLS encryption and implementing proper authorization for sensitive actions would be necessary to protect user data and system integrity.

- **Continuous Integration/Continuous Deployment (CI/CD)**: Implementing a CI/CD pipeline would enable automatic testing, building, and deployment, ensuring that changes to the application can be rolled out quickly and safely. This includes setting up automated unit and integration tests, containerizing the application (using Docker), and deploying to cloud environments such as Azure or AWS for seamless updates.
- **Monitoring and Metrics**: To ensure the health of the application in a production environment, integrating real-time monitoring (for example, Prometheus, Grafana) and metrics collection will help proactively detect and address issues before they impact end users. This also allows for performance benchmarking and helps to fine-tune the application's scaling capabilities.
- **Automated Testing and Test Coverage**: Although not included in this educational implementation, comprehensive automated testing is essential in a production system. This includes unit tests to validate core logic, integration tests to verify interactions between components, and end-to-end tests to simulate user workflows. Implementing tests early and integrating them into a CI/CD pipeline ensures code reliability, helps catch regressions before deployment, and improves maintainability over time. Frameworks such as xUnit, NUnit, or MSTest, along with tools such as Moq for mocking and Playwright for UI testing, can be used to build a robust test suite.

In summary, while the current implementation serves as a solid educational foundation for understanding the basics of **WebSocket** communication, transitioning to SignalR in production would offer significant advantages in terms of scalability, ease of use, and resilience. SignalR's built-in support for connection management, message broadcasting, and seamless scaling across multiple servers makes it the ideal solution for production-ready applications. Additionally, the current implementation lacks persistence, which is a key consideration for any production system—messages and user states should ideally be stored in a persistent store for recovery after server restarts or crashes. Incorporating robust error handling, security measures, performance optimizations, and persistence would ensure that the application can handle real-world traffic and provide a reliable, secure, and user-friendly experience. With these enhancements, the application would be well-equipped to meet the demands of a production environment while maintaining a smooth and efficient user experience.

Conclusion

In this chapter, we explored the design and implementation of a real-time chat application using **WebSockets** for communication between the client and server. The application highlights key concepts such as **CQRS**, event-based architectures, and the use of dependency injection to manage service lifecycles. We also examined how to structure the system with scalability, modularity, and flexibility in mind, while considering performance optimizations and thread safety. Although the application currently serves as an educational example, it provides valuable insights into building real-time, interactive systems. We also discussed how this approach can be enhanced with production-ready tools such as SignalR, persistence mechanisms, and additional performance considerations. This chapter serves as a foundation for understanding how to build robust, high-performance real-time applications while emphasizing best practices for maintainability and extensibility.

As we wrap up this book, the final chapter will reflect on the journey we have taken through the concepts, design principles, and practical techniques for building high-performance applications in C#. We will revisit the key takeaways, discuss how to apply these lessons in real-world scenarios, and explore how the evolving landscape of .NET can continue to shape the future of software development. Whether you are just starting or refining your skills, this concluding chapter will help solidify your understanding and inspire you to continue building powerful, efficient applications.

Points to Remember

- The sample chat application demonstrates real-time communication using **WebSockets** to expose low-level architectural concerns for educational purposes.
- Async/await is used throughout the client and server to handle I/O efficiently without blocking threads.
- Message sending is serialized and queued using **`Channel<T>`** to ensure order and protect against concurrency issues.
- The architecture prioritizes clarity, extensibility, and maintainability, making it ideal for educational exploration.
- Several improvements would be necessary for production readiness, including robust error handling, security, authentication, scalability with SignalR, and a complete testing strategy.

Multiple Choice Questions

1. Which technology was suggested as more appropriate for production use in place of raw **WebSockets**?
   a. gRPC
   b. SignalR
   c. HTTP/2 long polling
   d. Azure Functions
2. Which of the following is not currently implemented in the sample application?
   a. Real-time chat message delivery.
   b. User authentication and authorization.
   c. JSON-based polymorphic message serialization.
   d. Async/await-based message receiving.
3. What was the primary reason **WebSockets** were chosen for this sample chat application?
   a. **WebSockets** offer better security than other protocols.
   b. **WebSockets** are the industry standard for all production chat systems.
   c. **WebSockets** expose low-level communication concerns useful for learning purposes.
   d. **WebSockets** require less code than SignalR.
4. What is the main benefit of using **`async/await`** in the receive loops of both client and server?
   a. It increases the CPU usage for better performance.
   b. It simplifies the use of multithreading primitives like **`lock.`**
   c. It avoids dedicating background threads while keeping the loops responsive.
   d. It allows blocking socket operations to complete more quickly.

Answers

1. b
2. b
3. c
4. c

Questions

1. The client uses `Channel<T>` to queue messages for transmission. What would happen if the message volume spiked dramatically, and how might you adapt the implementation to handle backpressure or throttling?
2. The current implementation does not include a way for users to join chat rooms on their own (they must be invited by other users). What changes need to be made to add this feature?
3. The current server implementation keeps all chat state in memory. What strategies would you use to persist chat messages and user presence in a production environment without compromising performance?
4. Imagine integrating AI moderation to flag inappropriate messages. Where would you inject that logic in the current system, and what trade-offs would you need to consider?

Key Terms

- **WebSockets**: A full-duplex communication protocol over a single TCP connection, used here for real-time messaging between client and server.
- **Windows Presentation Foundation (WPF)**: A UI framework for building rich, responsive user experiences on Windows.
- **Model-View-ViewModel (MVVM)**: A pattern for building user interface code in a modular and testable way.
- **View:** In **MVVM**, the layer responsible for UI layout and presentation.
- **ViewModel:** In **MVVM**, the layer responsible for handling **View** behavior and acting as a mediator between the **View** and the **Model**.
- **Model:** The **MVVM** layer responsible for keeping application state and implementing business logic.
- **Command-Query Responsibility Segregation (CQRS)**: A design approach that separates read operations from write operations.

CHAPTER 15
Conclusion

Introduction

As we reach the final chapter of this journey into building high-performance applications in .NET, it is worth stepping back to reflect on how far we have come. From foundational threading concepts to sophisticated asynchronous patterns and parallel execution strategies, this book has focused on equipping you with the practical tools needed to write scalable, responsive, and efficient code. In this chapter, we will briefly recap the major topics we've covered, highlight key best practices, share real-world insights from the field, and suggest next steps for continuing your growth as a performance-minded developer.

Structure

This chapter will cover the following points:

- Recap of Topics Covered
    - Designing for Performance in .NET
    - Threading in .NET
    - Synchronization Primitives
    - Task-Based Programming
    - Parallel Programming Models
    - Asynchronous Programming
    - Concurrent Collections
    - Profiling
- Summary of Best Practices
    - Start with Measurement
    - Be **Intentional** About Concurrency
    - Reduce **Contention**
    - Make Performance a Habit
    - Use the Right Tools
- Real World Case Studies
    - Case 1: Scaling Text File Processing
    - Case 2: Modernizing Reporting
- Next Steps for the Reader
    - Start Small
    - Practice Continuously
    - Explore Advanced Concepts

- Final Thoughts
    - Performance Engineer Mindset
    - You Now Have the Tools
    - **Practicality Over Perfection**

Recap of Topics Covered

As we begin this final chapter, it is worth pausing to look back at the ground we've covered. This book has taken you through the essential techniques and tools for writing high-performance .NET applications, with a strong focus on parallelism and asynchronous programming. Section by section, we have explored how to effectively manage concurrency, leverage the `async` and `await` model, and use synchronization primitives and concurrent collections to build scalable systems. In this recap, we will summarize the key concepts you have learned, reinforcing how they work together to support robust, responsive, and modern software development.

Designing for Performance in .NET

Every performance-oriented application starts with thoughtful design. Throughout this book, we've emphasized that performance is not something to bolt on after the fact–it is a mindset that must be integrated from the beginning. In the .NET ecosystem, designing for performance means understanding how your application will execute under load, how it scales, and how it responds to increasing concurrency demands.

A performance-first design considers both the architecture and execution model. Do you need responsiveness on the UI thread? Should back-end services process data in parallel? Will asynchronous operations reduce blocking and improve throughput? These questions guide how you structure components, select abstractions, and plan your threading model.

By grounding our discussion in real-world use cases–such as data processing pipelines, high-throughput services, and responsive applications–we have seen how .NET provides powerful primitives including `Task`, `Parallel`, and `async/await` to help you achieve performance goals without sacrificing clarity or maintainability.

Threading in .NET

Our journey into concurrency began with the fundamentals: the Thread class. Working at this low level gave us a clear view of what is involved in manually creating, starting, and managing threads. It also highlighted the limitations–threads are expensive to create, difficult to scale, and prone to errors such as race conditions and deadlocks when not handled carefully.

To address these challenges, .NET offers more sophisticated tools built on top of its thread pool, which efficiently manages a pool of reusable threads behind the scenes. From there, we explored `Task` and the Task Parallel Library (TPL), which simplify concurrent programming by allowing developers to write scalable, responsive code without micromanaging threads.

Together, these abstractions strike a balance between control and productivity. By learning when to use each–from raw threads for edge cases to TPL for general-purpose parallelism–you now have a toolkit that adapts to your performance needs without sacrificing maintainability.

Synchronization Primitives

As we moved deeper into concurrency, we encountered one of the core challenges in multithreaded programming: safely coordinating access to shared resources. To address this, .NET provides a rich set of synchronization primitives, each suited to different patterns of use.

We began with traditional constructs such as **`Mutex`**, **`Monitor`**, and **`lock`**, which are essential for controlling access to critical sections in both single-process and inter-process scenarios. From there, we explored more specialized tools such as **`Semaphore`** and **`SemaphoreSlim`**, useful for limiting concurrency to a specific number of threads—ideal for managing resource pools such as database connections or I/O handles.

We also looked at signaling constructs such as **`AutoResetEvent`** and **`ManualResetEvent`**, which allow threads to communicate and coordinate execution order. Finally, we covered **`ReaderWriterLockSlim`**, which provides an efficient mechanism for enabling multiple readers while restricting write access—useful in scenarios where reads vastly outnumber writes.

Together, these primitives enable fine-grained control over synchronization, ensuring correctness without unnecessarily sacrificing performance. Knowing when and how to use them effectively is key to writing robust and scalable parallel code.

Task-Based Programming

Modern .NET development leans heavily on task-based programming to simplify concurrency while preserving readability and composability. Using **`Task`** and related APIs from the Task Parallel Library (TPL), developers can represent asynchronous or parallel work as objects that the runtime manages efficiently on the thread pool.

In this book, we explored how to create and run tasks using **`Task.Run()`**, **`Task.Factory.StartNew()`**, and **`Task.WhenAll()`**, and how to chain them with continuations. Unlike manual thread creation, tasks make it easy to write non-blocking, responsive code that scales well—whether you are handling CPU-intensive work or orchestrating multiple asynchronous operations.

Task-based programming also improves error handling and control. The ability to await completion, attach cancellation tokens, and catch aggregate exceptions allows developers to write safer and more predictable concurrent code. It also integrates seamlessly with higher-level constructs such as **`async/await`** for asynchronous programming.

Overall, **`Task`** serves as a building block for much of today's parallel and asynchronous .NET code—balancing power with simplicity and helping developers' reason clearly about the flow of concurrent operations.

Parallel Programming Models

Parallel programming models in .NET enable developers to take advantage of multiple cores in a system, facilitating the execution of independent tasks concurrently. Rather than focusing on managing individual threads, these models provide higher-level abstractions for parallel execution, allowing developers to express parallelism more naturally.

One of the key tools we explored is the **`Parallel`** class, specifically its **`Parallel.For()`** and **`Parallel.ForEach()`** methods. These constructs are designed for data parallelism, where a collection of data is divided into chunks and processed simultaneously by multiple threads. By abstracting away the complexities of thread management, these methods make it easy to process large datasets efficiently, balancing workload distribution and minimizing overhead.

In addition, we looked at the TPL, which allows for parallel execution using tasks. Unlike **`Parallel.For()`**, the TPL provides greater flexibility, enabling parallelism in situations beyond simple data loops. By creating and managing tasks, the TPL ensures scalability, particularly for larger applications where tasks may need to be executed in parallel with other asynchronous operations.

Together, these parallel programming models provide a rich set of tools to express parallelism efficiently, focusing on ease of use and scalability without delving into the complexities of low-level thread management.

Asynchronous Programming

As we move towards more efficient, non-blocking execution, asynchronous programming is an essential tool for modern .NET applications. By allowing code to run asynchronously without blocking threads, we can improve responsiveness and scalability, particularly in I/O-bound scenarios.

In this book, we explored the power of **`async/await`**, .NET's most user-friendly approach to asynchronous programming. By using **`async`** and **`await`**, we can write asynchronous code that looks almost identical to synchronous code, but without the drawbacks of thread-blocking operations. The **`async`** keyword marks a method as asynchronous, while **`await`** enables non-blocking execution of asynchronous tasks, yielding control back to the runtime until the operation is complete.

We covered how to leverage **`Task`** and **`Task<T>`** to perform asynchronous I/O operations, such as reading files or making HTTP requests, while keeping the application responsive. With **`async/await`**, these operations can run concurrently without blocking the main thread, making them particularly useful in GUI applications or server-side code that handles multiple client requests.

In addition to improving code readability, **`async/await`** helps developers avoid the "*callback hell*" that can arise with older asynchronous models, where callback functions are nested deeply. By allowing a more linear flow of control, **`async/await`** keeps asynchronous code clean and maintainable.

We also discussed important concepts such as cancellation tokens to cancel ongoing asynchronous operations and exception handling in asynchronous code, ensuring that errors are captured and managed correctly.

In summary, **`async/await`** offers a powerful abstraction for writing asynchronous code with minimal complexity, improving both the performance and clarity of your applications.

Concurrent Collections

When building multithreaded or parallel applications, managing shared data safely and efficiently is crucial. .NET provides a set of concurrent collections that help mitigate common challenges including race conditions and deadlocks, offering thread-safe operations out-of-the-box.

We began by exploring the **`ConcurrentBag<T>`**, a collection optimized for scenarios where threads need to add or take items in parallel. Unlike standard collections such as **`List<T>`**, **`ConcurrentBag<T>`** allows multiple threads to add and remove items without locking the entire collection, making it particularly useful for scenarios where thread **contention** is minimal.

We also examined the **`ConcurrentDictionary<TKey, TValue>`**, a thread-safe dictionary that allows multiple threads to read and write without requiring external synchronization. This collection supports atomic operations such as **`TryAdd()`**, **`TryUpdate()`**, and **`AddOrUpdate()`**, making it ideal for situations where you need to ensure consistency when modifying values in a concurrent environment.

Next, we looked at **`ConcurrentQueue<T>`** and **`ConcurrentStack<T>`**, both of which provide thread-safe implementations of FIFO and LIFO queues, respectively. These collections are particularly useful in producer-consumer scenarios, where multiple threads add items to a queue, and one or more other threads process them. Both collections guarantee safe operations, even when accessed concurrently from different threads.

Finally, we discussed the **`BlockingCollection<T>`**, a higher-level abstraction built on top of other concurrent collections. It provides a bounded buffer and supports blocking and bounding operations, making it useful for implementing the producer-consumer pattern where producers add items to the collection, and consumers take items from it in a thread-safe manner.

In all, these concurrent collections provide a rich set of tools for managing shared data in a multithreaded environment. By using these thread-safe structures, developers can focus on the core logic of their applications without worrying about manually managing synchronization or potential concurrency issues.

Profiling

Profiling is an essential technique for optimizing multi-threaded and asynchronous applications. It allows you to gather insights into your application's performance and identify potential bottlenecks, inefficiencies, and areas that can be improved. In this book, we focus primarily on Visual Studio's profiling tools, which provide powerful and integrated features for performance analysis.

We begin with Visual Studio's CPU and Memory Profilers, which are essential for understanding how your application uses system resources. The CPU Profiler tracks which methods consume the most processing time, helping you identify potential hotspots where optimization is needed. It provides detailed information on method calls, execution time, and thread activity, allowing you to pinpoint inefficient code paths. The Memory Profiler, on the other hand, helps you identify memory usage patterns, track allocations, and detect memory leaks. It also helps you optimize garbage collection by understanding object lifetimes and the impact of memory usage on application performance.

Another key tool is the Concurrency Visualizer, which provides a detailed view of how threads interact during execution. This tool visualizes thread activity over time, showing how threads are scheduled, where **contention** occurs, and if there are issues like excessive context switching or thread starvation. The Concurrency Visualizer makes it easier to analyze how your application manages concurrency and helps you identify potential bottlenecks in multithreaded applications.

While Visual Studio's profiling tools are powerful, third-party tools such as **`BenchmarkDotNet`** can complement your profiling efforts. **`BenchmarkDotNet`** is a precise benchmarking library for evaluating specific code changes or comparing different algorithms in a controlled environment. Though it is not the main focus of this book, it can be a valuable tool for measuring performance at a granular level.

By incorporating profiling tools like Visual Studio's CPU and Memory Profilers and the Concurrency Visualizer into your development process, you can make informed decisions about performance optimizations. Profiling ensures that performance is a priority throughout the lifecycle of your application, leading to better, more efficient software.

Summary of Best Practices

As we conclude our exploration of parallelism, asynchronous programming, and high-performance techniques, it is essential to consolidate the key practices that lead to successful and efficient applications. In this section, we will summarize the best practices that can help you design and implement high-performance, scalable software. These best practices encompass everything from choosing the right concurrency model to handling thread synchronization, managing resources effectively, and ensuring your application remains responsive under load. By following these guidelines, you will be better equipped to avoid common pitfalls, optimize your code, and deliver applications that perform well in production environments.

Start with Measurement

Before diving into optimization, it is crucial to measure. Performance improvements should never be based on assumptions; instead, rely on hard data to guide your decisions. To effectively optimize your application, you need to establish benchmarks that reflect real-world performance. This ensures that any changes you make contribute to a more efficient system, rather than inadvertently introducing new issues.

Start by using profiling tools to get a clear picture of how your application behaves under different conditions. Visual Studio's CPU and Memory Profiler, for example, can help identify where your application is spending most of its time and how resources are being consumed. Likewise, **`BenchmarkDotNet`** allows you to measure specific code paths and compare them against each other to identify the most efficient solutions.

It is also important to capture data over time and under varying loads. For instance, monitor performance during peak usage or under stress testing to see how well your application scales. Performance counters can provide ongoing insight into resource usage, such as CPU load, memory consumption, and thread activity, ensuring you are not only optimizing for a snapshot of performance but for long-term efficiency as well.

Lastly, do not forget the importance of measuring throughput, latency, and responsiveness. These factors can help identify inefficiencies that may not be immediately visible in CPU or memory usage but could still be affecting the overall user experience. By focusing on these key metrics, you ensure that your performance improvements are based on objective, actionable data.

In summary, the key to effective performance optimization is measurement. Establish a baseline, monitor key metrics, and let data drive your decisions. Without measurement, you cannot know where to focus your efforts or if the changes you make are having the desired impact.

Be Intentional about Concurrency

Concurrency is a powerful tool for improving performance, but it can also introduce complexity and subtle bugs if not approached **intentionally**. It is not enough to simply add parallelism or asynchronous operations for the sake of it–you must design with concurrency in mind from the outset.

First, understand the problem you are solving. Some tasks are inherently parallelizable, like processing independent data chunks in parallel loops, while others may benefit more from asynchronous programming, such as I/O-bound operations. Recognizing the appropriate concurrency model for your problem is key.

When implementing concurrency, always limit shared state. Shared resources are a source of **contention** and potential race conditions. Whenever possible, use immutable data or local copies of data that threads can operate on independently. For example, collections such as **`ConcurrentBag<T>`** or **`ConcurrentDictionary<TKey, TValue>`** allow you to avoid explicit locking, offering a more efficient way to manage shared data in a concurrent environment.

Next, carefully choose synchronization mechanisms. High-level abstractions, such as **`Task`** and **`Parallel.ForEach()`** can help reduce complexity by automatically managing threads and resource allocation, allowing you to focus on the logic rather than dealing with low-level threading issues. But even with these abstractions, be mindful of when you need synchronization primitives, such as **`Mutex`** or **`SemaphoreSlim`**, and use them judiciously to avoid performance bottlenecks.

It is also important to minimize blocking in concurrent applications. In threaded applications, blocking a thread while waiting for another can introduce inefficiencies and unnecessary delays. Using asynchronous programming models with **`async/await`** can help ensure that threads are not blocked waiting for I/O or other long-running operations, improving responsiveness and throughput.

Finally, test thoroughly. Concurrency can be difficult to get right, and issues such as race conditions or deadlocks can be subtle and elusive. Comprehensive unit and integration tests, combined with stress testing, can help identify potential issues early and ensure that your application behaves as expected under concurrent loads.

Being **intentional** about concurrency means designing with care, using the right tools for the job, and testing thoroughly. It is a proactive approach that pays off in the long run by producing efficient, maintainable, and scalable systems.

Reduce Contention

Contention occurs when multiple threads or tasks compete for the same resource, leading to delays and performance degradation. Reducing **contention** is essential for achieving high performance in concurrent applications. When threads are forced to wait for access to shared resources, the benefits of parallelism and concurrency are significantly diminished. Here are some strategies to minimize **contention** and improve overall performance.

Minimize Shared State

One of the most effective ways to reduce **contention** is to minimize shared state. When possible, design your application so that each thread or task works on its own independent data. Immutable data structures or thread-local storage can help eliminate the need for synchronization altogether. For instance, when processing data in parallel, ensure that each thread has its own copy of the data it needs, avoiding the need for locking mechanisms that can lead to **contention**.

Use Fine-Grained Locking

When shared resources are unavoidable, ensure that you lock only what is necessary. Fine-grained locking involves using locks around smaller sections of code, rather than locking entire blocks of code or larger data structures. This minimizes the scope of **contention** and allows other threads to work on non-conflicting sections of the application. For example, you can use **`ReaderWriterLockSlim`** to allow multiple threads to read from shared data while limiting write access to one thread at a time.

Leverage Higher-Level Concurrency Constructs

Higher-level abstractions such as the Task Parallel Library (TPL) and **`Parallel.ForEach()`** can often help minimize **contention** by efficiently managing threads and tasks behind the scenes. These abstractions intelligently distribute work across threads, ensuring that tasks are scheduled and executed in a way that reduces unnecessary blocking. Additionally, they help you avoid the complexity of manually managing thread pools or individual threads, which can lead to excessive **contention** if not done carefully.

Use Non-Blocking Algorithms

Where possible, consider using non-blocking algorithms. These algorithms allow threads to continue executing without waiting for other threads to release resources. Examples of non-blocking techniques include lock-free data structures, such as those found in the **`System.Collections.Concurrent`** namespace, or using atomic operations where supported. Non-blocking algorithms can be especially useful in highly concurrent environments where multiple threads need frequent access to shared resources.

Reduce Task Granularity

If tasks are too fine-grained, the overhead of managing them can lead to increased **contention**. It is important to balance task size so that the tasks are large enough to justify parallelism but not so large that they overload any individual thread. By choosing the right granularity for tasks, you ensure that threads are kept busy without excessive scheduling overhead, which can cause **contention** and inefficiency.

Profile and Identify Contention Hotspots

Ultimately, the best way to reduce **contention** is to profile your application. Using tools like Visual Studio's Concurrency Visualizer or CPU Profiler, you can pinpoint where **contention** is occurring in your application and identify potential solutions. Often, **contention** hotspots are the result of inefficient locking or poorly managed shared state, so profiling can reveal exactly where to focus your optimization efforts.

By following these strategies, you can minimize **contention** in your application, leading to more efficient thread execution and better overall performance. Remember, reducing **contention** is not just about minimizing the use of locks—it is about designing your system with concurrency in mind and choosing the right approach to handle shared resources.

Make Performance a Habit

Performance optimization should not be a one-time effort, but rather an ongoing habit throughout the software development lifecycle. Making performance a regular part of your development process helps you avoid costly last-minute fixes and ensures that your application remains efficient as it evolves. Here is how to incorporate performance-focused practices into your daily work:

Adopt a Performance-First Mindset

From the start of any project, establish a performance-first mindset. This means treating performance as a core requirement, not something to be tackled at the end of development. Think about performance early in the design phase, considering how your application will scale and handle concurrency. By prioritizing performance from the outset, you can make better design choices that optimize your application's ability to handle concurrent tasks and efficiently utilize system resources.

Write Efficient Code from the Beginning

Efficiency starts with writing clean, optimized code. Follow established coding practices, avoid common pitfalls such as excessive memory allocations, and write algorithms that are computationally efficient. Make use of high-performance libraries when available and ensure that data structures are chosen for their speed and suitability for concurrent access. Keep in mind that even small inefficiencies can add up in a large-scale application, so always strive for the most efficient solution without sacrificing readability.

Continuously Profile Your Application

Make profiling a regular part of your development routine. Instead of waiting until the end of the project to assess performance, profile your application regularly throughout development. This can help identify performance issues early on, allowing you to address them before they become bigger problems. Use tools such as Visual Studio's Profiler to monitor memory usage, CPU consumption, and thread activity as you develop new features or make changes to existing ones.

Measure before and after Optimization

When you make optimizations, always measure before and after. This ensures that the changes you have made are truly improving performance and not introducing new bottlenecks or issues. Without proper measurement, it is easy to assume that a change improved performance when it may have had little or no effect. Establish clear performance benchmarks and ensure that optimizations are validated through profiling and testing.

Iterate and Optimize in Small Increments

Instead of making large, sweeping optimizations all at once, optimize in small increments. Small changes are easier to measure and understand, and they reduce the risk of introducing bugs. Optimizing iteratively also allows you to test changes one at a time. ensuring that each tweak leads to measurable improvement. This iterative approach prevents you from overcomplicating your codebase with complex optimizations that may not even be necessary.

Foster a Culture of Performance

Encourage your team members to also prioritize performance in their work. Create a culture where performance is a shared responsibility, not just something for the performance team or final stages of development. Through regular code reviews, peer discussions, and shared knowledge, ensure that everyone is aware of the importance of performance and is equipped with the tools and techniques to maintain it.

Stay Up-to-Date with New Tools and Techniques

Performance optimization techniques and tools evolve constantly, so staying current is crucial. New libraries, frameworks, and performance profiling tools emerge regularly, and understanding the latest techniques can keep your application on the cutting edge. Continuously learning about new technologies allows you to incorporate the best solutions for your specific needs.

By making performance a habit, you will ensure that your applications are consistently efficient, scalable, and optimized for both concurrency and responsiveness. Performance is not something to tackle just once; it's an ongoing commitment that leads to better, more maintainable software over time.

Use the Right Tools

Building high-performance, concurrent applications is challenging–but the right tools make it manageable. Throughout this book, we have emphasized the importance of visibility and measurement, and .NET offers a rich toolset to support that effort.

Visual Studio Profiling Tools provide essential diagnostics. The CPU and Memory Usage tools identify bottlenecks and hotspots, while the Concurrency Visualizer reveals thread activity, synchronization, and core usage–especially useful when analyzing parallel loops, async workflows, or thread pool behavior.

For runtime insights, dotnet-counters and Event Tracing for Windows (ETW) expose valuable metrics such as garbage collection, thread pool usage, and **contention**–all without disrupting running systems. These tools are particularly effective for monitoring real-world performance.

While not a major focus here, tools including BenchmarkDotNet offer rigorous micro-benchmarking capabilities when testing small code paths or comparing algorithm performance.

In addition, diagnostic aids such as dotTrace, dotMemory, and logging frameworks (for example, Serilog, Application Insights) enhance visibility into behavior and performance trends–both during development and in production.

Lastly, don't neglect testing: frameworks such as xUnit and NBomber support automated performance and load testing, helping to validate concurrency strategies and catch regressions early.

Using the right tools allows you to profile effectively, measure improvements, and build performance-aware applications with confidence.

Real-World Case Studies

To ground the concepts covered in this book, this section highlights a few real-world projects from my own experience. Each case study illustrates a specific performance or concurrency challenge and how it was addressed using the techniques discussed throughout the book. These practical examples aim to reinforce key principles and provide insight into how performance-aware development plays out in actual applications.

Case 1: Scaling Text File Processing

This project involved building a web-based application that allowed users to upload text files containing structured data. Once uploaded, the data was parsed into memory and summarized using various grouping and aggregation operations. LINQ was chosen for its expressive syntax and ease of implementation during development. In testing with representative files, the application met all performance goals.

Challenge

After deployment, users began uploading significantly larger files–ranging from tens to hundreds of megabytes–far exceeding test scenarios. This increase in data volume led to noticeable slowdowns in processing. In some cases, the application appeared unresponsive or timed out entirely. Profiling revealed that LINQ queries over large in-memory data sets were consuming excessive CPU time on a single thread.

Approach

To address the issue, the application was updated to use PLINQ (Parallel LINQ) for the most computationally expensive queries. By converting key LINQ operations–such as grouping and aggregating–into parallel equivalents, the workload could be distributed across multiple cores. Care was taken to ensure thread safety, and the degree of parallelism was adjusted based on available hardware and observed performance.

Outcome

The change to PLINQ dramatically reduced processing time, cutting throughput times for large files by more than 70% in many cases. The application became responsive even under heavy input conditions, and no further timeouts were reported. Memory usage remained stable since the underlying data structures didn't change significantly–only the way they were processed.

Key Takeaways

- Code that performs well in controlled tests may not scale in real-world usage without profiling and stress testing.
- LINQ is convenient, but its sequential execution can become a bottleneck on large data sets.
- PLINQ offers an easy path to parallelism but still requires careful attention to side effects and performance tuning.
- Performance issues are often best solved by identifying hotspots and applying concurrency selectively, not universally.

Case 2: Modernizing Reporting

An internal reporting service, originally built several years prior, was responsible for collecting and aggregating operational data to generate detailed reports for business stakeholders. The core logic involved custom data structures and a series of `lock`-protected code blocks to coordinate access between threads. For years, the system met the company's needs, producing reports nightly during off-hours.

Challenge

As the company scaled, the volume of incoming data and the number of report requests increased substantially. What once took minutes to complete began taking hours. The serialized access enforced by numerous `lock` statements created **contention** and led to underutilized CPU cores, severely limiting the application's throughput. Attempts to add hardware yielded diminishing returns.

Approach

The solution involved a phased rewrite of the most critical sections of the code. The legacy data structures protected by locks were replaced with `ConcurrentDictionary`, `ConcurrentBag`, and other concurrent collections from the .NET framework. Where appropriate, `Interlocked` operations were used to safely update counters and shared state without explicit locks. This shift reduced **contention** and allowed the report generator to take full advantage of multicore systems.

Outcome

The new implementation reduced report generation time from hours to just minutes—even under peak loads. CPU usage increased (in a good way), spreading computation across multiple threads instead of waiting on locks. Reliability improved as well, with fewer deadlock or timeout-related support incidents reported.

Key Takeaways

- Excessive use of lock can create **contention** bottlenecks that limit scalability.
- Replacing lock-based coordination with concurrent collections and atomic operations can unlock dramatic performance improvements.
- Modern concurrent data structures in .NET simplify multithreaded programming without sacrificing correctness.
- As applications grow, older synchronization models may need to be reevaluated to keep up with demand.

Next Steps for the Reader

Mastering performance and concurrency in .NET is a journey, not a destination. While this book has covered foundational and practical concepts, the real growth happens through continuous application and exploration. Here are a few suggestions to keep moving forward.

- **Start Small**: Don't wait for a large-scale performance crisis to begin applying what you've learned. Start by profiling a small application, experimenting with `Parallel.For()`, or rewriting a tightly looped algorithm using `async` and `await`. These small efforts build confidence and often lead to meaningful insights—even in seemingly simple systems.
- **Practice Continuously**: Performance tuning and concurrent programming are skills best honed through regular use. Incorporate profiling into your development workflow, revisit

older code for improvement opportunities, and try re-implementing solutions using different models (for example, parallel loops versus `Task.Run()`). Over time, these habits form a strong performance intuition.

- **Explore Advanced Concepts:** Once you are comfortable with the basics, push further. Investigate lower-level features such as `Span<T>`, high-throughput messaging with `Channel<T>`, or reactive patterns using `System.Reactive`. Consider exploring topics such as memory layout, lock-free programming, or custom synchronization primitives to deepen your understanding and expand your toolkit.

Final Thoughts

Building high-performance applications in .NET requires more than just technical knowledge–it calls for a mindset attuned to system behavior, efficiency, and thoughtful tradeoffs. As you continue your journey, these final reflections aim to reinforce the perspective and confidence you have gained.

- **Performance Engineer Mindset**: The best performance work starts with curiosity. Performance engineers don't assume–they measure. They don't reach for concurrency for its own sake, but apply it purposefully when it solves a real problem. This mindset is rooted in observation, experimentation, and iteration. It means asking the right questions: *Is this fast enough? Where is the bottleneck? Is this scalable?* Over time, you will develop an instinct for spotting performance smells and opportunities alike.
- **You Now Have the Tools:** Throughout this book, you have encountered the core building blocks of modern high-performance .NET: threads, tasks, async/await, parallel loops, synchronization primitives, concurrent collections, and profiling tools. You have seen how to use them effectively–and, more importantly, when to use them. These tools don't solve problems on their own, but in your hands, they provide the foundation for responsive, scalable applications.
- **Practicality over Perfection:** High-performance code does not have to be complicated, and not every line of code needs to be optimized. Chasing theoretical perfection can lead to premature optimization and brittle solutions. Instead, focus on what matters: clarity, correctness, and measurable improvement where it counts. In practice, the most maintainable high-performance systems strike a balance between design elegance and real-world constraints.

Conclusion

As you step away from these pages and return to your own projects, remember that performance is not a destination–it is a discipline. Whether you are refining a single method or architecting a system from the ground up, the principles and techniques covered in this book can help you build software that is not just functional, but fast, efficient, and future-ready. Keep measuring, keep learning, and above all, keep building.

Points to Remember

- **Performance is a mindset**: Begin with measurement, question assumptions, and optimize where it matters.
- **Start small and iterate**: Real progress comes from steady, practical application over time.
- **Use the right tool for the job**: Threads, tasks, parallel loops, and concurrent collections each serve different purposes.
- **Profiling is essential**: Visual Studio's built-in tools help uncover real bottlenecks and guide optimization efforts.

- **Best practices matter**: Reduce **contention**, be **intentional** with concurrency, and prioritize maintainability alongside performance.
- **Aim for practicality, not perfection**: The goal is better performance, not the most complex or clever solution.
- **Continuous learning pays off**: Advanced concepts and tools become valuable as your experience grows.

Multiple Choice Questions

1. Which of the following is a common mistake when applying concurrency to an application?
   a. Using **`Parallel.ForEach()`** to handle large datasets.
   b. Employing **`ConcurrentDictionary`** to reduce lock **contention**.
   c. Adding threads without understanding shared state and synchronization.
   d. Measuring performance before and after optimization.
2. According to the book's guidance, which habit best supports long-term performance awareness?
   a. Making profiling and performance testing part of the regular development cycle.
   b. Learning C++ to improve low-level optimization.
   c. Refactoring code monthly to remove all lock statements.
   d. Writing all new code with **`async`** and **`await`** by default.
3. Why is "**practicality over perfection**" emphasized in performance engineering?
   a. Perfect code is always slower than practical code.
   b. Most performance issues are caused by over-engineering.
   c. Practical solutions always use the thread pool.
   d. Over-optimization can make code harder to maintain without significant benefit.
4. What is the recommended first step when addressing a performance issue?
   a. Rewrite the slowest code with unsafe pointers.
   b. Measure and profile the application to locate bottlenecks.
   c. Parallelize all CPU-bound operations immediately.
   d. Replace all collections with concurrent alternatives.

Answers

1. c
2. a
3. d
4. b

Questions

1. When does adding concurrency introduce more problems than it solves?
2. If performance is everyone's responsibility, how can a team ensure that it becomes part of the development culture–not just a late-stage concern?
3. How do you distinguish between code that is "fast enough" and code that truly needs optimization?
4. What are some ways to continue learning and practicing performance techniques beyond this book?

Key Terms

- **Contention**: A condition where multiple threads or tasks compete for the same resource, often leading to delays and performance degradation.
- **Practicality over Perfection**: Focusing on performance improvements that provide real-world benefits without sacrificing readability or maintainability.
- **Intentional Concurrency**: The practice of deliberately designing concurrency with awareness of trade-offs and impact.

Index

Symbols

R

U

V

W